© Copyright 1977

The Automobile Association
Fanum House
Basingstoke
Hampshire RG21 2EA
Tel. Basingstoke (0256) 20123

First published November 1977
Second Edition 1978

Produced by the Cartographic Department
Publications Division
The Automobile Association

Based upon the Ordnance Survey Maps with the
permission of the Controller of H.M. Stationery Office

The Ordnance Survey is not responsible for the
accuracy of the National Grid on this production

The contents of this publication are believed correct
at the time of printing, but the current position may
be checked through the AA. Nevertheless the
Publishers can accept no responsibility for errors or
omissions or for changes in the details given.

Printed in England by Sir Joseph Causton & Sons Ltd,
London and Eastleigh.

ISBN 0 09 211480 6   55521

MOTORISTS' ATLAS OF GREAT BRITAIN

THE AUTOMOBILE ASSOCIATION

Head Office

Fanum House

Basingstoke Hants RG21 2EA

Tel: Basingstoke 20123

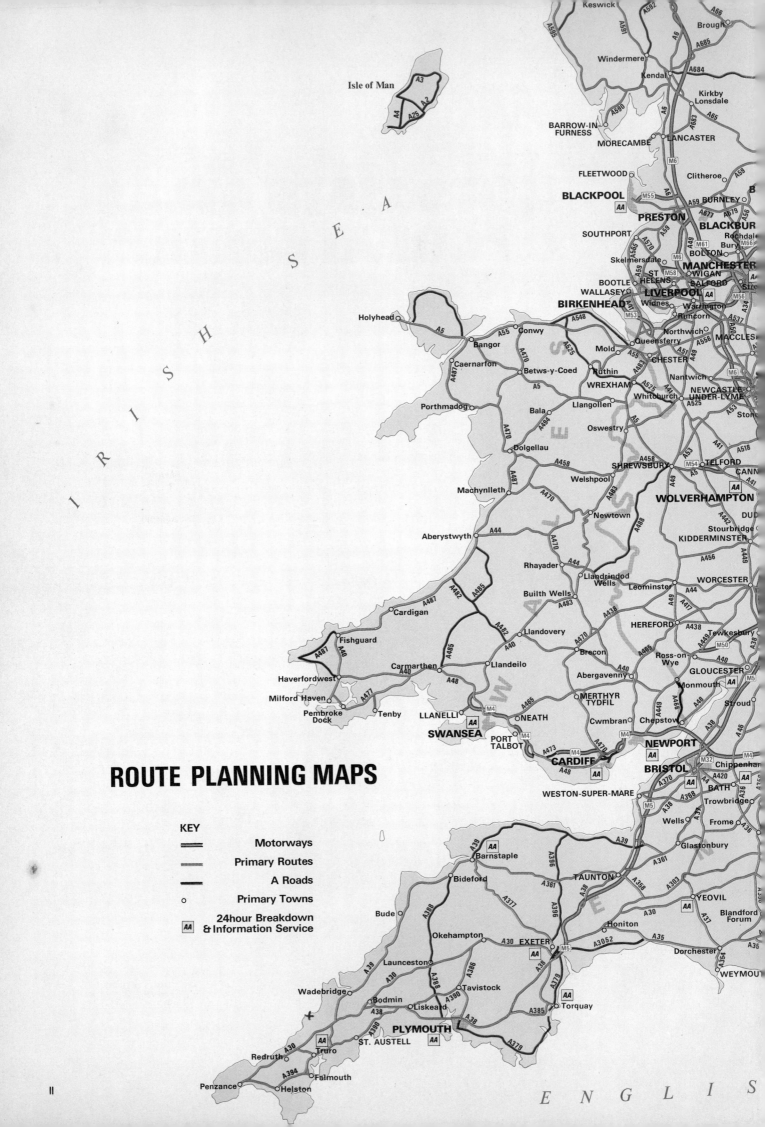

ROUTE PLANNING MAPS

KEY

Motorways	
Primary Routes	
A Roads	
○	Primary Towns
AA	24hour Breakdown & Information Service

Isle of Man

IRISH SEA

ENGLIS

II

MILEAGE CHART

Distances are given to the nearest mile and are measured along the normal AA recommended route.

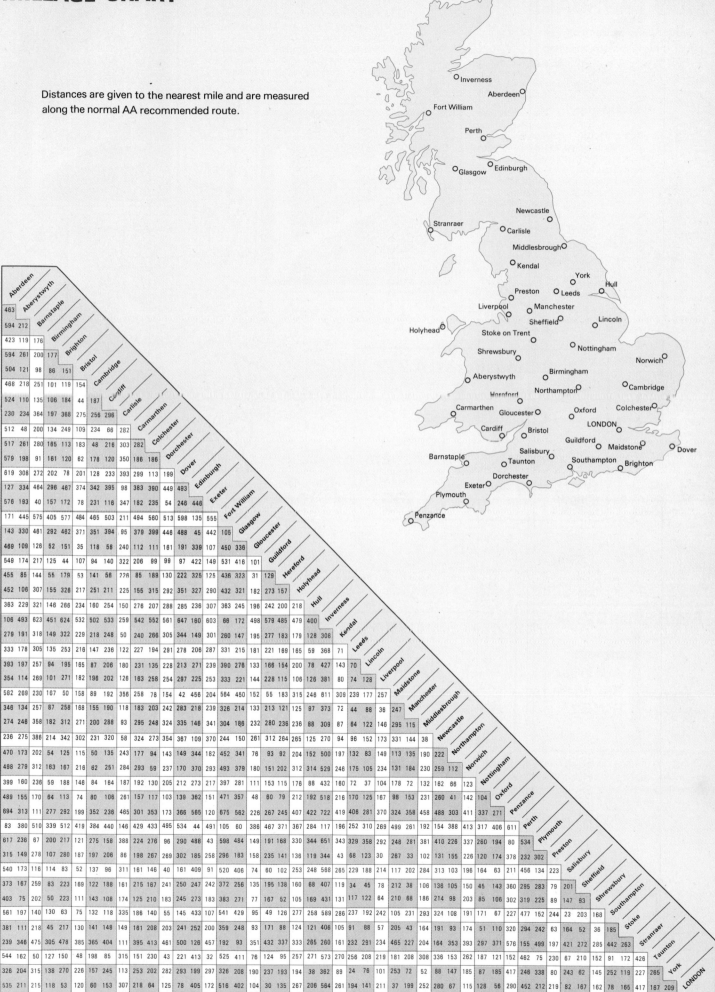

SIGN LANGUAGE

Understanding road signs- and their link with the map

MOTORWAYS

On the map - All Motorways are blue, Motorway signposts have white lettering on a blue background. Advance Direction signs approaching an interchange generally include the junction number in a black box. On the map the junction number appears in white on a blue circle.

Brighton
Crawley

Gatwick
A 23
✈

9

PRIMARY ROUTES

On the map - all the Primary Routes are green. The sign posts on Primary roads are also green, with white lettering and yellow numbers. Apart from the Motorways, Primary Routes are the most important traffic routes in both urban and rural areas. They form a network of throughroutes connecting 'Primary Towns', which are generally places of traffic importance. Usually Primary routes are along A roads.

Brighton A 23

Haywards Heath
Billingshurst
A 272
Lewes
(A 275)
Worthing
(A 24)

A ROADS

All A roads are shown in red on the map, unless part of the primary network when they are green. (as above) The signposts along these roads have black lettering on a white background. At a junction with a Primary Route the Primary Road number appears yellow in a green box.

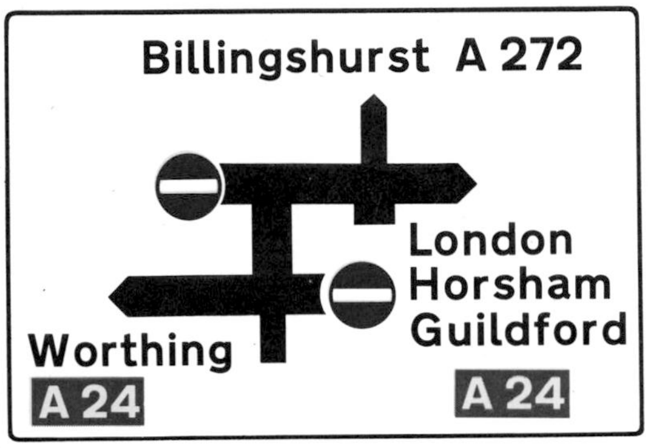

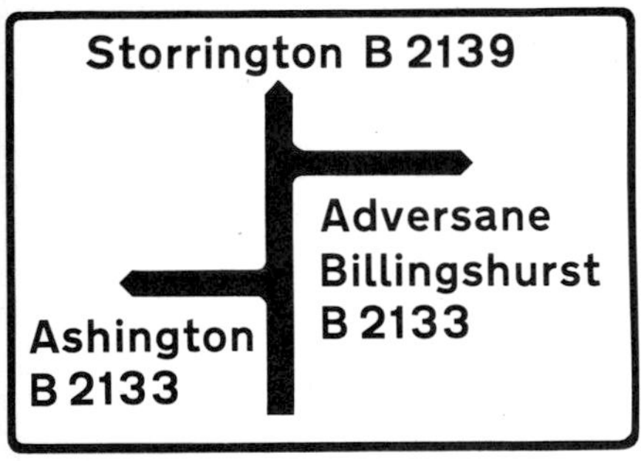

Billingshurst A 272

London
Horsham
Guildford
A 24

Worthing
A 24

B ROADS

On the map - all B roads not in the Primary network are signified by the colour yellow. The signs on B roads are black lettering on a white background, the same as for A roads.

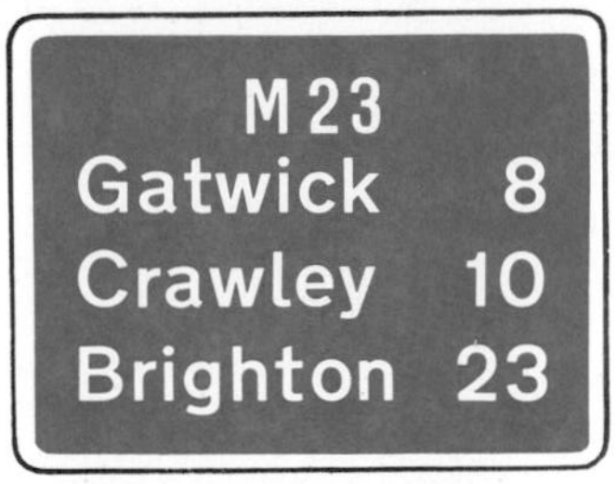

Storrington B 2139

Adversane
Billingshurst
B 2133

Ashington
B 2133

UNCLASSIFIED ROADS

On the map - all unclassified roads are white. New signposts along unclassified roads are usually of the Local Direction type. These have black lettering on a white background with a blue border. Local Direction signs may also appear in addition to Primary and non-Primary signs and indicate the route to local districts and amenities.

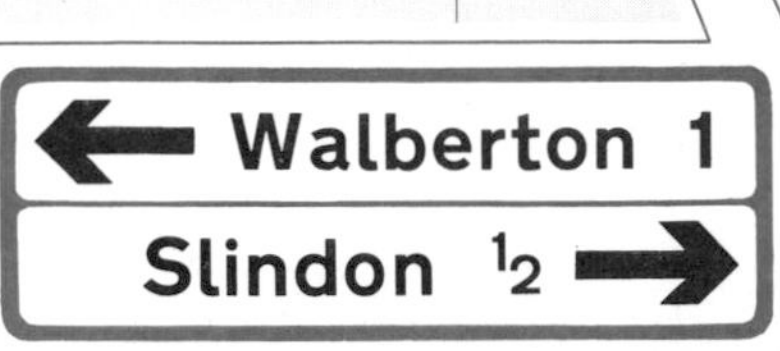

← Walberton 1
Slindon ½ →

CONFIRMATORY SIGNS

These often appear after important road junctions and confirm that drivers have taken their intended route. The colour of confirmatory signs differs according to the road classification, eg blue for Motor ways, green for Primary Routes, and white for A and B roads.

M 23
Gatwick   8
Crawley   10
Brighton 23

GRASP THE GRID

Indexing System & The National Grid.

To locate a place in the atlas, first check the index at the back of the book, eg:

Weyhill (Hants)	10 SU 3146
Weymouth (Dorset)	8 SY 6778
Whaddon (Bucks)	18 SP 8034

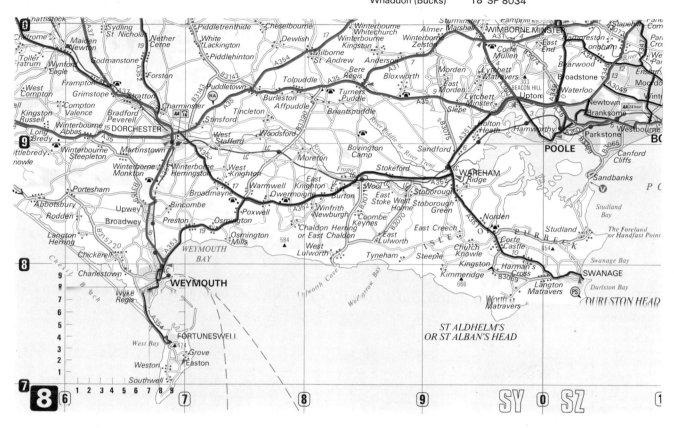

Using Weymouth as our example - this is the reference given in the index - 8 SY 6778

8 This is the number of the page on which Weymouth lies.

SY These first two letters show the major relevant area in which Weymouth is situated. They relate to an area labelled SY which is bound by heavy lines numbered in all cases O. (It can be seen that Poole lies in the next area labelled SZ).

67 The first set of numbers refer to the thin blue grid lines labelled along the bottom of the page. The 6 relates to the line of that number while the 7 is an estimated 7/10ths of the division between the 6 and 7.

78 The second set of figures refer to the numbers on the side of the page, the 7 relates to the line of that number, whereas the 8 is approximately 8/10ths of the division between 7 and 8.

If a line is drawn, from 67 vertically and from 78 horizontally, Weymouth should lie where the two intersect. Further examples of references given in the index, to the following appropriate towns may be checked against their locations in the map sample above:

Dorchester	8 SY 6990
Poole	8 SZ 0190
Swanage	8 SZ 0278
Wareham	8 SY 9287
Wool	8 SY 8486

It may be noted that, in every instance, it is the first set of figures after the area letters that applies to the number along the bottom of the grid. Therefore the second set will relate to the figures up the side of the page.

The National Grid

The National Grid provides a reference system common to maps of all scales. The country is divided into major grid squares (100kmsq), which are outlined on the map by heavy blue lines and each is designated two letters (eg SY) as its reference code. Each of these squares is then sub-divided into 100 10km sq, thus forming a finer grid which is numbered from 1 to 9, west to east, and south to north within each of the major lettered squares.

Thus each location can be referred to by first, two letters; showing the 100km square in which it lies, then a set of figures representing co-ordinates within the forementioned square, which gives precise location.

LEGEND

AUTOSTRADA	**AUTOBAHN**		**MOTORWAY**	**AUTOROUTE**
N. di autostrade	Autobahnnummer	M3	Motorway number	Numéro d'autoroute
Snodo con numero	Anschlusstelle mit Nummer	5	Junction with number	Jonction avec numéro
Snodo con entrata o uscita limitata	Anschlusstelle mit beschränkter Auf oder Abfahrt	7	Junction with limited entry or exit	Jonction à entrée ou sortie restreinte
Area di servizio	Tankstelle mit Raststätte	S	Service area	Zone services
Autostrada e Snodo i costruzione	Im Bau befindliche Autobahn und Anschlusstelle		Motorway & Junction under construction	Autoroute et Jonction en construction
STRADE	**STRASSEN**		**ROADS**	**ROUTES**
Rotta primaria	Hauptverbindungsstrasse	A9	Primary route	Route primaire
Altre strade A	Andere A Strasse	A130	Other A roads	Autres routes A
Strade Classe B	Strasse der Klasse B	B2137	B Roads	Routes catégorie B
Non-classificate	Nicht klassifizierte Strasse		Unclassified	Non classée
Corsia a due piste	Strasse mit getrennten Fahrbahnen	A7	Dual Carriageway	Route jumelée
In construzione	Im Bau befindliche Strasse		Under construction	En construction
Scozia : strade strette con aree di passaggio Scotland	Schottland: enge Strasse mit Uberholstellen		Scotland: narrow roads with passing places.	L'Écosse: Route étroite avec lieu de déplacement
SERVIZI AA DI SOCCORSO E DI INFORMAZIONI	**AA-PANNEN-UND INFORMATIONSDIENST**		**AA BREAKDOWN & INFORMATION SERVICES**	**SERVICES AA DEPANNAGE ET DE RENSEIGNEMENT**
Centro di servizio (24 ore ☎)	Dienststelle (24 Stunden ☎)	AA 24 hour	Service centre (24 hours ☎)	Station-service (24 heures ☎)
Centro di servizio (ore di lavoro normali)	Dienststelle (übliche Bürostunden)	AA	Service centre (normal office hours)	Station service (heures d'ouverture normales)
Centro di servizio autostrada	Autobahndienststelle	AA info	Motorway Information Centre	Centre-service d'autoroute
Centro di servizio strada	Strassendienststelle	AA 13	Road service centre	Centre-service de route
Centro di servizio porto	Hafendienststelle	AA	Port service centre	Centre-service de port
Telefoni AA & RAC	AA und RAC Telefonzellen	☎	AA & RAC telephones	Téléphones AA & RAC
Telefoni PTT in aree isolate	Öffentliche Telefonzellen in abgelegenen Gebieten (PO)	☎	PO telephones in isolated areas	Téléphones PTT dans endroits isolés
Area di riposo Area di pic-nic	Picknickplatz Rastzplatz	PS RA	Picnic site Rest area	Terrain de Pique-nique Aire de Repos
Punti di vista AA	AA-Aussichtspunkt	Bembridge Viewpoint	AA viewpoint	Points de vue AA
Inclinazione (la freccia indica in pendio)	Steigung (Pfeile weisen bergab)	←	Steep gradient (arrows point downhill)	Côte (la flèche est dirigée vers le bas)
Passaggio a livello	Bahnübergang	Toll	Road toll	Péage de route
Pedaggio strada	Gebührenpflichtige Strasse	LC	Level crossing	Passage à niveau
Traghetto veicoli (Gran Bretagna)	Autofähre (Grossbritannien)	V	Vehicle ferry (Gt Britain)	Bac pour véhicules (Grande-Bretagne)
Traghetto veicoli (continentale)	Autofähre (Kontinent)	CALAIS V	Vehicle ferry (continental)	Bac pour véhicules (Continental)
Aeroporto	Flughafen	✈	Airport	Aéroport
Area urbana	Stadtbezirk		Urban area	Zone urbaine
Confine nazionale	Nationale Grenze		National boundary	Frontière nationale
Confine di contea	Grafschaftsgrenze		County boundary	Frontière provinciale
Distanza in mille fra simboli	Entfernung zwischen Zeichen in Meilen	▼ 2 ▼	Distance in miles between symbols	Distance en milles entre symboles
A.S.M. in piedi	Ortshöhe nach Füssen	2525 ▲	Spot height in feet	Altitude en pieds anglais
Fiume e lago	Fluss und See		River and lake	Rivière et lac
Numeri di pagine di seguito	Hinweiszahlen für Anschlusskarten	13	Overlaps and numbers of continuing pages	Chiffres de guide pour cartes voisines

Scale 5 miles to 1 inch 1 : 316,800

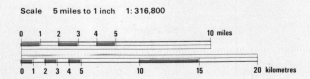

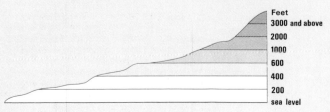

VIII

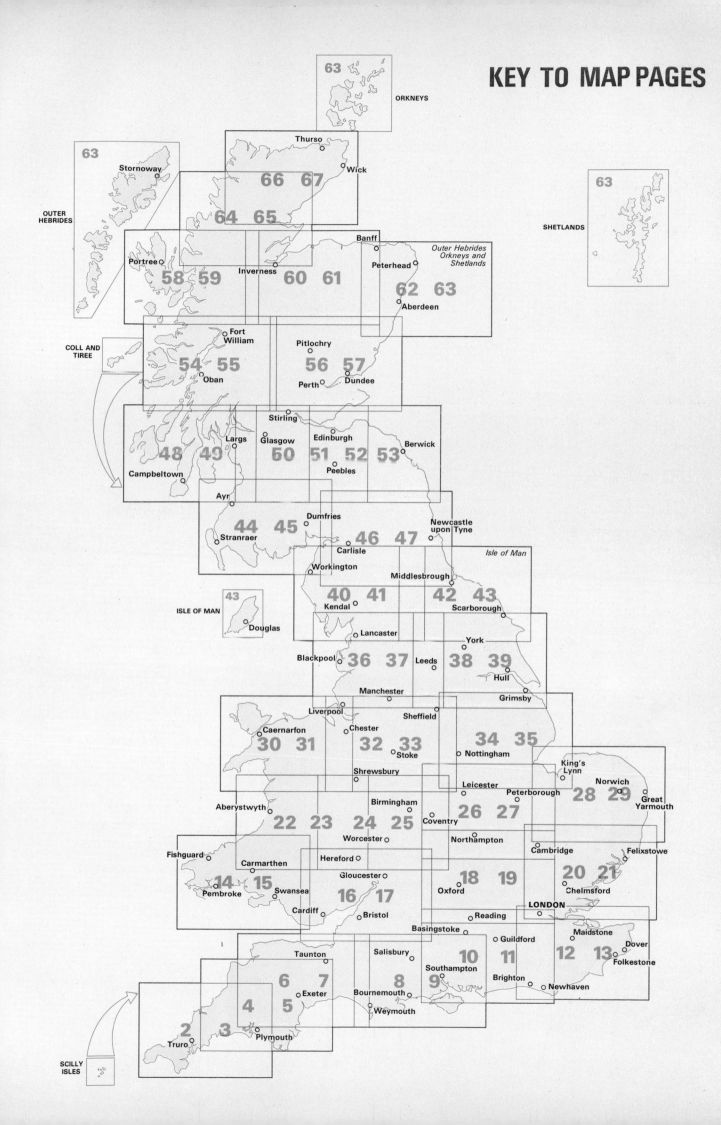

KEY TO MAP PAGES

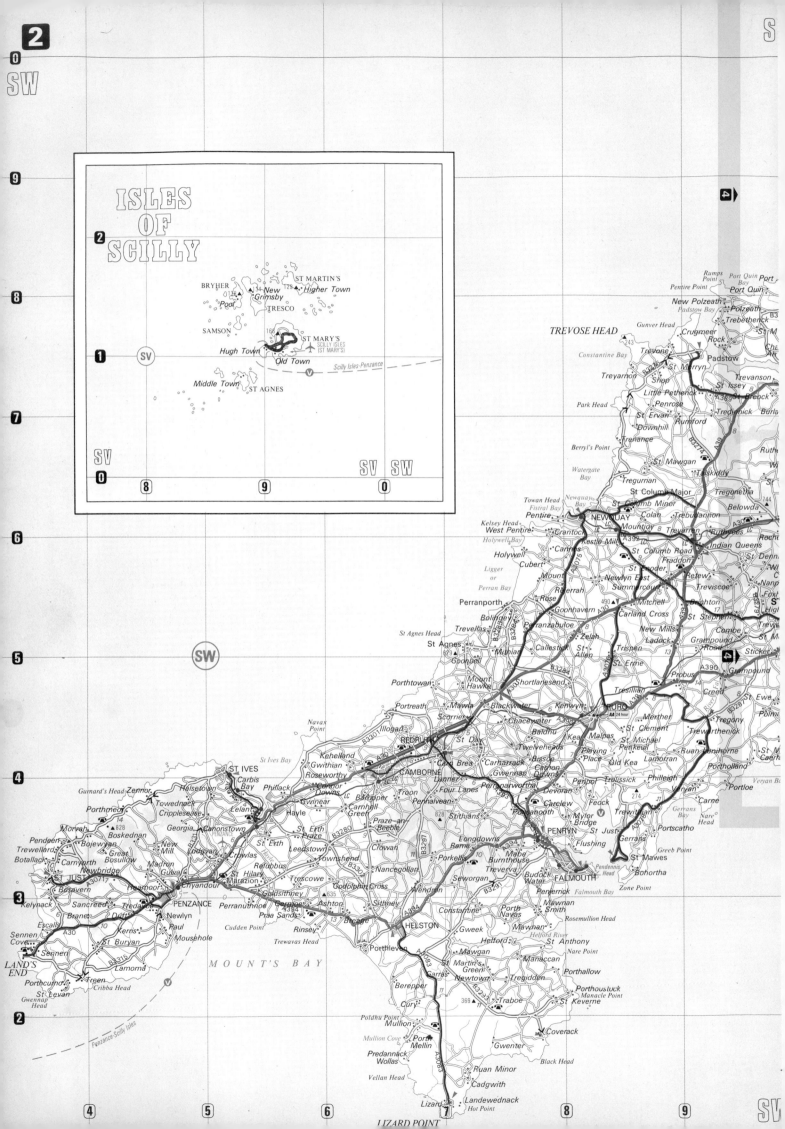

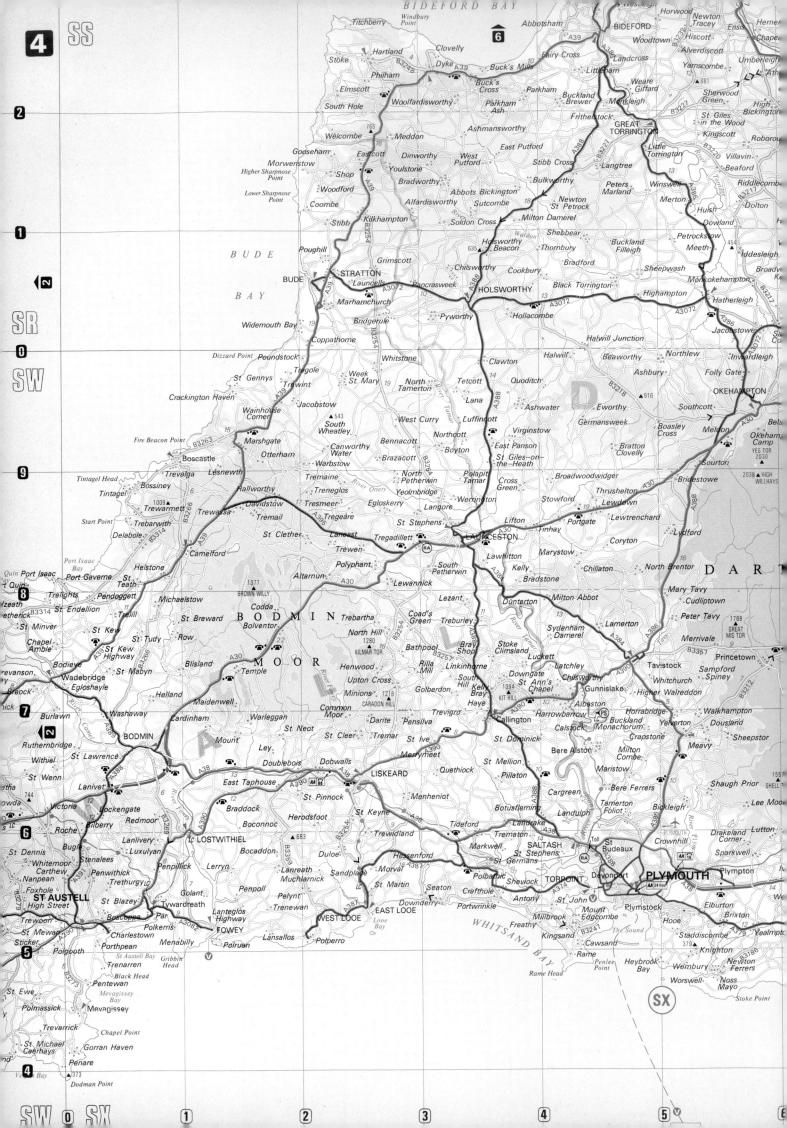

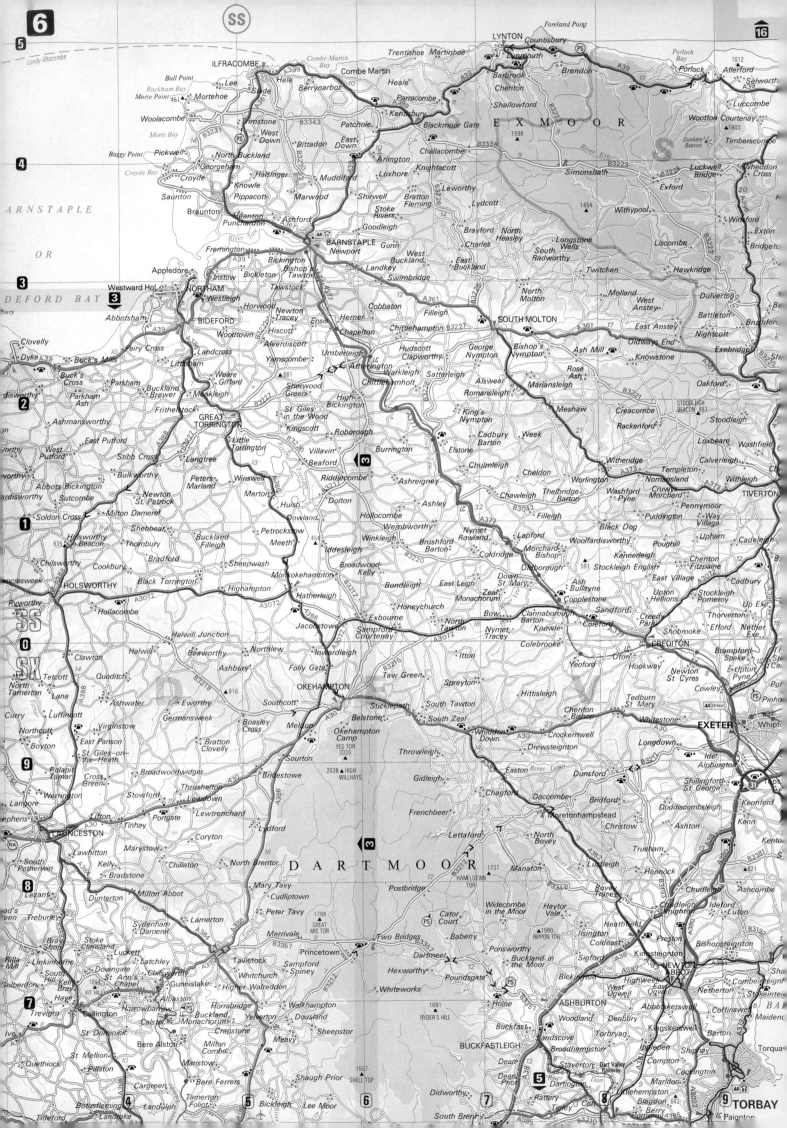

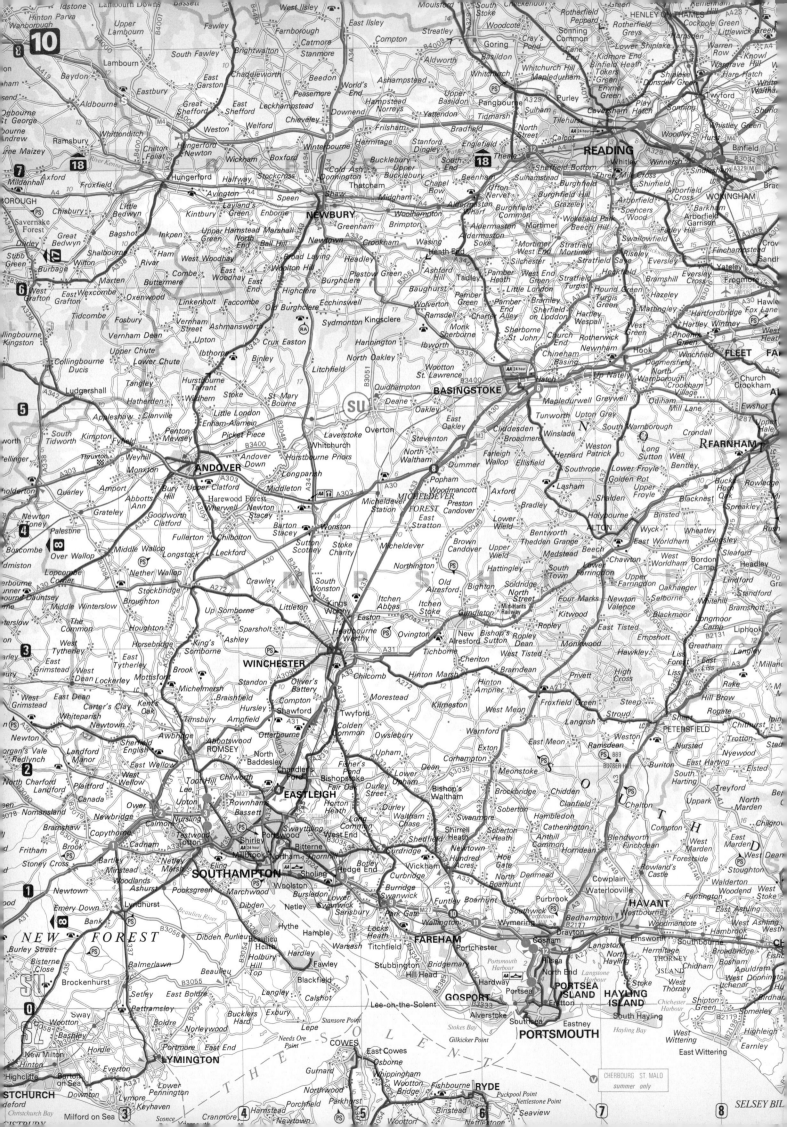

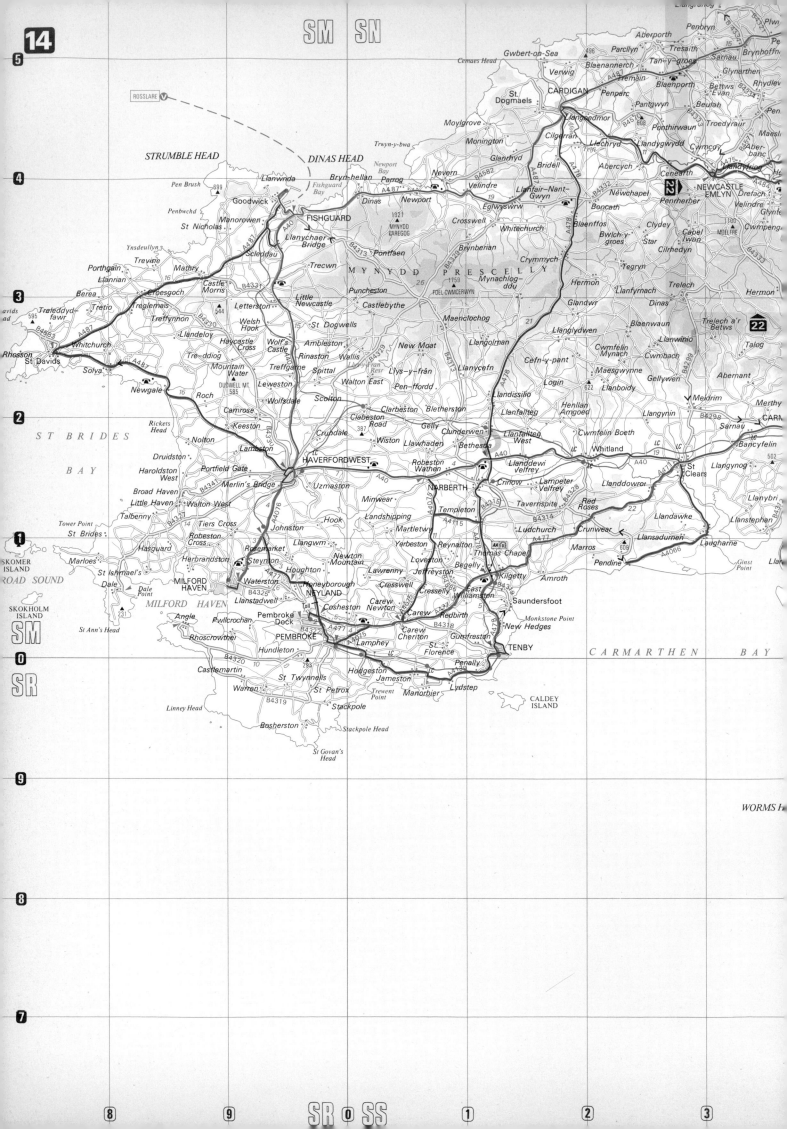

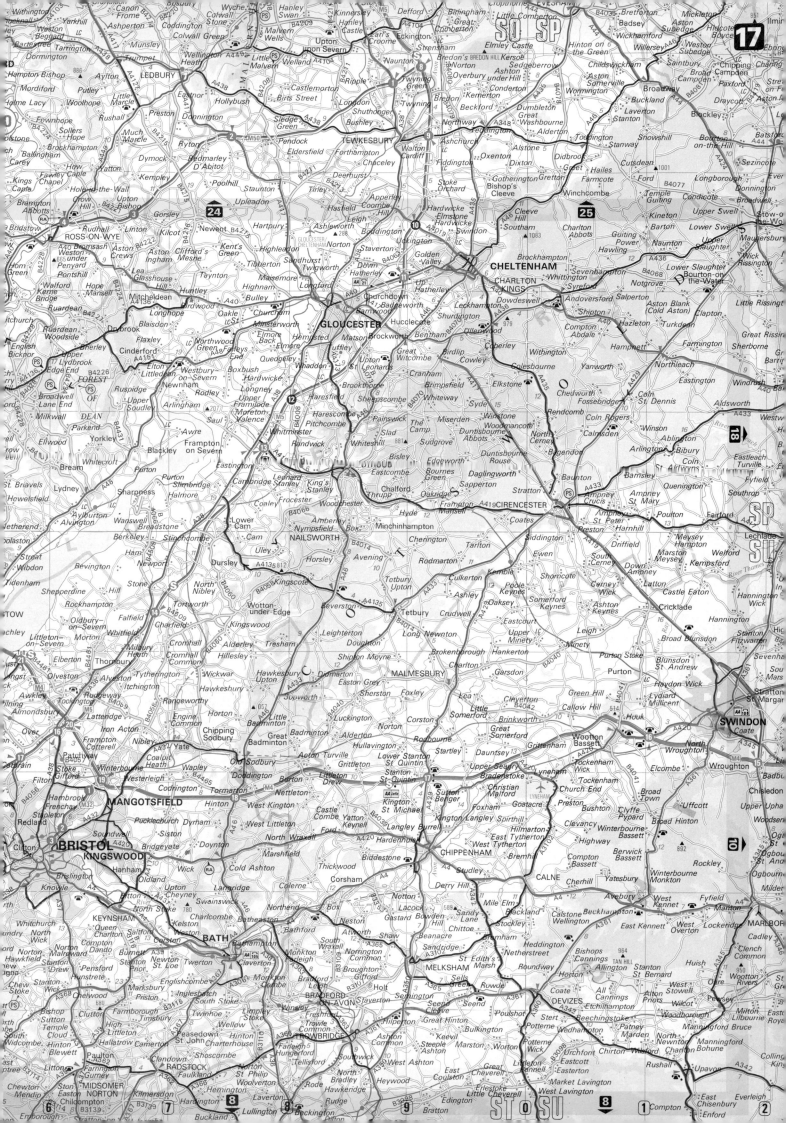

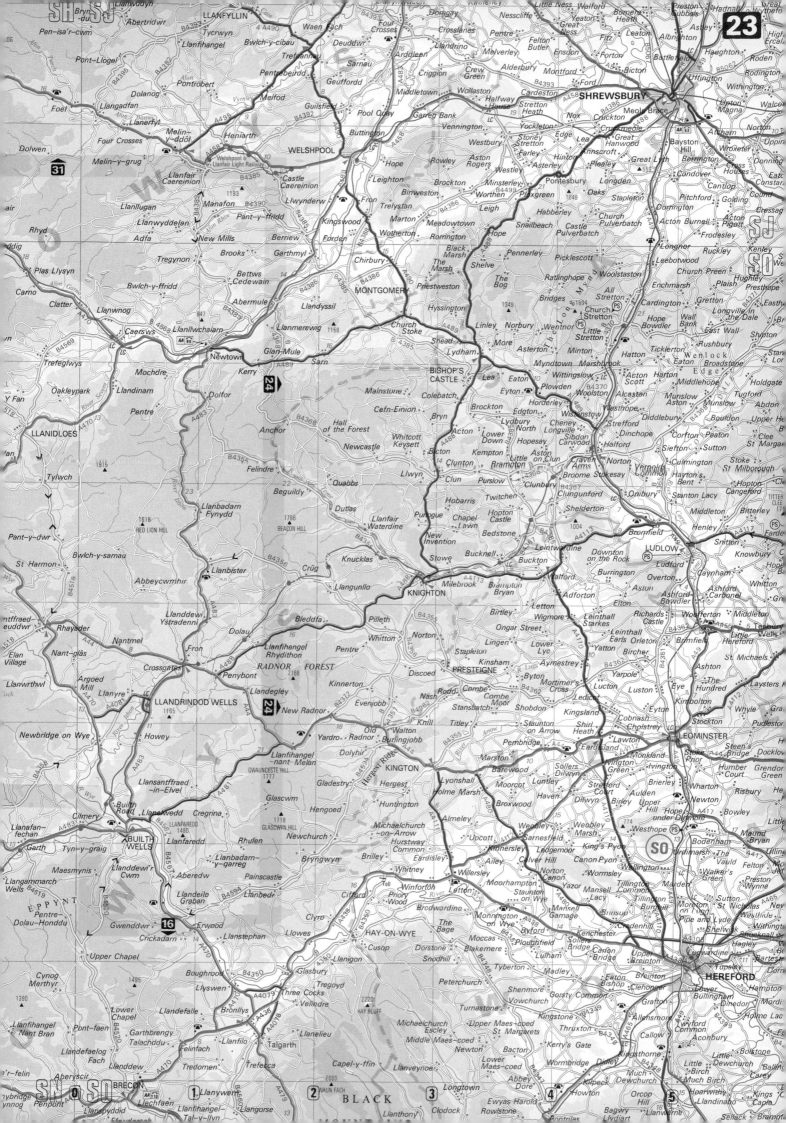

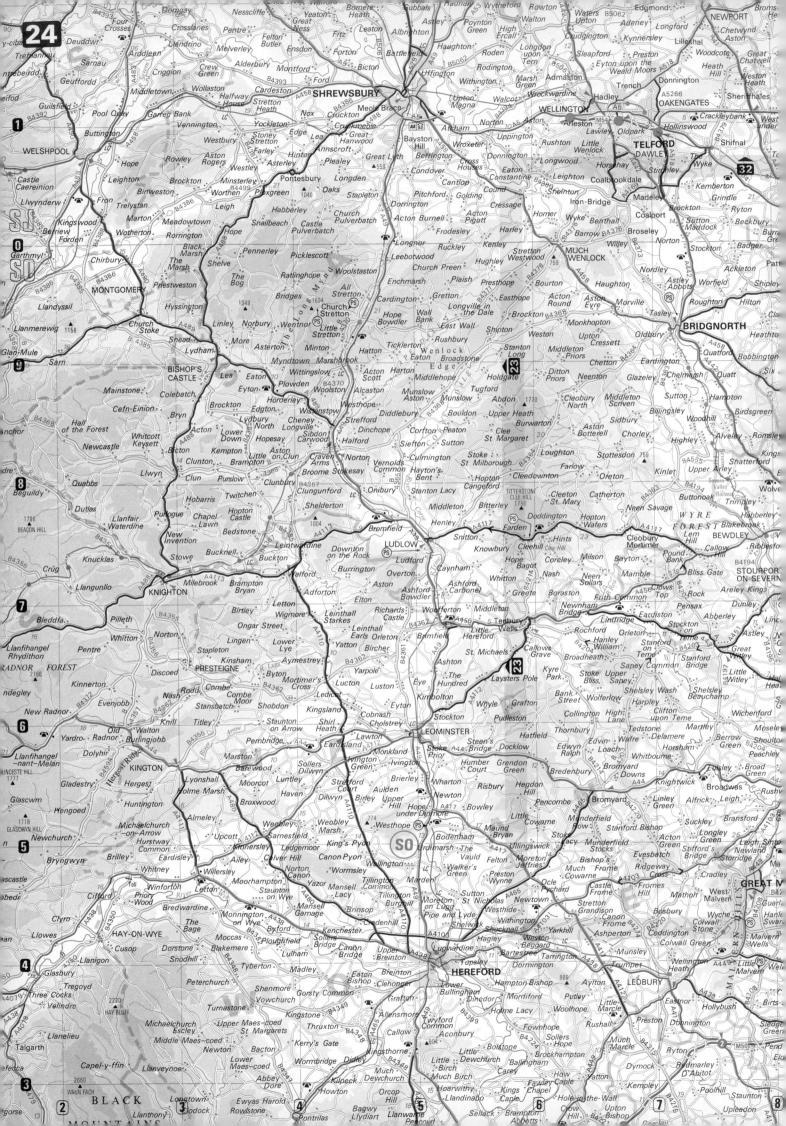

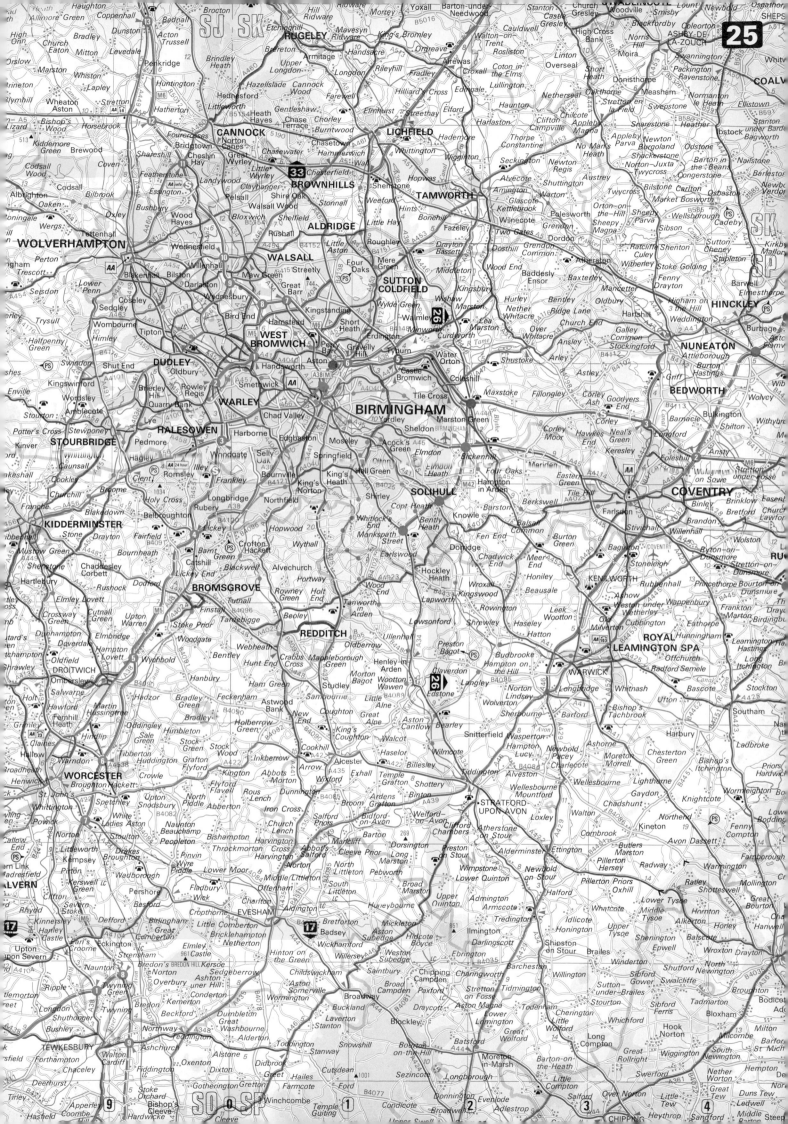

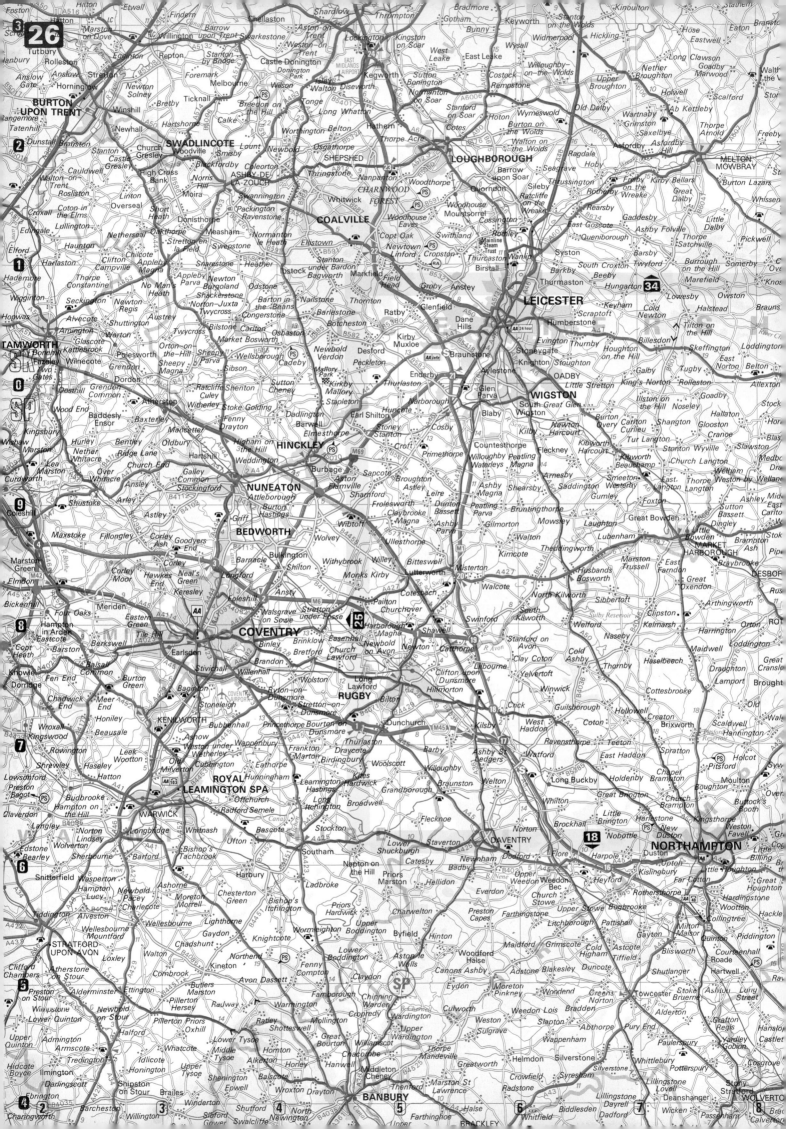

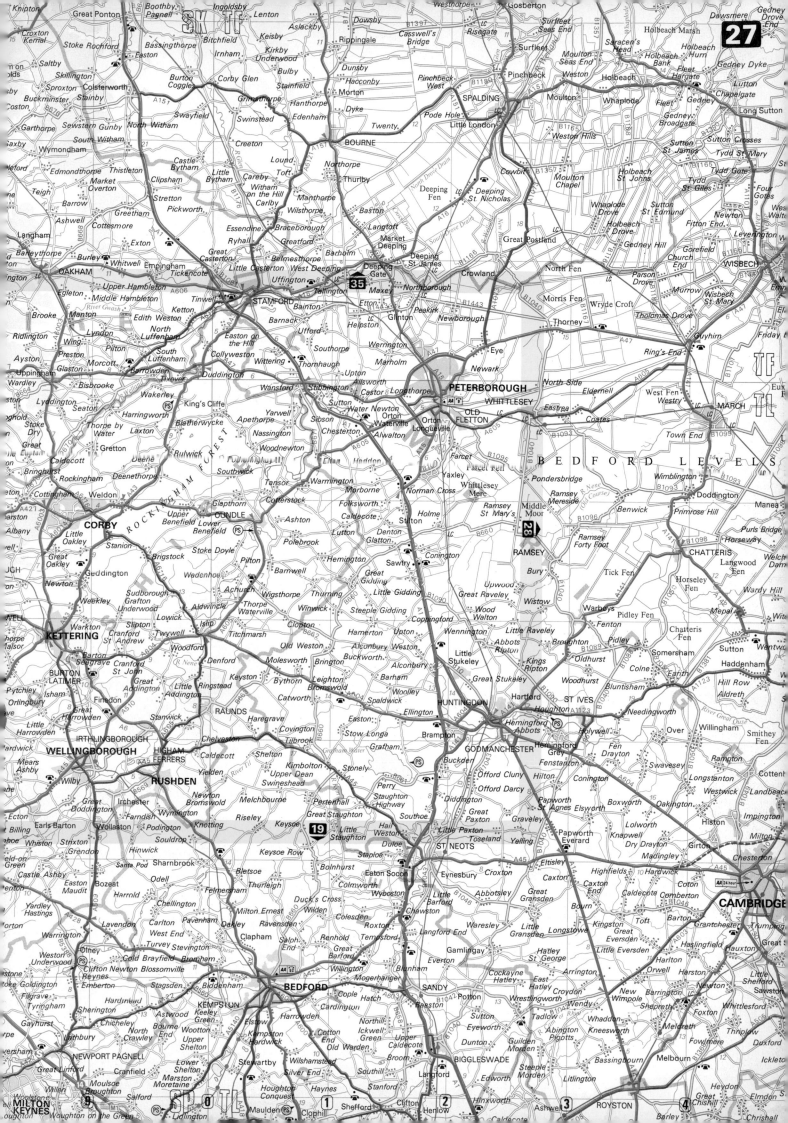

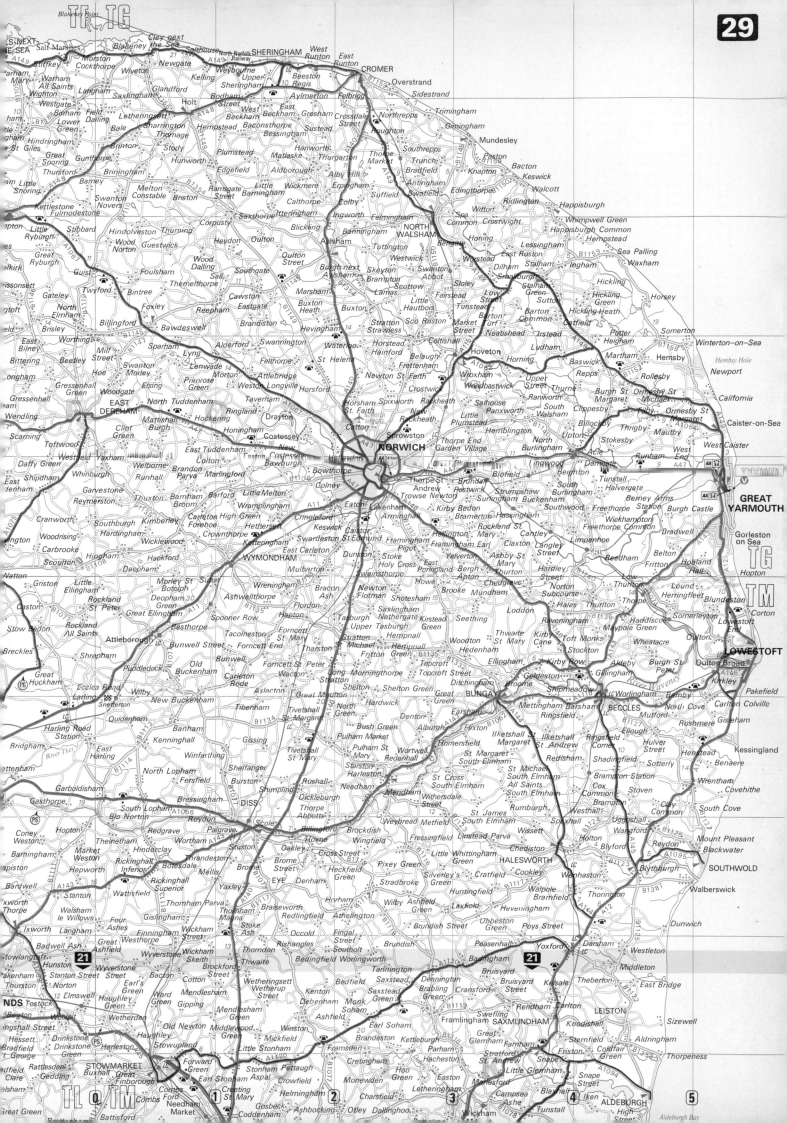

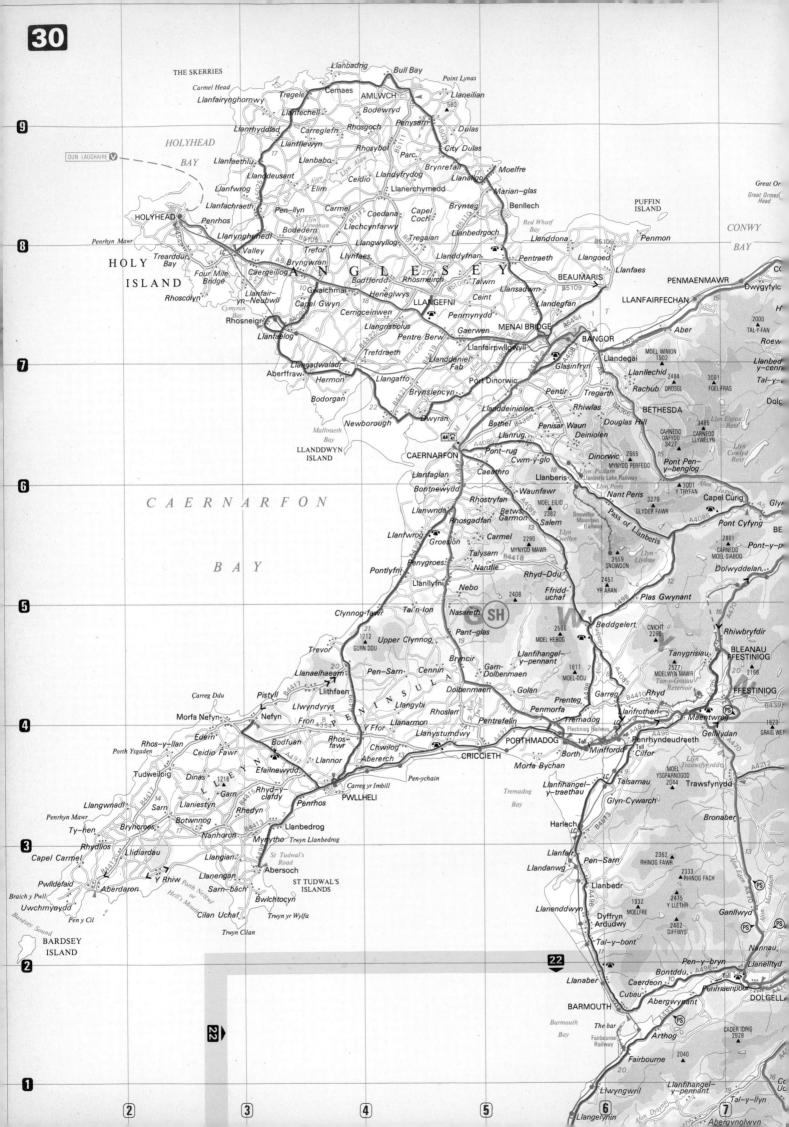

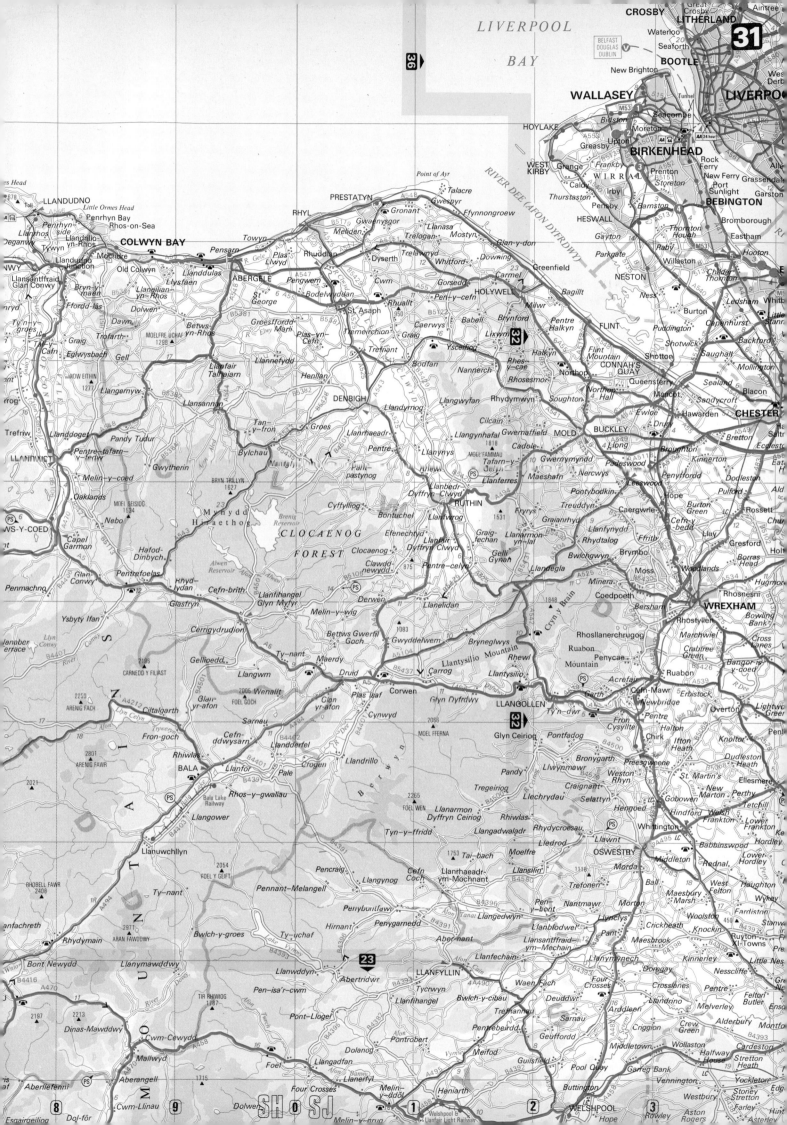

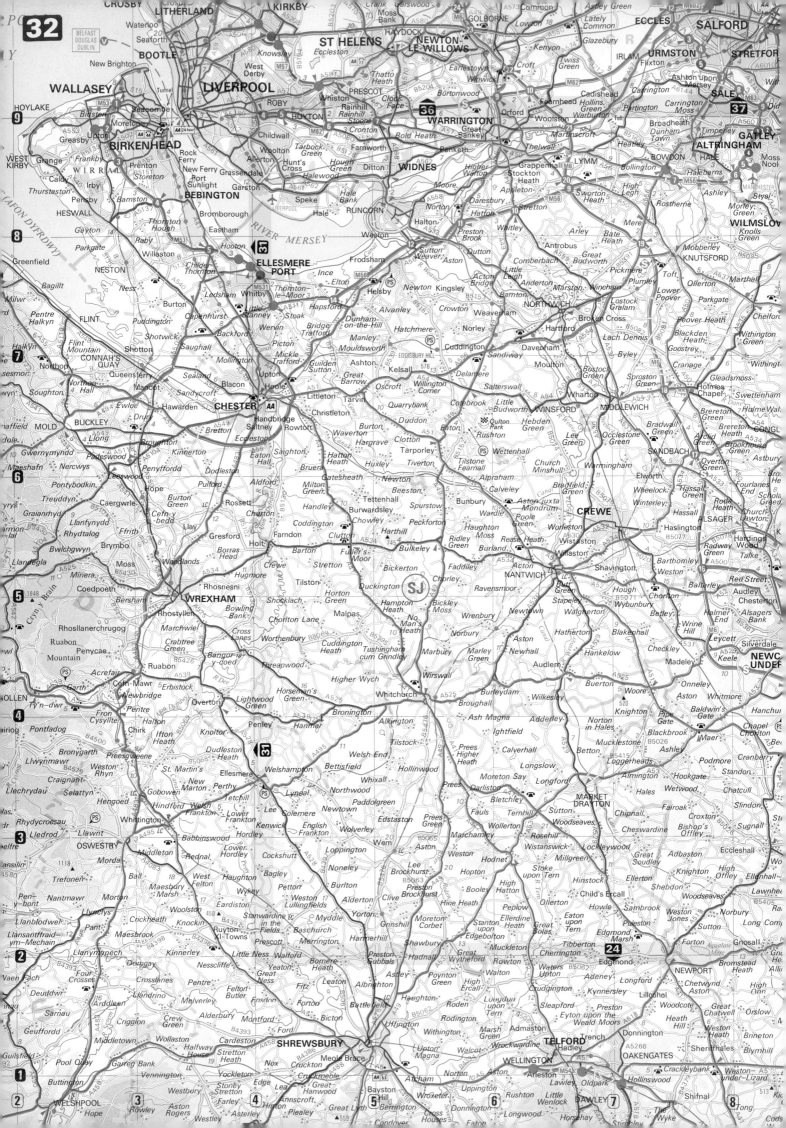

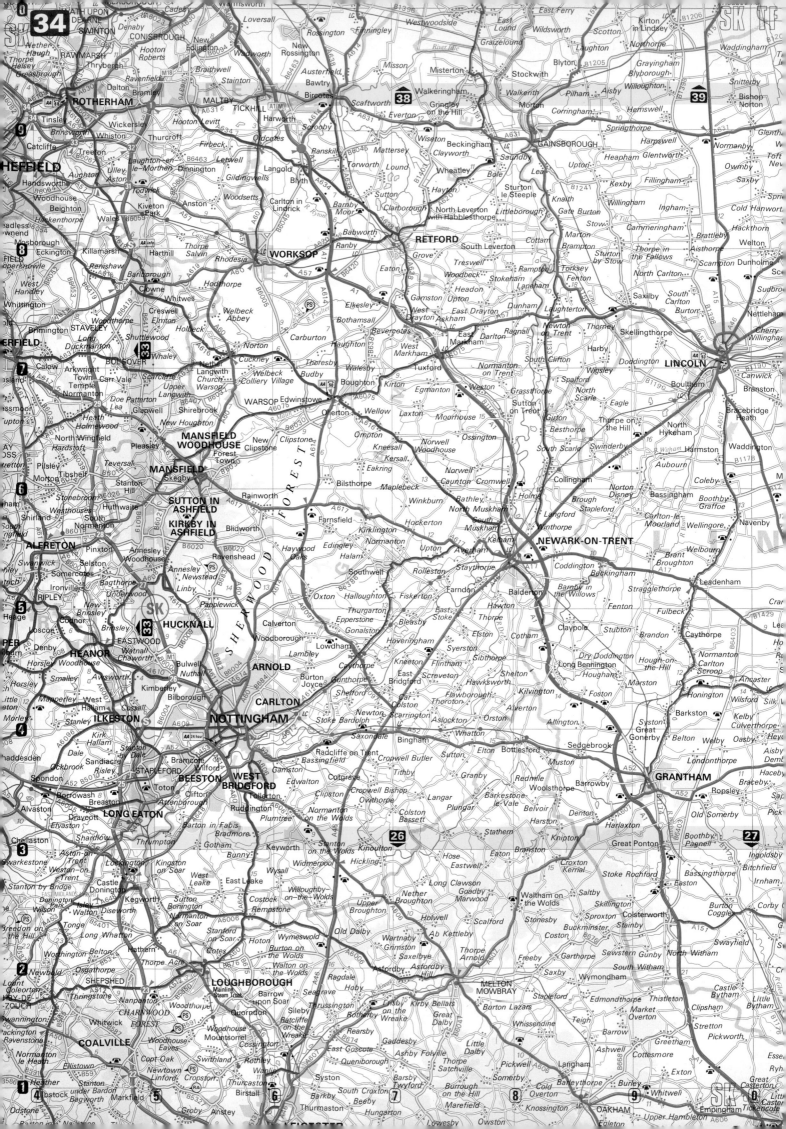

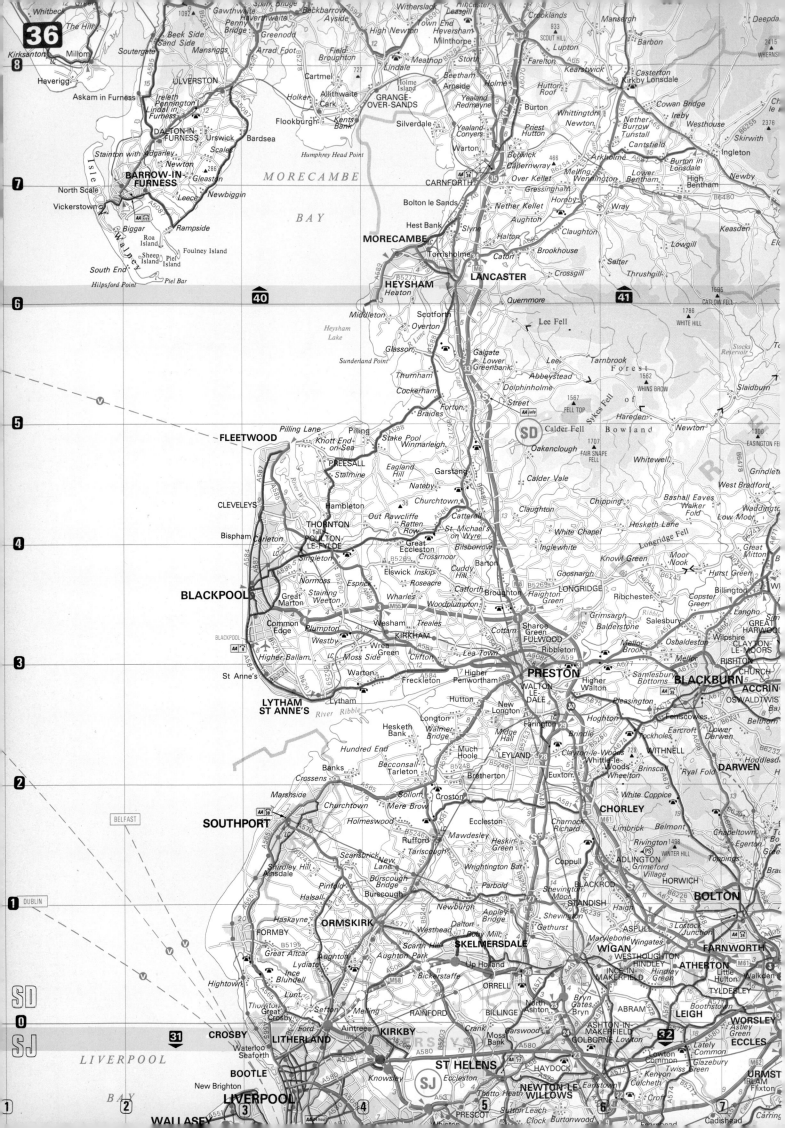

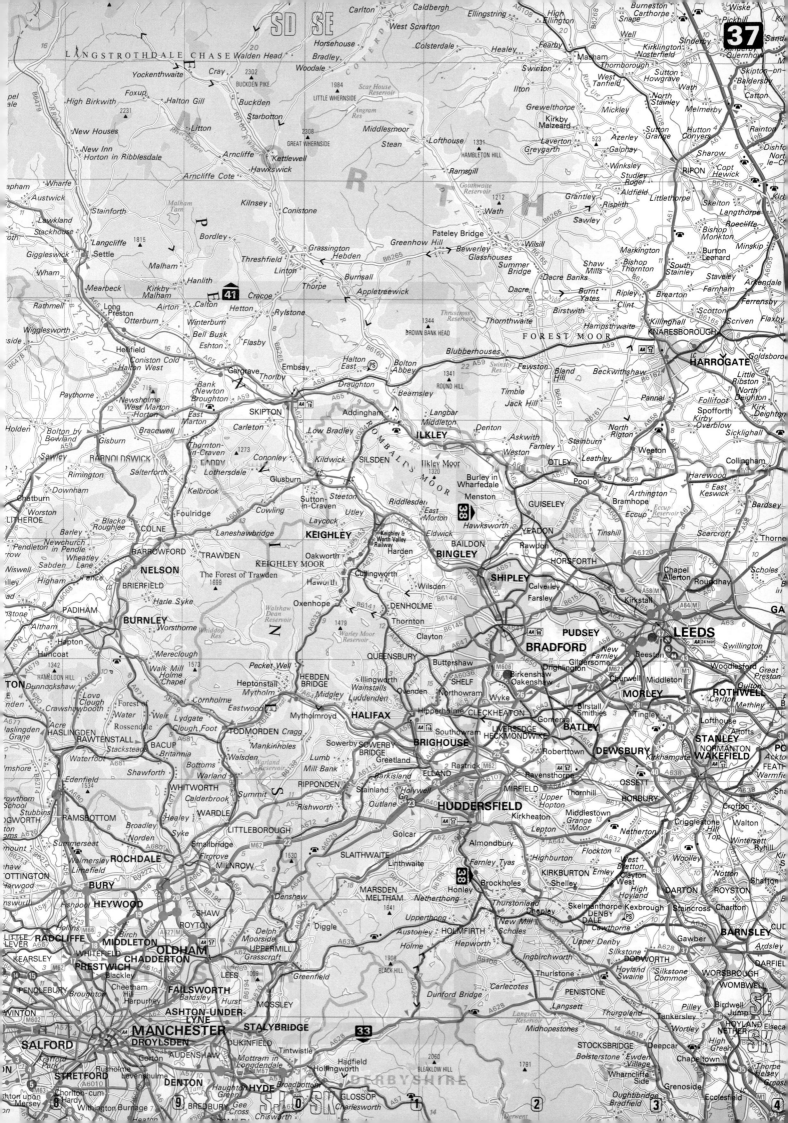

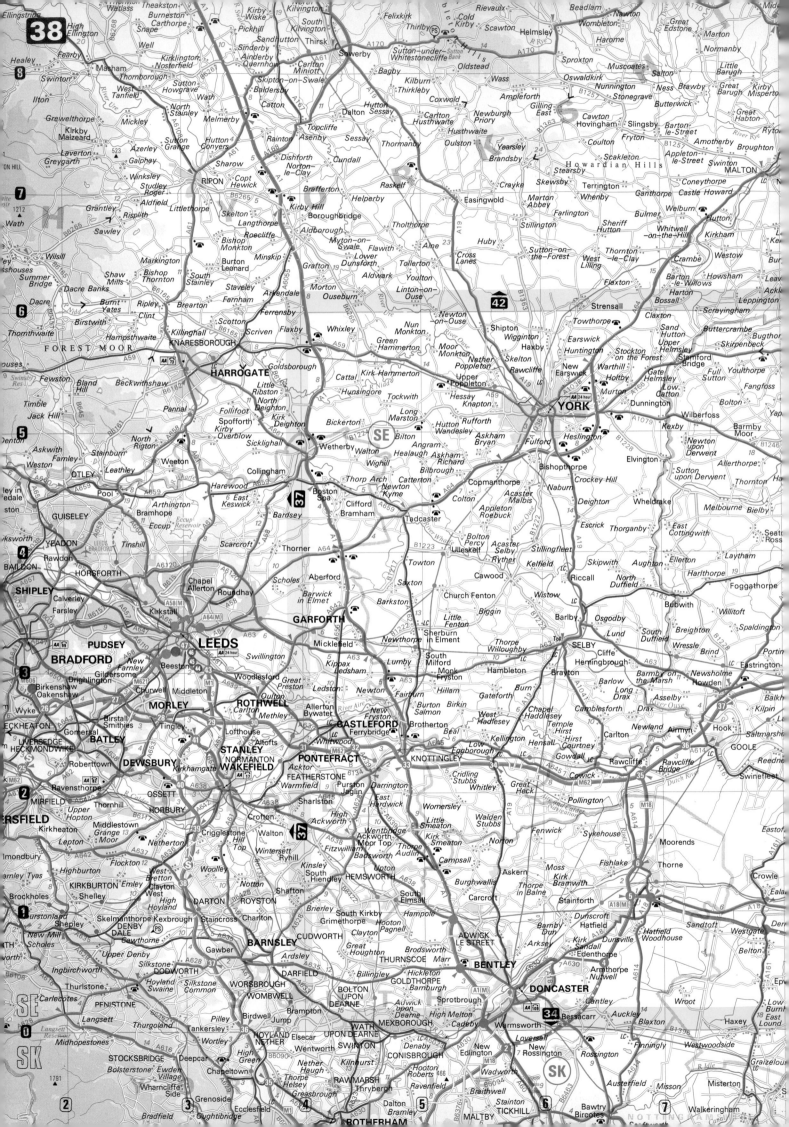

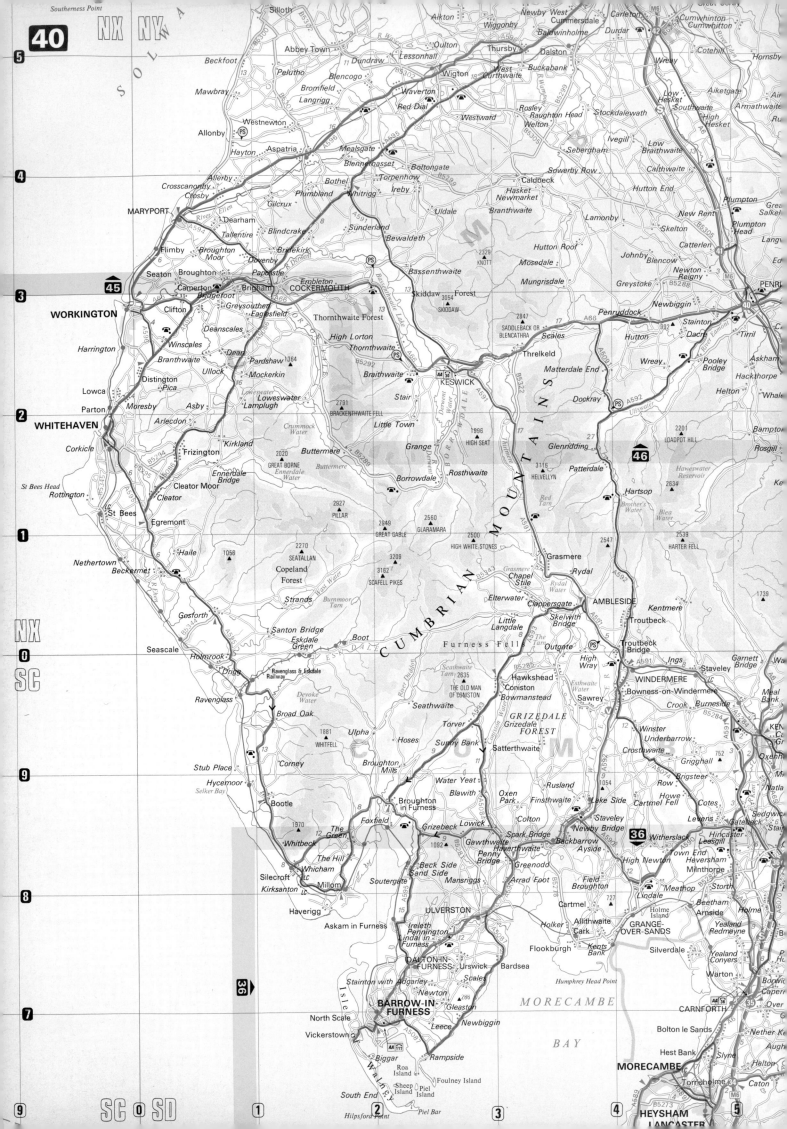

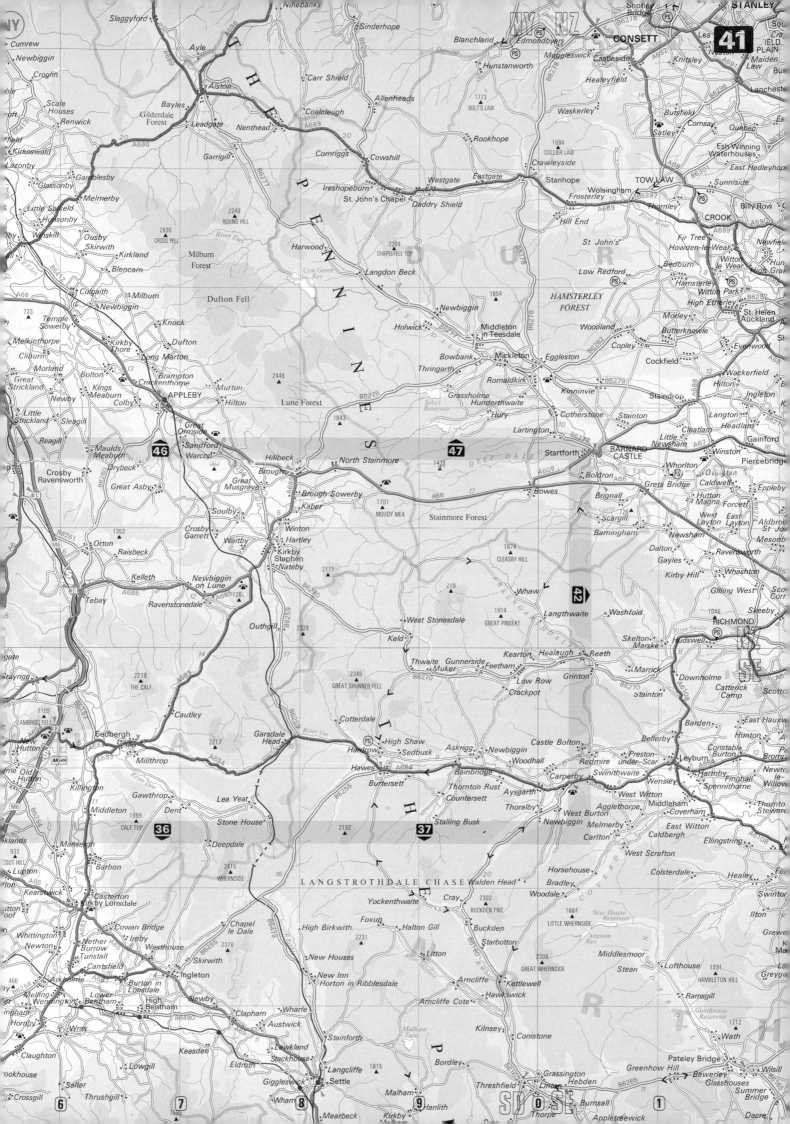

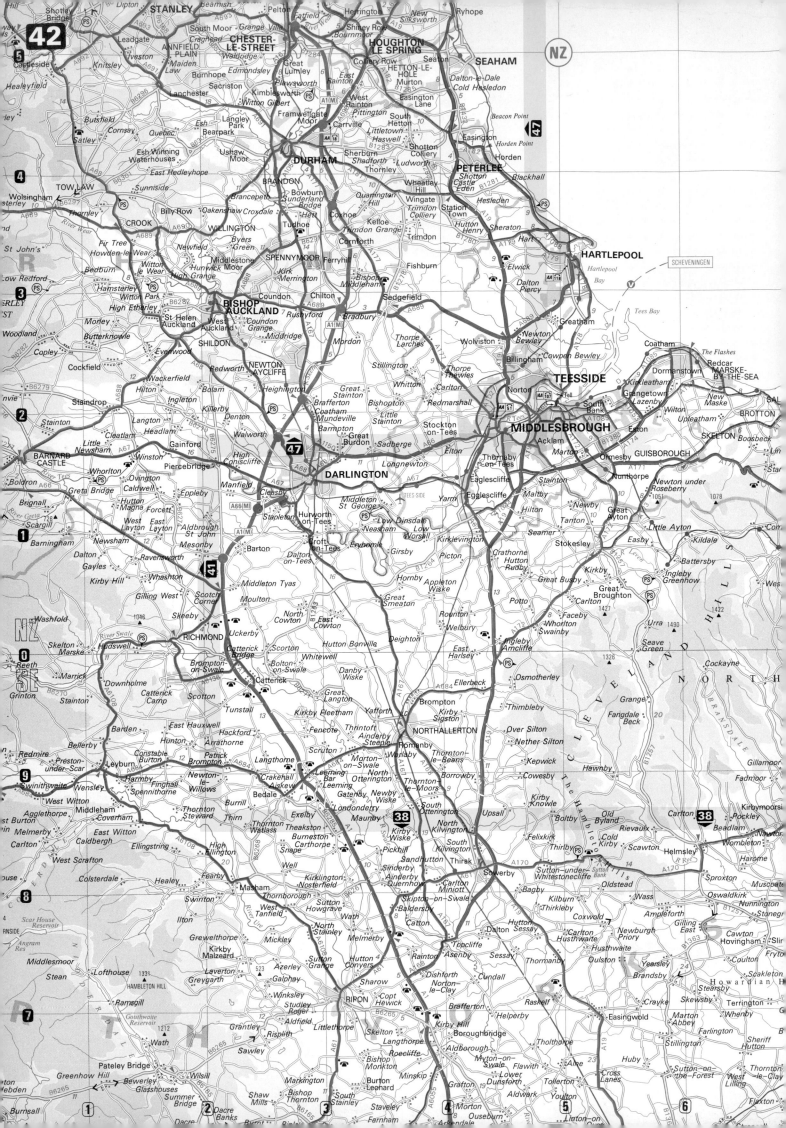

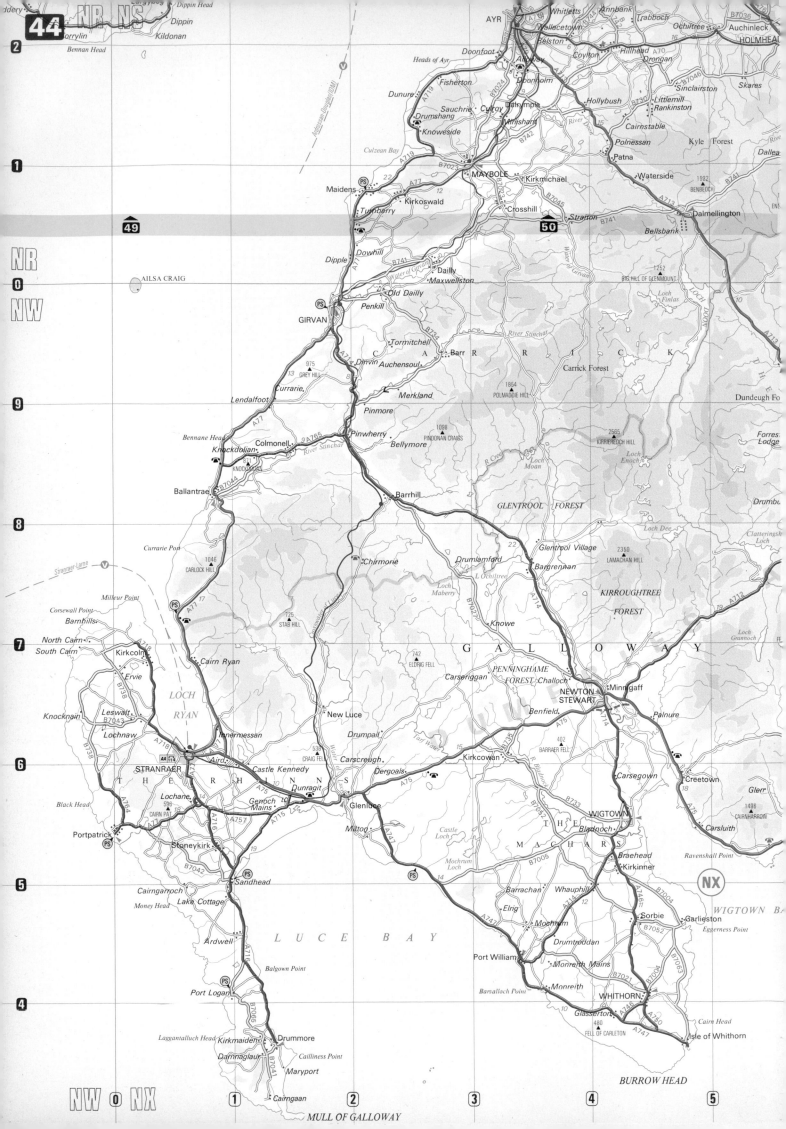

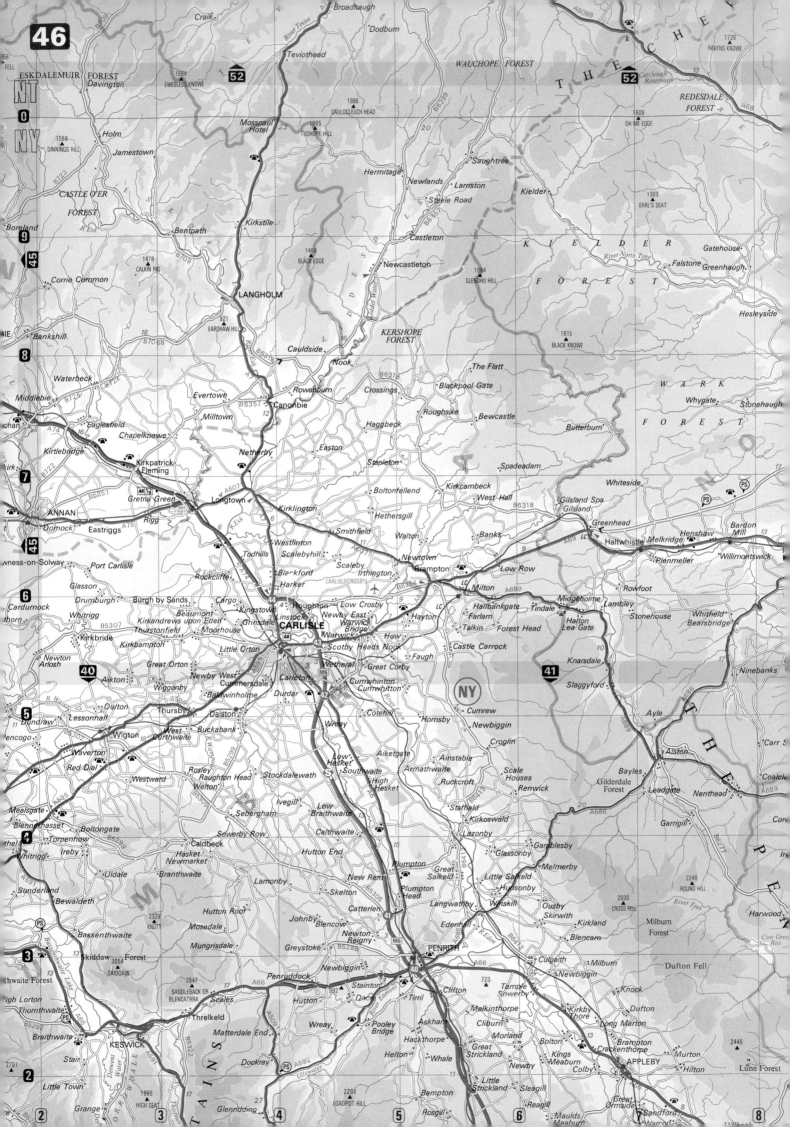

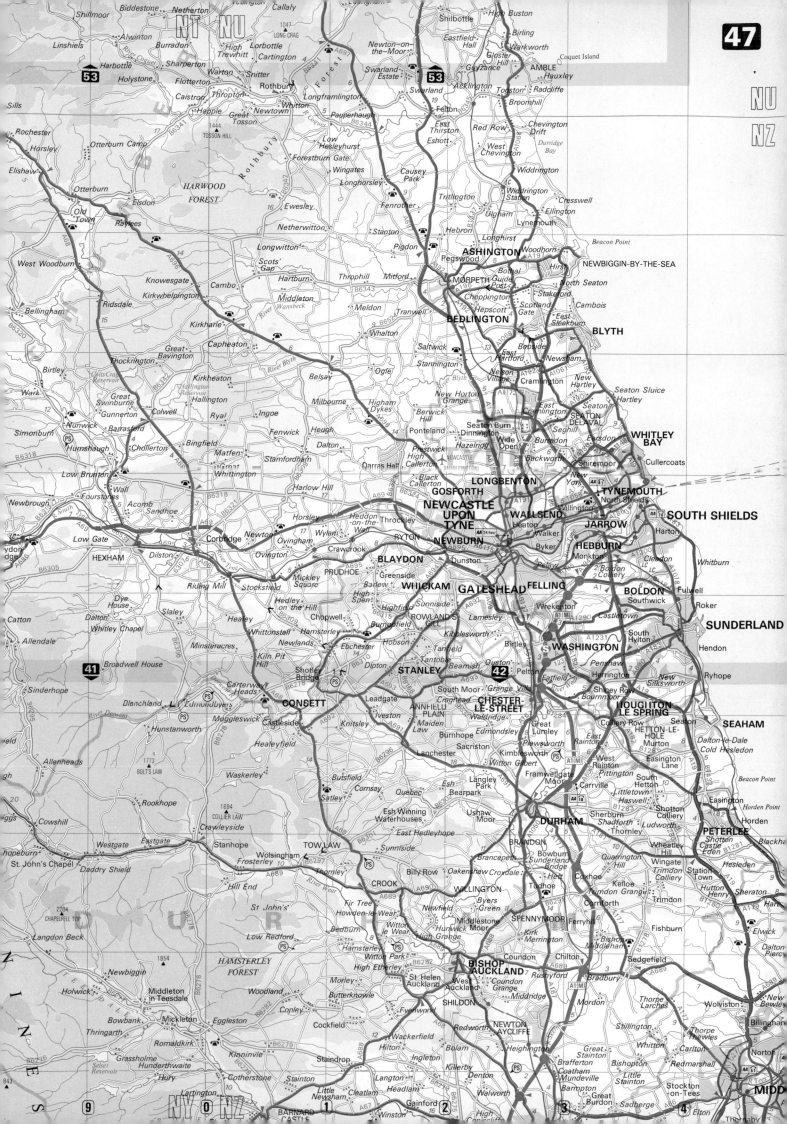

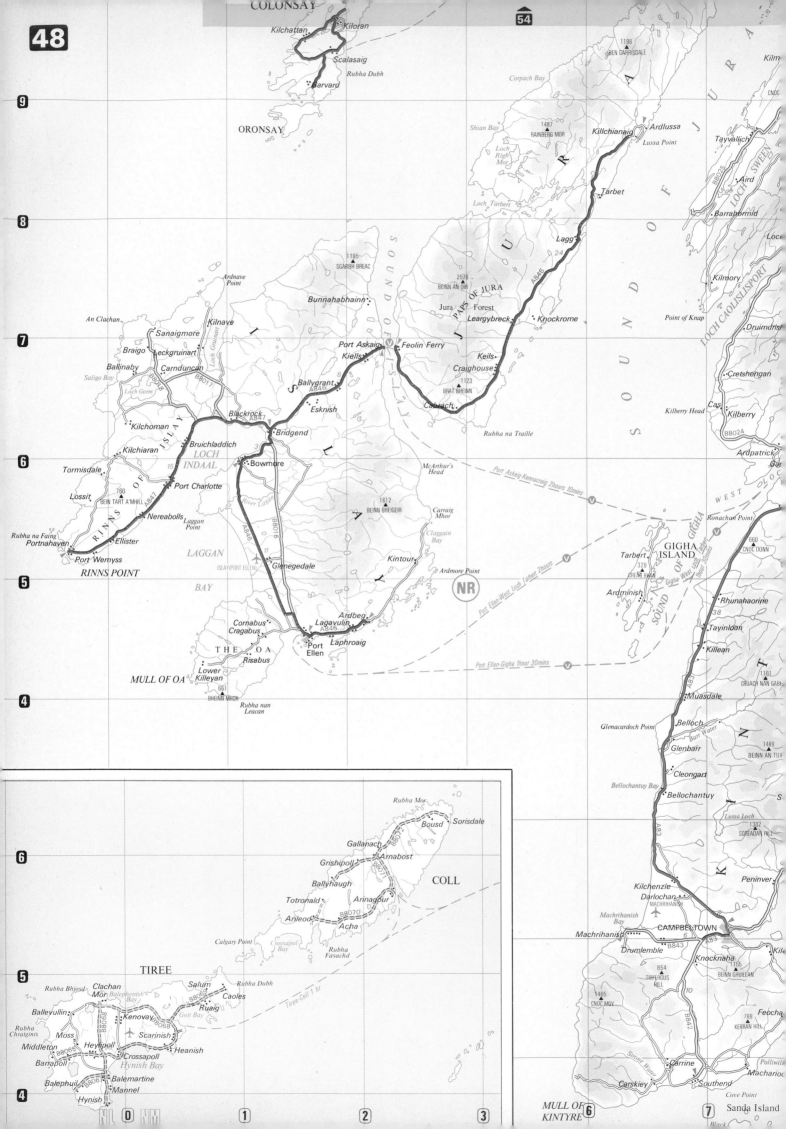

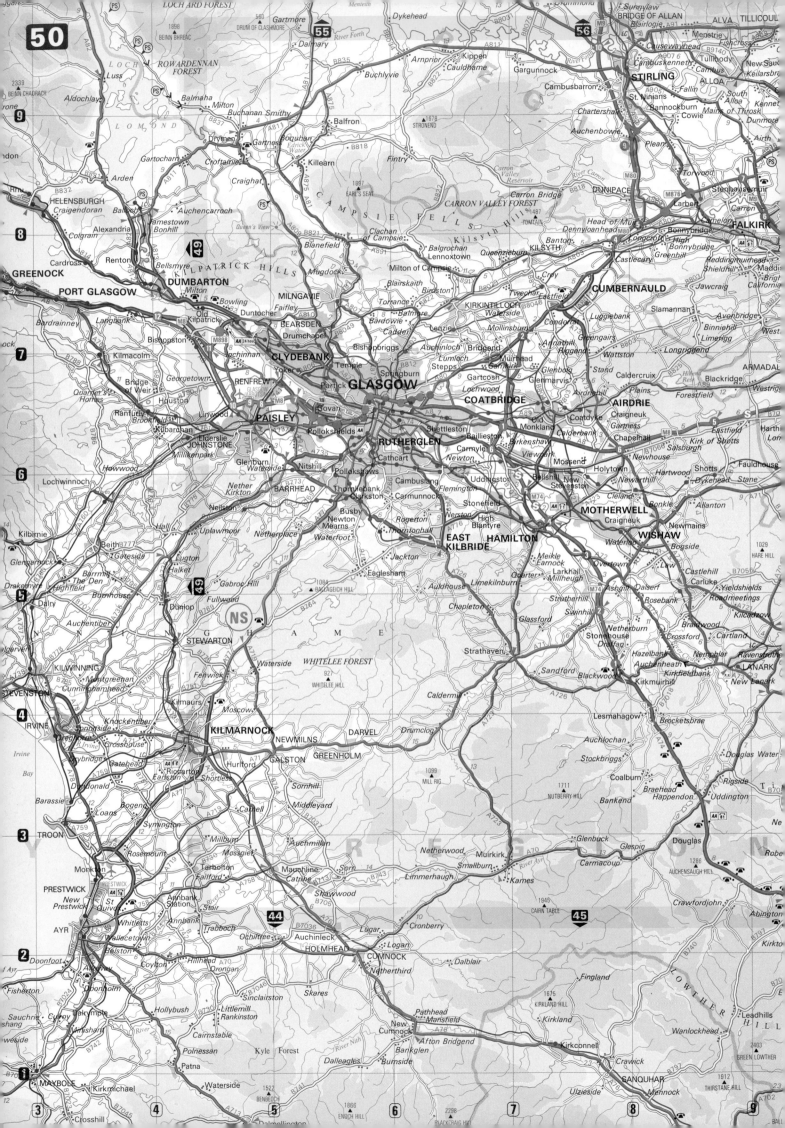

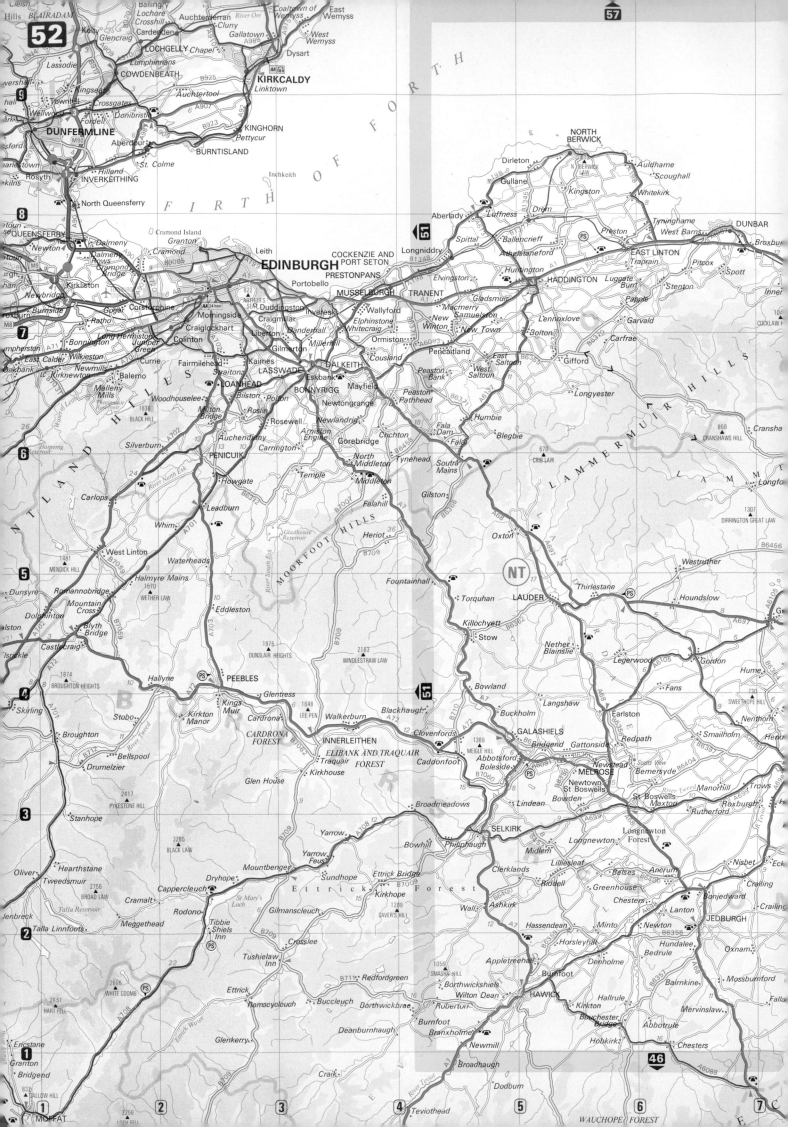

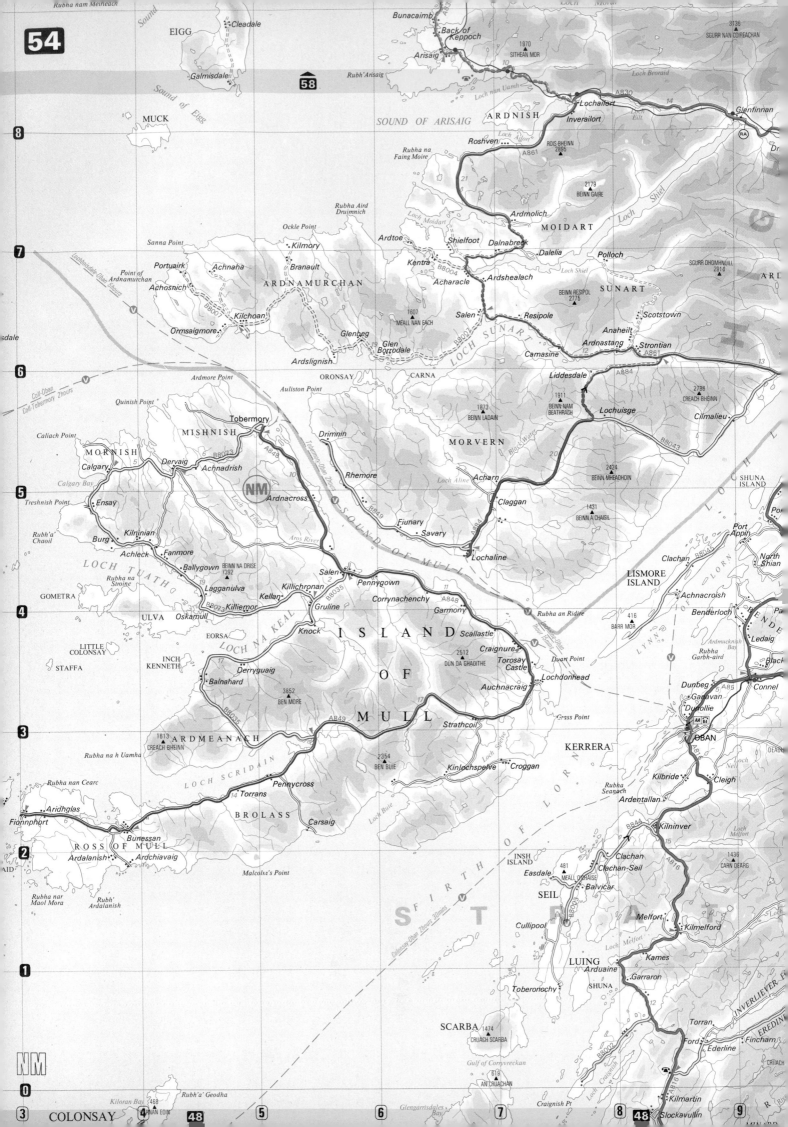

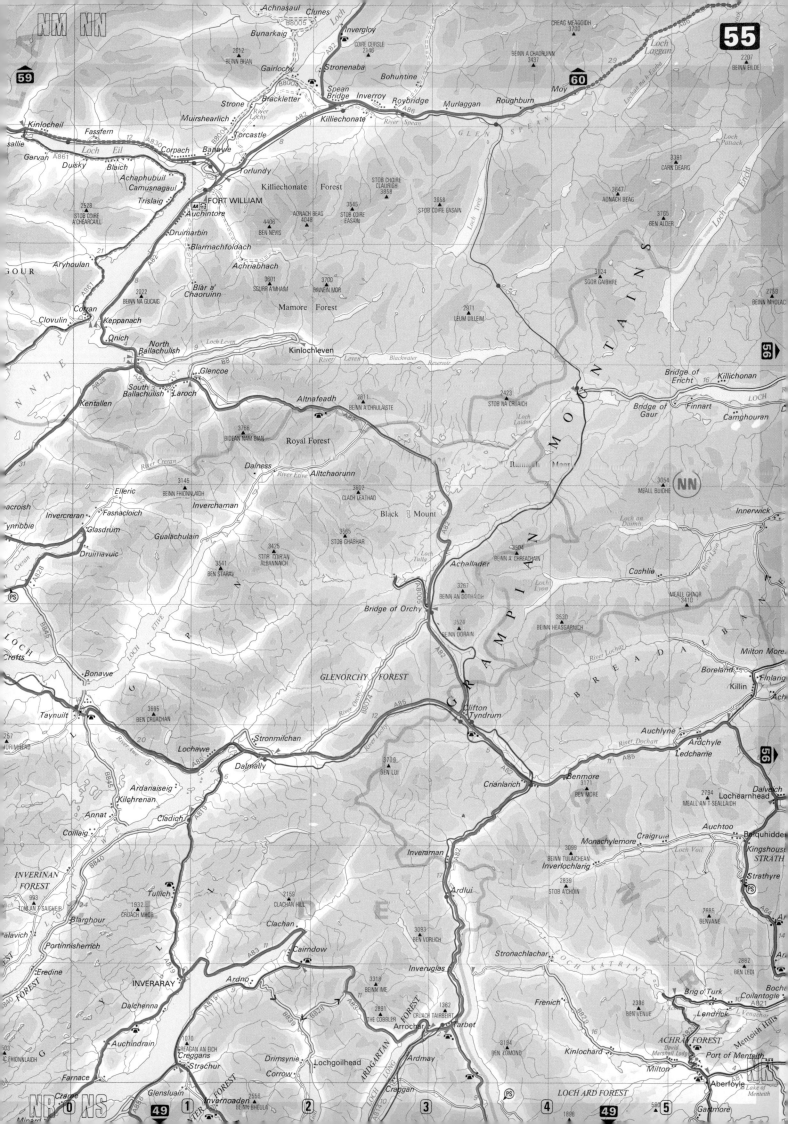

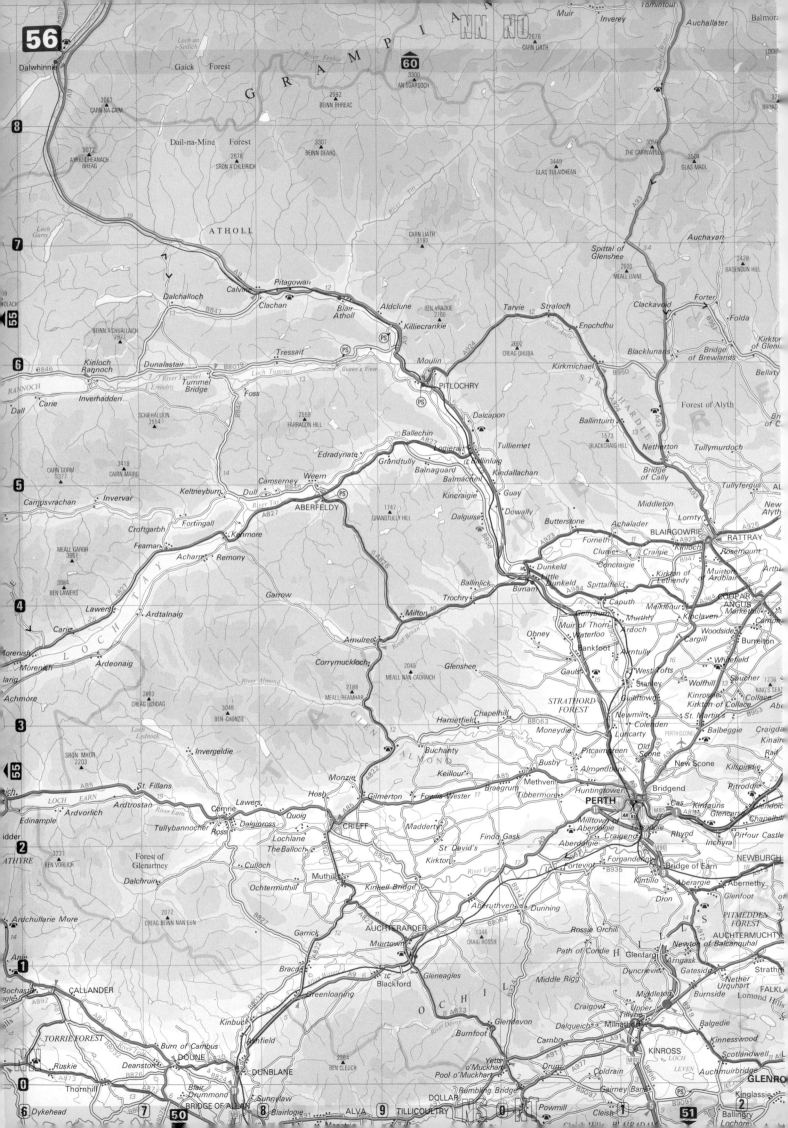

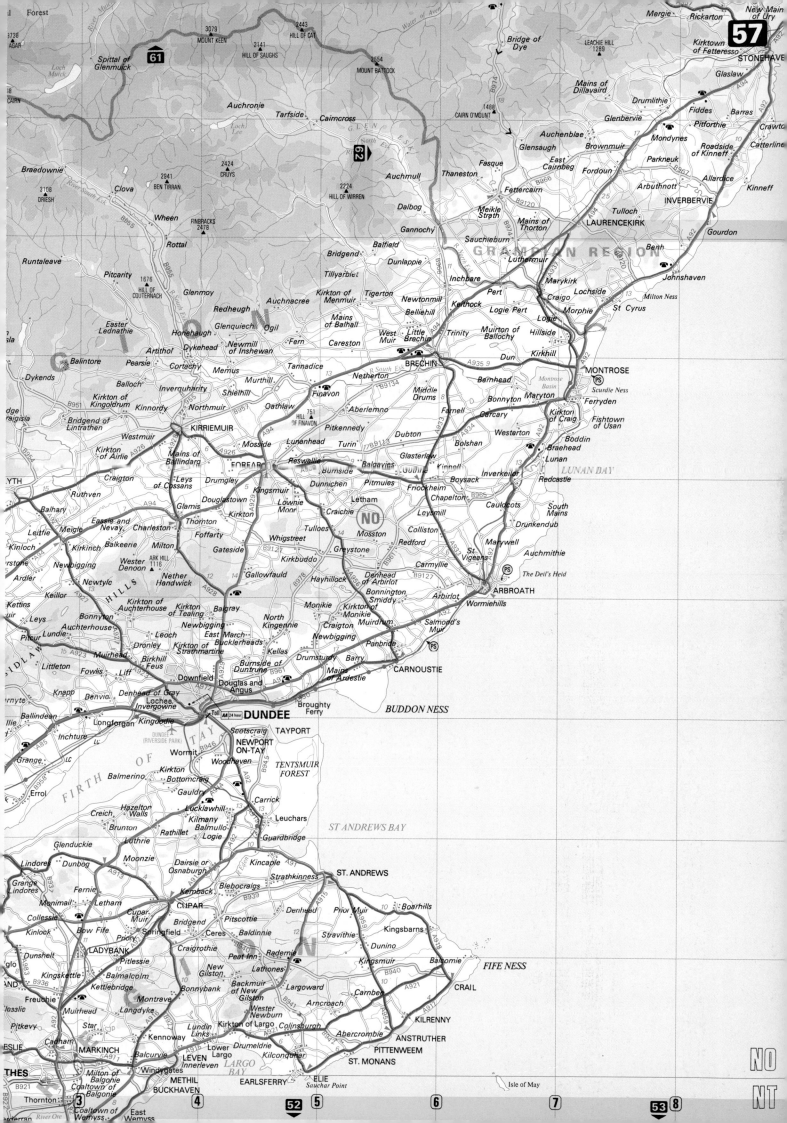

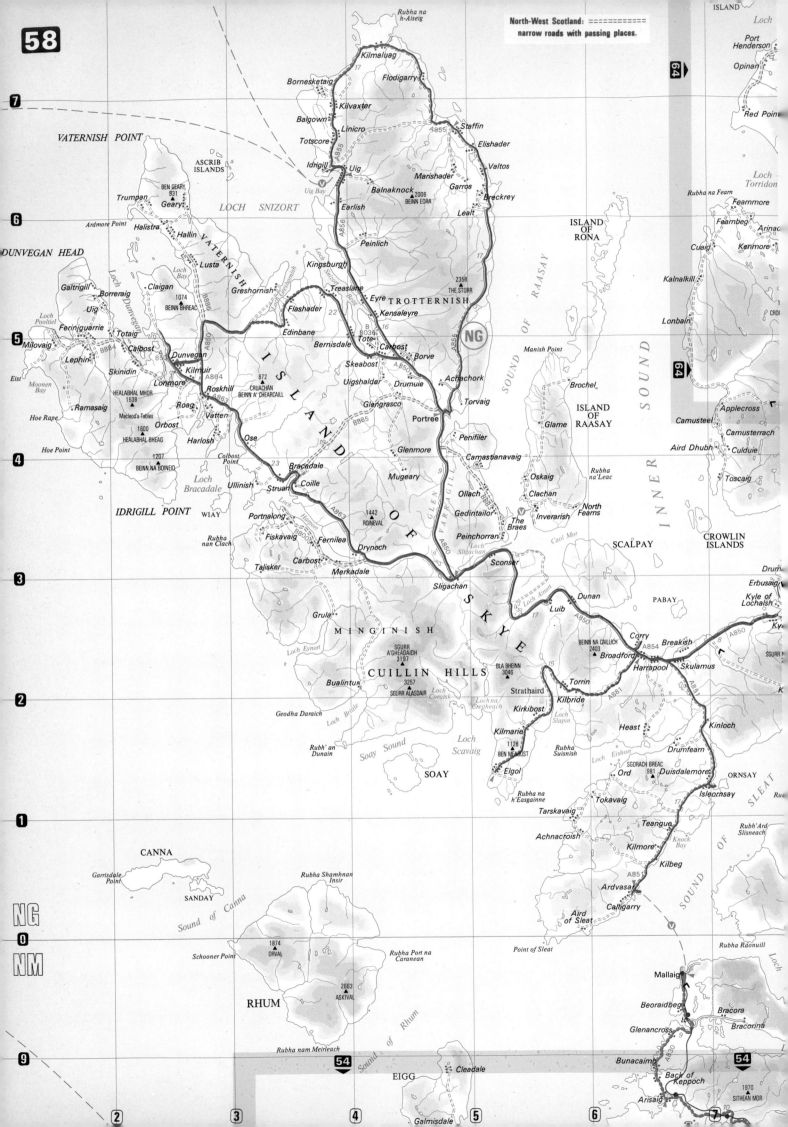

ISLAND

Rubha na
h-Aiseig

North-West Scotland: =============
narrow roads with passing places.

ISLAND
Loch

Port
Henderson
Opinan

Kilmaluag
Borneskeitaig   Flodigarry

Kilvaxter
Balgown
Linicro   Staffin
Totscore   A855   Elishader

Idrigill   Uig   Marishader
Uig Bay   Valtos
Balnaknock   Garros   Red Point
Earlish   2006   Breckrey
BEINN EDRA

VATERNISH POINT

Loch
Torridon

ASCRIB
ISLANDS
BEN GEARY   Peinlich   Lealt
931
Trumpan   Geary   LOCH SNIZORT   Fearnmore
Halistra   Rubha na Fearn   Fearnbeg
Ardmore Point   Arinac

DUNVEGAN HEAD   Hallin   Kingsburgh   ISLAND   Cuaig   Kenmore
Galtrigill   VATERNISH   OF   Kalnalkill
Borreraig   Lusta   Greshornish   RONA
Uig   Claigan   Treaslane   2358   Lonbain   CRO
Feriniquarrie   1074   Flashader   THE STORR
BEINN BHREAC   Edinbane   Eyre   TROTTERNISH
Milovaig   Totaig   22   Kensaleyre
Calbost   B   8036   NG   Manish Point
Lephin   Dunvegan   Tote   16
Skinidin   Kilmuir   Bernisdale   Carbost   Brochel
A864   872   Skeabost   Borve
Ramasaig   Lonmore   CRUACHAN   A850   Achachork   Glame   Applecross
Roskhill   BEINN A' CHEARCAILL   Uigshalder   Drumuie   ISLAND   Camusterrach
Roag   Torvaig   OF   Camusteel
Vatten   Glengrasco   RAASAY   Aird Dhubh   Culduie
1600   Orbost   Portree   Rubha
HEALABHAL BHEAG   Harlosh   Ose   na'Leac   Toscaig
Glenmore   Penifiler
BEINN NA BOINEID   Colbost   Bracadale   Camastianavaig   Oskaig   North
Point   23   Mugeary   9   Ollach   Clachan   Fearns
Ullinish   Coille   1442   Gedintailor   Inverarish
IDRIGILL POINT   WIAY   Struan   ROINEVAL   Peinchorran   The
Portnalong   Braes   SCALPAY   CROWLIN
Fiskavaig   B8009   Fernilea   Drynoch   Loch   ISLANDS
Carbost   Sligachan   Sconser
Talisker   Merkadale   Sligachan   Loch Ainort   Drum
Erbusaig
Grula   Dunan   PABAY   Kyle of
MINGINISH   Luib   Lochalsh
SGURR   17   Corry   Ky
A'GHEADAIDH   BEINN NA CAILLICH   Breakish
3197   2403   Broadford   A850   Ky
CUILLIN HILLS   BLA BHEINN   Harrapool   Skulamus   SGURR M
3046   15
Bualintur   3257   Torrin   Strathaird   Kilbride
SGURR ALASDAIR   Kilmarie   Heast   Kinloch
Geodha Daraich   Kirkibost   Drumfearn
Rubh' an   Loch Eynort   Kilmarie   Rubha Suisnish   ORNSAY
Dunain   1128   SGORACH BREAC   Duisdalemore
BEN MEABOST   Ord   981
Loch Scavaig   Elgol   Isleornsay
SOAY   Rubha na   Tokavaig
Soay Sound   h'Easgainne   Tarskavaig
Teangue   SLEAT
CANNA   Achnacroish   Kilmore   Knock   Rubh'Ard
Bay   Slisneach
Garrisdale   Kilbeg
Point   Rubha Shamhnan   A851
SANDAY   Insir   Ardvasar
Calligarry   SOUND
Sound of Canna   Aird   OF   Rubha Raonuill
of Sleat
Schooner Point   1874   Point of Sleat
ORVAL   Rubha Port na
Caranean

Mallaig

RHUM   Beoraidbeg   Bracora
Glenancross   Bracorina
2663
ASKIVAL

Bunacaimb
Rubha nam Meirleach   Back of
Keppoch   Arisaig   1970
EIGG   Cleadale   SITHEAN MOR
Rubha nam Meirleach   Galmisdale

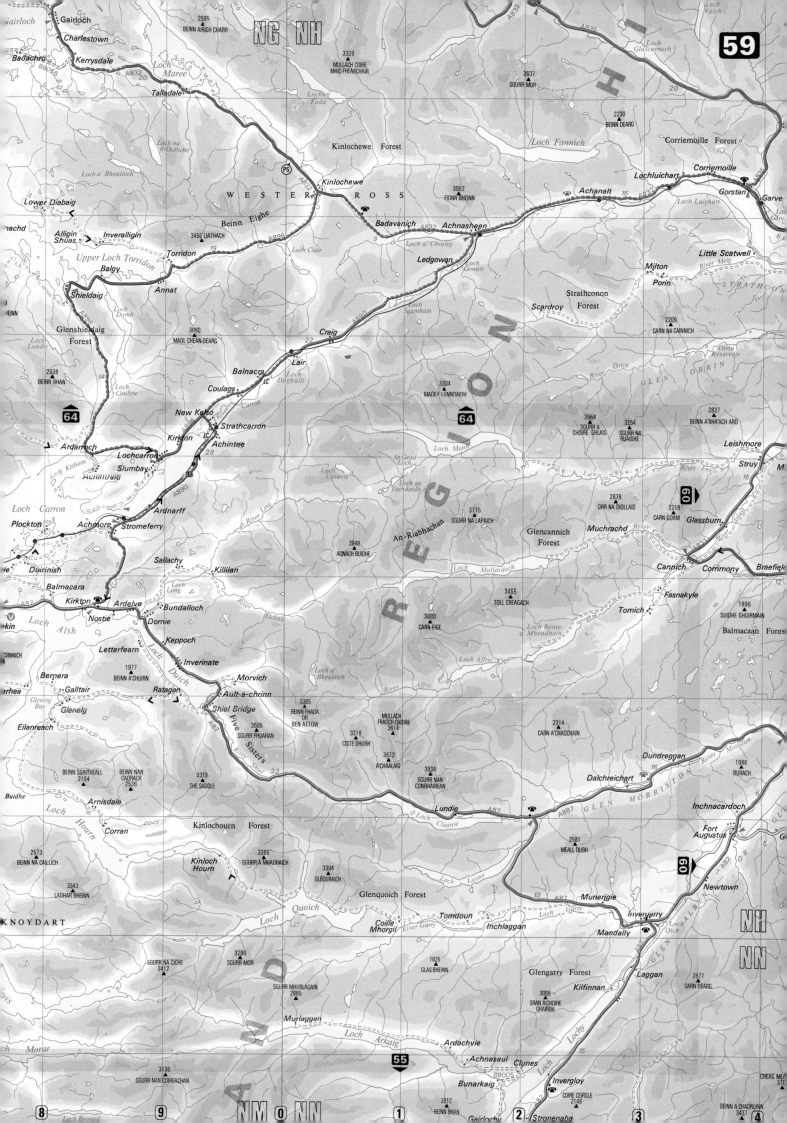

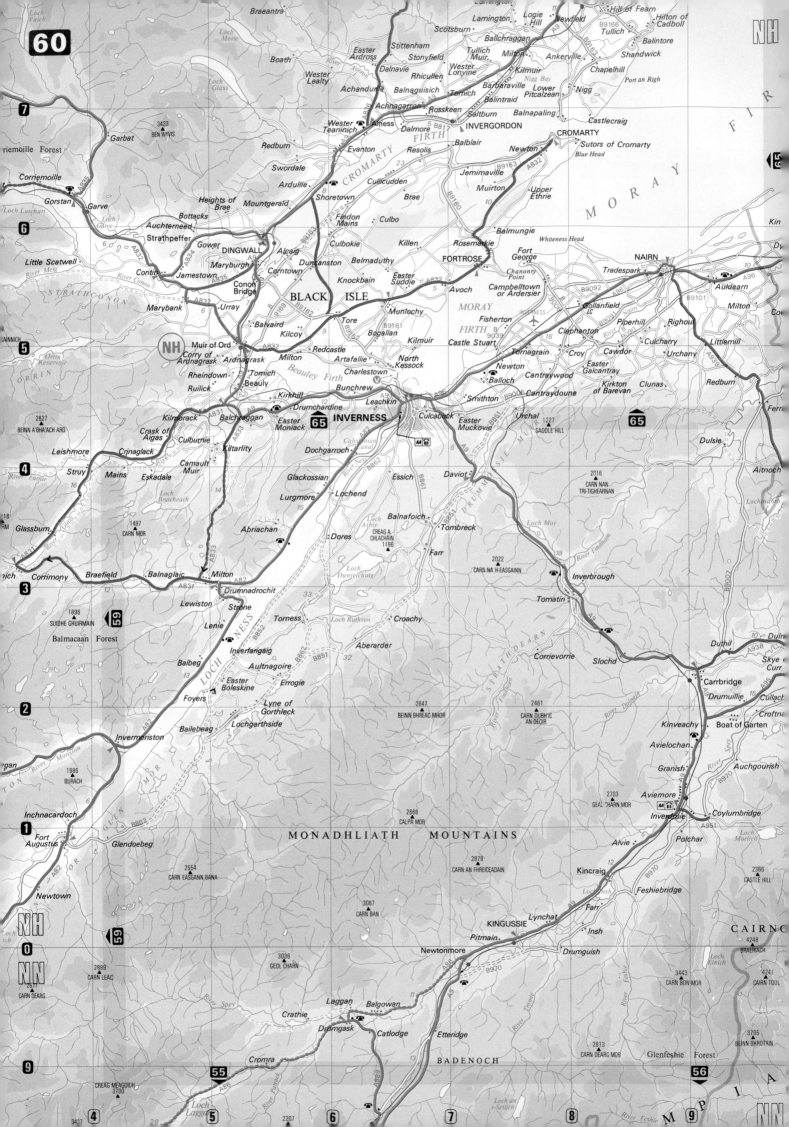

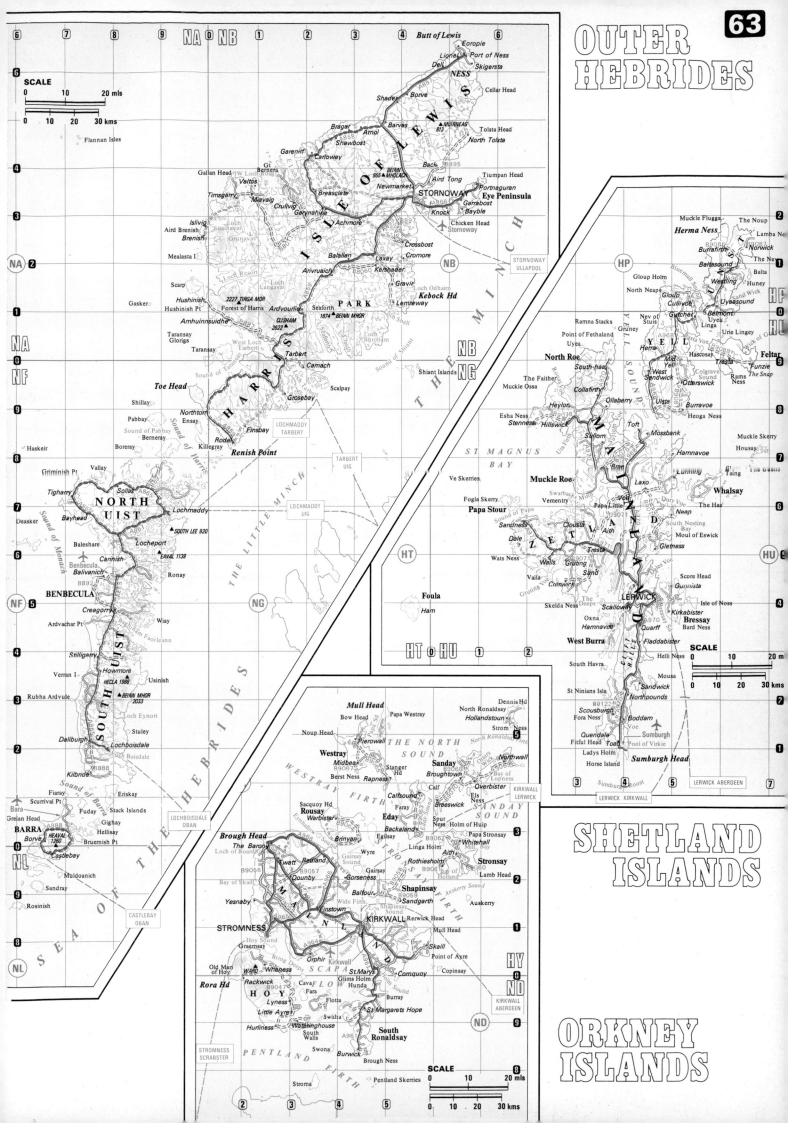

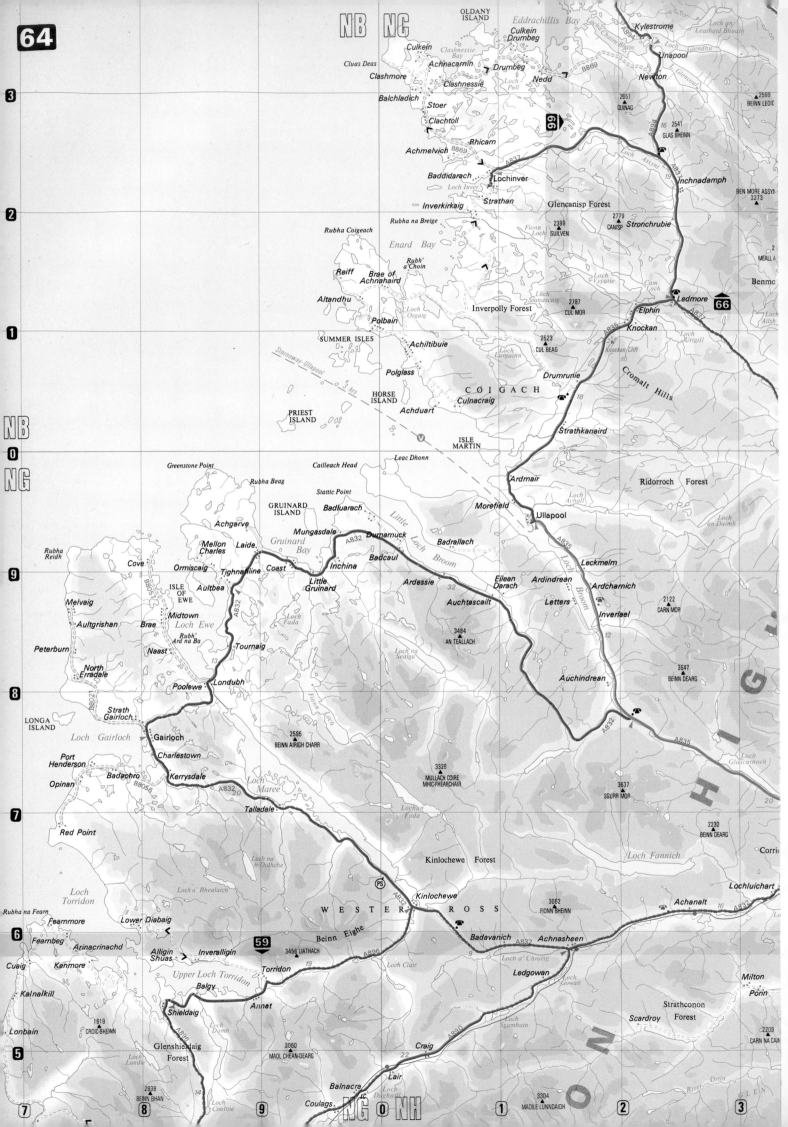

NC
NH

59

60

NH

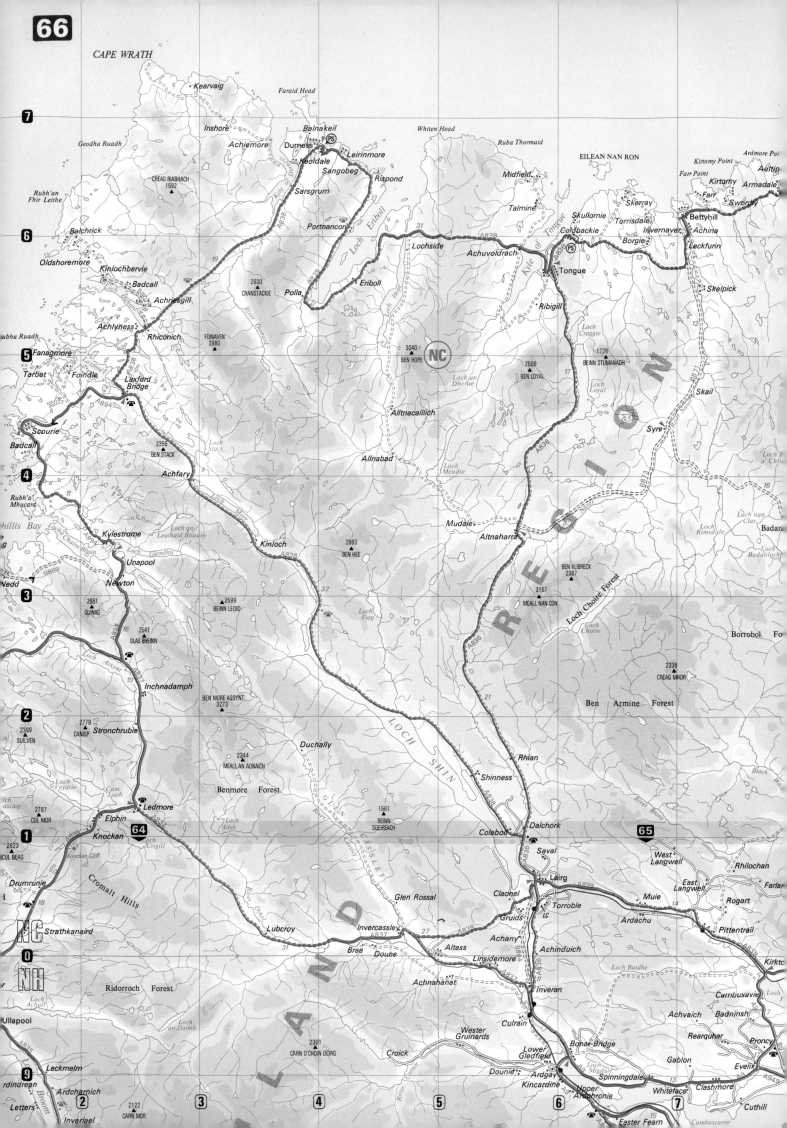

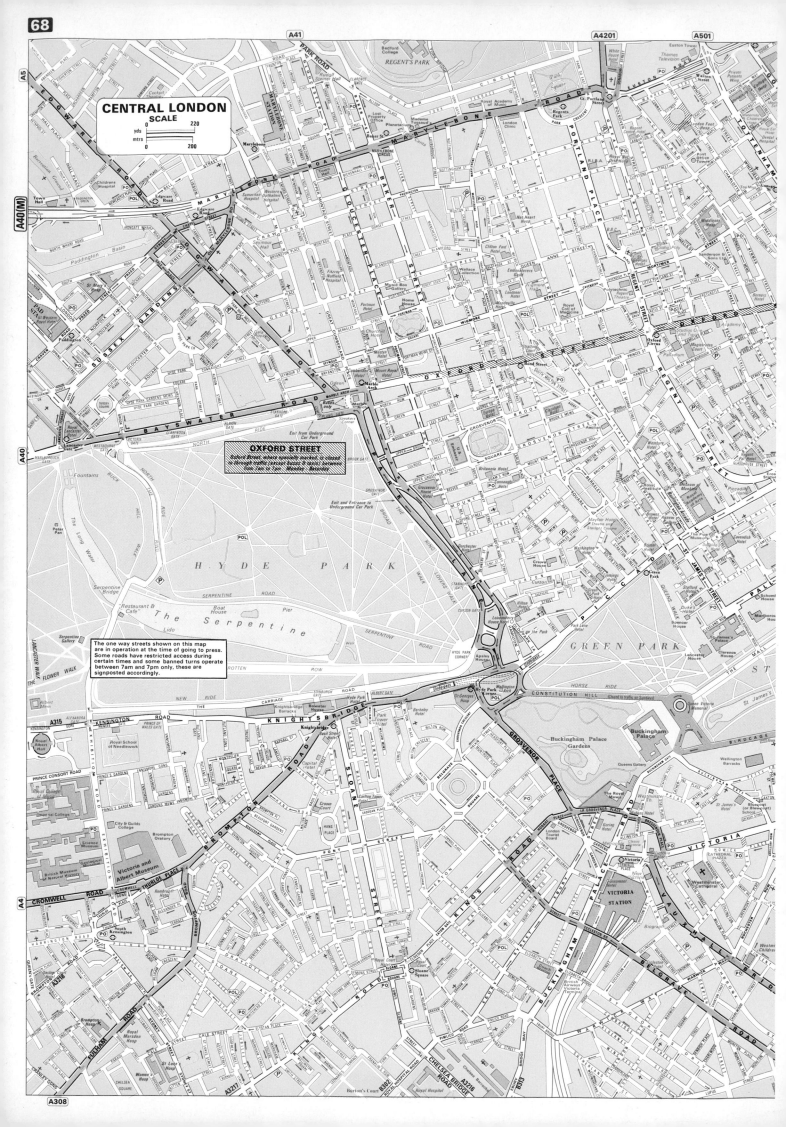

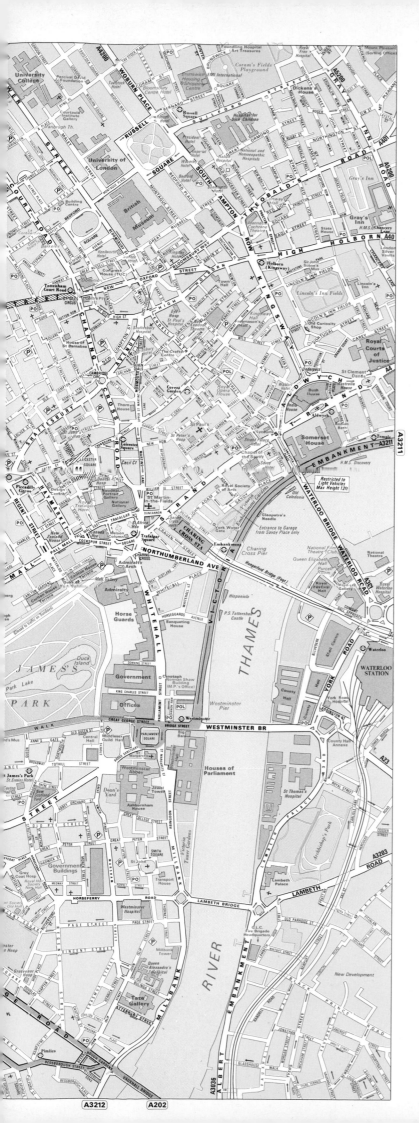

THEATRES IN CENTRAL LONDON

ADELPHI
The Strand WC2

ALBERY
St Martin's Lane WC2

ALDWYCH
Aldwych WC2

AMBASSADORS
West Street WC2

ARTS
(Theatre Club)
Gt Newport Street WC2

APOLLO
Shaftesbury Avenue W1

CAMBRIDGE
Earlham Street WC2

COCKPIT
Gateforth Street NW8

COLISEUM
St Martin's Lane WC2

COMEDY
Panton Street SW1

COTTESLOE
National Theatre, South Bank SE1

CRITERION
Piccadilly W1

DRURY LANE
Theatre Royal, Catherine Street WC2

DUCHESS
Catherine Street WC2

DUKE OF YORK'S
St Martin's Lane WC2

FORTUNE
Russell Street WC2

GARRICK
Charing Cross Road WC2

GLOBE
Shaftesbury Avenue W1

GREENWOOD
Weston Street SE1

HAYMARKET
Theatre Royal, Haymarket SW1

HER MAJESTY'S
Haymarket SW1

JEANNETTA COCHRANE
Theobalds Road WC1

KINGS ROAD THEATRE
Kings Road SW3

LYRIC
Shaftesbury Avenue W1

LYTTLETON
National Theatre, South Bank SE1

MAYFAIR
Stratton Street W1

MERMAID
Puddle Dock, Blackfriars EC4

NATIONAL THEATRE
(Cottesloe, Lyttleton &
Oliver Theatres), South Bank SE1

NEW LONDON
Parker Street, WC2

NEW VICTORIA
Wilton Road SW1

OLD VIC
Waterloo Road SE1

OLIVIER
National Theatre, South Bank SE1

OPEN AIR THEATRE
Inner Circle, Regents Park NW1

OPEN SPACE THEATRE
303/307 Euston Road NW1

PALACE
Shaftesbury Avenue W1

PALLADIUM
Argyll Street W1

PHOENIX
Charing Cross Road WC2

PICCADILLY
Denman Street W1

PRINCE OF WALES
Coventry Street W1

QUEEN'S
Shaftesbury Avenue W1

REGENT
Regent Street W1

ROYAL COURT
Sloane Square SW1

ROYAL OPERA HOUSE
Covent Garden WC2

ROYALTY
Portugal Street WC2

SADLER'S WELLS
Rosebery Avenue EC1

ST MARTIN'S
West Street WC2

SAVOY
Strand WC2

SHAFTESBURY
Shaftesbury Avenue WC2

SHAW
Euston Road NW1

STRAND
Aldwych WC2

VANBRUGH
62 Gower Street WC1

VAUDEVILLE
Strand WC2

VICTORIA PALACE
Victoria Street SW1

WESTMINSTER
Palace Street SW1

WHITEHALL
Whitehall SW1

WINDMILL
Gt Windmill Street W1

WYNDHAM'S
Charing Cross Road WC2

YOUNG VIC
The Cut SE1

CINEMAS IN CENTRAL LONDON

ABC BLOOMSBURY
Brunswick Square WC1

ABC
Fulham Road SW6

ABC 1 & 2
Shaftesbury Avenue WC2

ACADEMY 1, 2 & 3
Oxford Street W1

ASTORIA
Charing Cross Road WC2

BIOGRAPH
Wilton Road SW1

CARLTON
Haymarket SW1

CASINO
Old Compton Street W1

CENTA
Piccadilly W1

CINECENTA
Panton Street SW1

CLASSIC
Charing Cross Road WC2

CLASSIC
Moulin, Great Windmill Street W1

CLASSIC
Praed Street SW1

CLASSIC
Victoria Street SW1

COLUMBIA
Shaftesbury Avenue W1

CURZON
Curzon Street W1

DOMINION
Tottenham Court Road W1

EMI INTERNATIONAL FILM THEATRE
Golden Square W1

EMPIRE
Leicester Square WC2

EROS
Piccadilly Circus W1

GALA ROYAL
Marble Arch W2

INSTITUTE OF CONTEMPORARY ARTS
The Mall SW1

JACEY
Leicester Square WC2

JACEY
Trafalgar Square WC2

LEICESTER SQUARE THEATRE
Leicester Square WC2

LONDON PAVILION
Piccadilly Circus W1

METROPOLE
Victoria Street SW1

MINEMA
Knightsbridge SW7

NATIONAL FILM THEATRE 1 & 2
South Bank SE1

ODEON
Edgware Road W2

ODEON
Haymarket SW1

ODEON
Kings Road SW3

ODEON
Leicester Square WC2

ODEON
Marble Arch W2

ODEON
St Martin's Lane WC2

PARIS PULLMAN
Drayton Gardens SW10

PLAZA 1 & 2
Regent Street W1

PRINCE CHARLES
Leicester Place WC2

REGENT THEATRE
Regent Street W1

RIALTO
Coventry Street W1

RITZ
Leicester Square WC2

SCENE 1, 2, 3 & 4
Swiss Centre, Leicester Square WC2

STARLIGHT CINEMA
Mayfair Hotel, Stratton Street W1

STUDIO 1 & 2
Oxford Street W1

THE OTHER CINEMA
Tottenham Street W1

TIMES CENTA 1 & 2
Chiltern Court, Baker Street NW1

WARNER WEST END 1, 2, 3 & 4
Cranbourn Street WC2

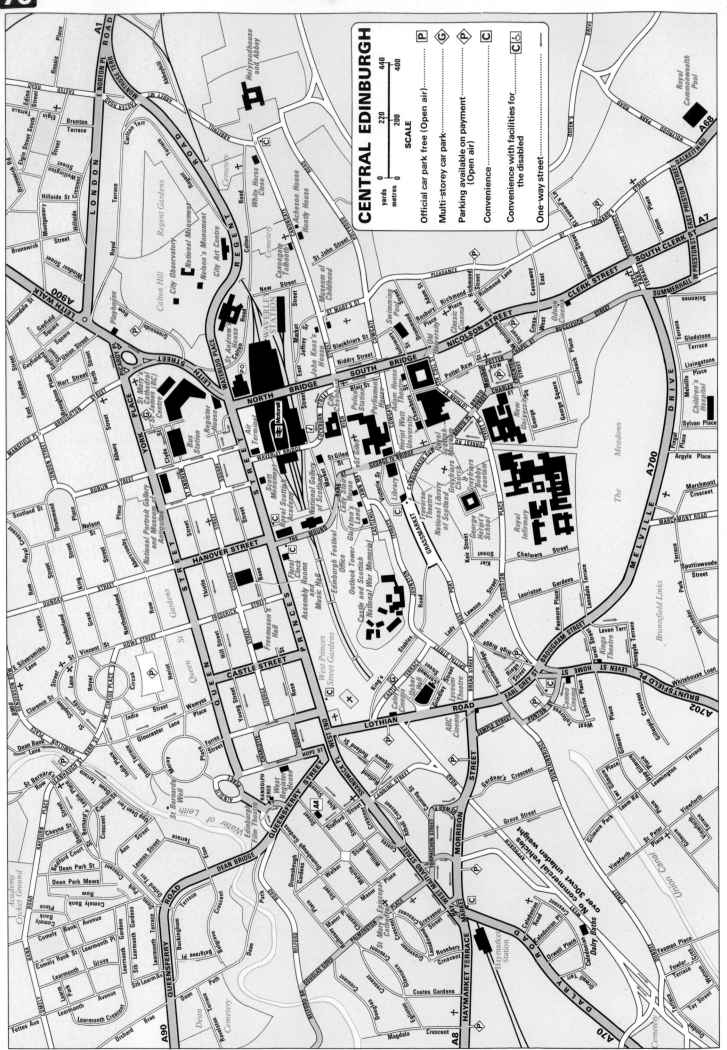

CENTRAL EDINBURGH

SCALE

yards 0   220   440
metres 0   200   400

P	Official car park free (Open air)
G	Multi-storey car park
P	Parking available on payment (Open air)
C	Convenience
C♿	Convenience with facilities for the disabled
→	One-way street

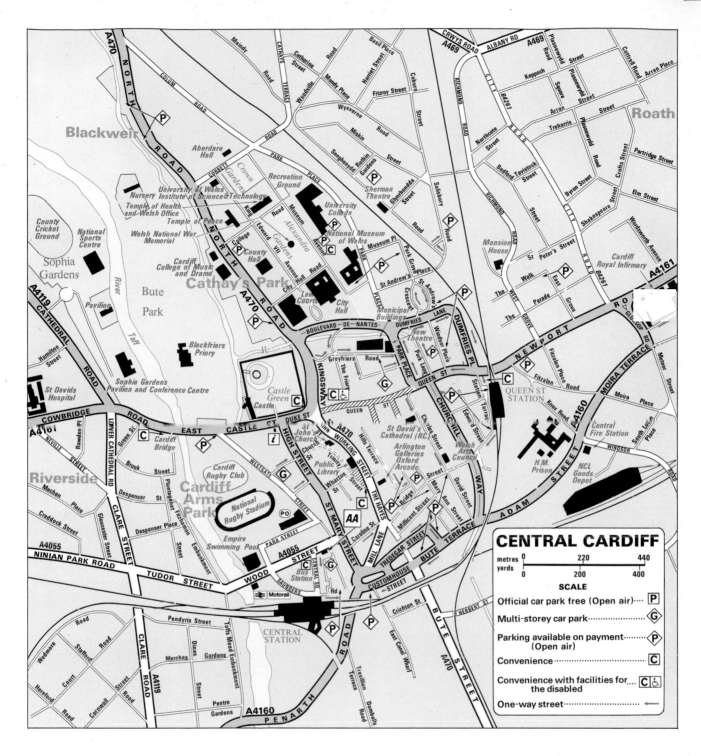

INDEX To Place Names

Ashby by Partney 73 Barton Turf

Ashby by Partney	35	TF 4266
Ashby cum Fenby	39	TA 2500
Ashby de la Launde	35	TF 0455
Ashby-de-la-Zouch	33	SK 3516
Ashby Folville	34	SK 7012
Ashby Magna	26	SP 5690
Ashby Parva	26	SP 5288
Ashby St. Ledgers	26	SP 5768
Ashby St. Mary	29	TG 3202
Ashchurch	25	SO 9233
Ashcombe	5	SX 9179
Ashcott	7	ST 4336
Ashdon	20	TL 5842
Asheldham	21	TL 9701
Ashen	20	TL 7442
Ashendon	18	SP 7014
Ashfield (Central)	56	NN 7803
Ashfield (Suff.)	21	TM 2062
Ashfield Green	29	TM 2673
Ashford (Derby.)	33	SK 1969
Ashford (Devon.)	6	SS 5335
Ashford (Kent)	13	TR 0142
Ashford (Surrey)	11	TQ 0671
Ashford Bowdler	24	SO 5170
Ashford Carbonel	24	SO 5270
Ashford Hill	10	SU 5562
Ashgill	50	NS 7849
Ashiesteel Hill	52	NT 4134
Ashill (Devon.)	7	ST 0811
Ashill (Norf.)	28	TF 8804
Ashill (Somer.)	7	ST 3217
Ashingdon	20	TQ 8693
Ashington (Northum.)	47	NZ 2687
Ashington (W Susx)	11	TQ 1315
Ashkirk	52	NT 4722
Ashleworth	17	SO 8125
Ashley (Cambs.)	20	TL 6961
Ashley (Devon.)	6	SS 6411
Ashley (Glos.)	17	ST 9394
Ashley (Hants.)	9	SU 3831
Ashley (Northants.)	26	SP 7991
Ashley (Staffs.)	32	SJ 7536
Ashley Green	19	SP 9705
Ashley Heath	8	SU 1105
Ash Magna	32	SJ 5739
Ashmansworth	10	SU 4156
Ashmansworthy	4	SS 3317
Ash Mill	6	SS 7823
Ashmore	8	ST 9117
Ashorne	26	SP 3057
Ashover	33	SK 3463
Ashow	26	SP 3170
Ashperton	24	SO 6441
Ashprington	5	SX 8157
Ash Priors	7	ST 1429
Ashreigney	6	SS 6213
Ashtead	11	TQ 1858
Ash Thomas	5	ST 0010
Ashton (Ches.)	32	SJ 5069
Ashton (Corn.)	2	SW 6028
Ashton (Devon.)	5	SX 8584
Ashton (Here. and Worc.)	24	SO 5164
Ashton (Northants.)	26	SP 7649
Ashton (Northants.)	27	TL 0588
Ashton Common	17	ST 8958
Ashton-in-Makerfield	32	SJ 5799
Ashton Keynes	17	SU 0494
Ashton under Hill	25	SO 9938
Ashton-under-Lyne	37	SJ 9399
Ashton upon Mersey	37	SJ 7792
Ashurst (Hants.)	9	SU 3310
Ashurst (Kent)	12	TQ 5038
Ashurst (W Susx)	11	TQ 1716
Ashurstwood	12	TQ 4236
Ashwater	4	SX 3895
Ashwell (Herts.)	19	TL 2639
Ashwell (Leic.)	34	SK 8613
Ashwellthorpe	29	TM 1397
Ashwick	8	ST 6447
Ashwicken	28	TF 7018
Askam in Furness	40	SD 2177
Askern	38	SE 5613
Askerswell	7	SY 5292
Askett	18	SP 8105
Askham (Cumbr.)	40	NY 5123
Askham (Notts.)	34	SK 7374
Askham Bryan	38	SE 5548
Askham Richard	38	SE 5347
Askrigg	41	SD 9491
Askwith	37	SE 1648
Aslackby	35	TF 0830
Aslacton	29	TM 1591
Aslockton	34	SK 7440
Asloun	62	NJ 5414
Aspatria	40	NY 1442
Aspenden	20	TL 3528
Aspley Guise	19	SP 9436
Aspley Heath	19	SP 9334
Aspull	36	SD 6108
Asselby	38	SE 7127
Assington	21	TL 9338
Astbury	33	SJ 8461
Astcote	26	SP 6753
Asterley	24	SJ 3707
Asterton	24	SO 3991
Asthall	18	SP 2811
Asthall Leigh	18	SP 3012
Astley (Here. and Worc.)	24	SO 7867
Astley (Salop)	32	SJ 5218
Astley (Warw.)	26	SP 3189
Astley Abbots	24	SO 7096
Astley Cross	24	SO 8069
Astley Green	32	SJ 7099
Aston (Berks.)	18	SU 7884
Aston (Ches.)	32	SJ 5578
Aston (Ches.)	32	SJ 6046
Aston (Derby.)	33	SK 1883
Aston (Here. and Worc.)	24	SO 4571
Aston (Herts.)	19	TL 2722
Aston (Oxon.)	18	SP 3302
Aston (Salop)	32	SJ 5228
Aston (Salop)	24	SJ 6109
Aston (Staffs.)	32	SJ 7540
Aston (Staffs.)	33	SJ 9131
Aston (S Yorks.)	33	SK 4685
Aston (W Mids)	25	SP 0789
Aston Abbotts	19	SP 8420
Aston Blank (Cold Aston)	17	SP 1219
Aston Botterell	24	SO 6284
Aston Cantlow	25	SP 1359
Aston Clinton	19	SP 8812
Aston Crews	17	SO 6723
Aston End	19	TL 2724
Aston Eyre	24	SO 6594
Aston Fields	25	SO 9669
Aston Flamville	26	SP 4692
Aston Ingham	17	SO 6823
Aston juxta Mondrum	32	SJ 6556
Aston le Walls	26	SP 4950
Aston Magna	25	SP 1935
Aston on Clun	24	SO 3981
Aston-on-Trent	33	SK 4129
Aston Rogers	23	SJ 3406
Aston Rowant	18	SU 7299
Aston Sandford	18	SP 7507
Aston Somerville	25	SP 0438
Aston Subedge	25	SP 1341
Aston Tirrold	18	SU 5586
Aston Upthorpe	18	SU 5586
Astwick	19	TL 2138
Astwood	27	SP 9547
Astwood Bank	25	SP 0362
Aswarby (Lincs.)	35	TF 0639
Aswardby (Lincs.)	35	TF 3770
Atcham	24	SJ 5408
Athelington	29	TM 2170
Athelney	7	ST 3428
Athelstaneford	52	NT 5377
Atherington	6	SS 5923
Atherstone	26	SP 3097
Atherstone on Stour	25	SP 2050
Atherton	36	SD 6703
Atlow	33	SK 2248
Attenborough	34	SK 5134
Attleborough (Norf.)	29	TM 0495
Attleborough (Warw.)	26	SP 3790
Attlebridge	29	TG 1216
Atwick	39	TA 1850
Atworth	17	ST 8565
Aubourn	34	SK 9262
Auchagallon	49	NR 8934
Aucharnie	62	NJ 6341
Auchattie	62	NO 6994
Auchenblae	57	NO 7278
Auchenbowie	50	NS 7988
Auchenbreck	49	NS 0281
Auchencairn	45	NX 7951
Auchencarroch	50	NS 4182
Auchencrow	53	NT 8560
Auchendinny	51	NT 2561
Auchengray	51	NS 9953
Auchengruith	45	NS 8209
Auchenhalrig	61	NJ 3661
Auchenheath	50	NS 8043
Auchentiber	50	NS 3647
Auchgourish	60	NH 9315
Auchindrain	55	NN 0303
Auchindrean	64	NH 1980
Auchininna	62	NJ 6446
Auchinleck (Dumf. and Galwy.)	44	NX 4570
Auchinleck (Strath.)	50	NS 5422
Auchinloch	50	NS 6670
Auchintore	55	NN 0972
Auchleuchries	62	NK 0136
Auchleven	62	NJ 6224
Auchlochan	50	NS 8037
Auchlyne	55	NN 5129
Auchmillan	50	NS 5129
Auchmithie	57	NO 6744
Auchmuirbridge	56	NO 2101
Auchnacree	57	NO 4663
Auchnagatt	62	NJ 9341
Auchronie	57	NO 4480
Auchterarder	56	NN 9312
Auchterderran	61	NT 2196
Auchterhouse	57	NO 3337
Auchtermuchty	56	NO 2311
Auchterneed	60	NH 4959
Auchtertool	51	NT 2190
Auchtoo	55	NN 5620
Auckingill	67	ND 3764
Auckley	38	SE 6501
Audenshaw	37	SJ 9196
Audlem	32	SJ 6543
Audley	32	SJ 7950
Auds	62	NJ 6564
Aughton (Humbs.)	38	SE 7038
Aughton (Lancs.)	36	SD 3804
Aughton (Lancs.)	41	SD 5467
Aughton (S Yorks.)	33	SK 4586
Aughton Park	36	SD 4106
Auldearn	60	NH 9155
Aulden	24	SO 4654
Auldhame	52	NT 5984
Auldhouse	50	NS 6250
Ault-a-chrinn	59	NG 9420
Aultbea	64	NG 8789
Aultgrishan	64	NG 7485
Aultiphurst	67	NC 8065
Aultmore (Grampn.)	61	NJ 4053
Aultnagoire	60	NH 5423
Aulton	62	NJ 6028
Aundorach	60	NH 9716
Aunsby	35	TF 0438
Auquhorthies	62	NJ 8329
Aust	17	ST 5789
Austerfield	38	SK 6594
Austonley	37	SE 1207
Austrey	33	SK 2906
Austwick	41	SD 7668
Authorpe	35	TF 3980
Authorpe Row	35	TF 5373
Avebury	17	SU 0969
Aveley	20	TQ 5680
Avening	17	ST 8797
Averham	34	SK 7654
Aveton Gifford	5	SX 6947
Avielochan	60	NH 9016
Aviemore	60	NH 8912
Avington	10	SU 3767
Avoch	60	NH 6955
Avon	8	SZ 1498
Avonbridge	50	NS 9072
Avon Castle	8	SU 1303
Avon Dassett	26	SP 4150
Avonmouth	16	ST 5177
Avonwick	5	SX 7158
Awbridge	9	SU 3323
Awkley	17	ST 5885
Awliscombe	5	ST 1301
Awre	17	SO 7008
Awsworth	33	SK 4843
Axbridge	16	ST 4254
Axford (Hants.)	10	SU 6043
Axford (Wilts.)	10	SU 2369
Axminster	7	SY 2998
Axmouth	5	SY 2591
Aylburton	17	SO 6101
Ayle	46	NY 7149
Aylesbeare	5	SY 0391
Aylesbury	18	SP 8213
Aylesby	39	TA 2007
Aylesford	12	TQ 7359
Aylesham	13	TR 2352
Aylestone	26	SK 5701
Aylmerton	29	TG 1839
Aylsham	29	TG 1926
Aylton	24	SO 6537
Aymestrey	24	SO 4265
Aynho	18	SP 5133
Ayot St. Lawrence	19	TL 1916
Ayot St. Peter	19	TL 2115
Ayr	50	NS 3321
Aysgarth	41	SE 0088
Ayside	40	SD 3983
Ayston	27	SK 8601
Aythorpe Roding	20	TL 5815
Ayton (Berwick.)	53	NT 9260
Ayton (N Yorks.)	43	SE 9884
Aywick (Yell)	63	HU 5386
Azerley	42	SE 2574
Babbinswood	32	SJ 3329
Babcary	7	ST 5628
Babel	15	SN 8235
Babell	31	SJ 1574
Babraham	20	TL 5150
Babworth	34	SK 6880
Back	63	NB 4840
Backaland	63	HY 5630
Backbarrow	40	SD 3584
Backford	32	SJ 3971
Backhill of Clackriach	62	NJ 9246
Backies	67	NC 8302
Backmuir of New Gilston	57	NO 4308
Back of Keppoch	54	NM 6587
Backwell	16	ST 4868
Backworth	47	NZ 2972
Bacon End	20	TL 6018
Baconsthorpe	29	TG 1237
Bacton (Here. and Worc.)	24	SO 3732
Bacton (Norf.)	29	TG 3434
Bacton (Suff.)	21	TM 0466
Bacup	37	SD 8622
Badachro	64	NG 7873
Badbury	17	SU 1980
Badby	26	SP 5559
Badcall (Highld.)	66	NC 1541
Badcall (Highld.)	66	NC 2355
Badcaul	64	NH 0191
Baddeley Green	33	SJ 9250
Baddesley Ensor	26	SP 2798
Baddidarach	64	NC 0923
Badenscoth	62	NJ 7038
Badenyon	61	NJ 3419
Badger	24	SO 7699
Badgers Mount	12	TQ 5061
Badgeworth (Glos.)	17	SO 9019
Badgworth (Somer.)	7	ST 3952
Badingham	21	TM 3067
Badlesmere	13	TR 0154
Badluarach	64	NG 9994
Badminton	17	ST 8082
Badrallach	64	NH 0691
Badsey	25	SP 0743
Badsworth	38	SE 4614
Badwell Ash	29	TL 9969
Bagby	42	SE 4680
Bagendon	17	SP 0006
Bagillt	32	SJ 2175
Baginton	26	SP 3474
Baglan	16	SS 7493
Bagley	32	SJ 4027
Bagnall	33	SJ 9250
Bagshot (Surrey)	11	SU 9163
Bagshot (Wilts.)	10	SU 3165
Bagthorpe (Norf.)	28	TF 7932
Bagthorpe (Notts.)	33	SK 4751
Bagworth	33	SK 4408
Bagwy Llydiart	16	SO 4427
Baildon	37	SE 1539
Baileboag	60	NH 5018
Baile Boidheach	48	NR 7473
Baile Mor		NM 2824
Baillieston	50	NS 6764
Bail Uachdraich	63	NF 8160
Bainbridge	41	SD 9390
Bainton (Cambs.)	35	TF 0906
Bainton (Humbs.)	39	SE 9652
Bairnkine	52	NT 6515
Baker's End	20	TL 3917
Baker Street	20	TQ 6381
Bakewell	33	SK 2168
Bala	31	SH 9236
Balallan	63	NB 2720
Balbeg	60	NH 4924
Balbeggie	56	NO 1629
Balbithan	62	NJ 7917
Balblair	65	NH 7066
Balchladich	64	NC 0330
Balchraggan	60	NH 5343
Balchrick	66	NC 1960
Balcombe	12	TQ 3130
Balcurvie	57	NO 3400
Baldersby	42	SE 3578
Balderstone	36	SD 6332
Balderton	34	SK 8151
Baldhu	2	SW 7743
Baldinnie	57	NO 4311
Baldock	19	TL 2434
Baldrine	43	SC 4281
Baldwin	43	SC 3581
Baldwinholme	46	NY 3351
Baldwin's Gate	32	SJ 7939
Bale	29	TG 0136
Balemartine	48	NL 9841
Balephuil	48	NL 9640
Balerno	51	NT 1666
Balfield	57	NO 5468
Balfour	63	HY 4716
Balfron	50	NS 5400
Balgaveny	62	NJ 6640
Balgavies	57	NO 5351
Balgedie	56	NO 1603
Balgonar	51	NT 0293
Balgove	62	NJ 8133
Balgowan	60	NN 6394
Balgown	58	NG 3868
Balgray	57	NO 4138
Balgrochan	50	NS 6278
Balhalgardy	62	NJ 7623
Balhary	57	NO 2646
Baliasta	63	HP 6009
Baligill	67	NC 8566
Balintore (Highld.)	65	NH 8675
Balintore (Tays.)	57	NO 2859
Balintraid	65	NH 7370
Balivanich	63	NF 7755
Balkeerie	57	NO 3244
Balkholme	38	SE 7828
Balkissock	44	NX 1381
Ball	32	SJ 3026
Ballabeg	43	SC 2470
Ballacannell	43	SC 4382
Ballacarnane Beg	43	SC 3088
Ballajora	43	SC 4790
Ballamodha	43	SC 2773
Ballantrae	44	NX 0882
Ballantrushal	63	NB 3853
Ballasalla (I. of M.)	43	SC 2870
Ballasalla (I. of M.)	43	SC 3497
Ballater	61	NO 3695
Ballaugh	43	SC 3493
Ballchraggan	65	NH 7775
Ballechin	56	NN 9353
Ballencrieff	52	NT 4878
Ballevullin	48	NL 9546
Ball Hill	10	SU 4263
Balliekine	49	NR 8739
Balliemore (Strath.)	54	NM 8228
Ballig	43	SC 2882
Ballinaby	48	NR 2267
Ballindean	57	NO 2529
Ballinger Common	19	SP 9103
Ballingham	24	SO 5731
Ballingry	56	NT 1797
Ballinluig	56	NN 9852
Ballintuim	56	NO 1054
Balloch (Highld.)	60	NH 7346
Balloch (Strath.)	50	NS 3981
Balloch (Tays.)	56	NN 8419
Balloch (Tays.)	57	NO 3557
Ballochan	61	NO 5290
Ballochroy	48	NR 7252
Balls Cross	11	SU 9826
Ballygown	54	NM 4343
Ballygrant	48	NR 3966
Ballymichael	49	NR 9231
Balmacara	59	NG 8028
Balmaclellan	45	NX 6578
Balmacneil	56	NN 9850
Balmae	45	NX 6845
Balmaha	50	NS 4290
Balmalcolm	57	NO 3108
Balmartin	63	NF 7273
Balmedie	62	NJ 9617
Balmerino	57	NO 3524
Balmerlawn	9	SU 3003
Balmore	50	NS 6073
Balmullo	57	NO 4220
Balmungie	60	NH 7359
Balnabodach	63	NF 7101
Balnacra	59	NG 9746
Balnafoich	60	NH 6835
Balnaguard	56	NN 9451
Balnaguisich	65	NH 6771
Balnahard	54	NM 4534
Balnahard	54	NR 4199
Balnakeil	66	NC 3968
Balnaknock	58	NG 4162
Balnamoon	57	NO 5463
Balnapaling	65	NH 7969
Balquhidder	55	NN 5320
Balranald	63	NF 7169
Balsall Common	26	SP 2377
Balscote	26	SP 3841
Balsham	20	TL 5850
Baltasound (Unst)	63	HP 6208
Balterley	32	SJ 7550
Balthangie	62	NJ 8351
Baltonsborough	7	ST 5434
Balvaird	60	NH 5452
Balvarran	56	NO 0762
Balvicar	54	NM 7616
Balvraid	60	NH 8231
Bamburgh	53	NU 1834
Bamford	33	SK 2083
Bampton (Cumbr.)	40	NY 5118
Bampton (Devon.)	6	SS 9522
Bampton (Oxon.)	18	SP 3103
Banavie	55	NN 1177
Banbury	18	SP 4540
Banc Cwmhelen	15	SN 6811
Banchory	62	NO 6995
Banchory-Devenick	62	NJ 9101
Bancyfelin	14	SN 3218
Banc-y-ffordd	15	SN 4037
Banff	62	NJ 6863
Bangor	30	SH 5872
Bangor-is-y-coed	32	SJ 3945
Banham	29	TM 0688
Bank	9	SU 2807
Bankend (Dumf. and Galwy.)	45	NY 0268
Bankend (Strath.)	50	NS 8033
Bankfoot	56	NO 0635
Bankglen	50	NS 5912
Bankhead (Grampn.)	62	NJ 6608
Bankhead (Grampn.)	62	NJ 8910
Bank Newton	37	SD 9152
Banknock	50	NS 7779
Banks (Cumbr.)	46	NY 5664
Banks (Lancs.)	36	SD 3820
Bankshill	46	NY 1981
Bank Street	24	SO 6362
Banningham	29	TG 2129
Bannister Green	20	TL 6920
Bannockburn	50	NS 8190
Banstead	11	TQ 2559
Bantham	5	SX 6643
Banton	50	NS 7479
Banwell	16	ST 3959
Bapchild	13	TQ 9363
Baramore	54	NM 6474
Barassie	50	NS 3232
Barbaraville	65	NH 7471
Barber Booth	33	SK 1184
Barbon	41	SD 6282
Barbrook	6	SS 7147
Barby	26	SP 5470
Barcheston	18	SP 2639
Barcombe	12	TQ 4214
Barcombe Cross	12	TQ 4216
Barden	42	SE 1493
Bardfield Saling	20	TL 6826
Bardister	63	HU 3577
Bardney	35	TF 1169
Bardon Mill	46	NY 7764
Bardowie	50	NS 5873
Bardrainney	50	NS 3372
Bardsea	40	SD 3074
Bardsey	37	SE 3643
Bardsley	37	SD 9201
Bardwell	29	TL 9473
Barewood	24	SO 3856
Barford (Norf.)	29	TG 1007
Barford (Warw.)	26	SP 2660
Barford St. Martin	8	SU 0531
Barford St. Michael	26	SP 4332
Barfreston	13	TR 2650
Bargoed	16	SO 1500
Bargrennan	44	NX 3476
Barham (Cambs.)	27	TL 1375
Barham (Kent)	13	TR 2050
Barham (Suff.)	21	TM 1451
Barholm	35	TF 0811
Barkby	34	SK 6309
Barkestone-le-Vale	34	SK 7734
Barkham	10	SU 7866
Barking (Gtr London)	20	TQ 4785
Barking (Suff.)	21	TM 0653
Barkingside	20	TQ 4489
Barkisland	37	SE 0419
Barkston (Lincs.)	34	SK 9241
Barkston (N Yorks.)	38	SE 4936
Barkway	20	TL 3835
Barkwith	35	TF 1681
Barlaston	33	SJ 8938
Barlavington	11	SU 9716
Barlborough	33	SK 4777
Barlby	38	SE 6334
Barlestone	26	SK 4205
Barley (Herts.)	20	TL 4038
Barley (Lancs.)	37	SD 8240
Barleythorpe	34	SK 8409
Barling	21	TQ 9289
Barlow (Derby.)	33	SK 3474
Barlow (N Yorks.)	38	SE 6428
Barlow (Tyne and Wear)	47	NZ 1560
Barmby Moor	38	SE 7748
Barmby on the Marsh	38	SE 6828
Barmer	28	TF 8133
Barmouth	22	SH 6115
Barmpton	42	NZ 3118
Barmston	39	TA 1659
Barnack	27	TF 0705
Barnacle	26	SP 3884
Barnard Castle	42	NZ 0516
Barnard Gate	18	SP 4010
Barnardiston	20	TL 7148
Barnburgh	38	SE 4803
Barnby	29	TM 4789
Barnby Dun	38	SE 6109
Barnby in the Willows	34	SK 8552
Barnby Moor	34	SK 6684
Barnes	11	TQ 2276
Barnet	19	TQ 2494
Barnetby le Wold	39	TA 0509
Barney	29	TF 9932
Barnham (Suff.)	20	TL 8779
Barnham (W Susx)	11	SU 9604
Barnham Broom	29	TG 0807
Barnhead	57	NO 6657
Barnhill	61	NJ 1457
Barnhills	44	NW 9871
Barningham (Durham)	42	NZ 0810
Barningham (Suff.)	29	TL 9676
Barnoldby le Beck	39	TA 2303
Barnoldswick	37	SD 8746
Barns Green	11	TQ 1227
Barnsley (Glos.)	17	SP 0705
Barnsley (S Yorks.)	37	SE 3406
Barnstaple	6	SS 5533
Barnston (Essex)	20	TL 6519
Barnston (Mers.)	32	SJ 2783
Barnt Green	25	SP 0073
Barnton	32	SJ 6374
Barnwell	27	TL 0485
Barnwood	17	SO 8518
Barr	44	NX 2794
Barrachan	44	NX 3649
Barrack	62	NJ 8942
Barraglom	63	NB 1634
Barrapoll	48	NL 9542
Barras	57	NO 8580
Barrasford	47	NY 9273
Barregarrow	43	SC 3288
Barrhead	50	NS 5058
Barrhill (Strath.)	44	NX 2382
Barrington (Cambs.)	20	TL 3949
Barrington (Somer.)	7	ST 3918
Barripper	2	SW 6338
Barrmill	50	NS 3651
Barrock	67	ND 2571
Barrow (Lancs.)	36	SD 7338
Barrow (Leic.)	34	SK 8815
Barrow (Salop)	24	SJ 6500
Barrow (Somer.)	8	ST 7231
Barrow (Suff.)	20	TL 7663
Barroway Drove	28	TF 5703
Barrowby	34	SK 8736
Barrowden	27	SK 9400
Barrowford	37	SD 8538
Barrow Gurney	16	ST 5267
Barrow-in-Furness	40	SD 1969
Barrow Street	8	ST 8330
Barrow upon Humber	39	TA 0721
Barrow upon Soar	34	SK 5717
Barrow upon Trent	33	SK 3528
Barry (Angus)	57	NO 5334
Barry (S Glam.)	16	ST 1168
Barry Island	16	ST 1166
Barsby	34	SK 6911
Barsham	29	TM 3989
Barston	25	SP 2078
Bartestree	24	SO 5641
Barthol Chapel	62	NJ 8134
Barthomley	32	SJ 7652
Bartley	9	SU 3012
Bartlow	20	TL 5845
Barton (Cambs.)	20	TL 4055
Barton (Ches.)	32	SJ 4454
Barton (Devon.)	5	SX 9067
Barton (Glos.)	17	SP 0925
Barton (Lancs.)	36	SD 5136
Barton (N Yorks.)	42	NZ 2208
Barton (Warw.)	25	SP 1051
Barton Bendish	28	TF 7105
Barton Common	29	TG 3522
Barton Hartshorn	18	SP 6431
Barton in Fabis	34	SK 5232
Barton in the Beans	33	SK 3906
Barton in the Clay	19	TL 0831
Barton-le-Street	38	SE 7274
Barton-le-Willows	38	SE 7163
Barton Mills	28	TL 7273
Barton Moss	32	SJ 7397
Barton on Sea	9	SZ 2493
Barton-on-the-Heath	18	SP 2532
Barton St. David	7	ST 5431
Barton Seagrave	27	SP 8877
Barton Stacey	10	SU 4340
Barton Turf	29	TG 3421

Barton-under-Needwood 74 Blarnaleyoch

Barton-under-Needwood 33 SK 1818
Barton-Upon-Humber 39 TA 0222
Barvas 63 NB 3649
Barway 28 TL 5475
Barwell 26 SP 4496
Barwick 7 ST 5513
Barwick in Elmet 37 SE 3937
Baschurch 32 SJ 4222
Bascote 26 SP 4063
Basford Green 33 SJ 9951
Bashall Eaves 36 SD 6943
Bashley 9 SZ 2496
Basildon (Berks.) 10 SU 6078
Basildon (Essex) 20 TQ 7189
Basing 10 SU 6652
Basingstoke 10 SU 6351
Baslow 33 SK 2572
Bason Bridge 7 ST 3445
Bassenthwaite 40 NY 2332
Bassett 9 SU 4116
Bassingbourn 20 TL 3344
Bassingfield 34 SK 6137
Bassingham 34 SK 9059
Bassingthorpe 34 SK 9628
Basta 63 HU 5294
Baston 35 TF 1114
Bastwick 29 TG 4217
Batcombe (Dorset.) 7 ST 6104
Batcombe (Somer.) 8 ST 6838
Bate Heath 32 SJ 6879
Bath 17 ST 7464
Bathampton 17 ST 7765
Bathealton 7 ST 0724
Batheaston 17 ST 7767
Bathford 17 ST 7866
Bathgate 51 NS 9768
Bathley 34 SK 7759
Bathpool 4 SX 2874
Batley 37 SE 2424
Batsford 25 SP 1834
Battersea 11 TQ 2876
Battisford 21 TM 0554
Battisford Tye 21 TM 0254
Battle (E Susx.) 12 TQ 7416
Battle (Powys) 15 SO 0031
Battlefield 24 SJ 5117
Battlesbridge 20 TQ 7794
Battlesden 19 SP 9628
Battleton 6 SS 9127
Battramsley 9 SZ 3099
Baughurst 10 SU 5859
Baulking 18 SU 3190
Baumber 35 TF 2174
Baunton 17 SP 0204
Baverstock 8 SU 0231
Bawburgh 29 TG 1508
Bawdeswell 29 TG 0420
Bawdrip 7 ST 3339
Bawdsey 21 TM 3440
Bawtry 38 SK 6592
Baxenden 37 SD 7726
Baxterley 26 SP 2796
Bayble 63 NB 5231
Baycliff 40 SD 2872
Baydon 10 SU 2877
Bayford 20 TL 3108
Bayhead 63 NF 7468
Bayles 46 NY 7044
Baylham 21 TM 1051
Bayston Hill 24 SJ 4809
Bayton 24 SO 6973
Beachampton 18 SP 7737
Beachley 16 ST 5591
Beacon 5 ST 1705
Beacon End 21 TL 9524
Beacon Hill (Dorset) 8 SY 9794
Beacon's Bottom 18 SU 7895
Beaconsfield 19 SU 9490
Beacontree 20 TQ 4886
Beacravik 63 NG 1190
Beadlam 42 SE 6584
Beadnell 53 NU 2329
Beaford 6 SS 5514
Beal (Northum.) 53 NU 0642
Beal (N Yorks.) 38 SE 5325
Bealings 21 TM 2348
Beaminster 7 ST 4801
Beamish 47 NZ 2253
Beamsley 37 SE 0752
Bean 12 TQ 5972
Beanacre 17 ST 9066
Beanley 53 NU 0818
Beaquoy 63 HY 3022
Beare Green 11 TQ 1842
Bearley 25 SP 1760
Bearpark 42 NZ 2343
Bearsbridge 46 NY 7857
Bearsden 50 NS 5471
Bearsted 12 TQ 8055
Bearwood 8 SZ 0496
Beattock 45 NT 0702
Beauchamp Roding 20 TL 5809
Beauchief 33 SK 3381
Beaufort 16 SO 1611
Beaulieu 9 SU 3801
Beauly 60 NH 5246
Beaumaris 30 SH 6076
Beaumont (Cumbr.) 46 NY 3459
Beaumont (Essex) 21 TM 1725
Beausale 26 SP 2470
Beaworthy 6 SX 4699
Beazley End 20 TL 7428
Bebington 32 SJ 3384
Bebside 47 NZ 2881
Beccles 29 TM 4290
Becconsall 36 SD 4422
Beckbury 24 SJ 7601
Beckenham 12 TQ 3769
Beckermet 40 NY 0206
Beckfoot (Cumbr.) 45 NY 0949
Beckfoot (Cumbr.) 40 NY 1600
Beck Foot (Cumbr.) 41 SD 6196
Beckford 25 SO 9735
Beckhampton 17 SU 0868
Beck Hole 43 NZ 8102
Beckingham (Lincs.) 34 SK 8753
Beckingham (Notts.) 34 SK 7790
Beckington 8 ST 7951
Beckley (E Susx.) 13 TQ 8423
Beckley (Oxon) 18 SP 5611
Beck Row 28 TL 6977
Beck Side 40 SD 2382
Beckton 20 TQ 4381
Bockwithshaw 37 SE 2653
Bedale 42 SE 2688
Bedburn 42 NZ 1031
Beddau 16 ST 0585
Beddgelert 30 SH 5848
Beddingham 12 TQ 4408
Beddington 12 TQ 3165
Bedfield 21 TM 2266
Bedford 27 TL 0449
Bedhampton 9 SU 6906
Bedingfield 21 TM 1768
Bedlington 47 NZ 2581
Bedlinog 16 SO 0901
Bedmond 19 TL 0903
Bednall 25 SJ 9517
Bedrule 52 NT 6017
Bedstone 24 SO 3675
Bedwas 16 ST 1689
Bedworth 26 SP 3587
Beeby 34 SK 6608
Beech (Hants.) 10 SU 6938
Beech (Staffs.) 33 SJ 8538
Beechamwell 28 TF 7405
Beech Hill 10 SU 6964
Beechingstoke 17 SU 0859
Beedon 10 SU 4877
Beeford 39 TA 1254
Beeley 33 SK 2667
Beelsby 39 TA 2001
Beenham 10 SU 5868
Beer 5 SY 2289
Beercrocombe 7 ST 3220
Beer Hackett 7 ST 5911
Beesby 35 TF 4680
Beeson 5 SX 8140
Beeston (Beds.) 27 TL 1648
Beeston (Ches.) 32 SJ 5358
Beeston (Norf.) 28 TF 9015
Beeston (Notts.) 34 SK 5336
Beeston (W Yorks.) 37 SE 2930
Beeston Regis 29 TG 1742
Beeswing 45 NX 8969
Beetham 40 SD 4979
Beetley 29 TF 9718
Begbroke 18 SP 4613
Begelly 14 SN 1107
Beguildy 23 SO 1979
Beighton (Norf.) 29 TG 3808
Beighton (S Yorks.) 33 SK 4483
Beith 50 NS 3454
Bekesbourne 13 TR 1955
Belaugh 29 TG 2818
Belbroughton 25 SO 9177
Belchamp Otten 20 TL 8041
Belchamp St. Paul 20 TL 7942
Belchamp Walter 20 TL 8240
Belchford 35 TF 2975
Belford 53 NU 1033
Belhelvie 62 NJ 9417
Bellabeg 61 NJ 3513
Bellanoch 49 NR 7992
Bellaty 57 NO 2459
Bell Busk 37 SD 9056
Belleau 35 TF 4078
Bellehiglash 61 NJ 1837
Bellerby 42 SE 1192
Belliehill 57 NO 5663
Bellingdon 19 SP 9405
Bellingham 47 NY 8383
Belloch 48 NR 6737
Bellochantuy 48 NR 6632
Bellsbank 44 NS 4804
Bellshill (Northum.) 53 NU 1230
Bellshill (Strath.) 50 NS 7360
Bellspool 51 NT 1635
Bellsquarry 51 NT 0465
Bells Yew Green 12 TQ 6136
Belmaduthy 60 NH 6556
Belmesthorpe 35 TF 0410
Belmont (Lancs.) 36 SD 6715
Belmont (Unst) 63 HP 5600
Belnacraig 61 NJ 3716
Belowda 2 SW 9661
Belper 33 SK 3447
Belsay 47 NZ 1078
Belses 52 NT 5725
Belsford 5 SX 7659
Belstead 21 TM 1341
Belston 50 NS 3820
Belstone 5 SX 6193
Belthorn 36 SD 7124
Beltoft 39 SE 8006
Belton (Humbs.) 38 SE 7806
Belton (Leic.) 33 SK 4420
Belton (Leic.) 26 SK 8101
Belton (Lincs.) 34 SK 9239
Belton (Norf.) 29 TG 4802
Belvedere 12 TQ 4978
Belvoir 34 SK 8133
Bembridge 9 SZ 6488
Bemersyde 52 NT 5933
Bempton 39 TA 1972
Benacre 29 TM 5184
Benenden 12 TQ 8033
Bengate 29 TG 3027
Benholm 57 NO 8069
Beningbrough 38 SE 5257
Benington (Herts.) 20 TL 3023
Benington (Lincs.) 35 TF 3946
Benllech 30 SH 5182
Benmore (Central) 55 NN 4125
Bennacott 4 SX 2991
Bennan (Island of Arran) 49 NR 9821
Bennecarrigan 49 NR 9423
Benniworth 35 TF 2081
Benover 12 TQ 7048
Benson 18 SU 6191
Benthall (Northum.) 53 NU 2328
Benthall (Salop) 24 SJ 6602
Bentham 17 SO 9116
Bentley (Hants.) 10 SU 7844
Bentley (Here. and Worc.) 25 SO 9966
Bentley (Humbs.) 39 TA 0135
Bentley (S Yorks.) 38 SE 5605
Bentley (Warw.) 26 SP 2895
Bentley Heath 25 SP 1676
Benton 6 SS 6536
Bentpath 46 NY 3190
Bentworth 10 SU 6640
Benvie 57 NO 3231
Benwick 27 TL 3490
Beoley 25 SP 0669
Beoraidbeg 58 NM 6793
Bepton 9 SU 8518
Berden 20 TL 4629
Berea 14 SM 7929
Bere Alston 4 SX 4466
Bere Ferrers 4 SX 4563
Berepper 2 SW 6522
Bere Regis 8 SY 8494
Bergh Apton 29 TG 3000
Berinsfield 18 SU 5696
Berkeley 17 ST 6899
Berkhamsted 19 SP 9907
Berkley 8 ST 8049
Berkswell 26 SP 2479
Bermondsey 12 TQ 3579
Bernisdale 58 NG 4050
Berrick Salome 18 SU 6293
Berriedale Water 67 ND 0630
Berriew 23 SJ 1801
Berrington (Northum.) 53 NU 0043
Berrington (Salop) 24 SJ 5206
Berrow 7 ST 2952
Berrow Green 24 SO 7458
Berry Hill 17 SO 5712
Berryhillock 61 NJ 5060
Berrynarbor 6 SS 5546
Berry Pomeroy 5 SX 8261
Bersham 32 SJ 3048
Berstane 63 HY 4610
Bersted 11 SU 9300
Berwick 12 TQ 5105
Berwick Bassett 17 SU 0973
Berwick Hill 47 NZ 1775
Berwick St. James 8 SU 0739
Berwick St. John 8 ST 9421
Berwick St. Leonard 8 ST 9233
Berwick-upon-Tweed 53 NT 9953
Besford 25 SO 9144
Bessacarr 38 SE 6101
Bessels Leigh 18 SP 4501
Bessingham 29 TG 1636
Besthorpe (Norf.) 29 TM 0695
Besthorpe (Notts.) 34 SK 8264
Beswick 39 TA 0148
Betchworth 11 TQ 2149
Bethel 30 SH 5265
Bethersden 13 TQ 9240
Bethesda (Dyfed) 14 SN 0918
Bethesda (Gwyn.) 30 SH 6266
Bethlehem 15 SN 6825
Bethnal Green 20 TQ 3583
Betley 32 SJ 7548
Betsham 12 TQ 6071
Betteshanger 13 TR 3152
Bettiscombe 7 SY 3999
Bettisfield 32 SJ 4535
Betton (Salop) 23 SJ 3102
Betton (Salop) 32 SJ 6836
Bettws (Gwent) 16 ST 2991
Bettws (Mid Glam.) 15 SS 9086
Bettws Bledrws 15 SN 5952
Bettws Cedewain 23 SO 1296
Bettws Evan 14 SN 3047
Bettws Gwerfil Goch 31 SJ 0346
Bettws Malpas 16 ST 3090
Bettws-Newydd 16 SO 3606
Bettyhill 66 NC 7061
Betws 15 SN 6311
Betws Garmon 30 SH 5357
Betws-y-coed 31 SH 7956
Betws-yn-Rhos 31 SH 9073
Beulah (Dyfed) 14 SN 2846
Beulah (Powys) 15 SN 9251
Bevendean 12 TQ 3406
Bevercotes 34 SK 6972
Beverley 39 TA 0339
Beverston 17 ST 8693
Bevington 17 ST 6596
Bewaldeth 40 NY 2134
Bewcastle 46 NY 5674
Bewdley 24 SO 7875
Bewerley 42 SE 1564
Bewholme 39 TA 1650
Bexhill 12 TQ 7407
Bexley 12 TQ 4973
Bexwell 28 TF 6303
Beyton 21 TL 9363
Bibury 17 SP 1106
Bicester 18 SP 5822
Bickenhall 7 ST 2818
Bickenhill 25 SP 1882
Bicker 35 TF 2237
Bickerstaffe 36 SD 4404
Bickerton (Ches.) 32 SJ 5052
Bickerton (N Yorks.) 38 SE 4450
Bickington (Devon.) 6 SS 5332
Bickington (Devon.) 5 SX 7972
Bickleigh (Devon.) 6 SS 9407
Bickleigh (Devon.) 4 SX 5262
Bickleton 6 SS 5031
Bickley 12 TQ 4268
Bickley Moss 32 SJ 5448
Bicknacre 20 TL 7802
Bicknoller 7 ST 1039
Bicknor 13 TQ 8658
Bickton 8 SU 1412
Bicton (Salop) 24 SJ 4415
Bicton (Salop) 23 SO 2882
Bidborough 12 TQ 5643
Biddenden 13 TQ 8538
Biddenham 27 TL 0250
Biddestone 17 ST 8673
Biddisham 7 ST 3853
Biddlesden 18 SP 6340
Biddlestone 47 NT 9508
Biddulph 33 SJ 8857
Biddulph Moor 33 SJ 9057
Bideford 4 SS 4526
Bidford-on-Avon 25 SP 1052
Bielby 38 SE 7843
Bieldside 62 NJ 8702
Bierley 9 SZ 5077
Bierton 19 SP 8415
Bigbury 5 SX 6646
Bigbury-on-Sea 5 SX 6544
Bigby 39 TA 0507
Biggar (Cumbr.) 40 SD 1966
Biggar (Strath.) 51 NT 0437
Biggin (Derby.) 33 SK 1559
Biggin (Derby.) 33 SK 2548
Biggin (N Yorks.) 38 SE 5434
Biggin Hill 12 TQ 4159
Biggleswade 27 TL 1944
Bighouse 67 NC 8964
Bighton 9 SU 6134
Bignor 11 SU 9814
Big Sand 64 NG 7579
Bilberry 4 SX 0159
Bilborough 34 SK 5241
Bilbrook 25 SJ 8703
Bilbrough 38 SE 5246
Bilbster 67 ND 2852
Bildeston 21 TL 9949
Billericay 20 TQ 6794
Billesdon 26 SK 7103
Billesley 25 SP 1456
Billingborough 35 TF 1134
Billinge 36 SD 5300
Billingford (Norf.) 29 TG 0120
Billingford (Norf.) 29 TM 1678
Billingham 42 NZ 4624
Billinghay 35 TF 1554
Billingley 38 SE 4304
Billingshurst 11 TQ 0825
Billingsley 24 SO 7085
Billington (Beds.) 19 SP 9422
Billington (Lancs.) 36 SD 7235
Billockby 29 TG 4213
Billy Row 42 NZ 1637
Bilsborrow 36 SD 5140
Bilsby 35 TF 4776
Bilsington 13 TR 0434
Bilsthorpe 34 SK 6560
Bilston (Lothian) 51 NT 2664
Bilston (W Mids) 25 SO 9496
Bilstone 33 SK 3606
Bilting 13 TR 0549
Bilton (Humbs.) 39 TA 1532
Bilton (Northum.) 53 NU 2210
Bilton (N Yorks.) 38 SE 4750
Bilton (Warw.) 26 SP 4873
Binbrook 39 TF 2093
Bincombe 8 SY 6884
Binegar 7 ST 6149
Binfield 11 SU 8471
Binfield Heath 10 SU 7478
Bingfield 47 NY 9772
Bingham 34 SK 7039
Bingham's Melcombe 8 ST 7701
Bingley 37 SE 1039
Binham 29 TF 9839
Binley (Hants.) 10 SU 4153
Binley (W Mids) 26 SP 3778
Binniehill 50 NS 8572
Binstead (I. of W.) 9 SZ 5792
Binsted (Hants.) 10 SU 7741
Binton 25 SP 1454
Bintree 29 TG 0123
Binweston 23 SJ 3004
Birch (Essex) 21 TL 9419
Birch (Gtr Mches.) 37 SD 8507
Bircham Newton 28 TF 7633
Bircham Tofts 28 TF 7732
Birchanger 20 TL 5122
Bircher 24 SO 4765
Birch Green 21 TL 9418
Birchgrove (S Glam.) 16 ST 1679
Birchgrove (W Glam.) 15 SS 7098
Birchington 13 TR 3069
Birchover 33 SK 2462
Birch Vale 33 SK 0286
Bircotes 38 SK 6391
Birdbrook 20 TL 7041
Bird End 25 SP 0193
Birdham 9 SU 8200
Birdingbury 26 SP 4368
Birdlip 17 SO 9214
Birdsgreen 24 SO 7685
Birdston 50 NS 6575
Birdwell 37 SE 3401
Birdwood 17 SO 7318
Birgham 53 NT 7939
Birkdale 36 SD 3214
Birkenhead 32 SJ 3188
Birkenhills 62 NJ 7445
Birkenshaw (Strath.) 50 NS 6962
Birkenshaw (W Yorks.) 37 SE 2028
Birkhall 61 NO 3493
Birkhill Feus 57 NO 3433
Birkin 38 SE 5226
Birley 24 SO 4553
Birling (Kent) 12 TQ 6860
Birling (Northum.) 47 NU 2406
Birlingham 25 SO 9343
Birmingham 25 SP 0787
Birnam 56 NO 0341
Birness 62 NJ 9933
Birse 62 NO 5596
Birsemore 61 NO 5297
Birstall 34 SK 5809
Birstall Smithies 37 SE 2226
Birstwith 37 SE 2459
Birtley (Here. and Worc.) 24 SO 3669
Birtley (Northum.) 47 NY 8778
Birtley (Tyne and Wear) 47 NZ 2755
Birts Street 24 SO 7836
Bisbrooke 27 SP 8899
Bishampton 25 SO 9851
Bishop Auckland 42 NZ 2029
Bishopbriggs 50 NS 6070
Bishop Burton 39 SE 9839
Bishop Middleham 42 NZ 3231
Bishop Monkton 42 SE 3266
Bishop Norton 39 SK 9892
Bishopsbourne 13 TR 1852
Bishops Cannings 17 SU 0364
Bishop's Castle 23 SO 3288
Bishop's Caundle 8 ST 6912
Bishop's Cleeve 17 SO 9527
Bishop's Frome 24 SO 6648
Bishop's Itchington 26 SP 3857
Bishops Lydeard 7 ST 1629
Bishop's Nympton 6 SS 7523
Bishop's Offley 32 SJ 7729
Bishop's Stortford 20 TL 4821
Bishop's Sutton 9 SU 6031
Bishop's Tachbrook 26 SP 3161
Bishop's Tawton 6 SS 5630
Bishopsteignton 5 SX 9173
Bishopstoke 9 SU 4619
Bishopston 15 SS 5889
Bishopstone (Bucks.) 18 SP 8010
Bishopstone (E Susx) 12 TQ 4701
Bishopstone (Here. and Worc.) 24 SO 4143
Bishopstone (Wilts.) 8 SU 0625
Bishopstone (Wilts.) 18 SU 2483
Bishop Sutton 17 ST 5859
Bishop's Waltham 9 SU 5517
Bishopswood (Somer.) 7 ST 2512
Bishop's Wood (Staffs.) 25 SJ 8309
Bishopsworth 17 ST 5768
Bishop Thornton 42 SE 2663
Bishopthorpe 38 SE 5947
Bishopton (Durham) 42 NZ 3621
Bishopton (Strath.) 50 NS 4371
Bishop Wilton 38 SE 7955
Bishton 16 ST 3887
Bisley (Glos.) 17 SO 9005
Bisley (Surrey) 11 SU 9559
Bispham 36 SD 3139
Bissoe 2 SW 7741
Bisterne Close 9 SU 2202
Bitchfield 34 SK 9828
Bittadon 6 SS 5441
Bittaford 5 SX 6557
Bittering 29 TF 9317
Bitterley 24 SO 5577
Bitterne 9 SU 4513
Bitteswell 26 SP 5385
Bitton 17 ST 6769
Bix 18 SU 7285
Bixter 63 HU 3352
Blaby 26 SP 5697
Blackacre 45 NY 0490
Blackadder 53 NT 8452
Blackawton 5 SX 8050
Blackborough 5 ST 0909
Blackborough End 28 TF 6614
Black Bourton 18 SP 2804
Blackboys 12 TQ 5220
Blackbrook 32 SJ 7639
Blackburn (Grampn.) 62 NJ 8212
Blackburn (Lancs.) 36 SD 6827
Blackburn (Lothian) 51 NS 9865
Black Callerton 47 NZ 1769
Black Clauchrie 44 NX 2984
Black Crofts 54 NM 9234
Blackden Heath 32 SJ 7871
Black Dog (Devon.) 6 SS 8009
Blackdog (Grampn.) 62 NJ 9514
Black Down (Devon.) 5 ST 0907
Black Down (Devon.) 4 SX 5081
Black Down (Dorset) 7 SY 6087
Blackfield 9 SU 4402
Blackford (Cumbr.) 46 NY 3962
Blackford (Somer.) 7 ST 4147
Blackford (Somer.) 8 ST 6526
Blackford (Tays.) 56 NN 8908
Blackfordby 33 SK 3318
Blackgang 9 SZ 4876
Blackhall Colliery 42 NZ 4539
Blackhalls Rocks 42 NZ 4739
Blackham 12 TQ 4839
Blackhaugh 52 NT 4238
Blackheath (Essex) 21 TM 0021
Blackheath (Surrey) 11 TQ 0346
Blackhill (Grampn.) 62 NK 0843
Blackland 17 SU 0168
Blackley 37 SD 8503
Blacklunans 56 NO 1560
Blackmill 15 SS 9386
Blackmoor 9 SU 7833
Blackmoor Gate 6 SS 6443
Blackmore 20 TL 6001
Blackmore End 20 TL 7430
Black Mount (Strath.) 55 NN 2842
Blackness 51 NT 0579
Blacknest 10 SU 7941
Black Notley 20 TL 7620
Blacko 37 SD 8541
Blackpill 15 SS 6290
Blackpool 36 SD 3035
Blackpool Gate 46 NY 5377
Blackridge 50 NS 8967
Blackrock (Gwent) 16 SO 2112
Blackrock (Islay) 48 NR 3063
Blackrod 36 SD 6110
Blackshaw 45 NY 0465
Blacksmith's Corner 21 TM 0131
Blackstone 11 TQ 2416
Blackthorn 18 SP 6219
Blackthorpe 21 TL 9063
Blacktoft 39 SE 8424
Blacktop 62 NJ 8604
Black Torrington 6 SS 4605
Blackwater (Corn.) 2 SW 7346
Blackwater (Hants.) 11 SU 8559
Blackwater (I. of W.) 9 SZ 5086
Blackwater (Suff.) 29 TM 5077
Blackwaterfoot 49 NR 8928
Blackwell (Derby.) 33 SK 1272
Blackwell (Durham.) 42 NZ 2712
Blackwell (Here. and Worc.) 25 SO 9972
Blackwood (Gwent) 16 ST 1797
Blackwood (Strath.) 50 NS 7943
Blackwood Hill 33 SJ 9255
Blacon 32 SJ 3767
Bladnoch 44 NX 4254
Bladon 18 SP 4414
Blaenannerch 14 SN 2449
Blaenau Ffestiniog 30 SH 7045
Blaenavon 16 SO 2509
Blaenawey 16 SO 2919
Blaen Dyryn 15 SN 9336
Blaengarw 15 SS 9092
Blaengwrach 15 SN 8605
Blaengwynfi 15 SS 8996
Blaenpennal 22 SN 6365
Blaenplwyf 22 SN 5775
Blaenporth 14 SN 2648
Blaenrhondda 15 SS 9299
Blaenwaun 14 SN 2327
Blagdon 5 SX 8561
Blagdon Hill 7 ST 2118
Blaich 55 NN 0476
Blaina 16 SO 2008
Blairadam Forest 51 NT 1693
Blair Atholl 56 NN 8765
Blair Castle (Tays.) (ant.) 56 NN 8666
Blairdenon Hill 56 NN 8601
Blair Drummond 56 NS 7398
Blairdrummond Moss 56 NS 7297
Blairfindy Castle (ant.) 61 NJ 1928
Blairgowrie 56 NO 1745
Blairhall 51 NT 0089
Blairingone 56 NS 9896
Blairlogie 56 NS 8396
Blairmore 49 NS 1982
Blairskaith 50 NS 5975
Blaisdon 17 SO 7016
Blakebrook 24 SO 8077
Blakedown 25 SO 8778
Blakelaw 53 NT 7730
Blakemere 24 SO 3641
Blakeney (Glos.) 17 SO 6707
Blakeney (Norf.) 29 TG 0243
Blakenhall (Ches.) 32 SJ 7247
Blakenhall (W Mids) 25 SO 9297
Blakeshall 25 SO 8381
Blakesley 26 SP 6250
Blanchland 47 NY 9650
Blandford Forum 8 ST 8806
Blandford St. Mary 8 ST 8805
Bland Hill 37 SE 2053
Blanefield 50 NS 5579
Blankney 35 TF 0660
Blarghour 55 NM 9913
Blarmachfoldach 55 NN 0969
Blarnaleyoch 64 NH 1490

Callow Hill 77 Chilton

Callow Hill (Wilts.) ... 17 ... SU 0385
Callows Grave ... 24 ... SO 5966
Calmore ... 9 ... SU 3314
Calmsden ... 17 ... SP 0408
Calne ... 17 ... ST 9971
Calow ... 33 ... SK 4071
Calshot ... 9 ... SU 4701
Calstock ... 4 ... SX 4368
Calthorpe ... 29 ... TG 1831
Calthwaite ... 40 ... NY 4640
Calton (N Yorks.) ... 37 ... SD 9059
Calton (Staffs.) ... 33 ... SK 1050
Calveley ... 32 ... SJ 5958
Calver ... 33 ... SK 2374
Calverhall ... 32 ... SJ 6037
Calver Hill ... 24 ... SO 3748
Calverleigh ... 6 ... SS 9214
Calverley ... 37 ... SE 2036
Calvert ... 18 ... SP 6824
Calverton (Bucks.) ... 18 ... SP 7938
Calverton (Notts.) ... 34 ... SK 6149
Calvine ... 56 ... NN 8066
Calzeat ... 51 ... NT 1136
Cam ... 17 ... ST 7599
Camas-luinie ... 59 ... NG 9128
Camastianavaig ... 58 ... NG 5039
Camasunary ... 58 ... NG 5119
Camault Muir ... 60 ... NH 5040
Camber ... 13 ... TQ 9619
Camberley ... 11 ... SU 8760
Camberwell ... 12 ... TQ 3376
Camblesforth ... 38 ... SE 6425
Cambo ... 47 ... NZ 0285
Cambois ... 47 ... NZ 3083
Camborne ... 2 ... SW 6440
Cambridge ... 20 ... TL 4658
Cambus ... 50 ... NS 8593
Cambusbarron ... 50 ... NS 7792
Cambuskenneth ... 50 ... NS 8094
Cambuslang ... 50 ... NS 6459
Camden ... 19 ... TQ 2784
Camelford ... 4 ... SX 1083
Camelon ... 50 ... NS 8680
Camelsdale ... 11 ... SU 8932
Camerory ... 61 ... NJ 0231
Camerton (Avon) ... 17 ... ST 6857
Camerton (Cumbr.) ... 40 ... NY 0330
Camghouran ... 55 ... NN 5556
Cammachmore ... 62 ... NO 9295
Cammeringham ... 34 ... SK 9482
Campbelltown or Ardersier ... 60 ... NH 7854
Campbelton ... 49 ... NS 1950
Campbeltown ... 48 ... NR 7120
Campmuir ... 56 ... NO 2137
Campsall ... 38 ... SE 5313
Campsea Ashe ... 21 ... TM 3356
Camp, The ... 17 ... SO 9308
Campton ... 19 ... TL 1238
Camrose ... 14 ... SM 9220
Camserney ... 56 ... NN 8149
Camusteel ... 58 ... NG 7042
Camusterrach ... 58 ... NG 7141
Camusvrachan ... 56 ... NN 6248
Canada ... 9 ... SU 2817
Canal Foot ... 40 ... SD 3177
Candlesby ... 35 ... TF 4567
Cane End ... 10 ... SU 6779
Canewdon ... 21 ... TQ 8994
Canford Bottom ... 8 ... SU 0300
Canford Cliffs ... 8 ... SZ 0689
Canisbay ... 67 ... ND 3472
Cann Common ... 8 ... ST 8920
Cannich ... 59 ... NH 3331
Cannington ... 7 ... ST 2539
Cannock ... 25 ... SJ 9710
Cannock Wood ... 25 ... SK 0412
Canonbie ... 46 ... NY 3976
Canon Bridge ... 24 ... SO 4341
Canon Frome ... 24 ... SO 6543
Canon Pyon ... 24 ... SO 4549
Canons Ashby ... 26 ... SP 5750
Canonstown ... 2 ... SW 5335
Canterbury ... 13 ... TR 1557
Cantley (Norf.) ... 29 ... TG 3704
Cantley (S Yorks.) ... 38 ... SE 6202
Cantlop ... 24 ... SJ 5205
Canton ... 16 ... ST 1577
Cantraydoune ... 60 ... NH 7946
Cantraywood ... 60 ... NH 7748
Cantsfield ... 41 ... SD 6172
Canwick ... 34 ... SK 9869
Canworthy Water ... 4 ... SX 2291
Caol ... 55 ... NN 1175
Caoles ... 48 ... NM 0848
Capel ... 11 ... TQ 1740
Capel Bangor ... 22 ... SN 6580
Capel Betws Lleucu ... 22 ... SN 6058
Capel Carmel ... 30 ... SH 1628
Capel Coch ... 30 ... SH 4582
Capel Curig ... 30 ... SH 7258
Capel Cynon ... 15 ... SN 3849
Capel Dewi ... 15 ... SN 4542
Capel Garmon ... 31 ... SH 8155
Capel Gwyn (Dyfed) ... 15 ... SN 4622
Capel Gwyn (Gwyn.) ... 30 ... SH 3575
Capel Gwynfe ... 15 ... SN 7222
Capel Hendre ... 15 ... SN 5911
Capel Isaac ... 15 ... SN 5927
Capel Iwan ... 14 ... SN 2836
Capel le Ferne ... 13 ... TR 2439
Capel Llanilterne ... 16 ... ST 0979
Capel St. Mary ... 21 ... TM 0838
Capel-y-ffin ... 23 ... SO 2531
Capenhurst ... 32 ... SJ 3673
Capernwray ... 40 ... SD 5372
Capheaton ... 47 ... NZ 0380
Cappercleuch ... 51 ... NT 2423
Capstone ... 12 ... TQ 7865
Capton ... 5 ... SX 8353
Caputh ... 56 ... NO 0940
Carbis Bay ... 2 ... SW 5339
Carbost (Island of Skye) ... 58 ... NG 3731
Carbost (Island of Skye) ... 58 ... NG 4248
Carbrooke ... 29 ... TF 9402
Carburton ... 34 ... SK 6173
Carcary ... 57 ... NO 6455
Carclew ... 2 ... SW 7838
Car Colston ... 34 ... SK 7142
Carcroft ... 38 ... SE 5409
Cardenden ... 51 ... NT 2195
Cardeston ... 24 ... SJ 3912
Cardiff ... 16 ... ST 1877
Cardigan ... 14 ... SN 1846
Cardington (Beds.) ... 27 ... TL 0847
Cardington (Salop) ... 24 ... SO 5095
Cardinham ... 4 ... SX 1268
Cardney House ... 56 ... NO 0545
Cardow ... 61 ... NJ 1942
Cardrona ... 51 ... NT 3038
Cardross (Strath.) ... 50 ... NS 3477
Cardurnock ... 46 ... NY 1758
Careby ... 34 ... TF 0216
Careston ... 57 ... NO 5260
Carew ... 14 ... SN 0403
Carew Cheriton ... 14 ... SN 0402
Carew Newton ... 14 ... SN 0404
Carey ... 24 ... SO 5631
Carfrae ... 52 ... NT 5769
Cargen ... 45 ... NX 9672
Cargenbridge ... 45 ... NX 9474
Cargill ... 56 ... NO 1536
Cargo ... 46 ... NY 3659
Cargreen ... 4 ... SX 4262
Carham ... 53 ... NT 7938
Carhampton ... 7 ... ST 0042
Carharrack ... 2 ... SW 7241
Carie (Tays.) ... 56 ... NN 6157
Carie (Tays.) ... 56 ... NN 6437
Carinish ... 63 ... NF 8159
Carisbrooke ... 9 ... SZ 4888
Cark ... 40 ... SD 3676
Carlby ... 35 ... TF 0414
Carlecotes ... 37 ... SE 1703
Carleton (Cumbr.) ... 46 ... NY 4253
Carleton (Lancs.) ... 36 ... SD 3339
Carleton (N Yorks.) ... 37 ... SD 9749
Carleton Forehoe ... 29 ... TG 0805
Carleton Rode ... 29 ... TM 1192
Carlingcott ... 17 ... ST 6958
Carlisle ... 46 ... NY 3955
Carlops ... 51 ... NT 1656
Carloway ... 63 ... NB 2042
Carlton (Beds.) ... 27 ... SP 9555
Carlton (Cambs.) ... 20 ... TL 6453
Carlton (Cleve.) ... 42 ... NZ 3921
Carlton (Leic.) ... 26 ... SK 3905
Carlton (Notts.) ... 34 ... SK 6141
Carlton (N Yorks.) ... 42 ... NZ 5004
Carlton (N Yorks.) ... 42 ... SE 0684
Carlton (N Yorks.) ... 42 ... SE 6086
Carlton (N Yorks.) ... 38 ... SE 6423
Carlton (Suff.) ... 21 ... TM 3864
Carlton (S Yorks.) ... 37 ... SE 3610
Carlton (W Yorks.) ... 37 ... SE 3327
Carlton Colville ... 29 ... TM 5190
Carlton Curlieu ... 26 ... SP 6997
Carlton Husthwaite ... 42 ... SE 4976
Carlton in Lindrick ... 34 ... SK 5984
Carlton-le-Moorland ... 34 ... SK 9058
Carlton Miniott ... 42 ... SE 3980
Carlton-on-Trent ... 34 ... SK 7963
Carlton Scroop ... 34 ... SK 9445
Carluke ... 50 ... NS 8450
Carmacoup ... 50 ... NS 7927
Carmarthen ... 15 ... SN 4120
Carmel (Clwyd) ... 31 ... SJ 1676
Carmel (Dyfed) ... 15 ... SN 5816
Carmel (Gwyn.) ... 30 ... SH 3882
Carmel (Gwyn.) ... 30 ... SH 4954
Carminish ... 63 ... NG 0284
Carmunnock ... 50 ... NS 5957
Carmyle ... 50 ... NS 6461
Carmyllie ... 57 ... NO 5542
Carna ... 54 ... NM 6259
Carnaby ... 39 ... TA 1465
Carnach (Harris) ... 63 ... NG 2297
Carnach (Highld.) ... 59 ... NH 0228
Carnan (South Uist) ... 63 ... NF 8143
Carnbee ... 57 ... NO 5306
Carnbo ... 56 ... NO 0503
Carne ... 2 ... SW 9138
Carnell ... 50 ... NS 4632
Carnforth ... 40 ... SD 4970
Carnhell Green ... 2 ... SW 6137
Carnie ... 62 ... NJ 8105
Carno ... 23 ... SN 9696
Carnock ... 51 ... NT 0489
Carnon Downs ... 2 ... SW 7940
Carnousie ... 62 ... NJ 6650
Carnoustie ... 57 ... NO 5634
Carnwath ... 51 ... NS 9746
Carnyorth ... 2 ... SW 3733
Carperby ... 41 ... SE 0089
Carradale ... 49 ... NR 8138
Carragrich ... 63 ... NG 2098
Carrbridge ... 60 ... NH 9022
Carreglefn ... 30 ... SH 3889
Carrick (Fife.) ... 57 ... NO 4422
Carrick (Strath.) ... 49 ... NS 1994
Carriden ... 51 ... NT 0181
Carrine ... 48 ... NR 6709
Carrington (Gtr Mches.) ... 32 ... SJ 7492
Carrington (Lincs.) ... 35 ... TF 3155
Carrington (Lothian) ... 51 ... NT 3160
Carrog ... 31 ... SJ 1043
Carron (Central) ... 50 ... NS 8882
Carron (Grampn.) ... 61 ... NJ 2241
Carronbridge (Dumf. and Galwy.) ... 45 ... NX 8697
Carronshore ... 50 ... NS 8983
Carr Shield ... 46 ... NY 8047
Carrutherstown ... 45 ... NY 1071
Carr Vale ... 33 ... SK 4669
Carrville ... 42 ... NZ 3043
Carsaig ... 54 ... NM 5421
Carseriggan ... 44 ... NX 3167
Carsethorn ... 45 ... NX 9959
Carshalton ... 11 ... TQ 2764
Carsington ... 33 ... SK 2553
Carskiey ... 48 ... NR 6508
Carsluith ... 44 ... NX 4854
Carsphairn ... 45 ... NX 5693
Carstairs ... 51 ... NS 9345
Carstairs Junction ... 51 ... NS 9545
Carswell Marsh ... 18 ... SU 3198
Carter's Clay ... 9 ... SU 3024
Carterton ... 18 ... SP 2706
Carthew ... 4 ... SX 0055
Carthorpe ... 42 ... SE 3083
Cartington ... 47 ... NU 0304
Cartland ... 50 ... NS 8646
Cartmel ... 40 ... SD 3778
Cartmel Fell ... 40 ... SD 4188
Carway ... 15 ... SN 4606
Cashmoor ... 8 ... ST 9813
Cassington ... 18 ... SP 4510
Casswell's Bridge ... 35 ... TF 1627
Castell Howell ... 15 ... SN 4448
Castell-y-bwch ... 16 ... ST 2792
Casterton ... 41 ... SD 6279
Castle Acre ... 28 ... TF 8115
Castle Ashby ... 27 ... SP 8659
Castle Bank ... 33 ... SJ 9021
Castlebay ... 63 ... NL 6698
Castle Bolton ... 42 ... SE 0391
Castle Bromwich ... 25 ... SP 1489
Castle Bytham ... 34 ... SK 9818
Castlebythe ... 14 ... SN 0229
Castle Caereinion ... 23 ... SJ 1605
Castle Camps ... 20 ... TL 6343
Castle Carrock ... 46 ... NY 5455
Castle Cary (Somer.) ... 8 ... ST 6332
Castlecary (Strath.) ... 50 ... NS 7878
Castle Combe ... 17 ... ST 8477
Castlecraig (Borders) ... 51 ... NT 1344
Castle Donington ... 33 ... SK 4427
Castle Douglas ... 45 ... NX 7662
Castle Eaton ... 17 ... SU 1495
Castle Eden ... 42 ... NZ 4338
Castleford ... 38 ... SE 4225
Castle Frome ... 24 ... SO 6645
Castle Green ... 40 ... SD 5287
Castle Gresley ... 33 ... SK 2718
Castle Heaton ... 53 ... NT 9041
Castle Hedingham ... 20 ... TL 7835
Castlehill (Strath.) ... 50 ... NS 8452
Castle Hill (Suff.) ... 21 ... TM 1646
Castle Kennedy ... 44 ... NX 1059
Castlemartin ... 14 ... SR 9198
Castle Morris ... 14 ... SM 9031
Castlemorton ... 24 ... SO 7937
Castle O'er ... 46 ... NY 2492
Castle Pulverbatch ... 24 ... SJ 4202
Castle Rising ... 28 ... TF 6624
Castleside ... 47 ... NZ 0748
Castle Stuart ... 60 ... NH 7449
Castlethorpe ... 26 ... SP 7944
Castleton (Borders) ... 46 ... NY 5190
Castleton (Derby.) ... 33 ... SK 1582
Castleton (Gwent) ... 16 ... ST 2583
Castleton (N Yorks.) ... 43 ... NZ 6808
Castle Toward ... 49 ... NS 1168
Castletown (Highld.) ... 67 ... ND 1967
Castletown (I. of M.) ... 43 ... SC 2667
Castletown (Tyne and Wear) ... 47 ... NZ 3558
Caston ... 29 ... TL 9598
Castor ... 27 ... TL 1298
Catacol ... 49 ... NR 9149
Catbrain ... 16 ... ST 5580
Catcliffe ... 33 ... SK 4288
Catcott ... 7 ... ST 3939
Caterham ... 12 ... TQ 3455
Catesby ... 26 ... SP 5159
Catfield ... 29 ... TG 3821
Catfirth (Shetld.) ... 63 ... HU 4354
Catford ... 12 ... TQ 3872
Catforth ... 36 ... SD 4735
Cathcart ... 50 ... NS 5960
[illegible]
Catherington ... 9 ... SU 6914
Catherton ... 24 ... SO 6578
Catlodge ... 60 ... NN 6392
Catlowdy ... 46 ... NY 4676
Catmore ... 10 ... SU 4579
Caton ... 40 ... SD 5364
Cator Court ... 5 ... SX 6877
Catrine ... 50 ... NS 5225
Cat's Ash ... 16 ... ST 3790
Catsfield ... 12 ... TQ 7213
Catshill ... 25 ... SO 9674
Cattal ... 38 ... SE 4454
Cattawade ... 21 ... TM 1033
Catterall ... 36 ... SD 4942
Catterick ... 42 ... SE 2397
Catterick Bridge ... 42 ... SE 2299
Catterick Camp ... 42 ... SE 1897
Catterlen ... 40 ... NY 4833
Catterline ... 57 ... NO 8678
Catterton ... 38 ... SE 5045
Catthorpe ... 26 ... SP 5578
Cattistock ... 7 ... SY 5999
Catton (Norf.) ... 29 ... TG 2312
Catton (Northum.) ... 46 ... NY 8257
Catton (N Yorks.) ... 42 ... SE 3778
Catwick ... 39 ... TA 1245
Catworth ... 27 ... TL 0873
Cauldcott ... 18 ... SP 5024
Cauldcots ... 57 ... NO 6547
Cauldhame ... 50 ... NS 6494
Cauldon ... 33 ... SK 0749
Cauldside ... 46 ... NY 4480
Cauldwell ... 33 ... SK 2517
Caulkerbush ... 45 ... NX 9257
Caunsall ... 25 ... SO 8481
Caunton ... 34 ... SK 7460
Causewayhead ... 50 ... NS 8195
Causeyend ... 62 ... NJ 9419
Causey Park ... 47 ... NZ 1794
Cautley ... 41 ... SD 6994
Cavendish ... 20 ... TL 8046
Cavenham ... 28 ... TL 7669
Caversfield ... 18 ... SP 5824
Caversham ... 10 ... SU 7274
Caver's Hill ... 51 ... NT 3921
Caversta ... 63 ... NB 3619
Caverswall ... 33 ... SJ 9442
Cawdor ... 60 ... NH 8450
Cawood ... 38 ... SE 5737
Cawsand ... 4 ... SX 4350
Cawston ... 29 ... TG 1324
Cawthorne ... 37 ... SE 2807
Cawton ... 42 ... SE 6476
Caxton ... 20 ... TL 3058
Caxton End ... 20 ... TL 3157
Caynham ... 24 ... SO 5473
Caythorpe (Lincs.) ... 34 ... SK 9348
Caythorpe (Notts.) ... 34 ... SK 6845
Cayton ... 43 ... TA 0583
Cefn-brith ... 31 ... SH 9350
Cefn Coch (Powys) ... 31 ... SJ 1026
Cefn-coed-y-cymmer ... 16 ... SO 0307
Cefn Cribwr ... 15 ... SS 8582
Cefn Cross ... 15 ... SS 8682
Cefn-ddwysarn ... 31 ... SH 9638
Cefn Einion ... 23 ... SO 2886
Cefn-mawr (Clywd) ... 32 ... SJ 2842
Cefn-y-bedd ... 32 ... SJ 3156
Cefn-y-coed ... 23 ... SO 2093
Cefn-y-pant ... 14 ... SN 1925
Ceidio ... 30 ... SH 4085
Ceint ... 30 ... SH 4874
Cellan ... 15 ... SN 6149
Cellarhead (Staffs.) ... 33 ... SJ 9547
Cemaes ... 30 ... SH 3793
Cemmaes ... 22 ... SH 8306
Cemmaes Road ... 22 ... SH 8204
Cenarth ... 14 ... SN 2641
Cennin ... 30 ... SH 4645
Ceres ... 57 ... NO 4011
Cerne Abbas ... 8 ... ST 6601
Cerney Wick ... 17 ... SU 0796
Cerrigceinwen ... 30 ... SH 4273
Cerrigydrudion ... 31 ... SH 9548
Cessford ... 52 ... NT 7323
Chaceley ... 25 ... SO 8530
Chacewater ... 2 ... SW 7444
Chackmore ... 18 ... SP 6835
Chacombe ... 26 ... SP 4943
Chadderton ... 37 ... SD 9005
Chaddesden ... 33 ... SK 3737
Chaddesley Corbett ... 25 ... SO 8973
Chaddleworth ... 10 ... SU 4177
Chadlington ... 18 ... SP 3221
Chadshunt ... 26 ... SP 3453
Chad Valley ... 25 ... SP 0385
Chadwell St. Mary ... 12 ... TQ 6478
Chadwick End ... 25 ... SP 2073
Chaffcombe ... 7 ... ST 3510
Chagford ... 5 ... SX 7087
Chailey ... 12 ... TQ 3919
Chainhurst ... 12 ... TQ 7347
Chalbury Common ... 8 ... SU 0206
Chaldon ... 12 ... TQ 3155
Chaldon Herring or East Chaldon ... 8 ... SY 7983
Chale ... 9 ... SZ 4877
Chale Green ... 9 ... SZ 4879
Chalfont St. Giles ... 19 ... SU 9993
Chalfont St. Peter ... 19 ... SU 9990
Chalford ... 17 ... SO 8902
Chalgrove ... 18 ... SU 6396
Chalk ... 12 ... TQ 6772
Challacombe ... 6 ... SS 6941
Challoch ... 44 ... NX 3867
Challock Lees ... 13 ... TR 0050
Chalton (Beds.) ... 19 ... TL 0326
Chalvington ... 12 ... TQ 5109
Chandler's Cross ... 19 ... TQ 0698
Chandler's Ford ... 9 ... SU 4320
Channerwick ... 63 ... HU 4023
Chantry (Somer.) ... 8 ... ST 7146
Chantry (Suff.) ... 21 ... TM 1443
Chapel ... 51 ... NT 2593
Chapel Allerton (Somer.) ... 7 ... ST 4050
Chapel Allerton (W Yorks.) ... 37 ... SE 2936
Chapel Amble ... 4 ... SW 9975
Chapel Brampton ... 26 ... SP 7266
Chapel Chorlton ... 32 ... SJ 8037
Chapelend Way ... 20 ... TL 7039
Chapel-en-le-Frith ... 33 ... SK 0580
Chapelgate ... 35 ... TF 4124
Chapel Haddlesey ... 38 ... SE 5826
Chapelhall ... 50 ... NS 7862
Chapel Hill (Grampn.) ... 62 ... NK 0635
Chapel Hill (Gwent) ... 16 ... SO 5200
Chapelhill (Highld.) ... 65 ... NH 8273
Chapel Hill (Lincs.) ... 35 ... TF 2054
Chapelhill (Tays.) ... 56 ... NO 0030
Chapel Hill (Tays.) ... 56 ... NO 2021
Chapelknowe ... 46 ... NY 3173
Chapel Lawn ... 23 ... SO 3176
Chapel Le Dale ... 41 ... SD 7377
Chapel of Garioch ... 62 ... NJ 7124
Chapel Row ... 10 ... SU 5669
Chapel St. Leonards ... 35 ... TF 5572
Chapel Stile ... 40 ... NY 3205
Chapelton (Devon.) ... 6 ... SS 5826
Chapelton (Strath.) ... 50 ... NS 6848
Chapelton (Tays.) ... 57 ... NO 6247
Chapeltown (Grampn.) ... 61 ... NJ 2421
Chapeltown (Lancs.) ... 36 ... SD 7315
Chapeltown (S Yorks.) ... 37 ... SK 3596
Chapmanslade ... 8 ... ST 8247
Chappel ... 21 ... TL 8928
Chard ... 7 ... ST 3208
Chardstock ... 7 ... ST 3004
Charfield ... 17 ... ST 7292
Charing ... 13 ... TQ 9549
Charing Heath ... 13 ... TQ 9148
Charingworth ... 25 ... SP 1939
Charlbury ... 18 ... SP 3519
Charlcombe ... 17 ... ST 7467
Charlecote ... 26 ... SP 2656
Charles ... 6 ... SS 6832
Charleston ... 57 ... NO 3845
Charlestown (Corn.) ... 4 ... SX 0351
Charlestown (Dorset) ... 8 ... SY 6579
Charlestown (Fife.) ... 51 ... NT 0683
Charlestown (Grampn.) ... 62 ... NJ 9300
Charlestown (Highld.) ... 64 ... NG 8174
Charlestown (Highld.) ... 60 ... NH 6448
Charlestown of Aberlour ... 61 ... NJ 2642
Charles Tye ... 21 ... TM 0252
Charlesworth ... 37 ... SK 0092
Charlinch ... 7 ... ST 2337
Charlton (Gtr London) ... 12 ... TQ 4278
Charlton (Here. and Worc.) ... 25 ... SP 0045
Charlton (Northants.) ... 18 ... SP 5236
Charlton (Wilts.) ... 8 ... ST 9021
Charlton (Wilts.) ... 17 ... ST 9689
Charlton (Wilts.) ... 17 ... SU 1155
Charlton (Wilts.) ... 8 ... SU 1723
Charlton (W Susx) ... 11 ... SU 8812
Charlton Abbots ... 17 ... SP 0324
Charlton Adam ... 7 ... ST 5328
Charlton Horethorne ... 8 ... ST 6623
Charlton Kings ... 17 ... SO 9620
Charlton Mackrell ... 7 ... ST 5228
Charlton Marshall ... 8 ... ST 8903
Charlton Musgrove ... 8 ... ST 7229
Charlton-on-Otmoor ... 18 ... SP 5615
Charlwood ... 11 ... TQ 2441
Charminster ... 8 ... SY 6792
Charmouth ... 7 ... SY 3693
Charndon ... 18 ... SP 6724
Charney Bassett ... 18 ... SU 3894
Charnock Richard ... 36 ... SD 5415
Charsfield ... 21 ... TM 2556
Charter Alley ... 10 ... SU 5957
Charterhouse ... 16 ... ST 4955
Chartershall ... 50 ... NS 7990
Charterville Allotments ... 18 ... SP 3110
Chartham ... 13 ... TR 1054
Chartham Hatch ... 13 ... TR 1056
Chartridge ... 19 ... SP 9303
Chart Sutton ... 12 ... TQ 8049
Charwelton ... 26 ... SP 5355
Chase Terrace ... 25 ... SK 0409
Chasetown ... 25 ... SK 0408
Chastleton ... 18 ... SP 2429
Chatburn ... 37 ... SD 7644
Chatcull ... 32 ... SJ 7934
Chatham ... 12 ... TQ 7567
Chathill ... 53 ... NU 1826
Chattenden ... 12 ... TQ 7672
Chatteris ... 27 ... TL 3986
Chattisham ... 21 ... TM 0942
Chatton ... 53 ... NU 0528
Chawleigh ... 6 ... SS 7112
Chawston ... 27 ... TL 1556
Chawton ... 10 ... SU 7037
Cheadle (Gtr Mches.) ... 33 ... SJ 8788
Cheadle (Staffs.) ... 33 ... SK 0043
Cheadle Hulme ... 33 ... SJ 8686
Cheam ... 11 ... TQ 2463
Chearsley ... 18 ... SP 7110
Chebsey ... 33 ... SJ 8528
Checkendon ... 10 ... SU 6682
Checkley (Ches.) ... 32 ... SJ 7245
Checkley (Staffs.) ... 33 ... SK 0237
Chedburgh ... 20 ... TL 7957
Cheddar ... 7 ... ST 4553
Cheddington ... 19 ... SP 9217
Cheddleton ... 33 ... SJ 9651
Cheddon Fitzpaine ... 7 ... ST 2427
Chedgrave ... 29 ... TM 3699
Chedington ... 7 ... ST 4805
Chediston ... 29 ... TM 3577
Chedworth ... 17 ... SP 0511
Chedzoy ... 7 ... ST 3337
Cheetham Hill ... 37 ... SD 8401
Cheldon ... 6 ... SS 7313
Chelford ... 32 ... SJ 8174
Chellaston ... 33 ... SK 3830
Chellington ... 27 ... SP 9656
Chelmarsh ... 24 ... SO 7187
Chelmondiston ... 21 ... TM 2037
Chelmorton ... 33 ... SK 1169
Chelmsford ... 20 ... TL 7006
Chelsfield ... 12 ... TQ 4864
Chelsworth ... 21 ... TL 9748
Cheltenham ... 17 ... SO 9422
Chelveston ... 27 ... SP 9969
Chelvey ... 16 ... ST 4668
Chelwood ... 17 ... ST 6361
Chelwood Gate ... 12 ... TQ 4130
Cheney Longville ... 24 ... SO 4184
Chenies ... 19 ... TQ 0198
Chepstow ... 16 ... ST 5393
Cherhill ... 17 ... SU 0370
Cherington (Glos.) ... 17 ... ST 9098
Cherington (Warw.) ... 18 ... SP 2936
Cheriton (Devon.) ... 6 ... SS 7346
Cheriton (Devon.) ... 5 ... ST 1001
Cheriton (Hants.) ... 9 ... SU 5828
Cheriton (Somer.) ... 8 ... ST 6825
Cheriton (W Glam.) ... 15 ... SS 4593
Cheriton Bishop ... 5 ... SX 7793
Cheriton Fitzpaine ... 6 ... SS 8606
Cherrington ... 32 ... SJ 6619
Cherry Burton ... 39 ... SE 9842
Cherry Cobb Sands ... 39 ... TA 2121
Cherry Hinton ... 20 ... TL 4857
Cherry Willingham ... 34 ... TF 0173
Chertsey ... 11 ... TQ 0466
Cheselbourne ... 8 ... SY 7699
Chesham ... 19 ... SP 9601
Chesham Bois ... 19 ... SU 9698
Cheshunt ... 20 ... TL 3502
Cheslyn Hay ... 25 ... SJ 9707
Chessington ... 11 ... TQ 1863
Chester ... 32 ... SJ 4066
Chesterblade ... 8 ... ST 6641
Chesterfield (Derby.) ... 33 ... SK 3871
Chesterfield (Staffs.) ... 25 ... SK 1005
Chester-le-Street ... 47 ... NZ 2751
Chesters (Borders) ... 52 ... NT 6210
Chesterton (Cambs.) ... 27 ... TL 1295
Chesterton (Cambs.) ... 20 ... TL 4560
Chesterton (Oxon.) ... 18 ... SP 5621
Chesterton (Staffs.) ... 32 ... SJ 8249
Chesterton Green ... 26 ... SP 3558
Chestfield ... 13 ... TR 1365
Cheswardine ... 32 ... SJ 7129
Cheswick ... 53 ... NU 0346
Chetnole ... 7 ... ST 6008
Chettiscombe ... 7 ... SS 9614
Chettisham ... 28 ... TL 5483
Chettle ... 8 ... ST 9513
Chetton ... 24 ... SO 6690
Chetwode ... 18 ... SP 6429
Chetwynd Aston ... 24 ... SJ 7517
Cheveley ... 20 ... TL 6760
Chevening ... 12 ... TQ 4857
Chevington ... 20 ... TL 7859
Chevington Drift ... 47 ... NZ 2699
Chevithorne ... 7 ... SS 9715
Chew Magna ... 17 ... ST 5763
Chew Stoke ... 16 ... ST 5561
Chewton Mendip ... 7 ... ST 5952
Chicheley ... 27 ... SP 9046
Chichester ... 9 ... SU 8605
Chickerell ... 8 ... SY 6480
Chicklade ... 8 ... ST 9134
Chidden ... 9 ... SU 6517
Chiddingfold ... 11 ... SU 9635
Chiddingly ... 12 ... TQ 5414
Chiddingstone ... 12 ... TQ 5045
Chiddingstone Causeway ... 12 ... TQ 5147
Chideock ... 7 ... SY 4292
Chidham ... 9 ... SU 7803
Chieveley ... 10 ... SU 4773
Chignall St. James ... 20 ... TL 6709
Chignall Smealy ... 20 ... TL 6611
Chigwell ... 20 ... TQ 4493
Chigwell Row ... 20 ... TQ 4693
Chilbolton ... 10 ... SU 3939
Chilcomb (Hants.) ... 9 ... SU 5028
Chilcombe (Dorset) ... 7 ... SY 5291
Chilcompton ... 8 ... ST 6452
Chilcote ... 33 ... SK 2811
Childer Thornton ... 32 ... SJ 3677
Child Okeford ... 8 ... ST 8312
Childrey ... 18 ... SU 3687
Child's Ercall ... 32 ... SJ 6625
Childswickham ... 25 ... SP 0738
Childwall ... 32 ... SJ 4089
Chilfrome ... 7 ... SY 5898
Chilgrove ... 9 ... SU 8314
Chilham ... 13 ... TR 0753
Chillaton ... 4 ... SX 4381
Chillenden ... 13 ... TR 2753
Chillerton ... 9 ... SZ 4883
Chillesford ... 21 ... TM 3852
Chillingham ... 53 ... NU 0625
Chillington (Devon.) ... 5 ... SX 7942
Chillington (Somer.) ... 7 ... ST 3811
Chilmark ... 8 ... ST 9632
Chilson ... 18 ... SP 3119
Chilsworthy (Corn.) ... 4 ... SX 4172
Chilsworthy (Devon.) ... 4 ... SS 3206
Chilthorne Domer ... 7 ... ST 5219
Chilton (Bucks.) ... 18 ... SP 6811
Chilton (Durham) ... 42 ... NZ 3031
Chilton (Oxon) ... 18 ... SU 4885

Dynevor Castle 81 Everton

Dynevor Castle ... 15 ... SN 6122
Dyrham ... 17 ... ST 7375
Dysart ... 51 ... NT 3093
Dyserth ... 31 ... SJ 0579

Eagland Hill ... 36 ... SD 4345
Eagle ... 34 ... SK 8767
Eaglescliffe ... 42 ... NZ 4215
Eaglesfield (Cumbr.) ... 40 ... NY 0928
Eaglesfield (Dumf. and Galwy.) ... 46 ... NY 2374
Eaglesham ... 50 ... NS 5751
Eairy ... 43 ... SC 2977
Eakring ... 34 ... SK 6762
Ealand ... 38 ... SE 7811
Ealing ... 19 ... TQ 1781
Eamont Bridge ... 40 ... NY 5228
Earby ... 37 ... SD 9046
Earcroft ... 36 ... SD 6824
Eardington ... 24 ... SO 7290
Eardisland ... 24 ... SO 4158
Eardisley ... 23 ... SO 3149
Eardiston (Here. and Worc.) ... 24 ... SO 6968
Eardiston (Salop) ... 32 ... SJ 3725
Earith ... 27 ... TL 3875
Earle ... 53 ... NT 9826
Earlestown ... 32 ... SJ 5795
Earlham ... 29 ... TG 1908
Earlish ... 58 ... NG 3861
Earls Barton ... 27 ... SP 8563
Earls Colne ... 20 ... TL 8528
Earl's Croome ... 25 ... SO 8642
Earlsdon ... 26 ... SP 3177
Earlsferry ... 57 ... NO 4800
Earlsford ... 62 ... NJ 8334
Earl's Green ... 21 ... TM 0366
Earlshall (ant.) ... 57 ... NO 4621
Earl's Hill ... 50 ... NS 7188
Earl Shilton ... 26 ... SP 4697
Earl Soham ... 21 ... TM 2363
Earl's Seat (Central) (mt.) ... 50 ... NS 5783
Earl's Seat (Northum.) ... 46 ... NY 7192
Earl Sterndale ... 33 ... SK 0967
Earlston (Borders) ... 52 ... NT 5738
Earlston (Strath.) ... 50 ... NS 4035
Earl Stonham ... 21 ... TM 1158
Earlstoun ... 45 ... NX 6183
Earlswood ... 25 ... SP 1174
Earlswood Common ... 16 ... ST 4595
Earnley ... 9 ... SZ 8096
Earsdon ... 47 ... NZ 3272
Earshaig ... 45 ... NT 0402
[illegible]
Earswick ... 38 ... SE 6157
Eartham ... 11 ... SU 9309
Easby ... 42 ... NZ 5708
Easdale (Strath.) ... 54 ... NM 7317
Easebourne ... 11 ... SU 8922
Easenhall ... 26 ... SP 4679
Easington (Bucks.) ... 18 ... SP 6810
Easington (Cleve.) ... 43 ... NZ 7418
Easington (Durham) ... 42 ... NZ 4143
Easington (Humbs.) ... 39 ... TA 3919
Easington (Northum.) ... 53 ... NU 1234
Easington (Oxon.) ... 18 ... SU 6697
Easington Lane ... 47 ... NZ 3646
Easingwold ... 38 ... SE 5269
Easole Street ... 13 ... TR 2652
Eassie and Nevay ... 57 ... NO 3345
East Aberthaw ... 16 ... ST 0367
East Allington ... 5 ... SX 7648
East Anstey ... 6 ... SS 8626
East Ashling ... 9 ... SU 8207
East Barming ... 12 ... TQ 7254
East Barnet ... 19 ... TQ 2794
East Barsham ... 28 ... TF 9133
East Beckham ... 29 ... TG 1640
East Bedfont ... 11 ... TQ 1074
East Bergholt ... 21 ... TM 0734
East Bilney ... 29 ... TF 9519
East Blatchington ... 12 ... TQ 4800
East Boldre ... 9 ... SU 3700
Eastbourne ... 12 ... TV 6199
East Bradenham ... 29 ... TF 9208
East Brent ... 7 ... ST 3452
East Bridge ... 21 ... TM 4566
East Bridgford ... 34 ... SK 6943
East Buckland ... 6 ... SS 6731
East Budleigh ... 5 ... SY 0684
East Burra ... 63 ... HU 3833
East Burrafirth ... 63 ... HU 3658
East Burton ... 8 ... SY 8386
Eastbury (Berks.) ... 10 ... SU 3477
Eastbury (Gtr London) ... 19 ... TQ 0991
East Cairnbeg ... 57 ... NO 7076
East Calder ... 51 ... NT 0867
East Carleton (Norf.) ... 29 ... TG 1802
East Carlton (Northants.) ... 26 ... SP 8389
East Chaldon or Chaldon Herring ... 8 ... SY 7983
East Challow ... 18 ... SU 3988
East Chiltington ... 12 ... TQ 3715
East Chisenbury ... 8 ... SU 1352
Eastchurch ... 13 ... TQ 9871
East Clandon ... 11 ... TQ 0651
East Claydon ... 18 ... SP 7325
Eastcombe (Glos.) ... 17 ... SO 8804
East Combe (Somer.) ... 7 ... ST 1631
Eastcote (Gtr London) ... 19 ... TQ 1188
Eastcote (W Mids) ... 25 ... SP 1979
Eastcott (Corn.) ... 4 ... SS 2515
Eastcott (Wilts.) ... 17 ... SU 0255
East Cottingwith ... 38 ... SE 7042
East Coulston ... 17 ... ST 9454
Eastcourt ... 17 ... ST 9792
East Cowes ... 9 ... SZ 5095
East Cowton ... 42 ... NZ 3103
East Cramlington ... 47 ... NZ 2876
East Creech ... 8 ... SY 9282
Eastdean (E Susx) ... 12 ... TV 5598
East Dean (Hants.) ... 9 ... SU 2726
East Dean (W Susx) ... 11 ... SU 9013
East Dereham ... 29 ... TF 9913
East Down ... 6 ... SS 5941
East Drayton ... 34 ... SK 7775
East End (Avon) ... 16 ... ST 4770
East End (Dorset) ... 8 ... SY 9998
Eastend (Essex) ... 21 ... TQ 9492
East End (Hants.) ... 10 ... SU 4161
East End (Hants.) ... 9 ... SZ 3697
East End (Herts.) ... 20 ... TL 4527
East End (Kent) ... 12 ... TQ 8335
East End (Oxon.) ... 18 ... SP 3914
Easter Ardross ... 65 ... NH 6373
Easter Balmoral ... 61 ... NO 2693
Easter Boleskine ... 60 ... NH 5122
Easter Compton ... 17 ... ST 5782
Easter Galcantray ... 60 ... NH 8147
Eastergate ... 11 ... SU 9405
Easter Kinkell ... 60 ... NH 5755
Easter Lednathie ... 57 ... NO 3363
Easter Moniack ... 60 ... NH 5543
Easter Muckovie ... 60 ... NH 7044
Eastern Green ... 26 ... SP 2780
Easter Ord ... 62 ... NJ 8304
Easter Skeld ... 63 ... HU 3044
Easter Stanhope ... 51 ... NT 1229
Easterton ... 17 ... SU 0154
Eastertown ... 16 ... ST 3454
East Farleigh ... 12 ... TQ 7353
East Farndon ... 26 ... SP 7185
East Ferry ... 39 ... SK 8199
Eastfield (N Yorks.) ... 43 ... TA 0484
Eastfield (Strath.) ... 50 ... NS 7574
Eastfield (Strath.) ... 50 ... NS 8964
Eastfield Hall ... 47 ... NU 2206
East Garston ... 10 ... SU 3676
Eastgate (Durham) ... 41 ... NY 9538
Eastgate (Norf.) ... 29 ... TG 1423
East Ginge ... 18 ... SU 4486
East Goscote ... 34 ... SK 6413
East Grafton ... 10 ... SU 2560
East Grimstead ... 9 ... SU 2227
East Grinstead ... 12 ... TQ 3938
East Guldeford ... 13 ... TQ 9321
East Haddon ... 26 ... SP 6668
East Hagbourne ... 18 ... SU 5388
East Halton ... 39 ... TA 1419
East Halton Skitter ... 39 ... TA 1423
East Ham (Essex) ... 20 ... TQ 4283
Eastham (Mers.) ... 32 ... SJ 3580
Easthampstead ... 11 ... SU 8667
East Hanney ... 18 ... SU 4192
East Hanningfield ... 20 ... TL 7601
East Hardwick ... 38 ... SE 4618
East Harling ... 29 ... TL 9986
East Harlsey ... 42 ... SE 4299
East Harptree ... 17 ... ST 5655
East Hartford ... 47 ... NZ 2679
East Harting ... 9 ... SU 7919
East Hatley ... 27 ... TL 2850
East Hauxwell ... 42 ... SE 1693
East Haven ... 57 ... NO 5836
East Heckington ... 35 ... TF 1944
East Hedleyhope ... 42 ... NZ 1540
East Hendred ... 18 ... SU 4588
East Heslerton ... 43 ... SE 9276
East Hoathly ... 12 ... TQ 5216
Easthope ... 24 ... SO 5695
Easthorpe ... 21 ... TL 9121
East Horrington ... 7 ... ST 5846
East Horsley ... 11 ... TQ 0952
Easthouses ... 51 ... NT 3465
East Huntspill ... 7 ... ST 3444
East Hyde ... 19 ... TL 1317
East Ilsley ... 10 ... SU 4981
Eastington (Glos.) ... 17 ... SO 7705
Eastington (Glos.) ... 17 ... SP 1213
East Kennett ... 17 ... SU 1167
East Keswick ... 37 ... SE 3544
East Kilbride ... 50 ... NS 6354
East Kirkby ... 35 ... TF 3362
East Knighton ... 8 ... SY 8185
East Knoyle ... 8 ... ST 8830
East Lambrook ... 7 ... ST 4319
East Langdon ... 13 ... TR 3346
East Langton ... 26 ... SP 7292
East Langwell ... 66 ... NC 7206
East Lavington ... 11 ... SU 9416
East Layton ... 42 ... NZ 1609
Eastleach Martin ... 17 ... SP 1905
Eastleach Turville ... 17 ... SP 1905
East Leake ... 34 ... SK 5526
East Leigh (Devon.) ... 6 ... SS 6905
Eastleigh (Hants.) ... 9 ... SU 4518
East Lexham ... 28 ... TF 8617
East Lilburn ... 53 ... NU 0423
Eastling ... 13 ... TQ 9656
East Linton ... 52 ... NT 5977
East Liss ... 9 ... SU 7827
East Lochussie ... 60 ... NH 5056
East Looe ... 4 ... SX 2553
East Lound ... 38 ... SK 7899
East Lulworth ... 8 ... SY 8581
East Mains ... 62 ... NO 6797
East Malling ... 12 ... TQ 7057
East March ... 57 ... NO 4436
East Marden ... 9 ... SU 8014
East Markham ... 34 ... SK 7472
East Marsh ... 14 ... SN 2808
East Marton ... 37 ... SD 9050
East Meon ... 9 ... SU 6822
East Mersea ... 21 ... TM 0414
East Molesey ... 11 ... TQ 1568
East Morden ... 8 ... SY 9194
East Morton ... 37 ... SE 1042
Eastney ... 9 ... SZ 6698
Eastnor ... 24 ... SO 7337
East Norton ... 26 ... SK 7800
East Oakley ... 10 ... SU 5749
Eastoft ... 39 ... SE 8016
East Ogwell ... 5 ... SX 8370
Easton (Cambs.) ... 27 ... TL 1371
Easton (Cumbr.) ... 46 ... NY 4372
Easton (Devon.) ... 5 ... SX 7288
Easton (Dorset) ... 8 ... SY 6871
Easton (Hants.) ... 9 ... SU 5132
Easton (I.of W.) ... 9 ... SZ 3485
Easton (Lincs.) ... 34 ... SK 9226
Easton (Norf.) ... 29 ... TG 1311
Easton (Somer.) ... 7 ... ST 5147
Easton (Suff.) ... 21 ... TM 2858
Easton Grey ... 17 ... ST 8787
Easton-in-Gordano ... 16 ... ST 5175
Easton Maudit ... 27 ... SP 8858
Easton on the Hill ... 27 ... TF 0004
Easton Royal ... 17 ... SU 2060
East Ord ... 53 ... NT 9851
East Panson ... 4 ... SX 3692
East Peckham ... 12 ... TQ 6649
East Pennard ... 7 ... ST 5937
East Plean ... 50 ... NS 8387
East Poringland ... 29 ... TG 2701
East Portlemouth ... 5 ... SX 7438
East Prawle ... 5 ... SX 7736
East Preston ... 11 ... TQ 0702
East Putford ... 4 ... SS 3616
East Quantoxhead ... 7 ... ST 1343
East Rainton ... 47 ... NZ 3347
East Ravendale ... 39 ... TF 2399
East Raynham ... 28 ... TF 8825
Eastrea ... 27 ... TL 2997
East Retford ... 34 ... SK 7080
Eastriggs ... 46 ... NY 2465
Eastrington ... 38 ... SE 7929
East Rudham ... 28 ... TF 8228
East Runton ... 29 ... TG 1942
East Ruston ... 29 ... TG 3427
Eastry ... 13 ... TR 3155
East Saltoun ... 52 ... NT 4767
East Shefford ... 10 ... SU 3974
East Sleekburn ... 47 ... NZ 2785
East Stoke (Dorset) ... 8 ... SY 8787
East Stoke (Notts.) ... 34 ... SK 7549
East Stour ... 8 ... ST 8022
East Stourmouth ... 13 ... TR 2662
East Stratton ... 10 ... SU 5440
East Studdal ... 13 ... TR 3149
East Taphouse ... 4 ... SX 1863
East Thirston ... 47 ... NZ 1999
East Tilbury ... 12 ... TQ 6877
East Tisted ... 9 ... SU 7032
East Torrington ... 35 ... TF 1483
East Tuddenham ... 29 ... TG 0811
East Tytherley ... 9 ... SU 2929
East Tytherton ... 17 ... ST 9674
East Village ... 6 ... SS 8405
Eastville ... 35 ... TF 4057
East Wall ... 24 ... SO 5293
East Walton ... 28 ... TF 7416
Eastwell ... 34 ... SK 7728
East Wellow ... 9 ... SU 3020
Eastwell Park ... 13 ... TR 0147
East Wemyss ... 57 ... NT 3396
East Whitburn ... 51 ... NS 9665
Eastwick ... 20 ... TL 4311
East Wickham ... 12 ... TQ 4576
East Williamston ... 14 ... SN 0905
East Winch ... 28 ... TF 6916
East Wittering ... 9 ... SZ 7996
East Witton ... 42 ... SE 1486
Eastwood (Essex) ... 20 ... TQ 8588
Eastwood (Notts.) ... 33 ... SK 4646
Eastwood (W Yorks.) ... 37 ... SD 9625
East Woodhay ... 10 ... SU 4061
East Worldham ... 10 ... SU 7538
East Wretham ... 28 ... TL 9190
East Yell ... 63 ... HU 5284
Eathorpe ... 26 ... SP 3969
Eaton (Ches.) ... 32 ... SJ 5763
Eaton (Ches.) ... 33 ... SJ 8765
Eaton (Leic.) ... 34 ... SK 7929
Eaton (Norf.) ... 29 ... TG 2006
Eaton (Notts.) ... 34 ... SK 7077
Eaton (Oxon.) ... 18 ... SP 4403
Eaton (Salop) ... 24 ... SO 3789
Eaton (Salop) ... 24 ... SO 4989
Eaton Bishop ... 24 ... SO 4439
Eaton Bray ... 19 ... SP 9720
Eaton Constantine ... 24 ... SJ 5906
Eaton Hastings ... 18 ... SU 2698
Eaton Socon ... 27 ... TL 1658
Eaton upon Tern ... 32 ... SJ 6523
Eaval (mt.) ... 63 ... NF 8960
Ebberston ... 43 ... SE 8983
Ebbesborne Wake ... 8 ... ST 9824
Ebbw Vale (Gwent) ... 16 ... ST 2094
Ebchester ... 47 ... NZ 1055
Ebford ... 5 ... SX 9887
Ebrington ... 25 ... SP 1840
Ecchinswell ... 10 ... SU 5060
Ecclaw ... 53 ... NT 7568
Ecclefechan ... 46 ... NY 1974
Eccles (Borders) ... 53 ... NT 7641
Eccles (Gtr Mches.) ... 37 ... SJ 7798
Eccles (Kent) ... 12 ... TQ 7260
Ecclesfield ... 37 ... SK 3393
Ecclesgrieg ... 57 ... NO 7365
Eccleshall ... 32 ... SJ 8329
Ecclesmachan ... 51 ... NT 0573
Eccles Road ... 29 ... TM 0190
Eccleston (Ches.) ... 32 ... SJ 4162
Eccleston (Lancs.) ... 36 ... SD 5216
Eccleston (Mers.) ... 32 ... SJ 4895
Eccup ... 37 ... SE 2842
Echt ... 62 ... NJ 7305
Eckford ... 52 ... NT 7125
Eckington (Derby.) ... 33 ... SK 4379
Eckington (Here. and Worc.) ... 25 ... SO 9241
Ecton ... 26 ... SP 8263
Edale ... 33 ... SK 1285
Eday Aerodrome ... 63 ... HY 5634
Edburton ... 11 ... TQ 2311
Edderton ... 65 ... NH 7184
Eddleston ... 51 ... NT 2447
Edenbridge ... 12 ... TQ 4446
Edenfield ... 37 ... SD 8019
Edenhall ... 41 ... NY 5632
Edenham ... 35 ... TF 0621
Eden Park ... 12 ... TQ 3868
Edensor ... 33 ... SK 2469
Edenthorpe ... 38 ... SE 6206
Ederline ... 54 ... NM 8702
Edern ... 30 ... SH 2739
Edgbaston ... 25 ... SP 0684
Edgcott ... 18 ... SP 6722
Edge ... 24 ... SJ 3908
Edgebolton ... 32 ... SJ 5721
Edge End ... 17 ... SO 5913
Edgefield ... 29 ... TG 0934
Edge Hill ... 26 ... SP 3747
Edgeworth ... 17 ... SO 9406
Edgmond ... 32 ... SJ 7119
Edgmond Marsh ... 32 ... SJ 7120
Edgton ... 24 ... SO 3885
Edgware ... 19 ... TQ 2091
Edgworth ... 36 ... SD 7416
Edinample ... 56 ... NN 6022
Edinbane ... 58 ... NG 3451
Edinburgh ... 51 ... NT 2674
Edingale ... 25 ... SK 2112
Edingley ... 34 ... SK 6655
Edingthorpe ... 29 ... TG 3132
Edington (Somer.) ... 7 ... ST 3939
Edington (Wilts.) ... 8 ... ST 9252
Edington Burtle ... 7 ... ST 3943
Edithmead ... 7 ... ST 3249
Edith Weston ... 27 ... SK 9205
Edlesborough ... 19 ... SP 9719
Edlingham ... 47 ... NU 1108
Edlington ... 35 ... TF 2371
Edmondbyers ... 47 ... NZ 0150
Edmondsham ... 8 ... SU 0611
Edmondsley ... 47 ... NZ 2348
Edmondthorpe ... 34 ... SK 8517
Edmonstone ... 63 ... HY 5220
Edmonton ... 20 ... TQ 3493
Ednam ... 52 ... NT 7337
Edradynate ... 56 ... NN 8852
Edrom ... 53 ... NT 8255
Edstaston ... 32 ... SJ 5131
Edstone ... 25 ... SP 1761
Edwalton ... 34 ... SK 5935
Edwardstone ... 21 ... TL 9442
Edwinsford ... 15 ... SN 6334
Edwinstowe ... 34 ... SK 6266
Edworth ... 27 ... TL 2241
Edwyn Ralph ... 24 ... SO 6457
Edzell ... 57 ... NO 5968
Efail Isaf ... 16 ... ST 0884
Efailnewydd ... 30 ... SH 3536
Efenechtyd ... 31 ... SJ 1155
Effingham ... 11 ... TQ 1253
Effirth ... 63 ... HU 3152
Efford ... 6 ... SS 8901
Egerton (Gtr Mches.) ... 36 ... SD 7014
Egerton (Kent) ... 13 ... TQ 9047
Eggardon Hill ... 7 ... SY 5494
Eggington ... 19 ... SP 9525
Egginton ... 33 ... SK 2628
Egglescliffe ... 42 ... NZ 4213
Eggleston ... 41 ... NZ 0023
Egham ... 11 ... TQ 0171
Egleton ... 34 ... SK 8707
Eglingham ... 53 ... NU 1019
Egloshayle ... 4 ... SX 0071
Egloskerry ... 4 ... SX 2786
Eglwysbach ... 31 ... SH 8070
Eglwys-Brewis ... 15 ... ST 0168
Eglwyswrw ... 14 ... SN 1438
Egmanton ... 34 ... SK 7368
Egremont ... 40 ... NY 0110
Egton ... 43 ... NZ 8006
Egton Bridge ... 43 ... NZ 8005
Eilanreach ... 59 ... NG 8017
Eilean Darach ... 64 ... NH 1087
Elan Village ... 23 ... SN 9365
Elberton (Avon) ... 17 ... ST 6088
Elburton (Devon.) ... 4 ... SX 5353
Elcho ... 56 ... NO 1620
Elcombe ... 17 ... SU 1280
Eldernell ... 27 ... TL 3298
Eldersfield ... 24 ... SO 7931
Elderslie ... 50 ... NS 4462
Eldroth ... 41 ... SD 7665
Eldwick ... 37 ... SE 1240
Elford (Northum.) ... 53 ... NU 1830
Elford (Staffs.) ... 25 ... SK 1810
Elgin ... 61 ... NJ 2162
Elgol ... 58 ... NG 5214
Elham ... 13 ... TR 1744
Elie ... 57 ... NO 4900
Elim ... 30 ... [illegible]
Eling ... 9 ... SU 3612
Elishader ... 58 ... NG 5065
Elishaw ... 47 ... NY 8694
Elkesley ... 34 ... SK 6875
Elkstone ... 17 ... SO 9612
Elland ... 37 ... SE 1020
Ellary ... 48 ... NR 7476
Ellastone ... 33 ... SK 1143
Ellemford ... 52 ... NT 7360
Ellenhall ... 33 ... SJ 8426
Ellen's Green ... 11 ... TQ 1035
Ellerbeck (N Yorks.) ... 42 ... SE 4396
Ellerby (Humbs.) ... 39 ... TA 1637
Ellerby (N Yorks.) ... 43 ... NZ 7914
Ellerdine Heath ... 32 ... SJ 6121
Ellerker ... 39 ... SE 9229
Ellerton (Humbs.) ... 38 ... SE 7039
Ellerton (Salop) ... 32 ... SJ 7126
Ellesborough ... 18 ... SP 8306
Ellesmere ... 32 ... SJ 3934
Ellesmere Port ... 32 ... SJ 4077
Ellingham (Norf.) ... 29 ... TM 3592
Ellingham (Northum.) ... 53 ... NU 1725
Ellingstring ... 42 ... SE 1783
Ellington (Cambs.) ... 27 ... TL 1671
Ellington (Northum.) ... 47 ... NZ 2792
Ellisfield ... 10 ... SU 6345
Ellistown ... 33 ... SK 4311
Ellon ... 62 ... NJ 9530
Ellough ... 29 ... TM 4486
Elloughton ... 39 ... SE 9428
Ellwood ... 17 ... SO 5808
Elm ... 35 ... TF 4607
Elmbridge ... 25 ... SO 8967
Elmdon (Essex) ... 20 ... TL 4639
Elmdon (W Mids) ... 25 ... SP 1783
Elmdon Heath ... 25 ... SP 1580
Elmesthorpe ... 26 ... SP 4696
Elmhurst ... 25 ... SK 1112
Elmley Castle ... 25 ... SO 9841
Elmley Lovett ... 25 ... SO 8669
Elmore ... 17 ... SO 7715
Elmore Back ... 17 ... SO 7716
Elm Park ... 20 ... TQ 5385
Elmscott ... 4 ... SS 2321
Elmsett ... 21 ... TM 0546
Elmstead Market ... 21 ... TM 0624
Elmsted Court ... 13 ... TR 1145
Elmstone ... 13 ... TR 2660
Elmstone Hardwicke ... 17 ... SO 9226
Elmswell ... 21 ... TL 9964
Elmton ... 34 ... SK 5073
Elphin ... 64 ... NC 2111
Elphinstone ... 51 ... NT 3970
Elrick ... 62 ... NJ 8206
Elrig ... 44 ... NX 3247
Elsdon ... 47 ... NY 9393
Elsecar ... 37 ... SE 3800
Elsenham ... 20 ... TL 5425
Elsfield ... 18 ... SP 5409
Elsham ... 39 ... TA 0312
Elsing ... 29 ... TG 0516
Elslack ... 37 ... SD 9349
Elsrickle ... 51 ... NT 0643
Elstead (Surrey) ... 11 ... SU 9043
Elsted (W Susx) ... 9 ... SU 8119
Elston ... 34 ... SK 7548
Elstone ... 6 ... SS 6716
Elstow ... 27 ... TL 0547
Elstree ... 19 ... TQ 1895
Elstronwick ... 39 ... TA 2232
Elswick ... 36 ... SD 4138
Elsworth ... 20 ... TL 3163
Elterwater ... 40 ... NY 3204
Eltham ... 12 ... TQ 4274
Eltisley ... 27 ... TL 2759
Elton (Cambs.) ... 27 ... TL 0893
Elton (Ches.) ... 32 ... SJ 4575
Elton (Cleve.) ... 42 ... NZ 4017
Elton (Derby.) ... 33 ... SK 2261
Elton (Glos.) ... 17 ... SO 6914
Elton (Here. and Worc.) ... 24 ... SO 4571
Elton (Notts.) ... 34 ... SK 7638
Elvanfoot ... 51 ... NS 9517
Elvaston ... 33 ... SK 4132
Elveden ... 28 ... TL 8279
Elvingston ... 52 ... NT 4674
Elvington (Kent) ... 13 ... TR 2750
Elvington (N Yorks.) ... 38 ... SE 6947
Elwick (Cleve.) ... 42 ... NZ 4532
Elwick (Northum.) ... 53 ... NU 1136
Elworth ... 32 ... SJ 7361
Elworthy ... 7 ... ST 0835
Ely (Cambs.) ... 28 ... TL 5380
Ely (S Glam.) ... 16 ... ST 1476
Emberton ... 27 ... SP 8849
Embleton (Cumbr.) ... 40 ... NY 1630
Embleton (Northum.) ... 53 ... NU 2322
Embo ... 65 ... NH 8192
Emborough ... 7 ... ST 6151
Embsay ... 37 ... SE 0053
Emery Down ... 9 ... SU 2808
Emley ... 37 ... SE 2413
Emmer Green ... 10 ... SU 7177
Emmington ... 18 ... SP 7402
Emneth ... 35 ... TF 4807
Emneth Hungate ... 28 ... TF 5107
Empingham ... 34 ... SK 9408
Empshott ... 9 ... SU 7731
Emsworth ... 9 ... SU 7405
Enaclete ... 63 ... NB 1228
Enborne ... 10 ... SU 4365
Enchmarsh ... 24 ... SO 4996
Enderby ... 26 ... SP 5399
End Moor ... 41 ... SD 5584
Endon ... 33 ... SJ 9253
Enfield ... 20 ... TQ 3296
Enford ... 8 ... SU 1351
Engine Common ... 17 ... ST 6984
Englefield ... 10 ... SU 6272
Englefield Green ... 11 ... SU 9870
English Bicknor ... 17 ... SO 5815
Englishcombe ... 17 ... ST 7162
English Frankton ... 32 ... SJ 4529
Enham-Alamein ... 10 ... SU 3648
Enmore ... 7 ... ST 2335
Ennerdale Bridge ... 40 ... NY 0615
Enoch ... 45 ... NS 8801
Enochdhu ... 56 ... NO 0662
Ensbury ... 8 ... SZ 0896
Ensdon ... 24 ... SJ 4016
Ensis ... 6 ... SS 5626
Enstone ... 18 ... SP 3725
Enterkinfoot ... 45 ... NS 8504
Enville ... 25 ... SO 8286
Eorabus ... 54 ... NM 3823
[illegible]
Epperstone ... 34 ... SK 6548
Epping ... 20 ... TL 4602
Epping Green (Essex) ... 20 ... TL 4305
Epping Green (Herts.) ... 19 ... TL 2906
Epping Upland ... 20 ... TL 4404
Eppleby ... 42 ... NZ 1713
Epsom ... 11 ... TQ 2160
Epwell ... 26 ... SP 3540
Epworth ... 38 ... SE 7803
Erbistock ... 32 ... SJ 3541
Erbusaig ... 59 ... NG 7629
Erdington ... 25 ... SP 1291
Eredine ... 55 ... NM 9609
Erlboll ... 66 ... NC 4356
Ericstane ... 51 ... NT 0710
Eridge Green ... 12 ... TQ 5535
Erines ... 49 ... NR 8575
Eriswell ... 28 ... TL 7278
Erith ... 12 ... TQ 5177
Erlestoke ... 8 ... ST 9853
Ermington ... 5 ... SX 6353
Erpingham ... 29 ... TG 1931
Errogie ... 60 ... NH 5622
Errol ... 57 ... NO 2522
Ersary ... 63 ... NF 7000
Ervie ... 44 ... NX 0067
Erwarton ... 21 ... TM 2234
Erwood ... 23 ... SO 0943
Eryholme ... 42 ... NZ 3208
Eryrys ... 32 ... SJ 2057
Escalls ... 2 ... SW 3627
Escrick ... 38 ... SE 6243
Esgairgeiliog ... 22 ... SH 7605
Esh ... 47 ... NZ 1944
Esher ... 11 ... TQ 1464
Eshott ... 47 ... NZ 2097
Eshton ... 37 ... SD 9356
Esh Winning ... 42 ... NZ 1942
Eskadale ... 60 ... NH 4539
Eskbank ... 51 ... NT 3266
Eskdale Green ... 40 ... NY 1400
Esprick ... 36 ... SD 4035
Essendine ... 35 ... TF 0412
Essendon ... 19 ... TL 2708
Essich ... 60 ... NH 6539
Essington ... 25 ... SJ 9603
Esslemont ... 62 ... NJ 9329
Eston ... 42 ... NZ 5518
Etal ... 53 ... NT 9339
Etchilhampton ... 17 ... SU 0460
Etchingham ... 12 ... TQ 7126
Etchinghill (Kent) ... 13 ... TR 1639
Etchinghill (Staffs.) ... 33 ... SK 0218
Eton ... 11 ... SU 9678
Etteridge ... 60 ... NN 6892
Ettington ... 26 ... SP 2649
Etton (Humbs.) ... 39 ... SE 9743
Etton (Northants.) ... 35 ... TF 1306
Ettrick ... 51 ... NT 2714
Ettrickbridge End ... 51 ... NT 3824
Etwall ... 33 ... SK 2732
Euston ... 28 ... TL 8978
Euxton ... 36 ... SD 5518
Evanton ... 65 ... NH 6066
Evedon ... 35 ... TF 0947
Evelix ... 65 ... NH 7690
Evenjobb ... 23 ... SO 2662
Evenley ... 18 ... SP 5834
Evenlode ... 18 ... SP 2229
Evenwood ... 42 ... NZ 1524
Everbay ... 63 ... HY 6725
Evercreech ... 8 ... ST 6438
Everdon ... 26 ... SP 5957
Everingham ... 39 ... SE 8042
Everleigh ... 8 ... SU 1953
Everley ... 43 ... SE 9789
Eversholt ... 19 ... SP 9933
Evershot ... 7 ... ST 5704
Eversley ... 10 ... SU 7762
Eversley Cross ... 10 ... SU 7961
Everton (Beds.) ... 27 ... TL 2051
Everton (Hants.) ... 9 ... SZ 2993
Everton (Notts.) ... 34 ... SK 6891

Evertown 46 NY 3576
Evesbatch 24 SO 6848
Evesham 25 SP 0344
Evington 26 SK 6203
Ewden Village 37 SK 2796
Ewe Hill 51 NT 0540
Ewell 11 TQ 2262
Ewell Minnis 13 TR 2643
Ewelme 18 SU 6491
Ewen 17 SU 0097
Ewenny 15 SS 9077
Ewerby 35 TF 1247
Ewesley 47 NZ 0592
Ewhurst (E Susx) 12 TQ 7924
Ewhurst (Surrey) 11 TQ 0940
Ewloe 32 SJ 3066
Eworthy 4 SX 4494
Ewshot 10 SU 8149
Ewyas Harold 16 SO 3828
Exbourne 6 SS 6002
Exbury 9 SU 4200
Exebridge 6 SS 9324
Exelby 42 SE 2986
Exeter 5 SX 9292
Exford 6 SS 8538
Exhall 25 SP 1055
Exminster 5 SX 9487
Exmouth 5 SY 0080
Exnaboe 63 HU 3912
Exning 20 TL 6265
Exton (Devon.) 5 SX 9886
Exton (Hants.) 9 SU 6121
Exton (Leic.) 34 SK 9211
Exton (Somer.) 6 SS 9233
Eyam 33 SK 2176
Eydon 26 SP 5450
Eye (Here. and Worc.) 24 SO 4963
Eye (Northants.) 27 TF 2202
Eye (Suffolk) 29 TM 1473
Eyemouth 53 NT 9464
Eyeworth 27 TL 2545
Eyhorne Street 12 TQ 8354
Eyke 21 TM 3151
Eynesbury 27 TL 1859
Eynsford 12 TQ 5365
Eynsham 18 SP 4309
Eype 7 SY 4491
Eyre 58 NG 4152
Eythorne 13 TR 2849
Eyton (Here. and Worc.) 24 SO 4761
Eyton (Salop) 24 SO 3687
Eyton upon the Weald Moors 24 SJ 6414

Faccombe 10 SU 3857
Faceby 42 NZ 4903
Faddiley 32 SJ 5752
Fadmoor 42 SE 6789
Faifley 50 NS 5073
Failand 16 ST 5272
Failford 50 NS 4526
Failsworth 37 SD 9002
Fairbourne 22 SH 6113
Fairburn 38 SE 4727
Fairfield 25 SO 9475
Fairford 17 SP 1501
Fairlie 49 NS 2155
Fairlight 13 TQ 8612
Fairmile 5 SY 0997
Fairmilehead 51 NT 2567
Fair Oak (Hants.) 9 SU 4918
Fairoak (Staffs.) 32 SJ 7632
Fairseat 12 TQ 6261
Fairstead (Essex) 20 TL 7616
Fairstead (Norf.) 29 TG 2723
Fairwarp 12 TQ 4626
Fairy Cross 4 SS 4024
Fakenham 29 TF 9229
Fala 52 NT 4361
Fala Dam 52 NT 4261
Falahill 51 NT 3956
Faldingworth 35 TF 0684
Falfield 17 ST 6893
Falkenham 21 TM 2939
Falkirk 50 NS 8880
Falkland 57 NO 2507
Falla 52 NT 7013
Fallin 50 NS 8391
Falmer 12 TQ 3508
Falmouth 2 SW 8032
Falstone 46 NY 7287
Fanagmore 66 NC 1750
Fangdale Beck 42 SE 5694
Fangfoss 38 SE 7653
Fan Hill 23 SN 9388
Fan Llia 15 SN 9318
Fanmore 54 NM 4244
Fans 52 NT 6140
Farcet 27 TL 2094
Far Cotton 26 SP 7458
Farden 24 SO 5776
Fareham 9 SU 5806
Farewell 25 SK 0811
Faringdon 18 SU 2895
Farington 36 SD 5425
Farlam 46 NY 5558
Farleigh 12 TQ 3660
Farleigh Hungerford 17 ST 7957
Farleigh Wallop 10 SU 6246
Farlesthorpe 35 TF 4774
Farleton 40 SD 5380
Farley (Salop) 24 SJ 3808
Farley (Staffs.) 33 SK 0644
Farley (Wilts.) 9 SU 2229
Farley Green 11 TQ 0645
Farley Hill 10 SU 7564
Farleys End 17 SO 7615
Farlington 38 SE 6167
Farlow 24 SO 6380
Farmborough 17 ST 6560
Farmcote 17 SP 0629
Farmers 15 SN 6444
Farmington 17 SP 1315
Farmoor 18 SP 4407
Farmtown 61 NJ 5051
Farnborough (Berks.) 10 SU 4381
Farnborough (Gtr London) 12 TQ 4464
Farnborough (Hants.) 11 SU 8753
Farnborough (Warw.) 26 SP 4349
Farncombe 11 SU 9755
Farndish 27 SP 9263
Farndon (Ches.) 32 SJ 4154
Farndon (Notts.) 34 SK 7651
Farnell 57 NO 6255
Farnham (Dorset) 8 ST 9514
Farnham (Essex) 20 TL 4724
Farnham (N Yorks.) 42 SE 3460
Farnham (Suff.) 21 TM 3660
Farnham (Surrey) 11 SU 8446
Farnham Common 19 SU 9584
Farnham Green 20 TL 4625
Farnham Royal 19 SU 9682
Farningham 12 TQ 5566
Farnley 37 SE 2147
Farnley Tyas 37 SE 1612
Farnsfield 34 SK 6456
Farnworth (Ches.) 32 SJ 5187
Farnworth (Gtr Mches.) 36 SD 7305
Farr (Highld.) 66 NC 7163
Farr (Highld.) 60 NH 6833
Farr (Highld.) 60 NH 8203
Farringdon 5 SY 0191
Farrington Gurney 17 ST 6255
Farsley 37 SE 2135
Farthinghoe 18 SP 5339
Farthingstone 26 SP 6155
Farway 5 SY 1895
Fasnacloich 55 NN 0247
Fasque 57 NO 6475
Fassfern 55 NN 0278
Fatfield 47 NZ 3053
Fattahead 62 NJ 6657
Faugh 46 NY 5154
Fauldhouse 51 NS 9260
Faulkbourne 20 TL 7917
Faulkland 17 ST 7354
Fauls 32 SJ 5933
Faversham 13 TR 0161
Favillar 61 NJ 2734
Fawfieldhead 33 SK 0763
Fawkham Green 12 TQ 5865
Fawler 18 SP 3717
Fawley (Berks.) 10 SU 3981
Fawley (Bucks.) 18 SU 7586
Fawley (Hants.) 9 SU 4503
Fawley Chapel 17 SO 5829
Faxfleet 39 SE 8624
Faygate 11 TQ 2134
Fazeley 25 SK 2001
Fearby 42 SE 1981
Fearnan 56 NN 7244
Fearnhead 32 SJ 6290
Fearnmore 64 NG 7260
Featherstone (Staffs.) 25 SJ 9305
Featherstone (W Yorks.) 38 SE 4222
Feckenham 25 SP 0061
Fedderate 62 NJ 8949
Feering 21 TL 8720
Feetham 41 SD 9898
Feizor 41 SD 7968
Felbridge 12 TQ 3739
Felbrigg 29 TG 2039
Felcourt 12 TQ 3841
Felden 19 TL 0404
Felindre (Dyfed) 15 SN 7027
Felindre (Powys) 23 SO 1681
Felindre (W Glam.) 15 SN 6302
Felinfach 23 SO 0933
Felinfoel 15 SN 5202
Felingwm Uchaf 15 SN 5024
Felixkirk 42 SE 4684
Felixstowe 21 TM 3034
Felkington 53 NT 9444
Felling 47 NZ 2762
Felmersham 27 SP 9957
Felmingham 29 TG 2529
Felpham 11 SZ 9599
Felsham 21 TL 9457
Felsted 20 TL 6720
Feltham 11 TQ 1072
Felthorpe 29 TG 1618
Felton (Avon) 16 ST 5165
Felton (Here. and Worc.) 24 SO 5748
Felton (Northum.) 47 NU 1800
Felton Butler 24 SJ 3917
Feltwell 28 TL 7190
Feltwell Anchor 28 TL 6789
Fence 37 SD 8237
Fendike Corner 35 TF 4560
Fen Ditton 20 TL 4860
Fen Drayton 20 TL 3468
Fen End 26 SP 2274
Feniscowles 36 SD 6425
Feniton 5 SY 1199
Fenny Bentley 33 SK 1750
Fenny Bridges 5 SY 1198
Fenny Compton 26 SP 4152
Fenny Drayton 26 SP 3597
Fenny Stratford 19 SP 8834
Fenrother 47 NZ 1792
Fenstanton 20 TL 3168
Fenton (Cambs.) 27 TL 3279
Fenton (Lincs.) 34 SK 8476
Fenton (Lincs.) 34 SK 8750
Fenton (Staffs.) 33 SJ 8944
Fenton Town 53 NT 9733
Fenwick (Northum.) 53 NU 0639
Fenwick (Northum.) 47 NZ 0572
Fenwick (Strath.) 50 NS 4643
Fenwick (S Yorks.) 38 SE 5916
Feock 2 SW 8238
Feolin Ferry 48 NR 4469
Feriniquarrie 58 NG 1750
Fern 57 NO 4861
Ferndale 15 SS 9997
Ferndown 8 SU 0700
Ferness 60 NH 9645
Fernham 18 SU 2991
Fernhill Heath 25 SO 8659
Fernhurst 11 SU 9028
Fernie 57 NO 3115
Fernilee 33 SK 0178
Fernlea 58 NG 3732
Ferrensby 42 SE 3660
Ferring 11 TQ 0902
Ferrybridge 38 SE 4824
Ferryden 57 NO 7156
Ferryhill 42 NZ 2832
Ferryside 15 SN 3610
Fersfield 29 TM 0682
Fersit 55 NN 3577
Feshiebridge 60 NH 8504
Fetcham 11 TQ 1555
Fetterangus 62 NJ 9850
Fettercairn 57 NO 6573
Fewston 37 SE 1954
Ffairfach 15 SN 6220
Ffestiniog 30 SH 7042
Fforest 15 SN 5804
Fforest-fach (W Glam.) 15 SS 6396
Ffostrasol 15 SN 3747
Ffrith 32 SJ 2855
Ffrwdgrech 15 SO 0227
Ffynnonddrain 15 SN 4021
Ffynnongroew 31 SJ 1382
Fiddes 57 NO 8181
Fiddington (Glos.) 25 SO 9231
Fiddington (Somer.) 7 ST 2140
Fiddlers Hamlet 20 TL 4701
Field 33 SK 0233
Field Broughton 40 SD 3881
Field Dalling 29 TG 0039
Field Head 33 SK 4909
Fifehead Magdalen 8 ST 7721
Fifehead Neville 8 ST 7610
Fifield (Berks.) 11 SU 9076
Fifield (Oxon.) 18 SP 2318
Figheldean 8 SU 1547
Fighting Cocks 42 NZ 3414
Filby 29 TG 4613
Filey 43 TA 1180
Filgrave 27 SP 8748
Filkins 18 SP 2304
Filleigh (Devon.) 6 SS 6628
Filleigh (Devon.) 6 SS 7410
Fillingham 34 SK 9485
Fillongley 26 SP 2787
Filton 17 ST 6079
Fimber 39 SE 8960
Finavon 57 NO 4957
Finavon Castle 57 NO 4956
Fincham 28 TF 6806
Finchampstead 10 SU 7963
Fincharn 54 NM 9003
Finchdean 9 SU 7312
Finchingfield 20 TL 6832
Finchley 19 TQ 2890
Findern 33 SK 3030
Findhorn 61 NJ 0464
Findhorn Bridge 60 NH 8027
Findochty 61 NJ 4667
Findo Gask 56 NO 0020
Findon (Grampn.) 62 NO 9397
Findon (W Susx) 11 TQ 1208
Findon Mains 65 NH 6060
Finedon 27 SP 9272
Fingal Street 29 TM 2169
Fingask 62 NJ 7827
Fingest 18 SU 7791
Finghall 42 SE 1889
Fingringhoe 21 TM 0220
Finmere 18 SP 6333
Finnart 55 NN 5157
Finningham 29 TM 0669
Finningly 38 SK 6699
Finnygaud 62 NJ 6054
Finsbay 63 NG 0786
Finsbury 20 TQ 3282
Finstall 25 SO 9869
Finsthwaite 40 SD 3687
Finstock 18 SP 3516
Finstown 63 HY 3514
Fintry (Central) 50 NS 6186
Fintry (Grampn.) 62 NJ 7554
Fionnphort (Island of Mull) 54 NM 2923
Firbeck 34 SK 5688
Firgrove 37 SD 9113
Firsby 35 TF 4563
Firth 63 HU 4473
Fir Tree 42 NZ 1334
Fishbourne (I of W) 9 SZ 5592
Fishbourne (W Susx) 9 SU 8304
Fishburn 42 NZ 3632
Fishcross 50 NS 8995
Fisherford 62 NJ 6635
Fisher's Pond 9 SU 4820
Fisherstreet 11 SU 9531
Fisherton (Highld.) 60 NH 7451
Fisherton (Strath.) 50 NS 2717
Fishguard 14 SM 9637
Fishlake 38 SE 6513
Fishpool 37 SD 8009
Fishtoft 35 TF 3642
Fishtoft Drove 35 TF 3148
Fishtown of Usan 57 NO 7254
Fishwick 53 NT 9151
Fiskavaig 58 NG 3234
Fiskerton (Lincs.) 35 TF 0472
Fiskerton (Notts.) 34 SK 7351
Fittleton 8 SU 1449
Fittleworth 11 TQ 0119
Fitton End 35 TF 4312
Fitz 24 SJ 4417
Fitzhead 7 ST 1228
Fitzwilliam 38 SE 4115
Five Ashes 12 TQ 5525
Fivehead 7 ST 3522
Five Oak Green 12 TQ 6445
Five Oaks 11 TQ 0928
Five Penny Borve 63 NB 4055
Five Penny Ness 63 NB 5364
Five Roads 15 SN 4905
Flackwell Heath 19 SU 8890
Fladbury 25 SO 9946
Fladdabister 63 HU 4332
Flagg 33 SK 1368
Flamborough 39 TA 2270
Flamstead 19 TL 0814
Flansham 11 SU 9601
Flasby 37 SD 9456
Flash 33 SK 0267
Flashader 58 NG 3553
Flatt, The 46 NY 5678
Flaunden 19 TL 0100
Flawborough 34 SK 7842
Flawith 38 SE 4865
Flax Bourton 16 ST 5069
Flaxby 37 SE 3957
Flaxley 17 SO 6915
Flaxpool 7 ST 1435
Flaxton 38 SE 6762
Fleckney 26 SP 6493
Flecknoe 26 SP 5163
Fleet (Hants.) 10 SU 8054
Fleet (Lincs.) 35 TF 3823
Fleetham 53 NU 1928
Fleet Hargate 35 TF 3925
Fleetwood 36 SD 3247
Flemingston 15 ST 0170
Flemington 50 NS 6559
Flempton 20 TL 8169
Fletching 12 TQ 4323
Flexford 11 SU 9350
Flimby 40 NY 0233
Flimwell 12 TQ 7131
Flint 32 SJ 2472
Flintham 34 SK 7446
Flint Mountain 32 SJ 2360
Flinton 39 TA 2136
Flitcham 28 TF 7226
Flitton 19 TL 0536
Flitwick 19 TL 0335
Flixborough 39 SE 8715
Flixton (Gtr Mches.) 32 SJ 7494
Flixton (N Yorks.) 43 TA 0479
Flixton (Suff.) 29 TM 3186
Flockton 37 SE 2314
Flodda (Benbecula) 63 NF 8455
Flodden 53 NT 9235
Flodigarry 58 NG 4671
Flookburgh 40 SD 3675
Flordon 29 TM 1897
Flore 26 SP 6460
Flotterton 47 NT 9902
Flowton 21 TM 0847
Flushing (Corn.) 2 SW 8034
Flushing (Grampn.) 62 NK 0546
Flyford Flavell 25 SO 9754
Fobbing 20 TQ 7183
Fochabers 61 NJ 3458
Fochriw 16 SO 1005
Fockerby 39 SE 8419
Fodder Fen 28 TL 5287
Fodderletter 61 NJ 1421
Fodderty 60 NH 5159
Foel 23 SH 9911
Foffarty 57 NO 4145
Foggathorpe 38 SE 7537
Fogo 53 NT 7749
Foindle 66 NC 1948
Folda 56 NO 1964
Fole 33 SK 0437
Foleshill 26 SP 3582
Folke 8 ST 6513
Folkestone 13 TR 2336
Folkingham 35 TF 0433
Folkington 12 TQ 5604
Folksworth 27 TL 1490
Folkton 43 TA 0579
Folla Rule 62 NJ 7333
Follifoot 37 SE 3452
Folly Gate 6 SX 5797
Fonthill Bishop 8 ST 9332
Fonthill Gifford 8 ST 9231
Fontmell Magna 8 ST 8616
Fontwell 11 SU 9407
Foolow 33 SK 1976
Foots Cray 12 TQ 4770
Forcett 42 NZ 1712
Ford (Bucks.) 18 SP 7709
Ford (Glos.) 17 SP 0829
Ford (Mers.) 32 SJ 3598
Ford (Northum.) 53 NT 9437
Ford (Salop) 24 SJ 4113
Ford (Staffs.) 33 SK 0654
Ford (Strath.) 54 NM 8603
Ford (Wilts.) 17 ST 8475
Ford (W Susx) 11 TQ 0003
Fordcombe 12 TQ 5240
Fordell 51 NT 1588
Forden 23 SJ 2201
Ford End 20 TL 6716
Fordham (Cambs.) 28 TL 6370
Fordham (Essex) 21 TL 9228
Fordham (Norf.) 28 TL 6199
Fordingbridge 8 SU 1413
Fordon 39 TA 0475
Fordoun 57 NO 7475
Fordstreet (Essex) 21 TL 9227
Ford Street (Somer.) 7 ST 1518
Fordwells 18 SP 3013
Fordwich 13 TR 1859
Fordyce 62 NJ 5563
Foremark 33 SK 3326
Forest 42 NY 8629
Forestburn Gate 47 NZ 0696
Forestfield 50 NS 8566
Forest Gate 20 TQ 4085
Forest Green 11 TQ 1241
Forest Hall 41 NY 5401
Forest Head 46 NY 5857
Forest Hill 18 SP 5807
Forest Mill 51 NS 9594
Forest Moor 37 SE 2256
Forest Row 12 TQ 4235
Forestside 9 SU 7512
Forest Town 34 SK 5662
Forfar 57 NO 4550
Forgandenny 56 NO 0818
Forgie 61 NJ 3954
Formby 36 SD 2907
Forncett End 29 TM 1493
Forncett St. Mary 29 TM 1694
Forncett St. Peter 29 TM 1693
Forneth 56 NO 0945
Fornham All Saints 20 TL 8367
Fornham St. Martin 20 TL 8566
Forres 61 NJ 0358
Forsbrook 33 SJ 9641
Forse 67 ND 2234
Forsinard 67 NC 8842
Forstal, The 13 TQ 8946
Forston 8 SY 6695
Fort Augustus 59 NH 3709
Forter 56 NO 1864
Forteviot 56 NO 0517
Fort George 60 NH 7656
Forth 51 NS 9453
Forthampton 25 SO 8532
Fortingall 56 NN 7447
Forton (Lancs.) 36 SD 4851
Forton (Salop) 24 SJ 4216
Forton (Somer.) 7 ST 3306
Forton (Staffs.) 32 SJ 7521
Fortree 62 NJ 9640
Fortrie 62 NJ 6645
Fortrose 60 NH 7256
Fortuneswell 8 SY 6873
Fort William 55 NN 1074
Forty Hill 20 TQ 3398
Forward Green 21 TM 1059
Fosbury 10 SU 3157
Fosdyke 35 TF 3133
Foss 56 NN 7958
Fossebridge 17 SP 0811
Foss-y-ffin 22 SN 4460
Foster Street 20 TL 4909
Foston (Derby.) 33 SK 1831
Foston (Lincs.) 34 SK 8542
Foston (N Yorks.) 38 SE 6965
Foston on the Wolds 39 TA 1055
Fotherby 39 TF 3191
Fotheringhay 27 TL 0593
Foulden (Borders) 53 NT 9355
Foulden (Norf.) 28 TL 7699
Foulis Castle 65 NH 5964
Foul Mile 12 TQ 6215
Foulridge 37 SD 8942
Foulsham 29 TG 0324
Fountainhall 52 NT 4349
Four Ashes 29 TM 0070
Fourcrosses (Gwyn.) 30 SH 3939
Four Crosses (Powys) 23 SJ 0508
Four Crosses (Powys) 32 SJ 2718
Four Crosses (Staffs.) 25 SJ 9509
Four Elms 12 TQ 4648
Four Forks 7 ST 2336
Four Gotes 35 TF 4516
Four Lanes 2 SW 6838
Fourlanes End 32 SJ 8059
Four Marks 9 SU 6634
Four Mile Bridge 30 SH 2778
Four Oaks (E Susx) 13 TQ 8624
Four Oaks (W Mids) 25 SP 1198
Four Oaks (W Mids) 26 SP 2480
Fourstones 47 NY 8967
Four Throws 12 TQ 7729
Fovant 8 SU 0028
Foveran 62 NJ 9824
Fowey 4 SX 1251
Fowlis 57 NO 3133
Fowlis Wester 56 NN 9223
Fowlmere 20 TL 4245
Fownhope 24 SO 5734
Foxdale 43 SC 2878
Foxearth 20 TL 8344
Foxfield 40 SD 2085
Foxham 17 ST 9777
Foxhole (Corn.) 2 SW 9654
Foxholes (N Yorks.) 39 TA 0173
Fox Lane 11 SU 8557
Foxley (Norf.) 29 TG 0321
Foxley (Wilts.) 17 ST 8985
Foxt 33 SK 0348
Foxton (Cambs.) 20 TL 4148
Foxton (Leic.) 26 SP 7090
Foxup 41 SD 8676
Foxwist Green 32 SJ 6168
Foy 17 SO 5928
Foyers 60 NH 4921
Fraddon 2 SW 9158
Fradley 25 SK 1513
Fradswell 33 SJ 9831
Fraisthorpe 39 TA 1561
Framfield 12 TQ 4920
Framingham Earl 29 TG 2702
Framingham Pigot 29 TG 2703
Framlingham 21 TM 2863
Frampton (Dorset) 8 SY 6294
Frampton (Lincs.) 35 TF 3239
Frampton Cotterell 17 ST 6582
Frampton Mansell 17 SO 9202
Frampton on Severn 17 SO 7407
Frampton West End 35 TF 3040
Framsden 21 TM 1959
Framwellgate Moor 47 NZ 2644
Franche 25 SO 8178
Frankby 32 SJ 2486
Frankley 25 SO 9980
Frankton 26 SP 4270
Frant 12 TQ 5835
Fraserburgh 62 NJ 9966
Frating Green 21 TM 0923
Fratton 9 SU 6600
Freathy 4 SX 3952
Freckenham 28 TL 6672
Freckleton 36 SD 4228
Freeby 34 SK 8020
Freeland 18 SP 4112
Freester 63 HU 4553
Freethorpe 29 TG 4105
Freethorpe Common 29 TG 4004
Freiston 35 TF 3743
Fremington 6 SS 5132
Frenchay 17 ST 6377
Frenchbeer 5 SX 6785
Frensham 11 SU 8441
Fresgoe 67 NC 9566
Freshfield 36 SD 2807
Freshford 17 ST 7860
Freshwater 9 SZ 3487
Freshwater Bay 9 SZ 3485
Freshwater West 14 SR 8899
Fressingfield 29 TM 2677
Freston 21 TM 1739
Freswick 67 ND 3667
Frettenham 29 TG 2417
Freuchie 57 NO 2806
Friar's Gate 12 TQ 4933
Friday Bridge 27 TF 4605
Fridaythorpe 39 SE 8759
Friern Barnet 19 TQ 2892
Friesthorpe 35 TF 0683
Frieth 18 SU 7990
Frilford 18 SU 4497
Frilsham 10 SU 5373
Frimley 11 SU 8758
Frindsbury 12 TQ 7369
Fring 28 TF 7334
Fringford 18 SP 6028
Frinsted 13 TQ 8957
Frinton-on-Sea 21 TM 2319
Friockheim 57 NO 5949
Frisby on the Wreake 34 SK 6917
Friskney 35 TF 4555
Friston (E Susx) 12 TV 5498
Friston (Suff.) 21 TM 4160
Fritchley 33 SK 3553
Fritham 9 SU 2413
Frith Bank 35 TF 3147
Frith Common 24 SO 6969
Frithelstock 6 SS 4619
Frithville 35 TF 3250
Frittenden 13 TQ 8141
Fritton (Norf.) 29 TG 4700
Fritton (Norf.) 29 TM 2293
Fritwell 18 SP 5229
Frizington 40 NY 0316
Frocester 17 SO 7803
Frodesley 24 SJ 5101
Frodsham 32 SJ 5177
Froggatt 33 SK 2476
Froghall 33 SK 0247
Frogmore 10 SU 8360
Frolesworth 26 SP 5090
Frome 8 ST 7747
Frome St. Quintin 7 ST 5902
Fromes Hill 24 SO 6846
Fron (Gwyn.) 30 SH 3539
Fron (Powys) 23 SJ 2203
Fron (Powys) 23 SO 0865
Fron Cysyllte 32 SJ 2741
Fron-goch 31 SH 9039
Frosterley 42 NZ 0237

Froxfield 83 Great Horkesley

Froxfield ... 10... SU 2967
Froxfield Green ... 9... SU 7025
Fryerning ... 20... TL 6400
Fryton ... 38... SE 6875
Fulbeck ... 34... SK 9450
Fulbourn ... 20... TL 5256
Fulbrook ... 18... SP 2513
Fulford (N Yorks.) ... 38... SE 6149
Fulford (Somer.) ... 7... ST 2129
Fulford (Staffs.) ... 33... SJ 9438
Fulham ... 11... TQ 2576
Fulking ... 11... TQ 2411
Fuller's Moor ... 32... SJ 4953
Fuller Street ... 20... TL 7415
Fullerton ... 10... SU 3739
Fulletby ... 35... TF 2973
Full Sutton ... 38... SE 7455
Fullwood ... 50... NS 4450
Fulmer ... 19... SU 9985
Fulmodeston ... 29... TF 9931
Fulnetby ... 35... TF 0979
Fulstow ... 39... TF 3297
Fulwell ... 47... NZ 3959
Fulwood (Lancs.) ... 36... SD 5331
Fulwood (S Yorks.) ... 33... SK 3085
Funtington ... 9... SU 7908
Funzie ... 63... HU 6689
Furnace ... 55... NN 0200
Furneux Pelham ... 20... TL 4327
Furzehill ... 6... SS 7245
Fyfett ... 7... ST 2314
Fyfield (Essex) ... 20... TL 5707
Fyfield (Glos.) ... 17... SP 2003
Fyfield (Hants.) ... 10... SU 2946
Fyfield (Oxon.) ... 18... SU 4298
Fyfield (Wilts.) ... 17... SU 1468
Fylingthorpe ... 43... NZ 9405
Fyvie ... 62... NJ 7637

Gabroc Hill ... 50... NS 4551
Gaddesby ... 34... SK 6813
Gaer ... 16... SO 1721
Gaerwen ... 30... SH 4871
Gagingwell ... 18... SP 4025
Gailey ... 25... SJ 9110
Gainford ... 42... NZ 1716
Gainsborough ... 34... SK 8189
Gainsford End ... 20... TL 7235
Gairloch ... 64... NG 8076
Gairlochy ... 55... NN 1784
Gairney Bank ... 56... NT 1299
Gaitsgill ... 46... NY 3946
Galashiels ... [illegible]... NT [illegible]
Galby ... 26... SK 6901
Galgate ... 36... SD 4855
Galhampton ... 8... ST 6329
Gall ... 56... NO 0734
Gallanach (Strath.) ... 54... NM 8226
Gallatown ... 51... NT 2994
Galley Common ... 26... SP 3192
Galleyend ... 20... TL 7103
Galleywood ... 20... TL 7002
Gallowfauld ... 57... NO 4342
Galltair ... 59... NG 8120
Galmisdale ... 54... NM 4784
Galmpton (Devon.) ... 5... SX 6940
Galmpton (Devon.) ... 5... SX 8856
Galphay ... 42... SE 2572
Galson ... 63... NB 4358
Galston ... 50... NS 5036
Galtrigill ... 58... NG 1854
Gamblesby ... 41... NY 6039
Gamlingay ... 27... TL 2452
Gamrie ... 62... NJ 7962
Gamston (Notts.) ... 34... SK 6037
Gamston (Notts.) ... 34... SK 7076
Ganarew ... 16... SO 5216
Ganavan ... 54... NM 8632
Ganllwyd ... 30... SH 7224
Gannachy ... 57... NO 5970
Ganstead ... 39... TA 1434
Ganthorpe ... 38... SE 6870
Ganton ... 43... SE 9877
Garbhallt (Strath.) ... 49... NS 0295
Garboldisham ... 29... TM 0081
Gardenstown ... 62... NJ 7964
Garderhouse ... 63... HU 3347
Gare Hill ... 8... ST 7840
Garelochhead ... 49... NS 2491
Garford ... 18... SU 4296
Garforth ... 38... SE 4033
Gargrave ... 37... SD 9354
Gargunnock ... 50... NS 7094
Garinin ... 63... NB 1944
Garlieston ... 44... NX 4746
Garlogie ... 62... NJ 7805
Garmond ... 62... NJ 8052
Garmouth ... 61... NJ 3364
Garn ... 30... SH 2734
Garnant ... 15... SN 6813
Garn-Dolbenmaen ... 30... SH 4944
Garnett Bridge ... 40... SD 5299
Garnkirk ... 50... NS 6768
Garrabost ... 63... NB 5133
Garraron ... 54... NM 8008
Garras ... 2... SW 7023
Garreg ... 30... SH 6141
Garreg Bank ... 23... SJ 2811
Garrick ... 56... NN 8412
Garrigill ... 41... NY 7441
Garros ... 58... NG 4963
Garrow ... 56... NN 8240
Garrynamonie ... 63... NF 7416
Garsdale ... 41... SD 7389
Garsdon ... 17... ST 9687
Garshall Green ... 33... SJ 9633
Garsington ... 18... SP 5802
Garstang ... 36... SD 4945
Garston ... 32... SJ 4083
Garswood ... 32... SJ 5599
Gartcosh ... 50... NS 6968
Garth (Clwyd) ... 32... SJ 2542
Garth (I. of M.) ... 43... SC 3177
Garth (Mid Glam.) ... 15... SS 8690
Garth (Powys) ... 15... SN 9549
Garth (Shetld.) ... 63... HU 2157
Garthbrengy ... 23... SO 0433
Gartheli ... 22... SN 5956
Garthmyl ... 23... SO 1999
Garthorpe (Humbs.) ... 39... SE 8419
Garthorpe (Leic.) ... 34... SK 8320
Gartmore ... 55... NS 5297
Gartness (Central) ... 50... NS 5086
Gartness (Strath.) ... 50... NS 7864
Gartocharn ... 50... NS 4286

Garton ... 39... TA 2635
Garton-on-the-Wolds ... 39... SE 9859
Gartymore ... 67... ND 0114
Garvald ... 52... NT 5870
Garvan ... 55... NM 9777
Garvard ... 48... NR 3691
Garve ... 65... NH 3961
Garveston ... 29... TG 0207
Garvock ... 49... NS 2571
Garway ... 16... SO 4522
Garynahine ... 63... NB 2331
Gastard ... 17... ST 8868
Gasthorpe ... 29... TL 9780
Gatcombe ... 9... SZ 4885
Gatebeck ... 41... SD 5485
Gate Burton ... 34... SK 8382
Gateforth ... 38... SE 5528
Gatehead ... 50... NS 3936
Gate Helmsley ... 38... SE 6955
Gatehouse ... 46... NY 7988
Gatehouse of Fleet ... 45... NX 5956
Gatelawbridge ... 45... NX 9096
Gateley ... 29... TF 9624
Gatenby ... 42... SE 3287
Gateshead ... 47... NZ 2562
Gatesheath ... 32... SJ 4760
Gateside (Fife.) ... 56... NO 1809
Gateside (Strath.) ... 50... NS 3653
Gateside (Tays.) ... 57... NO 3749
Gateside (Tays.) ... 57... NO 4344
Gathurst ... 36... SD 5307
Gatley ... 32... SJ 8387
Gattonside ... 52... NT 5435
Gauldry ... 57... NO 3723
Gaunt's Common ... 8... SU 0205
Gautby ... 35... TF 1772
Gavinton ... 53... NT 7652
Gawber ... 37... SE 3207
Gawcott ... 18... SP 6831
Gawsworth ... 33... SJ 8869
Gawthrop ... 41... SD 6987
Gawthwaite ... 40... SD 2784
Gaydon ... 26... SP 3654
Gayhurst ... 27... SP 8446
Gayles ... 42... NZ 1207
Gay Street ... 11... TQ 0820
Gayton (Mers.) ... 32... SJ 2680
Gayton (Norf.) ... 28... TF 7219
Gayton (Northants.) ... 26... SP 7054
Gayton (Staffs.) ... 33... SJ 9728
Gayton le Marsh ... 35... TF 4284
Gayton Thorpe ... 28... TF 7418
Gaywood ... 28... TF 6320
Gazeley ... 20... TL 7264
[illegible] ... [illegible]... NG [illegible]
Gedding ... 21... TL 9457
Geddington ... 27... SP 8983
Gedintailor ... 58... NG 5235
Gedney ... 35... TF 4024
Gedney Broadgate ... 35... TF 4022
Gedney Drove End ... 35... TF 4629
Gedney Dyke ... 35... TF 4126
Gedney Hill ... 35... TF 3311
Gee Cross ... 37... SJ 9593
Geilston ... 50... NS 3477
Geise ... 67... ND 1064
Geldeston ... 29... TM 3891
Gell ... 31... SH 8569
Gelligaer ... 16... ST 1397
Gelli Gynan ... 32... SJ 1854
Gellilydan ... 30... SH 6839
Gellioedd ... 31... SH 9344
Gelly ... 14... SN 0819
Gellyburn ... 56... NO 0939
Gellywen ... 14... SN 2723
Gelston ... 45... NX 7758
Genoch Mains ... 44... NX 1356
Gentleshaw ... 25... SK 0511
Geocrab ... 63... NG 1190
Georgeham ... 6... SS 4639
George Nympton ... 6... SS 7023
Georgetown ... 50... NS 4567
Georgia ... 2... SW 4836
Georth ... 63... HY 3625
Germansweek ... 4... SX 4394
Germoe ... 2... SW 5829
Gerrans ... 2... SW 8735
Gerrards Cross ... 19... TQ 0088
Geshader ... 63... NB 1131
Gestingthorpe ... 20... TL 8138
Geuffordd ... 23... SJ 2114
Gibraltar ... 35... TF 5558
Gidea Park ... 20... TQ 5390
Gidleigh ... 5... SX 6788
Gifford ... 52... NT 5368
Giggleswick ... 41... SD 8163
Gilberdyke ... 39... SE 8329
Gilchriston ... 52... NT 4865
Gilcrux ... 40... NY 1138
Gildersome ... 37... SE 2429
Gildingwells ... 34... SK 5585
Gileston ... 15... ST 0167
Gilfach ... 16... ST 1598
Gilfach Goch ... 15... SS 9890
Gilfachrheda ... 22... SN 4058
Gillamoor ... 43... SE 6890
Gilling East ... 42... SE 6176
Gillingham (Dorset) ... 8... ST 8026
Gillingham (Kent) ... 12... TQ 7768
Gillingham (Norf.) ... 29... TM 4191
Gilling West ... 42... NZ 1805
Gillow Heath ... 33... SJ 8858
Gills ... 67... ND 3172
Gilmerton (Lothian) ... 51... NT 2968
Gilmerton (Tays.) ... 56... NN 8823
Gilmorton ... 26... SP 5787
Gilsland ... 46... NY 6366
Gilsland Spa ... 46... NY 6367
Gilston ... 52... NT 4456
Gilwern ... 16... SO 2414
Gimingham ... 20... TG 2036
Gipping ... 21... TM 0763
Gipsey Bridge ... 35... TF 2850
Girlsta ... 63... HU 4250
Girsby ... 42... NZ 3508
Girthon ... 45... NX 6053
Girton (Cambs.) ... 20... TL 4262
Girton (Notts.) ... 34... SK 8266
Girvan ... 44... NX 1897
Gisburn ... 37... SD 8248
Gisleham ... 29... TM 5188
Gislingham ... 29... TM 0771
Gissing ... 29... TM 1485
Gittisham ... 5... SY 1398
Glackossian ... 60... NH 5938
Gladestry ... 23... SO 2355
Gladsmuir ... 52... NT 4573

Glais ... 15... SN 7000
Glaisdale (N Yorks.) ... 43... NZ 7705
Glamis ... 57... NO 3846
Glanaber Terrace ... 30... SH 7547
Glanaman ... 15... SN 6713
Glan-Conwy ... 31... SH 8352
Glandford ... 29... TG 0441
Glandwr (Dyfed) ... 14... SN 1928
Glandwr (Gwent) ... 16... SO 2101
Glangrwyne ... 16... SO 2316
Glan-Mule ... 23... SO 1690
Glanrhyd ... 14... SN 1442
Glanton ... 53... NU 0714
Glanton Pike ... 53... NU 0514
Glanvilles Wootton ... 8... ST 6708
Glan-y-don ... 31... SJ 1679
Glan-yr-afon (Clwyd-Gwyn.) ... 31... SJ 0242
Glan-yr-afon (Gwyn.) ... 31... SH 9141
Glapthorn ... 27... TL 0290
Glapwell ... 33... SK 4766
Glasbury ... 23... SO 1739
Glascote ... 26... SK 2203
Glascwm ... 23... SO 1553
Glasdrum ... 55... NN 0046
Glasfryn ... 31... SH 9150
Glasgow ... 50... NS 5865
Glasinfryn ... 30... SH 5868
Glaspwll ... 22... SN 7397
Glasserton ... 44... NX 4238
Glassford ... 50... NS 7247
Glasshouse Hill ... 17... SO 7020
Glasshouses ... 42... SE 1764
Glasslaw ... 62... NJ 8659
Glasslie ... 56... NO 2305
Glasson (Cumbr.) ... 46... NY 2560
Glasson (Lancs.) ... 36... SD 4455
Glassonby ... 41... NY 5738
Glasterlaw ... 57... NO 6051
Glaston ... 27... SK 8900
Glastonbury ... 7... ST 4938
Glatton ... 27... TL 1586
Glazebury ... 32... SJ 6796
Glazeley ... 24... SO 7088
Gleadless Townend ... 33... SK 3883
Gleadsmoss ... 33... SJ 8469
Gleaston ... 40... SD 2570
Glemsford ... 20... TL 8247
Glenalmond (Tays.) ... 56... NN 9627
Glenancross ... 58... NM 6691
Glen Auldyn ... 43... SC 4393
Glenbarr ... 48... NR 6736
Glen Barry ... 62... NJ 5554
Glen Bernisdale ... 58... NG 4048
Glenbervie ... 57... NO 7680
Glenboig ... 50... NS 7268
Glenbranter ... 55... NS 1097
Glen Breackerie ... 48... NR 6511
Glenbreck ... 51... NT 0521
Glenbuck ... 50... NS 7429
Glenburn ... 50... NS 4761
Glencaple ... 45... NX 9968
Glencarse ... 56... NO 1922
Glencloy ... 49... NS 0036
Glencoe (Highld.) ... 55... NN 1058
Glencraig ... 51... NT 1795
Glendaruel ... 49... NR 9985
Glendevon (Tays.) ... 56... NN 9804
Glendoick ... 56... NO 2022
Glenduckie ... 57... NO 2818
Glenegedale ... 48... NR 3351
Glenelg ... 59... NG 8119
Glenfarg (Tays.) ... 56... NO 1310
Glenfield ... 34... SK 5306
Glenfinnan (Highld.) ... 54... NM 9080
Glenfoot ... 56... NO 1715
Glengarnock ... 50... NS 3252
Glengrasco ... 58... NG 4444
Glenkindie ... 61... NJ 4313
Glenlee (Dumf. and Galwy.) ... 45... NX 6080
Glenlivet ... 61... NJ 2126
Glenluce ... 44... NX 1957
Glenmaye ... 43... SC 2380
Glenmore (Island of Skye) ... 58... NG 4340
Glenmore (Strath.) ... 54... NM 8412
Glen Parva ... 26... SP 5798
Glenridding ... 40... NY 3817
Glenrothes ... 57... NO 2600
Glensaugh ... 57... NO 6778
Glenshee (Tays.) ... 56... NN 9834
Glensluain ... 55... NS 0999
Glenstockadale ... 44... NX 0061
Glenstriven ... 49... NS 0878
Glentham ... 34... TF 0090
Glentress ... 51... NT 2839
Glentrool Village ... 44... NX 3578
Glentworth ... 34... SK 9488
Glen Village ... 50... NS 8878
Glen Vine ... 43... SC 3378
Glespin ... 50... NS 8028
Gletness ... 63... HU 4651
Glewstone ... 16... SO 5522
Glinton ... 35... TF 1506
Glooston ... 26... SP 7596
Glossop ... 37... SK 0393
Gloster Hill ... 47... NU 2504
Gloucester ... 17... SO 8318
Gloup ... 63... HP 5004
Glusburn ... 37... SE 0344
Gluss ... 63... HU 3477
Glympton ... 18... SP 4221
Glyn ... 30... SH 7457
Glynarthen ... 14... SN 3148
Glyn Ceiriog ... 32... SJ 2038
Glyncorrwg ... 15... SS 8799
Glyn-Cywarch ... 30... SH 6034
Glynde ... 12... TQ 4509
Glyndebourne ... 12... TQ 4510
Glyn Dyfrdwy ... 31... SJ 1542
Glyn-Neath ... 15... SN 8806
Glyntaff ... 16... ST 0889
Glynteg ... 15... SN 3637
Glyntrefnant ... 22... SN 9192
Gnosall ... 32... SJ 8220
Gnosall Heath ... 33... SJ 8419
Goadby ... 26... SP 7598
Goadby Marwood ... 34... SK 7826
Goatacre ... 17... SU 0176
Goathill ... 8... ST 6717
Goathland ... 43... NZ 8301
Goathurst ... 7... ST 2534
Gobowen ... 32... SJ 3033
Godalming ... 11... SU 9743
Godmanchester ... 27... TL 2470
Godmanstone ... 8... SY 6697
Godmersham ... 13... TR 0650
Godney ... 7... ST 4842
Godolphin Cross ... 2... SW 6031

Godre'r-graig ... 15... SN 7507
Godshill (Hants.) ... 8... SU 1714
Godshill (I. of W.) ... 9... SZ 5281
Godstone ... 12... TQ 3551
Goetre ... 16... SO 3205
Goff's Oak ... 20... TL 3202
Gogar ... 51... NT 1672
Goginan ... 22... SN 6981
Golan ... 30... SH 5242
Golant ... 4... SX 1254
Golberdon ... 4... SX 3271
Golborne ... 32... SJ 6097
Golcar ... 37... SE 0915
Goldcliff ... 16... ST 3683
Golden Cross ... 12... TQ 5312
Golden Green ... 12... TQ 6348
Golden Grove ... 15... SN 5919
Goldenhill ... 33... SJ 8553
Golden Pot ... 10... SU 7143
Golden Valley (Glos.) ... 17... SO 9022
Golders Green ... 19... TQ 2488
Goldhanger ... 21... TL 9009
Golding ... 24... SJ 5403
Goldsborough (N Yorks.) ... 43... NZ 8314
Goldsborough (N Yorks.) ... 37... SE 3856
Goldsithney ... 2... SW 5430
Goldthorpe ... 38... SE 4604
Gollanfield ... 60... NH 8052
Golspie ... 65... NH 8399
Golval ... 67... NC 8962
Gomersal ... 37... SE 2026
Gomshall ... 11... TQ 0847
Gonalston ... 34... SK 6847
Gonfirth (Shetld.) ... 63... HU 3661
Good Easter ... 20... TL 6212
Gooderstone ... 28... TF 7602
Goodleigh ... 6... SS 5934
Goodmanham ... 39... SE 8842
Goodnestone (Kent) ... 13... TR 0461
Goodnestone (Kent) ... 13... TR 2554
Goodrich ... 17... SO 5719
Goodrington ... 5... SX 8958
Goodwick ... 14... SM 9438
Goodworth Clatford ... 10... SU 3642
Goodyers End ... 26... SP 3385
Goole ... 38... SE 7423
Goole Fields ... 38... SE 7519
Goonbell ... 2... SW 7249
Goonhavern ... 2... SW 7953
Gooseham ... 4... SS 2316
Goosetrey ... 32... SJ 7769
Goosey ... 18... SU 3591
Goosnargh ... 36... SD 5536
Gordon ... 52... NT 6443
Gordonbush ... 67... NC 8409
Gordonstoun ... 61... NJ 1368
Gordonstown (Grampn.) ... 62... NJ 5656
Gordonstown (Grampn.) ... 62... NJ 7138
Gorebridge ... 51... NT 3461
Gorefield ... 35... TF 4112
Goring ... 10... SU 6000
Goring-by-Sea ... 11... TQ 1102
Gorleston on Sea ... 29... TG 5203
Gorley ... 8... SU 1511
Gorrachie ... 62... NJ 7358
Gorran Haven ... 4... SX 0141
Gors ... 22... SN 6277
Gorsedd ... 31... SJ 1476
Gorseinon ... 15... SS 5998
Gors-goch ... 23... SN 9393
Gorslas ... 15... SN 5713
Gorsley ... 17... SO 6826
Gorsness ... 63... HY 4119
Gorstan ... 65... NH 3862
Gorsty Common ... 24... SO 4537
Gorton ... 37... SJ 8996
Gosbeck ... 21... TM 1555
Gosberton ... 35... TF 2331
Gosfield ... 20... TL 7829
Gosforth (Cumbr.) ... 40... NY 0603
Gosforth (Tyne and Wear) ... 47... NZ 2467
Gosmore ... 19... TL 1927
Gosport ... 9... SZ 6199
Gossabrough ... 63... HU 5383
Goswick ... 53... NU 0545
Gotham ... 34... SK 5330
Gotherington ... 17... SO 9629
Gott Bay ... 48... NM 0546
Goudhurst ... 12... TQ 7337
Goulceby ... 35... TF 2579
Gourdas ... 62... NJ 7741
Gourdon ... 57... NO 8270
Gourock ... 49... NS 2477
Govan ... 50... NS 5464
Gowanhill ... 62... NK 0363
Gowdall ... 38... SE 6122
Gowerton ... 15... SS 5896
Gowkhall ... 51... NT 0589
Goxhill (Humbs.) ... 39... TA 1021
Goxhill (Humbs.) ... 39... TA 1844
Graffham (W Susx) ... 11... SU 9216
Grafham (Cambs.) ... 27... TL 1669
Grafton (Here. and Worc.) ... 24... SO 4937
Grafton (Here. and Worc.) ... 24... SO 5761
Grafton (N Yorks.) ... 38... SE 4163
Grafton (Oxon.) ... 18... SP 2600
Grafton Flyford ... 25... SO 9655
Grafton Regis ... 26... SP 7546
Grafton Underwood ... 27... SP 9280
Grafty Green ... 13... TQ 8748
Graianrhyd ... 32... SJ 2156
Graig (Clwyd) ... 31... SJ 0872
Graig (Gwyn.) ... 31... SH 8071
Graig-fechan ... 31... SJ 1454
Grain ... 13... TQ 8876
Grainsby ... 39... TF 2799
Grainthorpe ... 39... TF 3896
Graizelound ... 38... SK 7798
Grampound ... 2... SW 9348
Grampound Road ... 2... SW 9150
Gramsdale ... 63... NF 8255
Granborough ... 18... SP 7625
Granby ... 34... SK 7536
Grandborough ... 26... SP 4866
Grandtully ... 56... NN 9152
Grange (Cumbr.) ... 40... NY 2517
Grange (Mers.) ... 32... SJ 2286
Grange (N Yorks.) ... 42... SE 5796
Grange (Tays.) ... 57... NO 2725
Grange Crossroads ... 61... NJ 4754
Grange Hill ... 20... TQ 4492
Grange Moor ... 37... SE 2216
Grangemouth ... 51... NS 9281
Grange of Lindores ... 57... NO 2516
Grange-over-Sands ... 40... SD 4077
Grangepans ... 51... NT 0282
Grangetown ... 42... NZ 5420

Grange Villa ... 47... NZ 2352
Granish ... 60... NH 8914
Gransmoor ... 39... TA 1259
Granston ... 14... SM 8934
Grantchester ... 20... TL 4355
Grantham ... 34... SK 9135
Grantlodge ... 62... NJ 7017
Granton (Dumf. and Galwy.) ... 45... NT 0709
Granton (Lothian) ... 51... NT 2277
Grantown-on-Spey ... 61... NJ 0327
Grantshouse ... 53... NT 8065
Grappenhall ... 32... SJ 6385
Grasby ... 39... TA 0804
Grasmere (Cumbr.) ... 40... NY 3307
Grasscroft ... 37... SD 9804
Grassendale ... 32... SJ 3985
Grassholme ... 41... NY 9221
Grassington ... 41... SE 0064
Grassmoor ... 33... SK 4067
Grassthorpe ... 34... SK 7967
Grateley ... 10... SU 2741
Gratwich ... 33... SK 0231
Graveley (Cambs.) ... 27... TL 2564
Graveley (Herts.) ... 19... TL 2328
Gravelly Hill ... 25... SP 1090
Gravels ... 23... SJ 3300
Graveney ... 13... TR 0562
Gravesend ... 12... TQ 6473
Gravir ... 63... NB 3715
Grayingham ... 39... SK 9395
Grayrigg ... 41... SD 5797
Grays ... 12... TQ 6177
Grayshott ... 11... SU 8735
Grayswood ... 11... SU 9234
Grazeley ... 10... SU 6966
Greasbrough ... 38... SK 4195
Greasby ... 32... SJ 2587
Great Abington ... 20... TL 5348
Great Addington ... 27... SP 9575
Great Alne ... 25... SP 1159
Great Altcar ... 36... SD 3206
Great Amwell ... 20... TL 3712
Great Asby ... 41... NY 6813
Great Ashfield ... 21... TM 0068
Great Ayton ... 42... NZ 5510
Great Baddow ... 20... TL 7204
Great Badminton ... 17... ST 8082
Great Bardfield ... 20... TL 6730
Great Barford ... 27... TL 1352
Great Barr ... 25... SP 0495
Great Barrington ... 17... SP 2013
Great Barrow ... 32... SJ 4668
Great Barton ... 21... TL 8967
Great Barugh ... [illegible]... SE [illegible]
Great Bavington ... 47... NY 9880
Great Bedwyn ... 10... SU 2764
Great Bentley ... 21... TM 1121
Great Billing ... 26... SP 8162
Great Bircham ... 28... TF 7632
Great Blakenham ... 21... TM 1150
Great Bolas ... 32... SJ 6421
Great Bookham ... 11... TQ 1454
Great Bosullow ... 2... SW 4133
Great Bourton ... 26... SP 4545
Great Bowden ... 26... SP 7488
Great Bradley ... 20... TL 6753
Great Braxted ... 20... TL 8614
Great Bricett ... 21... TM 0350
Great Brickhill ... 19... SP 9030
Great Bridgeford ... 33... SJ 8827
Great Brington ... 26... SP 6665
Great Bromley ... 21... TM 0826
Great Broughton ... 42... NZ 5406
Great Budworth ... 32... SJ 6677
Great Burdon ... 42... NZ 3116
Great Burstead ... 20... TQ 6892
Great Busby ... 42... NZ 5105
Great Canfield ... 20... TL 5917
Great Carlton ... 35... TF 4185
Great Casterton ... 34... TF 0009
Great Chart ... 13... TQ 9842
Great Chatwell ... 24... SJ 7914
Great Chesterford ... 20... TL 5042
Great Cheverell ... 17... ST 9858
Great Chishill ... 20... TL 4238
Great Clacton ... 21... TM 1716
Great Coates ... 39... TA 2310
Great Comberton ... 25... SO 9542
Great Corby ... 46... NY 4754
Great Cornard ... 21... TL 8840
Great Coxwell ... 18... SU 2693
Great Cransley ... 26... SP 8376
Great Cressingham ... 28... TF 8501
Great Crosby ... 32... SJ 3199
Great Cubley ... 33... SK 1637
Great Dalby ... 34... SK 7414
Great Doddington ... 27... SP 8864
Great Driffield ... 39... TA 0257
Great Dunham ... 28... TF 8714
Great Dunmow ... 20... TL 6221
Great Durnford ... 8... SU 1338
Great Easton (Essex) ... 20... TL 6125
Great Easton (Leic.) ... 27... SP 8493
Great Eccleston ... 36... SD 4240
Great Edstone ... 43... SE 7084
Great Ellingham ... 29... TM 0196
Great Elm ... 8... ST 7449
Great Eversden ... 20... TL 3653
Great Fen ... 28... TL 5978
Great Finborough ... 21... TM 0157
Greatford ... 35... TF 0811
Great Fransham ... 28... TF 8913
Great Gaddesden ... 19... TL 0211
Great Gidding ... 27... TL 1183
Great Givendale ... 39... SE 8153
Great Glemham ... 21... TM 3361
Great Glen ... 26... SP 6597
Great Gonerby ... 34... SK 8938
Great Gransden ... 27... TL 2756
Great Green (Norf.) ... 29... TM 2789
Great Green (Suff.) ... 21... TL 9155
Great Habton ... 43... SE 7576
Great Hallingbury ... 20... TL 5119
Greatham (Cleve.) ... 42... NZ 4927
Greatham (Hants.) ... 9... SU 7730
Greatham (W Susx) ... 11... TQ 0415
Great Hanwood ... 24... SJ 4309
Great Harrowden ... 27... SP 8871
Great Harwood ... 36... SD 7332
Great Haseley ... 18... SP 6401
Great Hatfield ... 39... TA 1842
Great Heck ... 38... SE 5920
Great Henny ... 21... TL 8738
Great Hinton ... 17... ST 9058
Great Hockham ... 29... TL 9592
Great Holland ... 21... TM 2119
Great Horkesley ... 21... TL 9731

Great Hormead 84 Haselbech

Great Hormead 20 TL 4030
Great Horwood 18 SP 7731
Great Houghton (Northants.) 26 SP 7958
Great Houghton (S Yorks.) 38 SE 4206
Great Hucklow 33 SK 1777
Great Kelk 39 TA 1058
Great Kingshill 19 SU 8798
Great Langton 42 SE 2996
Great Leighs 20 TL 7317
Great Limber 39 TA 1308
Great Linford 27 SP 8542
Great Livermere 28 TL 8871
Great Longstone 33 SK 1971
Great Lumley 47 NZ 2949
Great Lyth 24 SJ 4507
Great Malvern 24 SO 7845
Great Maplestead 20 TL 8034
Great Marton 36 SD 3335
Great Massingham 28 TF 7922
Great Milton 18 SP 6302
Great Missenden 19 SP 8901
Great Mitton 36 SD 7138
Great Mongeham 13 TR 3451
Great Moulton 29 TM 1690
Great Musgrave 41 NY 7613
Great Ness 32 SJ 3918
Great Oakley (Essex) 21 TM 1927
Great Oakley (Northants.) 27 SP 8686
Great Offley 19 TL 1427
Great Ormside 41 NY 7017
Great Orton 46 NY 3254
Great Oxendon 26 SP 7383
Great Palgrave 28 TF 8312
Great Parndon 20 TL 4308
Great Paxton 27 TL 2164
Great Plumstead 29 TG 2910
Great Ponton 34 SK 9230
Great Postland 35 TF 2612
Great Preston 38 SE 4029
Great Raveley 27 TL 2581
Great Rissington 17 SP 1917
Great Rollright 18 SP 3231
Great Ryburgh 29 TF 9527
Great Ryle 53 NU 0212
Great Saling 20 TL 7025
Great Salkeld 41 NY 5536
Great Sampford 20 TL 6435
Great Sankey 32 SJ 5688
Great Saxham 20 TL 7862
Great Shefford 10 SU 3875
Great Shelford 20 TL 4652
Great Smeaton 42 NZ 3404
Great Snoring 29 TF 9434
Great Somerford 17 ST 9682
Great Soudley 32 SJ 7228
Great Stainton 42 NZ 3322
Great Stambridge 21 TQ 8991
Great Staughton 27 TL 1264
Great Steeping 35 TF 4364
Great Stonar 13 TR 3359
Greatstone-on-Sea 13 TR 0822
Great Strickland 41 NY 5522
Great Stukeley 27 TL 2275
Great Sturton 35 TF 2176
Great Swinburne 47 NY 9375
Great Tew 18 SP 3929
Great Tey 21 TL 8925
Great Torrington 6 SS 4919
Great Tosson 47 NU 0300
Great Totham (Essex) 20 TL 8511
Great Totham (Essex) 20 TL 8613
Great Wakering 21 TQ 9487
Great Waldingfield 21 TL 9143
Great Walsingham 29 TF 9437
Great Waltham 20 TL 6913
Great Warley 20 TQ 5890
Great Washbourne 25 SO 9834
Great Welnetham 21 TL 8759
Great Wenham 21 TM 0738
Great Whittington 47 NZ 0070
Great Wigborough 21 TL 9615
Great Wilbraham 20 TL 5557
Great Wishford 8 SU 0835
Great Witcombe 17 SO 9014
Great Witley 24 SO 7566
Great Wolford 18 SP 2434
Greatworth 26 SP 5542
Great Wratting 20 TL 6848
Great Wyrley 25 SJ 9907
Great Wytheford 32 SJ 5719
Great Yarmouth 29 TG 5207
Great Yeldham 20 TL 7638
Greenbank 36 SD 5254
Greenburn 51 NS 9360
Greendikes 53 NU 0628
Greenfield (Beds.) 19 TL 0534
Greenfield (Clwyd) 32 SJ 1977
Greenfield (Gtr Mches.) 37 SD 9904
Greenfield (Highld.) 59 NH 2000
Greenfield (Oxon.) 18 SU 7191
Greenford 19 TQ 1382
Greengairs 50 NS 7870
Greenham 10 SU 4865
Green Hammerton 38 SE 4656
Greenhaugh 46 NY 7987
Greenhead (Northum.) 46 NY 6665
Greenhill (Central) 50 NS 8278
Greenhill (Gtr London) 19 TQ 1688
Green Hill (Northum.) 47 NY 8647
Greenhill (S Yorks.) 33 SK 3481
Green Hill (Wilts.) 17 SU 0686
Greenhithe 12 TQ 5974
Greenholm 50 NS 5637
Greenholme 41 NY 5905
Greenhow Hill 42 SE 1164
Greenigo 63 HY 4107
Greenland 67 ND 2367
Greenlaw (Borders) 52 NT 7145
Greenloaning 56 NN 8307
Greenmount 37 SD 7714
Greenock 50 NS 2776
Greenodd 40 SD 3182
Green Ore 7 ST 5749
Greenside 47 NZ 1362
Greenskairs 62 NJ 7863
Greens Norton 26 SP 6649
Greenstead Green 20 TL 8227
Greensted 20 TL 5302
Green Street 19 TQ 1998
Green Street Green 12 TQ 4563
Green, The (Cumbr.) 40 SD 1784
Green, The (Wilts.) 8 ST 8731
Greenwich 12 TQ 4077
Greet 26 SP 0230
Greete 24 SO 5770
Greetham (Leic.) 34 SK 9214
Greetham (Lincs.) 35 TF 3070
Greetland 37 SE 0821
Greinton 7 ST 4136
Grendon (Northants.) 27 SP 8760
Grendon (Warw.) 26 SK 2800
Grendon Common 26 SP 2799
Grendon Green 24 SO 5957
Grendon Underwood 18 SP 6720
Grenitote 63 NF 8274
Grenoside 37 SK 3394
Gresford 32 SJ 3454
Gresham 29 TG 1738
Greshornish 58 NG 3454
Gress 63 NB 4842
Gressenhall 29 TF 9615
Gressenhall Green 29 TF 9616
Gressingham 41 SD 5769
Greta Bridge 42 NZ 0813
Gretna 46 NY 3167
Gretna Green 46 NY 3268
Gretton (Glos.) 25 SP 0030
Gretton (Northants.) 27 SP 8994
Gretton (Salop) 24 SO 5195
Grewelthorpe 42 SE 2276
Greysouthen 40 NY 0729
Greystoke 40 NY 4330
Greystone 57 NO 5343
Greywell 10 SU 7151
Gribun 54 NM 4533
Griff 26 SP 3588
Griffithstown 16 ST 2999
Grigghall 40 SD 4691
Grimeford Village 36 SD 6112
Grimethorpe 38 SE 4109
Griminish 63 NF 7851
Grimista 63 HU 4643
Grimley 25 SO 8360
Grimness (S. Ronaldsay) 63 ND 4793
Grimoldby 35 TF 3988
Grimsargh 36 SD 5834
Grimsby 39 TA 2810
Grimscote 26 SP 6553
Grimscott 4 SS 2606
Grimshader 63 NB 4025
Grimsthorpe 35 TF 0423
Grimston (Leic.) 34 SK 6821
Grimston (Norf.) 28 TF 7221
Grimstone 8 SY 6393
Grindale 39 TA 1371
Grindle 24 SJ 7403
Grindleford 33 SK 2477
Grindleton 37 SD 7545
Grindlow 33 SK 1877
Grindon (Northum.) 53 NT 9144
Grindon (Staffs.) 33 SK 0854
Gringley on the Hill 34 SK 7390
Grinsdale 46 NY 3758
Grinshill 32 SJ 5223
Grinton 42 SE 0498
Gristhorpe 43 TA 0882
Griston 29 TL 9499
Gritley 63 HY 5605
Grittenham 17 SU 0382
Grittleton 17 ST 8579
Grizebeck 40 SD 2384
Grizedale 40 SD 3394
Grobister 63 HY 6524
Groby 34 SK 5207
Groes (Clwyd) 31 SJ 0064
Groes (W Glam.) 15 SS 7986
Groes-faen 16 ST 0780
Groesffordd Marli 31 SJ 0073
Groeslon 30 SH 4755
Grogport 49 NR 8044
Gronant 31 SJ 0883
Groombridge 12 TQ 5337
Grosebay 63 NG 1592
Grosmont (Gwent) 16 SO 4024
Grosmont (N Yorks.) 43 NZ 8205
Groton 21 TL 9641
Grove (Dorset) 8 SY 6972
Grove (Kent) 13 TR 2362
Grove (Notts.) 34 SK 7379
Grove (Oxon.) 18 SU 4090
Grovely Wood 8 SU 0534
Grove Park 12 TQ 4172
Grovesend 15 SN 5900
Gruids 66 NC 5604
Gruinart 48 NR 2866
Grula 58 NG 3826
Gruline 54 NM 5440
Grunasound 63 HU 3733
Grundisburgh 21 TM 2251
Gruting 63 HU 2748
Grutness 63 HU 4009
Grwyne Fechan 16 SO 2324
Gualachulain 55 NN 1145
Guardbridge 57 NO 4519
Guarlford 25 SO 8145
Guay 56 NO 0049
Guestling Green 13 TQ 8513
Guestwick 29 TG 0627
Gugh 2 SV 8908
Guide Post 47 NZ 2585
Guilden Morden 27 TL 2744
Guilden Sutton 32 SJ 4468
Guildford 11 TQ 0049
Guildtown 56 NO 1331
Guilsborough 26 SP 6773
Guilsfield 23 SJ 2111
Guisborough 42 NZ 6115
Guiseley 37 SE 1941
Guist 29 TF 9925
Guiting Power 17 SP 0924
Gulberwick 63 HU 4437
Gulf of Corryvreckan 54 NM 6901
Gullane 52 NT 4882
Gulval 2 SW 4831
Gumfreston 14 SN 1101
Gumley 26 SP 6890
Gunby (Humbs.) 38 SE 7135
Gunby (Lincs.) 34 SK 9021
Gundleton 9 SU 6133
Gunn 6 SS 6333
Gunnerside 41 SD 9598
Gunnerton 47 NY 9074
Gunness 39 SE 8411
Gunnislake 4 SX 4371
Gunnista 63 HU 5043
Gunthorpe (Norf.) 29 TG 0135
Gunthorpe (Notts.) 34 SK 6744
Gurnard 9 SZ 4795
Gurney Slade 8 ST 6249
Gurnos 15 SN 7709
Gussage All Saints 8 SU 0010
Gussage St. Michael 8 ST 9811
Guston 13 TR 3244
Gutcher 63 HU 5498
Guthrie 57 NO 5650
Guyhirn 27 TF 3903
Guy's Head 35 TF 4825
Guy's Marsh 8 ST 8420
Guyzance 47 NU 2103
Gwaenysgor 31 SJ 0780
Gwalchmai 30 SH 3975
Gwaun-Cae-Gurwen 15 SN 7011
Gwbert-on-Sea 14 SN 1650
Gweek 2 SW 7026
Gwehelog 16 SO 3804
Gwenddwr 23 SO 0643
Gwennap 2 SW 7340
Gwenter 2 SW 7418
Gwernaffield 32 SJ 2064
Gwernesney 16 SO 4101
Gwernogle 15 SN 5234
Gwernymynydd 32 SJ 2162
Gwespyr 31 SJ 1183
Gwinear 2 SW 5937
Gwithian 2 SW 5841
Gwrhyd 15 SN 9339
Gwrych Castle 31 SH 9277
Gwyddelwern 31 SJ 0746
Gwyddgrug 15 SN 4635
Gwytherin 31 SH 8761
Gylchedd 31 SH 8644
Gypsey Race 39 TA 0970

Habberley (Here. and Worc.) 24 SO 8077
Habberley (Salop) 24 SJ 3903
Habost (Isle of Lewis) 63 NB 3219
Habost (Isle of Lewis) 63 NB 5362
Habrough 39 TA 1514
Haccombe 5 SX 8970
Hacconby 35 TF 1025
Haceby 34 TF 0236
Hacheston 21 TM 3059
Hackenthorpe 33 SK 4183
Hacketts 20 TL 3208
Hackford 29 TG 0502
Hackforth 42 SE 2493
Hackland 63 HY 3920
Hacklete 63 NB 1534
Hackleton 26 SP 8055
Hackness (N Yorks.) 43 SE 9690
Hackness (South Walls) 63 ND 3391
Hackney 20 TQ 3585
Hackthorn 34 SK 9882
Hackthorpe 41 NY 5423
Hadden 53 NT 7836
Haddenham (Bucks.) 18 SP 7408
Haddenham (Cambs.) 27 TL 4675
Haddington 52 NT 5174
Haddiscoe 29 TM 4497
Haddon 27 TL 1392
Hademore 25 SK 1708
Hadfield 37 SK 0296
Hadham Cross 20 TL 4218
Hadham Ford 20 TL 4321
Hadleigh (Essex) 20 TQ 8087
Hadleigh (Suff.) 21 TM 0242
Hadley 24 SJ 6712
Hadley End 33 SK 1320
Hadlow 12 TQ 6349
Hadlow Down 12 TQ 5324
Hadnall 32 SJ 5210
Hadstock 20 TL 5645
Hadzor 25 SO 9162
Haffenden Quarter 13 TQ 8841
Hafod-Dinbych 31 SH 8953
Hafodunos 31 SH 8666
Haggbeck 46 NY 4774
Hagley (Here. and Worc.) 24 SO 5641
Hagley (Here. and Worc.) 25 SO 9181
Hagworthingham 35 TF 3469
Haigh 36 SD 6108
Haighton Green 36 SD 5634
Haile 40 NY 0308
Hailes 25 SP 0530
Hailey (Herts.) 20 TL 3710
Hailey (Oxon.) 18 SP 3512
Hailsham 12 TQ 5909
Hail Weston 27 TL 1662
Hainault 20 TQ 4691
Hainford 29 TG 2218
Hainton 35 TF 1784
Haisthorpe 39 TA 1264
Halam 34 SK 6754
Halberton 7 ST 0012
Halcro 67 ND 2260
Hale (Ches.) 32 SJ 4682
Hale (Gtr Mches.) 32 SJ 7786
Hale (Hants.) 8 SU 1919
Hale (Lincs.) 35 TF 1443
Hale Bank 32 SJ 4784
Halebarns 32 SJ 7985
Hales (Norf.) 29 TM 3897
Hales (Staffs.) 32 SJ 7134
Halesowen 25 SO 9683
Hales Place 13 TR 1459
Hale Street 12 TQ 6749
Halesworth 29 TM 3877
Halewood 32 SJ 4585
Halford (Salop) 24 SO 4383
Halford (Warw.) 26 SP 2545
Halfpenny Green 25 SO 8292
Halfway (Berks.) 10 SU 4068
Halfway (Dyfed) 15 SN 6430
Halfway (Dyfed) 15 SN 8232
Halfway House 23 SJ 3411
Halfway Houses 13 TQ 9373
Halifax 37 SE 0825
Halistra 58 NG 2459
Halket 50 NS 4252
Halkirk 67 ND 1359
Halkyn 32 SJ 2071
Halland 12 TQ 5016
Hallaton 26 SP 7896
Hallatrow 17 ST 6356
Hallbankgate 46 NY 5859
Hall Dunnerdale 40 SD 2195
Hallen 16 ST 5479
Hall Green 25 SP 1181
Hallin 58 NG 2559
Halling 12 TQ 7063
Hallington 47 NY 9875
Halloughton 34 SK 6851
Hallow 25 SO 8258
Hallrule 52 NT 5914
Halls 52 NT 6572
Hallsands 5 SX 8138
Hall's Green 19 TL 2728
Halltoft End 35 TF 3645
Hallworthy 4 SX 1787
Hallyburton 52 NT 6748
Hallyne 51 NT 1940
Halmer End 32 SJ 7949
Halmore 17 SO 6902
Halmyre Mains 51 NT 1749
Halnaker 11 SU 9108
Halsall 36 SD 3710
Halse (Northants.) 18 SP 5640
Halse (Somer.) 7 ST 1327
Halsetown 2 SW 5038
Halsham 39 TA 2627
Halsinger 6 SS 5138
Halstead (Essex) 20 TL 8130
Halstead (Kent) 12 TQ 4961
Halstead (Leic.) 26 SK 7505
Halstock 7 ST 5308
Haltham 35 TF 2463
Halton (Bucks.) 19 SP 8710
Halton (Ches.) 32 SJ 5381
Halton (Clwyd) 32 SJ 3039
Halton (Lancs.) 40 SD 5065
Halton East 37 SE 0454
Halton Gill 41 SD 8876
Halton Holegate 35 TF 4165
Halton Lea Gate 46 NY 6558
Halton West 37 SD 8454
Haltwhistle 46 NY 7064
Halvergate 29 TG 4206
Halwell 5 SX 7753
Halwill 4 SX 4299
Halwill Junction 4 SS 4400
Ham (Bressay) 63 HU 4939
Ham (Foula) 63 HT 9739
Ham (Glos.) 17 ST 6898
Ham (Gtr London) 11 TQ 1672
Ham (Highld.) 67 ND 2373
Ham (Kent) 13 TR 3354
Ham (Wilts.) 10 SU 3262
Hamble 9 SU 4806
Hambleden (Bucks.) 18 SU 7886
Hambledon (Hants.) 9 SU 6414
Hambledon (Surrey) 11 SU 9638
Hambleton (Lancs.) 36 SD 3742
Hambleton (N Yorks.) 38 SE 5430
Hambridge 7 ST 3921
Hambrook (Avon) 17 ST 6378
Hambrook (W Susx) 9 SU 7806
Hameringham 35 TF 3167
Hamerton 27 TL 1379
Ham Green (Avon) 16 ST 5575
Ham Green (Here. and Worc.) 25 SP 0063
Hamilton 50 NS 7255
Hammersmith 11 TQ 2279
Hammerwich 25 SK 0707
Hammoon 8 ST 8114
Hamnavoe (Shetld.) 63 HU 4971
Hamnavoe (West Burra) 63 HU 3635
Hamnavoe (Yell) 63 HU 4980
Hampden 19 SP 8603
Hampden Park 12 TQ 6002
Hampden Row 19 SP 8402
Hampnett 17 SP 0915
Hampole 38 SE 5010
Hampreston 8 SZ 0598
Hampstead 19 TQ 2485
Hampstead Norris 10 SU 5276
Hampsthwaite 37 SE 2558
Hampton (Gtr London) 11 TQ 1369
Hampton (Salop) 24 SO 7486
Hampton Bishop 24 SO 5538
Hampton Heath 32 SJ 4949
Hampton in Arden 25 SP 2081
Hampton Lovett 25 SO 8865
Hampton Lucy 26 SP 2557
Hampton on the Hill 26 SP 2564
Hampton Poyle 18 SP 5015
Hamsey 12 TQ 4112
Hamstall Ridware 33 SK 1019
Hamstead (I. of W.) 9 SZ 3991
Hamstead (W Mids) 25 SP 0593
Hamstead Marshall 10 SU 4165
Hamsterley (Durham) 42 NZ 1131
Hamsterley (Durham) 47 NZ 1156
Hamstreet (Kent) 13 TR 0034
Ham Street (Somer.) 7 ST 5534
Hamtoun 63 HT 9637
Hamworthy 8 SY 9990
Hanbury (Here and Worc.) 25 SO 9663
Hanbury (Staffs.) 33 SK 1727
Hanchurch 32 SJ 8441
Handbridge 32 SJ 4164
Handcross 11 TQ 2630
Handforth 33 SJ 8883
Handley 32 SJ 4657
Handsacre 25 SK 0916
Handsworth (S Yorks.) 33 SK 4086
Handsworth (W Mids) 25 SP 0490
Hanford 33 SJ 8642
Hanging Langford 8 SU 0237
Hanham 17 ST 6372
Hankelow 32 SJ 6645
Hankerton 17 ST 9690
Hankham 12 TQ 6105
Hanley 33 SJ 8847
Hanley Castle 25 SO 8342
Hanley Childe 24 SO 6565
Hanley Swan 25 SO 8143
Hanley William 24 SO 6765
Hanlith 41 SD 9061
Hanmer 32 SJ 4540
Hannington (Hants.) 10 SU 5355
Hannington (Northants.) 26 SP 8171
Hannington (Wilts.) 17 SU 1793
Hannington Wick 17 SU 1795
Hanslope 26 SP 8046
Hanthorpe 35 TF 0824
Hanwell 26 SP 4343
Hanworth (Gtr London) 11 TQ 1271
Hanworth (Norf.) 29 TG 1935
Happendon 50 NS 8533
Happisburgh 29 TG 3731
Happisburgh Common 29 TG 3729
Hapsford 32 SJ 4774
Hapton (Lancs.) 37 SD 7931
Hapton (Norf.) 29 TM 1796
Harberton 5 SX 7758
Harbertonford 5 SX 7856
Harbledown 13 TR 1358
Harborne 25 SP 0384
Harborough Magna 26 SP 4779
Harbottle 47 NT 9304
Harbury 26 SP 3759
Harby (Leic.) 34 SK 7431
Harby (Notts.) 34 SK 8770
Harcombe 5 SY 1590
Harden 37 SE 0838
Hardenhuish 17 ST 9074
Hardgate 62 NJ 7801
Hardham 11 TQ 0317
Hardingham 29 TG 0403
Hardingstone 26 SP 7657
Hardings Wood 32 SJ 8054
Hardington 8 ST 7452
Hardington Mandeville 7 ST 5111
Hardington Marsh 7 ST 5009
Hardley 9 SU 4205
Hardley Street 29 TG 3801
Hardmead 27 SP 9347
Hardrow 41 SD 8691
Hardstoft 33 SK 4463
Hardway (Hants.) 9 SU 6101
Hardway (Somer.) 8 ST 7134
Hardwick (Bucks.) 18 SP 8019
Hardwick (Cambs.) 20 TL 3758
Hardwick (Norf.) 29 TM 2290
Hardwick (Northants.) 27 SP 8569
Hardwick (Oxon.) 18 SP 3706
Hardwick (Oxon.) 18 SP 5729
Hardwicke (Glos.) 17 SO 7912
Hardwicke (Glos.) 17 SO 9127
Hareby 35 TF 3365
Hareden 36 SD 6350
Harefield 19 TQ 0590
Hare Hatch 10 SU 8077
Harehope 53 NU 0920
Harescombe 17 SO 8410
Haresfield 17 SO 8110
Hare Street 20 TL 3929
Harewood 37 SE 3245
Harford 5 SX 6359
Hargrave (Ches.) 32 SJ 4862
Hargrave (Northants.) 27 TL 0370
Hargrave Green 20 TL 7759
Haringey 20 TQ 3290
Harker 46 NY 3960
Harkstead 21 TM 1935
Harlaston 25 SK 2111
Harlaxton 34 SK 8832
Harlech 30 SH 5831
Harlesden 19 TQ 2383
Harleston (Norf.) 29 TM 2483
Harleston (Suff.) 21 TM 0160
Harlestone 26 SP 7064
Harle Syke 37 SD 8634
Harley 24 SJ 5901
Harling Road 29 TL 9788
Harlington 19 TL 0330
Harlosh 58 NG 2841
Harlow 20 TL 4711
Harlow Hill 47 NZ 0768
Harlthorpe 38 SE 7337
Harlton 20 TL 3852
Harman's Cross 8 SY 9880
Harmby 42 SE 1289
Harmer Green 19 TL 2516
Harmer Hill 32 SJ 4822
Harmston 34 SK 9762
Harnhill 17 SP 0600
Harold Hill 20 TQ 5391
Haroldston West 14 SM 8615
Haroldswick (Unst) 63 HP 6312
Harold Wood 20 TQ 5590
Harome 42 SE 6482
Harpenden 19 TL 1314
Harpford 5 SY 0890
Harpham 39 TA 0961
Harpley (Here. and Worc.) 24 SO 6861
Harpley (Norf.) 28 TF 7826
Harpole 26 SP 6961
Harpsdale 67 ND 1256
Harpsden 10 SU 7680
Harpswell 34 SK 9389
Harpurhey 37 SD 8701
Harpur Hill 33 SK 0671
Harrapool 58 NG 6523
Harrietfield 56 NN 9829
Harrietsham 13 TQ 8753
Harrington (Cumbr.) 40 NX 9926
Harrington (Lincs.) 35 TF 3671
Harrington (Northants.) 26 SP 7780
Harringworth 27 SP 9197
Harriseahead 33 SJ 8656
Harrogate 37 SE 3055
Harrold 27 SP 9456
Harrow 19 TQ 1388
Harrowbarrow 4 SX 3969
Harrowden 27 TL 0646
Harrow on the Hill 19 TQ 1586
Harsgeir 63 NB 1040
Harston (Cambs.) 20 TL 4251
Harston (Leic.) 34 SK 8331
Hart 42 NZ 4735
Hartburn 47 NZ 0886
Hartest 20 TL 8352
Hartfield 12 TQ 4735
Hartford (Cambs.) 27 TL 2572
Hartford (Ches.) 32 SJ 6372
Hartfordbridge 10 SU 7757
Hartford End 20 TL 6817
Harthill (Ches.) 32 SJ 4955
Harthill (Lothian) 50 NS 9064
Harthill (S Yorks.) 33 SK 4980
Hartington 33 SK 1360
Hartland 4 SS 2624
Hartland Quay 4 SS 2224
Hartlebury 25 SO 8470
Hartlepool 42 NZ 5032
Hartley (Cumbr.) 41 NY 7808
Hartley (Kent) 12 TQ 6166
Hartley (Kent) 12 TQ 7634
Hartley (Northum.) 47 NZ 3475
Hartley Wespall 10 SU 6958
Hartley Wintney 10 SU 7756
Hartlip 12 TQ 8364
Harton (N Yorks.) 38 SE 7061
Harton (Salop) 24 SO 4888
Harton (Tyne and Wear) 47 NZ 3864
Hartpury 17 SO 7924
Hartshill 26 SP 3293
Hartshorne 33 SK 3221
Hartsop 40 NY 4013
Hartwell 26 SP 7850
Hartwood 50 NS 8459
Harvel 12 TQ 6563
Harvington 25 SP 0548
Harvington Cross 25 SP 0549
Harwell 18 SU 4989
Harwich 21 TM 2431
Harwood (Durham) 41 NY 8133
Harwood (Gtr Mches.) 36 SD 7411
Harwood Dale 43 SE 9595
Harworth 38 SK 6291
Hascombe 11 TQ 0039
Haselbech 26 SP 7177

Hollandstoun 86 Jurby West

Hollandstoun 63 HY 7553
Hollesley 21 TM 3544
Hollingbourne 13 TQ 8455
Hollington (Derby.) 33 SK 2239
Hollington (E Susx) 12 TQ 7911
Hollington (Staffs.) 33 SK 0538
Hollingworth 37 SK 0096
Hollins 37 SD 8108
Hollinsclough 33 SK 0666
Hollins Green 32 SJ 6990
Hollinswood 24 SJ 6909
Hollinwood 32 SJ 5236
Hollocombe 6 SS 6311
Holloway 33 SK 3256
Hollowell 26 SP 6972
Hollybush (Gwent) 16 SO 1603
Hollybush (Here. and Worc.) 24 SO 7636
Hollybush (Strath.) 50 NS 3914
Holly End 28 TF 4906
Hollym 39 TA 3425
Holm (Isle of Lewis) 63 NB 4531
Holmbury St. Mary 11 TQ 1144
Holme (Cambs.) 27 TL 1987
Holme (Cumbr.) 40 SD 5278
Holme (Notts.) 34 SK 8059
Holme (W Yorks.) 37 SE 1005
Holme Chapel 37 SD 8728
Holme Hale 28 TF 8807
Holme Lacy 24 SO 5535
Holme Marsh 23 SO 3354
Holme next the Sea 28 TF 7043
Holme on the Wolds 39 SE 9646
Holmer 24 SO 5042
Holmer Green 19 SU 9097
Holmes Chapel 32 SJ 7667
Holmesfield 33 SK 3277
Holmeswood 36 SD 4316
Holme upon Spalding Moor 39 SE 8138
Holmewood 33 SK 4365
Holmfirth 37 SE 1408
Holmhead 50 NS 5620
Holmpton 39 TA 3623
Holmrook 40 SD 0799
Holmsgarth 63 HU 4642
Holne 5 SX 7069
Holnest 8 ST 6509
Holsworthy 4 SS 3403
Holsworthy Beacon 4 SS 3508
Holt (Clwyd) 32 SJ 4053
Holt (Dorset) 8 SU 0203
Holt (Here. and Worc.) 25 SO 8262
Holt (Norf.) 29 TG 0738
Holt (Wilts.) 17 ST 8661
Holtby 38 SE 6754
Holt End 25 SP 0769
Holt Heath 25 SO 8163
Holton (Lincs.) 35 TF 1181
Holton (Oxon.) 18 SP 6006
Holton (Somerset) 8 ST 6826
Holton (Suff.) 29 TM 4077
Holton Heath 8 SY 9491
Holton le Clay 39 TA 2802
Holton le Moor 39 TF 0797
Holton St. Mary 21 TM 0537
Holwell (Herts.) 19 TL 1633
Holwell (Leic.) 34 SK 7323
Holwell (Oxon.) 18 SP 2309
Holwick 41 NY 9026
Holworth 8 SY 7683
Holybourne 10 SU 7341
Holy Cross 25 SO 9279
Holyhead 30 SH 2482
Holymoorside 33 SK 3369
Holyport 11 SU 8977
Holystone 47 NT 9502
Holytown 50 NS 7760
Holywell (Cambs.) 27 TL 3370
Holywell (Clwyd) 32 SJ 1875
Holywell (Corn.) 2 SW 7658
Holywell (Dorset) 7 ST 5904
Holywell Green 37 SE 0918
Holywell Lake 7 ST 1020
Holywell Row 28 TL 7077
Holywood 45 NX 9480
Homer 24 SJ 6101
Homersfield 29 TM 2885
Hom Green 17 SO 5822
Homington 8 SU 1226
Honeyborough 14 SM 9506
Honeybourne 25 SP 1144
Honeychurch 6 SS 6202
Honey Hill 13 TR 1161
Honiley 26 SP 2472
Honing 29 TG 3227
Honingham 29 TG 1011
Honington (Lincs.) 34 SK 9443
Honington (Suff.) 28 TL 9174
Honington (Warw.) 26 SP 2642
Honiton 5 ST 1600
Honley 37 SE 1311
Hoo (Kent) 12 TQ 7872
Hooe (Devon.) 4 SX 5052
Hooe (E Susx) 12 TQ 6809
Hoo Green 21 TM 2559
Hook (Dyfed) 14 SM 9811
Hook (Hants.) 10 SU 7254
Hook (Humbs.) 38 SE 7525
Hook (Surrey) 11 TQ 1764
Hook (Wilts.) 17 SU 0784
Hooke (Dorset) 7 ST 5300
Hookgate 32 SJ 7435
Hook Norton 18 SP 3533
Hookway 6 SX 8598
Hookwood 11 TQ 2643
Hoole 32 SJ 4367
Hooton 32 SJ 3679
Hooton Levitt 38 SK 5291
Hooton Pagnell 38 SE 4808
Hooton Roberts 38 SK 4897
Hope (Clwyd) 32 SJ 3058
Hope (Derby.) 33 SK 1783
Hope (Devon.) 5 SX 6740
Hope (Powys) 23 SJ 2507
Hope (Salop) 23 SJ 3401
Hope Bagot 24 SO 5874
Hope Bowdler 24 SO 4792
Hopeman 61 NJ 1469
Hope Mansell 17 SO 6219
Hopesay 24 SO 3883
Hope under Dinmore 24 SO 5052
Hopton (Norf.) 29 TG 5200
Hopton (Salop) 32 SJ 5926
Hopton (Staffs.) 33 SJ 9426
Hopton (Suff.) 29 TL 9979
Hopton Cangeford 24 SO 5480
Hopton Castle 24 SO 3678
Hopton Wafers 24 SO 6476
Hopwas 25 SK 1705
Hopwood 25 SP 0375
Horam 12 TQ 5717
Horbling 35 TF 1135
Horbury 37 SE 2918
Horden 42 NZ 4441
Horderley 24 SO 4086
Hordle 9 SZ 2795
Hordley 32 SJ 3730
Horeb 15 SN 3942
Horham 29 TM 2172
Horkesley Heath 21 TL 9829
Horkstow 39 SE 9818
Horley (Oxon.) 26 SP 4143
Horley (W Susx) 11 TQ 2843
Hornblotton Green 7 ST 5833
Hornby (Lancs.) 41 SD 5868
Hornby (N Yorks) 42 NZ 3605
Horncastle 35 TF 2669
Hornchurch 20 TQ 5487
Horncliffe 53 NT 9249
Horndean 9 SU 7013
Horndon on the Hill 20 TQ 6683
Horne 12 TQ 3344
Horn Hill 19 TQ 0292
Horning 29 TG 3417
Horninghold 26 SP 8097
Horninglow 33 SK 2324
Horningsea 20 TL 4962
Horningsham 8 ST 8241
Horningtoft 29 TF 9323
Hornsby 46 NY 5150
Hornsea 39 TA 2047
Hornsey 20 TQ 3089
Hornton 26 SP 3945
Horrabridge 4 SX 5169
Horringer 20 TL 8261
Horsebridge (E Susx) 12 TQ 5911
Horsebridge (Hants.) 9 SU 3430
Horse Bridge (Staffs.) 33 SJ 9553
Horsebrook 25 SJ 8810
Horsehay 24 SJ 6707
Horseheath 20 TL 6147
Horsehouse 42 SE 0481
Horsell 11 SU 9959
Horseman's Green 32 SJ 4441
Horseway 27 TL 4287
Horsey 29 TG 4523
Horsford 29 TG 1915
Horsforth 37 SE 2337
Horsham (Here. and Worc.) 24 SO 7357
Horsham (W Susx) 11 TQ 1730
Horsham St. Faith 29 TG 2114
Horsington (Lincs.) 35 TF 1868
Horsington (Somer.) 8 ST 7023
Horsley (Derby.) 33 SK 3744
Horsley (Glos.) 17 ST 8398
Horsley (Northum.) 47 NY 8496
Horsley (Northum.) 47 NZ 0966
Horsley Cross 21 TM 1227
Horsleycross Street 21 TM 1228
Horsleyhill 52 NT 5319
Horsley Woodhouse 33 SK 3945
Horsmonden 12 TQ 7040
Horspath 18 SP 5704
Horstead 29 TG 2619
Horsted Keynes 12 TQ 3828
Horton (Avon) 17 ST 7684
Horton (Berks.) 11 TQ 0175
Horton (Bucks.) 19 SP 9219
Horton (Dorset) 8 SU 0307
Horton (Lancs.) 37 SD 8550
Horton (Northants.) 26 SP 8254
Horton (Northum.) 53 NU 0230
Horton (Staffs.) 33 SJ 9457
Horton (W Glam.) 15 SS 4785
Horton (Wilts.) 17 SU 0463
Horton Green 32 SJ 4549
Horton Heath 9 SU 4916
Horton in Ribblesdale 41 SD 8172
Horton Kirby 12 TQ 5668
Horwich 36 SD 6311
Horwood 6 SS 5027
Hose 34 SK 7329
Hosh 56 NN 8523
Hoswick 63 HU 4124
Hotham 39 SE 8934
Hothfield 13 TQ 9644
Hoton 34 SK 5722
Houbie 63 HU 6390
Hough 32 SJ 7151
Hougham 34 SK 8844
Hougharry 63 NF 7071
Hough Green 32 SJ 4885
Hough-on-the-Hill 34 SK 9246
Houghton (Cambs.) 27 TL 2871
Houghton (Cumbr.) 46 NY 4159
Houghton (Dyfed) 14 SM 9807
Houghton (Hants.) 9 SU 3331
Houghton (W Susx) 11 TQ 0111
Houghton Conquest 27 TL 0441
Houghton le Spring 47 NZ 3450
Houghton on the Hill 26 SK 6703
Houghton Regis 19 TL 0224
Houghton St. Giles 29 TF 9235
Houlsyke 43 NZ 7308
Hound Green 10 SU 7259
Houndslow 52 NT 6347
Houndwood 53 NT 8464
Hounslow 11 TQ 1276
Housetter 63 HU 3684
Houston 50 NS 4067
Houstry 67 ND 1534
Hove 11 TQ 2805
Hoveringham 34 SK 6946
Hoveton 29 TG 3018
Hovingham 38 SE 6675
How 46 NY 5056
How Caple 24 SO 6030
Howden 38 SE 7428
Howden-le-Wear 42 NZ 1633
Howe (Cumbr.) 40 SD 4588
Howe (Highld.) 67 ND 3062
Howe (Norf.) 29 TM 2799
Howe Green 20 TL 7403
Howell 35 TF 1346
Howe of Teuchar 62 NJ 7947
Howe Street (Essex) 20 TL 6914
Howe Street (Essex) 20 TL 6934
Howe, The 43 SC 1967
Howey 23 SO 0558
Howgate 51 NT 2457
Howick 53 NU 2517
Howlaws 52 NT 7242
Howle 32 SJ 6823
Howlett End 20 TL 5834
Howmore 63 NF 7636
Hownam 53 NT 7719
Hownam Law 53 NT 7921
Hownam Mains 53 NT 7820
Howsham (Humbs.) 39 TA 0404
Howsham (N Yorks.) 38 SE 7362
Howton 16 SO 4129
Howwood 50 NS 3960
Hoxne 29 TM 1877
Hoylake 32 SJ 2189
Hoyland Nether 37 SE 3600
Hoyland Swaine 37 SE 2604
Hubbert's Bridge 35 TF 2643
Huby 38 SE 5665
Hucclecote 17 SO 8717
Hucking 12 TQ 8358
Hucknall 34 SK 5349
Huddersfield 37 SE 1416
Huddington 25 SO 9457
Hudswell 42 NZ 1400
Huggate 39 SE 8855
Hughenden Valley 19 SU 8695
Hughley 24 SO 5697
Hugh Town 2 SV 9010
Hugmore 32 SJ 3752
Huish (Devon.) 6 SS 5311
Huish (Wilts.) 17 SU 1463
Huish Champflower 7 ST 0429
Huish Episcopi 7 ST 4226
Hulcott 19 SP 8516
Hulland 33 SK 2447
Hullavington 17 ST 8982
Hullbridge 20 TQ 8194
Hulme End 33 SK 1059
Hulme Walfield 33 SJ 8465
Hulne Park 53 NU 1514
Hulver Street 29 TM 4686
Humber Court 24 SO 5356
Humberston 39 TA 3105
Humberstone 34 SK 6206
Humbie 52 NT 4562
Humbleton (Humbs.) 39 TA 2234
Humbleton (Northum.) 53 NT 9728
Hume 52 NT 7041
Humshaugh 47 NY 9171
Huna 67 ND 3573
Huncoat 37 SD 7730
Huncote 26 SP 5197
Hundalee 52 NT 6418
Hunderthwaite 41 NY 9821
Hundleby 35 TF 3966
Hundleton 14 SM 9600
Hundon 20 TL 7348
Hundred Acres 9 SU 5911
Hundred End 36 SD 4122
Hundred, The 24 SO 5264
Hungarton 34 SK 6807
Hungerford (Berks.) 10 SU 3368
Hungerford (Hants.) 8 SU 1612
Hungerford Newtown 10 SU 3571
Hunmanby 43 TA 0977
Hunningham 26 SP 3768
Hunsdon 20 TL 4114
Hunsingore 38 SE 4253
Hunsonby 41 NY 5835
Hunspow 67 ND 2172
Hunstanton 28 TF 6741
Hunstanworth 47 NY 9449
Hunston (Suff.) 21 TL 9768
Hunston (W Susx) 9 SU 8601
Hunstrete 17 ST 6462
Hunt End 25 SP 0364
Hunter's Quay 49 NS 1879
Huntingdon 27 TL 2371
Huntingfield 29 TM 3374
Huntington (Here. and Worc.) 23 SO 2553
Huntington (Lothian) 52 NT 4875
Huntington (N Yorks.) 38 SE 6156
Huntington (Staffs.) 25 SJ 9713
Huntingtower 56 NO 0725
Huntley 17 SO 7219
Huntly 62 NJ 5339
Hunton (Kent) 12 TQ 7149
Hunton (N Yorks.) 42 SE 1892
Hunt's Cross 32 SJ 4385
Huntsham 7 ST 0020
Huntspill 7 ST 3045
Huntworth 7 ST 3134
Hunwick 42 NZ 1832
Hunworth 29 TG 0635
Hurdsfield 33 SJ 9274
Hurley (Berks.) 18 SU 8283
Hurley (Warw.) 26 SP 2495
Hurlford 50 NS 4536
Hurliness 63 ND 2888
Hurn 8 SZ 1296
Hursley 9 SU 4225
Hurst (Berks.) 10 SU 7972
Hurst (Gtr Mches.) 37 SD 9400
Hurst (N Yorks.) 42 NZ 0402
Hurstbourne Priors 10 SU 4346
Hurstbourne Tarrant 10 SU 3853
Hurst Green (E Susx) 12 TQ 7327
Hurst Green (Lancs.) 36 SD 6838
Hurst Green (Surrey) 12 TQ 3951
Hurstpierpoint 11 TQ 2816
Hurtwood Common 11 TQ 0743
Hurworth 42 NZ 3010
Hury 41 NY 9619
Husbands Bosworth 26 SP 6484
Husborne Crawley 19 SP 9535
Husinish 63 NA 9812
Husthwaite 38 SE 5175
Huthwaite 33 SK 4659
Huttoft 35 TF 5176
Hutton (Avon) 16 ST 3458
Hutton (Borders) 53 NT 9053
Hutton (Cumbr.) 40 NY 4326
Hutton (Essex) 20 TQ 6394
Hutton (Lancs.) 36 SD 4926
Hutton (N Yorks.) 38 SE 7667
Hutton Bonville 42 NZ 3300
Hutton Buscel 43 SE 9784
Hutton Conyers 42 SE 3273
Hutton Cranswick 39 TA 0252
Hutton End 40 NY 4538
Hutton Henry 42 NZ 4236
Hutton-le-Hole 43 SE 7090
Hutton Magna 42 NZ 1212
Hutton Roof (Cumbr.) 40 NY 3734
Hutton Roof (Cumbr.) 41 SD 5777
Hutton Rudby 42 NZ 4606
Hutton Sessay 42 SE 4776
Hutton Wandesley 38 SE 5050
Huxley 32 SJ 5061
Huxter (Shetld.) 63 HU 5662
Huyton 32 SJ 4490
Hycemoor 40 SD 0989
Hyde (Glos.) 17 SO 8801
Hyde (Gtr Mches.) 37 SJ 9294
Hyde Heath 19 SP 9300
Hydestile 11 SU 9740
Hynish 48 NL 9839
Hyssington 23 SO 3194
Hythe (Hants.) 9 SU 4207
Hythe (Kent) 13 TR 1635
Hythe End 11 TQ 0172
Hythie 62 NK 0051

Ibberton 8 ST 7807
Ible 33 SK 2457
Ibsley 8 SU 1509
Ibstock 33 SK 4010
Ibstone 18 SU 7593
Ibthorpe 10 SU 3753
Ibworth 10 SU 5654
Ickburgh 28 TL 8195
Ickenham 19 TQ 0786
Ickford 18 SP 6407
Ickham 13 TR 2258
Ickleford 19 TL 1831
Icklesham 13 TQ 8816
Ickleton 20 TL 4943
Icklingham 28 TL 7772
Ickwell Green 27 TL 1545
Icomb 17 SP 2122
Idbury 18 SP 2320
Iddesleigh 6 SS 5608
Ide 5 SX 8990
Ideford 5 SX 8977
Ide Hill 12 TQ 4851
Iden 13 TQ 9123
Iden Green 12 TQ 8031
Idlicote 26 SP 2844
Idmiston 8 SU 1937
Idridgehay 33 SK 2849
Idrigil 58 NG 3863
Idstone 18 SU 2584
Idvies 57 NO 5347
Ifield (W Susx) 11 TQ 2537
Ifield or Singlewell (Kent) 12 TQ 6471
Ifold 11 TQ 0231
Iford 12 TQ 4007
Ifton Heath 32 SJ 3236
Ightfield 32 SJ 5938
Ightham 12 TQ 5956
Iken 21 TM 4155
Ilam 33 SK 1351
Ilchester 7 ST 5222
Ilderton 53 NU 0121
Ilford 20 TQ 4586
Ilfracombe 6 SS 5147
Ilkeston 33 SK 4642
Ilketshall St. Andrew 29 TM 3887
Ilketshall St. Margaret 29 TM 3485
Ilkley 37 SE 1147
Illey 25 SO 9881
Illingworth 37 SE 0728
Illogan 2 SW 6643
Illston on the Hill 26 SP 7099
Ilmer 18 SP 7605
Ilmington 25 SP 2143
Ilminster 7 ST 3614
Ilsington 5 SX 7876
Ilston 15 SS 5590
Ilton (N Yorks.) 42 SE 1878
Ilton (Somer.) 7 ST 3517
Imachar 49 NR 8640
Imber 8 ST 9648
Immingham 39 TA 1714
Impington 20 TL 4463
Ince 32 SJ 4476
Ince Blundell 36 SD 3203
Ince-in-Makerfield 36 SD 5903
Inchbare 57 NO 6065
Inchberry 61 NJ 3155
Inchinnan 50 NS 4768
Inchlaggan 59 NH 1801
Inchnacardoch 59 NH 3710
Inchnadamph 64 NC 2522
Inchture 57 NO 2728
Inchyra 56 NO 1820
Indian Queens 2 SW 9158
Ingatestone 20 TQ 6499
Ingbirchworth 37 SE 2205
Ingestre 33 SJ 9724
Ingham (Lincs.) 34 SK 9483
Ingham (Norf.) 29 TG 3825
Ingham (Suff.) 28 TL 8570
Ingleby Arncliffe 42 NZ 4400
Ingleby Greenhow 42 NZ 5806
Inglesbatch 17 ST 7061
Inglesham 17 SU 2098
Ingleton (Durham) 42 NZ 1720
Ingleton (N Yorks.) 41 SD 6972
Inglewhite 36 SD 5439
Ingoe 47 NZ 0374
Ingoldisthorpe 28 TF 6832
Ingoldmells 35 TF 5668
Ingoldsby 34 TF 0030
Ingram 53 NU 0116
Ingrave 20 TQ 6292
Ings 40 SD 4498
Ingst 17 ST 5887
Ingworth 29 TG 1929
Inkberrow 25 SP 0157
Inkhorn 62 NJ 9239
Inkpen 10 SU 3564
Inkstack 67 ND 2570
Innellan 49 NS 1469
Innerleithen 51 NT 3336
Innerleven 57 NO 3700
Innermessan 44 NX 0863
Innerwick (Lothian) 52 NT 7273
Innerwick (Tays.) 56 NN 5947
Insch 62 NJ 6327
Insh 60 NH 8101
Inskip 36 SD 4537
Instow 6 SS 4730
Inver (Grampn.) 61 NO 2393
Inver (Highld.) 65 NH 8682
Inver (Tays.) 56 NO 0142
Inverailort 54 NM 7681
Inveralligin 59 NG 8457
Inverallochy 62 NK 0464
Inveramsay 62 NJ 7424
Inveran 65 NH 5797
Inveraray 55 NN 0908
Inverarish 58 NG 5535
Inverarity 57 NO 4444
Inverarnan 55 NN 3118
Inverasdale 64 NG 8286
Inverbervie 57 NO 8372
Invercreran 55 NN 0147
Inverdruie 60 NH 9010
Inverebrie 62 NJ 9233
Inveresk 51 NT 3471
Inverey 56 NO 0889
Inverfarigaig 60 NH 5224
Invergarry 59 NH 3101
Invergeldie 56 NN 7427
Invergordon 65 NH 7168
Invergowrie 57 NO 3430
Inverguseran 58 NG 7407
Inverhadden 56 NN 6757
Inverharroch 61 NJ 3831
Inverie 59 NG 7600
Inverinan 55 NM 9917
Inverinate 59 NG 9122
Inverkeilor 57 NO 6649
Inverkeithing 51 NT 1383
Inverkeithny 62 NJ 6246
Inverkip 49 NS 2071
Inverkirkaig 64 NC 0819
Inverlael 64 NH 1885
Inverlochlarig 55 NN 4318
Inver Mallie 55 NN 1388
Invermoriston 60 NH 4117
Invernaver 66 NC 7060
Inverness 60 NH 6645
Invernoaden 55 NS 1197
Inverquharity 57 NO 4057
Inverquhomery 62 NK 0246
Inverroy 55 NN 2581
Inverugie 62 NK 0947
Inveruglas 55 NN 3109
Inverurie 62 NJ 7721
Invervar 56 NN 6648
Inwardleigh 6 SX 5599
Inworth 21 TL 8717
Iping 9 SU 8522
Ipplepen 5 SX 8366
Ipsden 18 SU 6385
Ipstones 33 SK 0249
Ipswich 21 TM 1744
Irby 32 SJ 2584
Irby in the Marsh 35 TF 4763
Irby upon Humber 39 TA 1904
Irchester 27 SP 9265
Ireby (Cumbr.) 40 NY 2338
Ireby (Lancs.) 41 SD 6575
Ireland (Shetld.) 63 HU 3722
Ireleth 40 SD 2277
Ireshopeburn 41 NY 8638
Irlam 32 SJ 7194
Irnham 34 TF 0226
Iron Acton 17 ST 6783
Iron-Bridge 24 SJ 6703
Iron Cross 25 SP 0552
Ironside 62 NJ 8852
Ironville 33 SK 4351
Irstead 29 TG 3620
Irthington 46 NY 4961
Irthlingborough 27 SP 9470
Irton 43 TA 0084
Irvine 50 NS 3239
Isauld 67 NC 9765
Isbister (Shetld.) 63 HU 3791
Isbister (Whalsay) 63 HU 5763
Isfield 12 TQ 4417
Isham 27 SP 8873
Islawr-dref 22 SH 6815
Isle Abbotts 7 ST 3520
Isle Brewers 7 ST 3621
Isleham 28 TL 6474
Isle of Whithorn 44 NX 4736
Isleornsay 58 NG 6912
Islesburgh 63 HU 3369
Isleworth 11 TQ 1675
Isley Walton 33 SK 4225
Islington 20 TQ 3085
Islip (Northants.) 27 SP 9879
Islip (Oxon.) 18 SP 5214
Islivig 63 NA 9927
Istead Rise 12 TQ 6369
Itchen Abbas 9 SU 5332
Itchen Stoke 9 SU 5532
Itchingfield 11 TQ 1328
Itchington 17 ST 6586
Itteringham 29 TG 1430
Itton (Devon.) 6 SX 6898
Itton (Gwent) 16 ST 4896
Ivegill 40 NY 4143
Ivelet 41 SD 9398
Iver 19 TQ 0381
Iver Heath 19 TQ 0283
Iveston 47 NZ 1350
Ivinghoe 19 SP 9416
Ivinghoe Aston 19 SP 9518
Ivington 24 SO 4756
Ivington Green 24 SO 4656
Ivybridge 5 SX 6356
Ivychurch 13 TR 0227
Ivy Hatch 12 TQ 5854
Iwade 13 TQ 9067
Iwerne Courtney or Shroton 8 ST 8512
Iwerne Minster 8 ST 8614
Ixworth 29 TL 9370
Ixworth Thorpe 28 TL 9172

Jack Hill 37 SE 1951
Jackstown 62 NJ 7531
Jackton 50 NS 5953
Jacobstow (Corn.) 4 SX 1995
Jacobstowe (Devon.) 6 SS 5801
Jameston 14 SS 0599
Jamestown (Dumf. and Galwy.) 46 NY 2996
Jamestown (Highld.) 60 NH 4756
Jamestown (Strath.) 50 NS 3981
Janetstown 67 ND 1932
Jarrow 47 NZ 3265
Jawcraig 50 NS 8475
Jaywick 21 TM 1513
Jedburgh 52 NT 6520
Jeffreyston 14 SN 0906
Jemimaville 65 NH 7165
Jevington 12 TQ 5601
Johnby 40 NY 4333
Johnshaven 57 NO 7966
Johnston (Dyfed) 14 SM 9310
Johnstone (Strath.) 50 NS 4263
Johnstonebridge 45 NY 1091
Jordans 19 SU 9791
Jordanston 14 SM 9132
Jump 37 SE 3701
Juniper Green 51 NT 2068
Jurby East 43 SC 3899
Jurby West 43 SC 3598

Kaber 87 Kneeton

Place	Page	Grid ref.
Kaber	41	NY 7911
Kaimes (Lothian)	51	NT 2767
Kames (Strath.)	54	NM 8211
Kames (Strath.)	49	NR 9771
Kames (Strath.)	50	NS 6926
Kea	2	SW 8042
Keadby	39	SE 8311
Keal	35	TF 3763
Keal Coates	35	TF 3661
Kearsley	37	SD 7504
Kearstwick	41	SD 6079
Kearton	41	SD 9999
Keasden	41	SD 7266
Keddington (Lincs.)	35	TF 3388
Kedington (Suff.)	20	TL 7046
Kedleston	33	SK 2941
Keelby	39	TA 1610
Keele	32	SJ 8045
Keeley Green	27	TL 0046
Keeston	14	SM 9019
Keevil	17	ST 9157
Kegworth	33	SK 4826
Kehelland	2	SW 6241
Keig	62	NJ 6119
Keighley	37	SE 0641
Keilarsbrae	50	NS 8993
Keilhill	62	NJ 7259
Keillmore	48	NR 6880
Keillor	57	NO 2640
Keillour	56	NN 9725
Keils	48	NR 5268
Keinton Mandeville	7	ST 5430
Keir Mill	45	NX 8593
Keisby	35	TF 0328
Keiss	67	ND 3461
Keith	61	NJ 4350
Keithock	57	NO 6063
Kelbrook	37	SD 9044
Kelby	34	TF 0041
Keld (Cumbr.)	41	NY 5514
Keld (N Yorks.)	41	NY 8901
Keldholme	43	SE 7086
Kelfield	38	SE 5938
Kelham	34	SK 7755
Kellan	54	NM 5240
Kellas (Grampn.)	61	NJ 1654
Kellas (Tays.)	57	NO 4535
Kellaton	5	SX 8039
Kelleth	41	NY 6605
Kelling	29	TG 0942
Kellington	38	SE 5524
Kelloe	42	NZ 3435
Kelly	4	SX 3981
Kelly Bray	4	SX 3571
Kelmarsh	26	SP 7379
Kelmscot	18	SU 2499
Kelsale	21	TM 3865
Kelsall	32	SJ 5268
Kelshall	20	TL 3236
Kelso	52	NT 7333
Kelstern	35	TF 2590
Kelston	17	ST 6966
Keltneyburn (Tays.)	56	NN 7749
Kelty	51	NT 1494
Kelvedon	20	TL 8618
Kelvedon Hatch	20	TQ 5698
Kelynack	2	SW 3729
Kemback	57	NO 4115
Kemberton	24	SJ 7204
Kemble	17	ST 9897
Kemerton	25	SO 9437
Kemeys Commander	16	SO 3405
Kemnay	62	NJ 7315
Kempley	17	SO 6729
Kempsey	25	SO 8549
Kempsford	17	SU 1596
Kempston	27	TL 0347
Kempston Hardwick	27	TL 0244
Kempton	24	SO 3582
Kemp Town	12	TQ 3303
Kemsing	12	TQ 5558
Kenardington	13	TQ 9732
Kenchester	24	SO 4343
Kencot	18	SP 2504
Kendal	40	SD 5192
Kenderchurch	16	SO 4028
Kenfig	15	SS 8081
Kenfig Hill	15	SS 8483
Kenilworth	26	SP 2872
Kenley (Gtr London)	12	TQ 3259
Kenley (Salop)	24	SJ 5600
Kenmore (Highld.)	58	NG 7557
Kenmore (Tays.)	56	NN 7745
Kenn (Avon)	16	ST 4168
Kenn (Devon.)	5	SX 9285
Kennacley	63	NG 1794
Kennerleigh	5	SS 8107
Kennet	51	NS 9291
Kennethmont	62	NJ 5328
Kennett	20	TL 6968
Kennford	5	SX 9186
Kenninghall	29	TM 0386
Kennington (Kent)	13	TR 0245
Kennington (Oxon.)	18	SP 5202
Kennoway	57	NO 3402
Kennyhill	28	TL 6680
Kennythorpe	38	SE 7865
Kenovay	48	NL 9946
Kensaleyre	58	NG 4251
Kensington and Chelsea	11	TQ 2778
Kensworth	19	TL 0318
Kensworth Common	19	TL 0317
Kentallen	55	NN 0057
Kentchurch	16	SO 4125
Kentford	20	TL 7066
Kentisbeare	5	ST 0608
Kentisbury	6	SS 6144
Kentmere	40	NY 4504
Kenton (Devon.)	5	SX 9583
Kenton (Suff.)	21	TM 1965
Kentra	54	NM 6568
Kents Bank	40	SD 3975
Kent's Green	17	SO 7423
Kent's Oak	9	SU 3224
Kenwick	32	SJ 4230
Kenwyn	2	SW 8145
Kenyon	32	SJ 6295
Keoldale	66	NC 3866
Keose	63	NB 3521
Keppanach	55	NN 0262
Keppoch	59	NG 9621
Kepwick	42	SE 4690
Keresley	26	SP 3182
Kerne Bridge	17	SO 5819
Kerridge	33	SJ 9376
Kerris	2	SW 4427
Kerry	23	SO 1490
Kerrycroy	49	NS 1061
Kerry's Gate	24	SO 3933
Kersall	34	SK 7162
Kersey	21	TM 0044
Kershader	63	NB 3419
Kershopefoot	46	NY 4782
Kersoe	25	SO 9939
Kerswell	5	ST 0806
Kerswell Green	25	SO 8646
Kesgrave	21	TM 2245
Kessingland	29	TM 5286
Kestle Mill	2	SW 8459
Keston	12	TQ 4164
Keswick (Cumbr.)	40	NY 2723
Keswick (Norf.)	29	TG 2004
Keswick (Norf.)	29	TG 3533
Kettering	27	SP 8778
Ketteringham	29	TG 1503
Kettins	56	NO 2338
Kettlebaston	21	TL 9650
Kettlebridge	57	NO 3007
Kettlebrook	25	SK 2103
Kettleburgh	21	TM 2660
Kettleness	43	NZ 8315
Kettleshulme	33	SJ 9879
Kettlesing Bottom	37	SE 2257
Kettlestone	29	TF 9631
Kettlethorpe	34	SK 8475
Kettlewell	41	SD 9772
Ketton	27	SK 9704
Kew	11	TQ 1877
Kewstoke	16	ST 3363
Kexbrough	37	SE 3009
Kexby (Lincs.)	34	SK 8785
Kexby (N Yorks.)	38	SE 7050
Key Green	33	SJ 8963
Keyham	34	SK 6606
Keyhaven	9	SZ 3091
Keyingham	39	TA 2425
Keymer	12	TQ 3115
Keynsham	17	ST 6568
Keysoe	27	TL 0763
Keysoe Row	27	TL 0861
Keyston	27	TL 0475
Keyworth	34	SK 6130
Kibblesworth	47	NZ 2456
Kibworth Beauchamp	26	SP 6893
Kibworth Harcourt	26	SP 6894
Kidbrooke	12	TQ 4076
Kiddemore Green	25	SJ 8509
Kidderminster	25	SO 8376
Kiddington	18	SP 4122
Kidlington	18	SP 4913
Kidmore End	10	SU 6979
Kidsgrove	32	SJ 8354
Kidstones	41	SD 9581
Kidwelly	15	SN 4106
Kielder	46	NY 6293
Kiells	48	NR 4168
Kilbarchan	50	NS 4063
Kilbeg	58	NG 6506
Kilberry	48	NR 7164
Kilbirnie	50	NS 3154
Kilbride (Island of Skye)	58	NG 5820
Kilbride (South Uist)	63	NF 7514
Kilbride (Strath.)	54	NM 8525
Kilburn (Derby.)	33	SK 3845
Kilburn (N Yorks.)	42	SE 5179
Kilby	26	SP 6295
Kilcadzow	50	NS 8848
Kilchattan (Bute)	49	NS 1054
Kilchattan (Colonsay)	48	NR 3795
Kilchenzie	48	NR 6725
Kilcheran	54	NM 8238
Kilchiaran	48	NR 2060
Kilchoan	54	NM 4963
Kilchoman	48	NR 2163
Kilchrenan	55	NN 0322
Kilconquhar	57	NO 4802
Kilcot	17	SO 6925
Kilcoy	60	NH 5751
Kilcreggan	49	NS 2380
Kildale	42	NZ 6009
Kildalloig	48	NR 7518
Kildavanan	49	NS 0266
Kildonan (Highld.)	67	NC 9121
Kildonan (Island of Arran)	49	NS 0321
Kildonnan	54	NM 4985
Kildrummy	61	NJ 4617
Kildwick	37	SE 0145
Kilfinan	49	NR 9378
Kilfinnan	59	NN 2795
Kilgetty	14	SN 1207
Kilgwrrwg Common	16	ST 4797
Kilham (Humbs.)	39	TA 0564
Kilham (Northum.)	53	NT 8832
Kilkenneth	48	NL 9444
Kilkerran	44	NS 3003
Kilkhampton	4	SS 2511
Killamarsh	33	SK 4680
Killay	15	SS 6092
Killchianaig	48	NR 6486
Killean	48	NR 6944
Killearn	50	NS 5286
Killen	60	NH 6758
Killerby	42	NZ 1919
Killichonan	55	NN 5458
Killichronan	54	NM 5441
Killiechanate	55	NN 2481
Killiecrankie	56	NN 9162
Killilan	59	NG 9430
Killimster	67	ND 3156
Killin	55	NN 5732
Killinghall	37	SE 2858
Killingholme	39	TA 1416
Killington	41	SD 6188
Killochyett	52	NT 4545
Killocraw	48	NR 6630
Killundine	54	NM 5849
Kilmacolm	50	NS 3569
Kilmahumaig	48	NR 7893
Kilmaluag	58	NG 4374
Kilmany	57	NO 3821
Kilmarie	58	NG 5417
Kilmarnock	50	NS 4237
Kilmaron Castle	57	NO 3516
Kilmartin	54	NR 8398
Kilmaurs	50	NS 4141
Kilmelfort	54	NM 8413
Kilmeny	48	NR 3865
Kilmersdon	8	ST 6952
Kilmeston	9	SU 5825
Kilmichael Glassary	49	NR 8593
Kilmichael of Inverlussa	49	NR 7785
Kilmington (Devon.)	7	SY 2798
Kilmington (Wilts.)	8	ST 7736
Kilmorack	60	NH 4944
Kilmore (Island of Skye)	58	NG 6507
Kilmore (Strath.)	54	NM 8824
Kilmory (Highld.)	54	NM 5270
Kilmory (Island of Arran)	49	NR 9621
Kilmory (Rhum)	58	NG 3603
Kilmory (Strath.)	48	NR 7075
Kilmory Castle	49	NR 8686
Kilmuir (Highld.)	60	NH 6749
Kilmuir (Highld.)	65	NH 7573
Kilmuir (Island of Skye)	58	NG 2547
Kilmun	49	NS 1781
Kilnave	48	NR 2871
Kilndown	12	TQ 7035
Kilnhurst	38	SK 4697
Kilninian	54	NM 3945
Kilninver	54	NM 8221
Kiln Pit Hill	47	NZ 0454
Kilnsea	39	TA 4015
Kilnsey	41	SD 9767
Kilnwick	39	SE 9949
Kiloran	54	NR 3996
Kilpatrick	49	NR 9027
Kilpeck	24	SO 4430
Kilpheder	63	NF 7419
Kilphedir	67	NC 9818
Kilpin	38	SE 7726
Kilrenny	57	NO 5705
Kilsby	26	SP 5671
Kilspindie	56	NO 2225
Kilsyth	50	NS 7178
Kiltarlity	60	NH 5041
Kilton	7	ST 1644
Kilvaxter	58	NG 3869
Kilve	7	ST 1443
Kilvington	34	SK 7942
Kilwinning	50	NS 3043
Kimberley (Norf.)	29	TG 0704
Kimberley (Notts.)	33	SK 4944
Kimble	18	SP 8206
Kimblesworth	47	NZ 2547
Kimble Wick	18	SP 8007
Kimbolton (Cambs.)	27	TL 0967
Kimbolton (Here. and Worc.)	24	SO 5261
Kimcote	26	SP 5886
Kimmeridge	8	SY 9179
Kimmerston	53	NT 9535
Kimpton (Hants.)	10	SU 2746
Kimpton (Herts.)	19	TL 1718
Kinbrace	67	NC 8631
Kinbuck	56	NN 7905
Kincaple	57	NO 4518
Kincardine (Fife.)	51	NS 9387
Kincardine (Highld.)	65	NH 6089
Kincardine O'Neil	62	NO 5999
Kinclaven	56	NO 1538
Kincorth	62	NJ 9302
Kincraig	60	NH 8305
Kincraigie	56	NN 9849
Kindallachan	56	NN 9950
Kineton (Glos.)	17	SP 0926
Kineton (Warw.)	26	SP 3351
Kinfauns	56	NO 1622
Kingarth	49	NS 0956
Kingcoed	16	SO 4205
Kingerby	34	TF 0592
Kingham	18	SP 2523
Kingholm Quay	45	NX 9773
Kinghorn	51	NT 2686
Kinglassie	56	NT 2298
Kingoodie	57	NO 3320
Kingsand	4	SX 4350
Kingsbarns	57	NO 5912
Kingsbridge (Devon.)	5	SX 7344
Kingsbridge (Somer.)	7	SS 9837
King's Bromley	25	SK 1216
Kingsburgh	58	NG 3955
Kingsbury (Gtr London)	19	TQ 1989
Kingsbury (Warw.)	25	SP 2196
Kingsbury Episcopi	7	ST 4320
Kings Caple	17	SO 5628
Kingsclere	10	SU 5258
King's Cliffe	27	TL 0097
Kingscote	17	ST 8196
Kingscott	6	SS 5318
King's Coughton	25	SP 0858
Kingscross	49	NS 0428
King's Delph	27	TL 2595
Kingsdon	7	ST 5126
Kingsdown	13	TR 3748
Kingseat	51	NT 1290
Kingsey	18	SP 7406
Kingsfold	11	TQ 1636
Kingsford	25	SO 8281
Kingshall Street	21	TL 9161
King's Heath	25	SP 0781
Kingshouse	55	NN 5620
Kingskerswell	5	SX 8767
Kingskettle	57	NO 3008
Kingsland	24	SO 4461
Kings Langley	19	TL 0702
Kingsley (Ches.)	32	SJ 5474
Kingsley (Hants.)	10	SU 7838
Kingsley (Staffs.)	33	SK 0047
Kingsley Green	11	SU 8930
King's Lynn	28	TF 6220
Kings Meaburn	41	NY 6221
Kings Muir (Borders)	51	NT 2539
Kingsmuir (Fife)	57	NO 5409
Kingsmuir (Tays.)	57	NO 4849
Kingsnorth	13	TR 0039
King's Norton (Leic.)	26	SK 6800
King's Norton (W Mids)	25	SP 0579
King's Nympton	6	SS 6819
King's Pyon	24	SO 4350
Kings Ripton	27	TL 2576
King's Somborne	9	SU 3631
King's Stag	8	ST 7210
King's Stanley	17	SO 8103
King's Sutton	18	SP 4936
Kingstanding	25	SP 0794
Kingsteignton	5	SX 8773
King Sterndale	33	SK 0972
Kingsthorne	24	SO 4932
Kingsthorpe	26	SP 7563
Kingston (Cambs.)	20	TL 3455
Kingston (Devon.)	5	SX 6347
Kingston (Dorset)	8	ST 7509
Kingston (Dorset)	8	SY 9579
Kingston (Grampn.)	61	NJ 3365
Kingston (Hants.)	8	SU 1401
Kingston (I. of W.)	9	SZ 4781
Kingston (Kent)	13	TR 1951
Kingston (Lothian)	52	NT 5482
Kingston Bagpuize	18	SU 4098
Kingston Blount	18	SU 7399
Kingston by Sea	11	TQ 2205
Kingston Deverill	8	ST 8436
Kingstone (Here. and Worc.)	24	SO 4235
Kingstone (Somer.)	7	ST 3713
Kingstone (Staffs.)	33	SK 0629
Kingston Lisle	18	SU 3287
Kingston near Lewes	12	TQ 3908
Kingston on Soar	34	SK 5027
Kingston Russell	7	SY 5891
Kingston St. Mary	7	ST 2229
Kingston Seymour	16	ST 3966
Kingston upon Hull	39	TA 0929
Kingston upon Thames	11	TQ 1869
Kingstown	46	NY 3959
King's Walden	19	TL 1623
Kingswear	5	SX 8851
Kingswells	62	NJ 8606
Kingswinford	25	SO 8888
Kingswood (Avon)	17	ST 6473
Kingswood (Bucks.)	18	SP 6819
Kingswood (Glos.)	17	ST 7491
Kingswood (Kent)	12	TQ 8351
Kingswood (Powys)	23	SJ 2402
Kingswood (Surrey)	11	TQ 2455
Kingswood (Warw.)	25	SP 1871
Kingswood Common	23	SO 2854
Kings Worthy	9	SU 4932
Kington (Here. and Worc.)	23	SO 2956
Kington (Here. and Worc.)	25	SO 9955
Kington Langley	17	ST 9276
Kington Magna	8	ST 7622
Kington St. Michael	17	ST 9077
Kingussie	60	NH 7500
Kingweston	7	ST 5230
Kinharrachie	62	NJ 9231
Kinkell Bridge	56	NN 9316
Kinknockie	62	NK 0041
Kinlet	24	SO 7280
Kinloch (Fife.)	57	NO 2812
Kinloch (Highld.)	66	NC 3434
Kinloch (Tays.)	56	NO 1444
Kinloch (Tays.)	57	NO 2644
Kinlochard	55	NN 4502
Kinlochbervie	66	NC 2156
Kinlocheil	55	NM 9779
Kinlochewe	64	NH 0261
Kinloch Hourn	59	NG 9407
Kinlochleven	55	NN 1861
Kinlochmore	55	NN 1962
Kinloch Rannoch	56	NN 6658
Kinloss	61	NJ 0661
Kinmel Bay	31	SH 9881
Kinmuck	62	NJ 8119
Kinmundy	62	NJ 8817
Kinnadie	62	NJ 9643
Kinnaird	57	NO 2428
Kinneff	57	NO 8574
Kinnelhead	45	NT 0201
Kinnell	57	NO 6050
Kinnerley	32	SJ 3321
Kinnersley (Here. and Worc.)	23	SO 3449
Kinnersley (Here. and Worc.)	25	SO 8743
Kinnerton (Ches.)	32	SJ 3361
Kinnerton (Powys)	23	SO 2463
Kinnesswood	56	NO 1702
Kinninvie	42	NZ 0521
Kinnordy	57	NO 3654
Kinoulton	34	SK 6730
Kinross	56	NO 1102
Kinrossie	56	NO 1832
Kinsham	24	SO 3664
Kinsley	38	SE 4114
Kinson	8	SZ 0696
Kintbury	10	SU 3866
Kintessack	61	NJ 0060
Kintillo	56	NO 1317
Kintocher	62	NJ 5709
Kintore	62	NJ 7916
Kintra	48	NR 3248
Kinuachdrach Harbour	54	NR 7098
Kinveachy	60	NH 9118
Kinver	25	SO 8483
Kippax	38	SE 4130
Kippen	50	NS 6594
Kippford or Scaur	45	NX 8355
Kirbister (Orkney)	63	HY 3607
Kirbuster	63	HY 2825
Kirby Bedon	29	TG 2705
Kirby Cane	29	TM 3794
Kirby Cross	21	TM 2120
Kirby Grindalythe	39	SE 9067
Kirby Hill (N Yorks.)	42	NZ 1306
Kirby Hill (N Yorks.)	42	SE 3868
Kirby Knowle	42	SE 4687
Kirby le Soken	21	TM 2222
Kirby Mills	43	SE 7185
Kirby Misperton	43	SE 7779
Kirby Muxloe	26	SK 5104
Kirby Row	29	TM 3792
Kirby Sigston	42	SE 4194
Kirby Underdale	39	SE 8158
Kirby Wiske	42	SE 3784
Kirdford	11	TQ 0226
Kirivick	63	NB 2041
Kirk	67	ND 2859
Kirkabister	63	HU 4938
Kirkandrews upon Eden	46	NY 3558
Kirkbampton	46	NY 3056
Kirkbean	45	NX 9859
Kirk Bramwith	38	SE 6111
Kirkbride	46	NY 2356
Kirkbuddo	57	NO 5043
Kirkburn (Humbs.)	39	SE 9855
Kirkburton	37	SE 1912
Kirkby (Lincs.)	39	TF 0692
Kirkby (Mers.)	32	SJ 4098
Kirkby (N Yorks.)	42	NZ 5306
Kirkby Bellars	34	SK 7117
Kirkby Fleetham	42	SE 2894
Kirkby Green	35	TF 0857
Kirkby in Ashfield	33	SK 4956
Kirkby la Thorpe	35	TF 0946
Kirkby Lonsdale	41	SD 6178
Kirkby Malham	41	SD 8960
Kirkby Mallory	26	SK 4500
Kirkby Malzeard	42	SE 2374
Kirkbymoorside	43	SE 6986
Kirkby on Bain	35	TF 2362
Kirkby Overblow	37	SE 3249
Kirkby Stephen	41	NY 7708
Kirkby Thore	41	NY 6325
Kirkby Underwood	35	TF 0727
Kirkcaldy	51	NT 2791
Kirkcambeck	46	NY 5368
Kirkcarswell	45	NX 7549
Kirkcolm	44	NX 0268
Kirk Connel (Dumf. and Galwy.)	50	NS 7312
Kirkcowan	44	NX 3260
Kirkcudbright	45	NX 6851
Kirk Deighton	37	SE 3950
Kirk Ella	39	TA 0129
Kirkfieldbank	50	NS 8643
Kirkgunzeon	45	NX 8666
Kirk Hallam	33	SK 4540
Kirkham (Lancs.)	36	SD 4231
Kirkham (N Yorks.)	38	SE 7365
Kirkhamgate	37	SE 2922
Kirk Hammerton	38	SE 4655
Kirkharle	47	NZ 0182
Kirkheaton (Northum.)	47	NZ 0177
Kirkheaton (W Yorks.)	37	SE 1817
Kirkhill (Highld.)	60	NH 5545
Kirkhill (Tays.)	57	NO 6860
Kirkhope (Borders)	51	NT 3823
Kirkhouse	51	NT 3233
Kirkibost (Island of Skye)	58	NG 5417
Kirkibost (Isle of Lewis)	63	NB 1835
Kirkinch	57	NO 3144
Kirkinner	44	NX 4251
Kirkintilloch	50	NS 6573
Kirk Ireton	33	SK 2650
Kirkland (Cumbr.)	40	NY 0718
Kirkland (Cumbr.)	41	NY 6432
Kirkland (Dumf. and Galwy.)	50	NS 7214
Kirkland (Dumf. and Galwy.)	45	NX 8090
Kirk Langley	33	SK 2838
Kirkleatham	42	NZ 5921
Kirklevington	42	NZ 4309
Kirkley	29	TM 5491
Kirkleyditch	33	SJ 8778
Kirklington (Notts.)	34	SK 6757
Kirklington (N Yorks.)	42	SE 3181
Kirklinton	46	NY 4366
Kirkliston	51	NT 1274
Kirkmaiden	44	NX 1236
Kirk Merrington	42	NZ 2631
Kirk Michael (I. of M.)	43	SC 3190
Kirkmichael (Strath.)	44	NS 3408
Kirkmichael (Tays.)	56	NO 0860
Kirkmond le Mire	39	TF 1892
Kirkmuirhill	50	NS 7943
Kirknewton (Lothian)	51	NT 1166
Kirknewton (Northum.)	53	NT 9130
Kirk of Shotts	50	NS 8462
Kirkoswald (Cumbr.)	41	NY 5541
Kirkoswald (Strath.)	44	NS 2407
Kirkpatrick Durham	45	NX 7870
Kirkpatrick-Fleming	46	NY 2770
Kirk Sandall	38	SE 6007
Kirksanton	40	SD 1380
Kirk Smeaton	38	SE 5116
Kirkstall	37	SE 2635
Kirkstead	35	TF 1762
Kirkstile (Dumf. and Galwy.)	46	NY 3690
Kirkton (Borders)	52	NT 5413
Kirkton (Dumf. and Galwy.)	45	NX 9781
Kirkton (Fife.)	57	NO 3625
Kirkton (Grampn.)	62	NJ 6112
Kirkton (Grampn.)	62	NJ 6425
Kirkton (Grampn.)	62	NJ 6950
Kirkton (Grampn.)	62	NJ 8243
Kirkton (Grampn.)	62	NK 1050
Kirkton (Highld.)	59	NG 9141
Kirkton (Highld.)	65	NH 7998
Kirkton (Tays.)	56	NN 9618
Kirkton (Tays.)	57	NO 4246
Kirkton Manor	51	NT 2137
Kirkton of Airlie	57	NO 3151
Kirkton of Auchterhouse	57	NO 3338
Kirkton of Barevan	60	NH 8347
Kirkton of Collace	56	NO 1931
Kirkton of Craig	57	NO 7055
Kirkton of Culsalmond	62	NJ 6432
Kirkton of Durris	62	NO 7796
Kirkton of Glenbuchat	61	NJ 3715
Kirkton of Glenisla	56	NO 2160
Kirkton of Kingoldrum	57	NO 3354
Kirkton of Largo	57	NO 4203
Kirkton of Lethendy	56	NO 1241
Kirkton of Logie Buchan	62	NJ 9829
Kirkton of Maryculter	62	NO 8599
Kirkton of Menmuir	57	NO 5364
Kirkton of Monikie	57	NO 5138
Kirkton of Rayne	62	NJ 6930
Kirkton of Skene	62	NJ 8007
Kirkton of Strathmartine	57	NO 3735
Kirkton of Tealing	57	NO 4037
Kirktown	62	NK 0952
Kirktown of Alvah	62	NJ 6760
Kirktown of Auchterless	62	NJ 7141
Kirktown of Bourtie	62	NJ 8024
Kirktown of Deskford	61	NJ 5061
Kirktown of Fetteresso	57	NO 8585
Kirkwall	63	HY 4410
Kirkwhelpington	47	NY 9984
Kirk Yetholm	53	NT 8227
Kirmington	39	TA 1011
Kirn	49	NS 1878
Kirriemuir	57	NO 3854
Kirstead Green	29	TM 2997
Kirtlebridge	46	NY 2372
Kirtling	20	TL 6857
Kirtling Green	20	TL 6855
Kirtlington	18	SP 4919
Kirtomy	66	NC 7463
Kirton (Lincs.)	35	TF 3038
Kirton (Notts.)	34	SK 6869
Kirton (Suff.)	21	TM 2779
Kirton End	35	TF 2840
Kirton Holme	35	TF 2642
Kirton in Lindsey	39	SK 9398
Kishorn	59	NG 8340
Kislingbury	26	SP 6959
Kites Hardwick	26	SP 4668
Kittybrewster	62	NJ 9208
Kitwood	9	SU 6633
Kiveton Park	33	SK 4982
Knaith	34	SK 8284
Knap Corner	8	ST 8023
Knaphill	11	SU 9658
Knapp (Somer.)	7	ST 3025
Knapp (Tays.)	57	NO 2831
Knapton (Norf.)	29	TG 3034
Knapton (N Yorks.)	38	SE 5652
Knapton (N Yorks.)	39	SE 8775
Knapwell	20	TL 3362
Knaresborough	37	SE 3557
Knarsdale	46	NY 6753
Knaven	62	NJ 8943
Knayton	42	SE 4387
Knebworth	19	TL 2520
Kneesall	34	SK 7064
Kneesworth	20	TL 3444
Kneeton	34	SK 7146

Little Garway 89 Loosley Row

Little Garway 16 SO 4424
Little Gidding 27 TL 1382
Little Glemham 21 TM 3458
Little Gransden 27 TL 2755
Little Gruinard River 64 NG 9484
Little Hadham 20 TL 4422
Little Hallingbury 20 TL 5017
Littleham (Devon.) 4 SS 4323
Littleham (Devon.) 5 SY 0281
Littlehampton 11 TQ 0202
Little Harrowden 27 SP 8771
Little Haseley 18 SP 6400
Little Hautbois 29 TG 2521
Little Haven 14 SM 8513
Little Hay 25 SK 1202
Little Haywood 33 SK 0021
Littlehempston 5 SX 8162
Little Hereford 24 SO 5568
Little Hill 23 SO 1267
Little Horkesley 21 TL 9531
Little Horsted 12 TQ 4718
Little Horwood 18 SP 7930
Little Houghton (Northants.) 26 SP 8059
Littlehoughton (Northum.) 53 NU 2316
Little Hucklow 33 SK 1678
Little Hulton 36 SD 7103
Little Kingshill 19 SU 8999
Little Langford 8 SU 0436
Little Laver 20 TL 5409
Little Leigh 32 SJ 6175
Little Leighs 20 TL 7116
Little Lever 37 SD 7507
Little London (E Susx) 12 TQ 5420
Little London (Hants.) 10 SU 3749
Little London (Hants.) 10 SU 6259
Little London (Lincs.) 35 TF 2321
Little Longstone 33 SK 1871
Little Malvern 24 SO 7741
Little Maplestead 20 TL 8233
Little Marcle 24 SO 6736
Little Marlow 19 SU 8788
Little Massingham 28 TF 7924
Little Melton 29 TG 1506
Little Mill (Gwent) 16 SO 3102
Littlemill (Highld.) 60 NH 9150
Littlemill (Strath.) 50 NS 4515
Little Milton 18 SP 6100
Little Missenden 19 SU 9298
Littlemore 18 SP 5302
Little Ness (Salop) 32 SJ 4019
Little Newcastle 14 SM 9829
Little Newsham 42 NZ 1217
Little Oakley (Essex) 21 TM 2229
Little Oakley (Northants.) 27 SP 8985
Little Orton 46 NY 3555
Littleover 33 SK 3234
Little Paxton 27 TL 1862
Little Petherick 2 SW 9172
Little Plumstead 29 TG 3112
Littleport 28 TL 5686
Little Raveley 27 TL 2579
Little Ribston 37 SE 3853
Little Rissington 17 SP 1819
Little Ryburgh 29 TF 9628
Little Ryle 53 NU 0211
Little Salkeld 41 NY 5636
Little Sampford 20 TL 6533
Little Saxham 20 TL 7963
Little Scatwell 59 NH 3756
Little Shelford 20 TL 4551
Little Smeaton 38 SE 5216
Little Snoring 29 TF 9532
Little Somerford 17 ST 9684
Little Stainton 42 NZ 3420
Little Stanney 32 SJ 4173
Little Staughton 27 TL 1062
Little Steeping 35 TF 4362
Littlestone-on-Sea 13 TR 0824
Little Stonham 21 TM 1160
Little Stretton (Leic.) 26 SK 6600
Little Stretton (Salop) 24 SO 4491
Little Strickland 41 NY 5619
Little Stukeley 27 TL 2075
Little Tew 18 SP 3828
Little Thetford 28 TL 5376
Littlethorpe 42 SE 3269
Little Thurrock 12 TQ 6477
Littleton (Ches.) 32 SJ 4366
Littleton (Hants.) 9 SU 4532
Littleton (Somer.) 7 ST 4830
Littleton (Surrey) 11 TQ 0768
Littleton (Tays.) 57 NO 2633
Littleton Drew 17 ST 8280
Littleton-on-Severn 17 ST 5990
Littleton Pannell 17 ST 9954
Little Torrington 6 SS 4816
Little Totham 21 TL 8812
Little Town (Cumbr.) 40 NY 2319
Littletown (Durham) 42 NZ 3343
Little Wakering 21 TQ 9388
Little Walden 20 TL 5441
Little Waldingfield 21 TL 9245
Little Walsingham 29 TF 9336
Little Waltham 20 TL 7012
Little Warley 20 TQ 6090
Little Weighton 39 SE 9833
Little Welnetham 21 TL 8859
Little Wenlock 24 SJ 6406
Little Whittingham Green 29 TM 2877
Littlewick Green 10 SU 8379
Little Wilbraham 20 TL 5458
Little Witley 24 SO 7863
Little Wittenham 18 SU 5693
Little Wolford 18 SP 2635
Littleworth (Here. and Worc.) 25 SO 8850
Littleworth (Oxon.) 18 SU 3197
Littleworth (Staffs.) 25 SK 0111
Little Wyrley 25 SK 0105
Little Yeldham 20 TL 7739
Litton (Derby.) 33 SK 1674
Litton (N Yorks.) 41 SD 9074
Litton (Somer.) 17 ST 5954
Litton Cheney 7 SY 5490
Liverpool 32 SJ 3591
Liversedge 37 SE 2024
Liverton 43 NZ 7115
Livingston 51 NT 0568
Livingston Village 51 NT 0366
Lixwm 31 SJ 1671
Lizard 2 SW 6912
Llanaber 30 SH 6018
Llanaelhaearn 30 SH 3844
Llanafan 22 SN 6872
Llanafan-fechan 15 SN 9650
Llanallgo 30 SH 5085
Llanarmon 30 SH 4239
Llanarmon Dyffryn Ceiriog 31 SJ 1532
Llanarmon-yn-Ial 32 SJ 1856
Llanarth (Dyfed) 22 SN 4257
Llanarth (Gwent) 16 SO 3711
Llanarthney 15 SN 5320
Llanasa 31 SJ 1081
Llanbabo 30 SH 3786
Llanbadarn Fawr 22 SN 6080
Llanbadarn Fynydd 23 SO 0977
Llanbadarn-y-garreg 23 SO 1148
Llanbadrig 30 SH 3794
Llanbeder 16 ST 3890
Llanbedr (Gwyn.) 30 SH 5826
Llanbedr (Powys) 23 SO 1346
Llanbedr (Powys) 16 SO 2320
Llanbedr-Dyffryn-Clwyd 31 SJ 1459
Llanbedrgoch 30 SH 5180
Llanbedrog 30 SH 3231
Llanbedr-y-cennin 30 SH 7569
Llanberis 30 SH 5760
Llanbister 23 SO 1073
Llanblethian 15 SS 9873
Llanboidy 14 SN 2123
Llanbradach 16 ST 1490
Llanbrynmair 22 SH 9002
Llancarfan 16 ST 0570
Llancayo 16 SO 3603
Llancynfelyn 22 SN 6492
Llandaff 16 ST 1578
Llandanwg 30 SH 5728
Llandawke 14 SN 2811
Llanddaniel Fab 30 SH 4970
Llanddarog 15 SN 5016
Llanddeiniol 22 SN 5672
Llanddeiniolen 30 SH 5465
Llandderfel 31 SH 9837
Llanddeusant (Dyfed) 15 SN 7724
Llanddeusant (Gwyn.) 30 SH 3485
Llanddew 23 SO 0530
Llanddewi 15 SS 4689
Llanddewi Brefi 22 SN 6655
Llanddewi'r Cwm 23 SO 0348
Llanddewi Rhydderch 16 SO 3412
Llanddewi Velfrey 14 SN 1417
Llanddewi Ystradenni 23 SO 1068
Llanddoget 31 SH 8063
Llanddona 30 SH 5779
Llanddowror 14 SN 2514
Llanddulas 31 SH 9078
Llanddyfnan 30 SH 5078
Llandebie 15 SN 6215
Llandefaelog 15 SN 4111
Llandefaelog Fach 23 SO 0332
Llandefaelog-tre'r-graig 23 SO 1230
Llandefalle 23 SO 1135
Llandegai 30 SH 5970
Llandegfan 30 SH 5674
Llandegla 32 SJ 1952
Llandegley 23 SO 1363
Llandegveth 16 ST 3395
Llandeilo 15 SN 6322
Llandeilo Graban 23 SO 0944
Llandeilo'r Fan 15 SN 8934
Llandeloy 14 SM 8526
Llandenny 16 SO 4104
Llandevenny 16 ST 4186
Llandinabo 16 SO 5128
Llandinam 23 SO 0288
Llandissilio 14 SN 1221
Llandogo 16 SO 5204
Llandough (S Glam.) 15 SS 9972
Llandough (S Glam.) 16 ST 1673
Llandovery 15 SN 7634
Llandow 15 SS 9473
Llandre (Dyfed) 22 SN 6286
Llandrillo 31 SJ 0337
Llandrillo-yn-Rhos 31 SH 8380
Llandrindod Wells 23 SO 0561
Llandrinio 23 SJ 2917
Llandudno 31 SH 7782
Llandudno Junction 31 SH 7977
Llandwrog 30 SH 4556
Llandyfan 15 SN 6417
Llandyfodwg 15 SS 9587
Llandyfriog 14 SN 3241
Llandyfrydog 30 SH 4485
Llandygwydd 14 SN 2443
Llandyrnog 31 SJ 1064
Llandyssil 23 SO 1995
Llandyssul 15 SN 4140
Llanedeyrn 16 ST 2182
Llanegryn 22 SH 5905
Llanegwad 15 SN 5121
Llaneilian 30 SH 4692
Llanelian-yn-Rhos 31 SH 8376
Llanelidan 31 SJ 1050
Llanelieu 23 SO 1834
Llanellen 16 SO 3010
Llanelli (Dyfed) 15 SN 5000
Llanelltyd 30 SH 7119
Llanelly (Gwent) 16 SO 2314
Llanelwedd 23 SO 0451
Llanenddwyn 30 SH 5823
Llanengan 30 SH 2927
Llanerchymedd 30 SH 4183
Llanerfyl 23 SJ 0309
Llanfachraeth 30 SH 3182
Llanfachreth 30 SH 7522
Llanfaelog 30 SH 3373
Llanfaes 30 SH 6077
Llanfaethlu 30 SH 3186
Llanfaglan 30 SH 4760
Llanfair 30 SH 5729
Llanfair Caereinion 23 SJ 1006
Llanfair Clydogau 15 SN 6251
Llanfair Dyffryn Clwyd 31 SJ 1355
Llanfairfechan 30 SH 6874
Llanfair-Nant-Gwyn 14 SN 1637
Llanfairpwllgwyngyll 30 SH 5371
Llanfair Talhaiarn 31 SH 9269
Llanfair Waterdine 23 SO 2476
Llanfairynghornwy 30 SH 3290
Llanfair-yn-Neubwll 30 SH 3077
Llanfallteg 14 SN 1520
Llanfallteg West 14 SN 1519
Llanfaredd 23 SO 0651
Llanfechain 31 SJ 1820
Llanfechell 30 SH 3691
Llanfendigaid 22 SH 5605
Llanferres 31 SJ 1860
Llanfflewyn 30 SH 3689
Llanfihangel 23 SJ 0817
Llanfihangel ar-Arth 15 SN 4539
Llanfihangel Crucorney 16 SO 3220
Llanfihangel Glyn Myfyr 31 SH 9849
Llanfihangel Nant Bran 15 SN 9434
Llanfihangel-nant-Melan 23 SO 1758
Llanfihangel Rhydithon 23 SO 1466
Llanfihangel Rogiet 16 ST 4487
Llanfihangel-Tal-y-llyn 16 SO 1128
Llanfihangel uwch-Gwili 15 SN 4822
Llanfihangel-y-Creuddyn 22 SN 6676
Llanfihangel-y-pennant (Gwyn.) 30 SH 5245
Llanfihangel-y-Pennant (Gwyn.) 22 SH 6708
Llanfihangel-y-traethau 30 SH 5935
Llanfilo 23 SO 1133
Llanfoist 16 SO 2813
Llanfor 31 SH 9336
Llanfrechfa 16 ST 3193
Llanfrothen 30 SH 6241
Llanfrynach 16 SO 0726
Llanfwrog (Clwyd) 31 SJ 1157
Llanfwrog (Gwyn.) 30 SH 3083
Llanfyllin 31 SJ 1419
Llanfynydd (Clwyd) 32 SJ 2756
Llanfynydd (Dyfed) 15 SN 5527
Llanfyrnach 14 SN 2231
Llangadfan 23 SJ 0010
Llangadog 15 SN 7028
Llangadwaladr (Clwyd) 31 SJ 1730
Llangadwaladr (Gwyn.) 30 SH 3869
Llangaffo 30 SH 4468
Llangain 15 SN 3815
Llangammarch Wells 15 SN 9347
Llangan 15 SS 9577
Llangarron 16 SO 5221
Llangasty-Talyllyn 16 SO 1426
Llangathen 15 SN 5822
Llangattock 16 SO 2117
Llangattock Lingoed 16 SO 3620
Llangattock-Vibon-Avel 16 SO 4515
Llangedwyn 32 SJ 1824
Llangefni 30 SH 4575
Llangeinor 15 SS 9187
Llangeinwen 30 SH 4365
Llangeitho 22 SN 6159
Llangeler 15 SN 3739
Llangelynin 22 SH 5707
Llangendeirne 15 SN 4514
Llangennech 15 SN 5601
Llangennith 15 SS 4291
Llangenny 16 SO 2418
Llangernyw 31 SH 8767
Llangian 30 SH 2928
Llangiwg 15 SN 7205
Llanglydwen 14 SN 1826
Llangoed 30 SH 6079
Llangoedmor 14 SN 2046
Llangollen 32 SJ 2141
Llangolman 14 SN 1127
Llangorse 16 SO 1327
Llangorwen 22 SN 6084
Llangovan 16 SO 4505
Llangower 31 SH 9032
Llangranog 14 SN 3154
Llangristiolus 30 SH 4373
Llangrove 16 SO 5219
Llangua 16 SO 3926
Llangunllo 23 SO 2171
Llangunnor 15 SN 4219
Llangurig 22 SN 9080
Llangwm (Clwyd) 31 SH 9644
Llangwm (Dyfed) 14 SM 9909
Llangwm (Gwent) 16 ST 4299
Llangwm-isaf 16 SO 4200
Llangwnadl 30 SH 2033
Llangwyfan 31 SJ 1266
Llangwyllog 30 SH 4379
Llangwyryfon 22 SN 5970
Llangybi (Dyfed) 15 SN 6053
Llangybi (Gwent) 16 ST 3796
Llangybi (Gwyn.) 30 SH 4240
Llangyfelach 15 SS 6499
Llangynhafal 31 SJ 1263
Llangynidr 16 SO 1519
Llangynin 14 SN 2519
Llangynog (Dyfed) 14 SN 3316
Llangynog (Powys) 31 SJ 0526
Llanhamlach 16 SO 0926
Llanharan 15 ST 0083
Llanharry 15 ST 0080
Llanhennock 16 ST 3592
Llanhilleth 16 SO 2101
Llanidloes 23 SN 9584
Llaniestyn 30 SH 2633
Llanigon 23 SO 2139
Llanilar 22 SN 6275
Llanilid 15 SS 9781
Llanishen (Gwent) 16 SO 4703
Llanishen (S Glam.) 16 ST 1781
Llanllechid 30 SH 6268
Llanlleonfel 15 SN 9350
Llanllowell 16 ST 3998
Llanllugan 23 SJ 0402
Llanllwch 15 SN 3818
Llanllwchaiarn 23 SO 1192
Llanllyfni 30 SH 4651
Llanmadoc 15 SS 4493
Llanmaes 15 SS 9869
Llanmartin 16 ST 3989
Llanmerewig 23 SO 1593
Llanmihangel 15 SS 9771
Llanmorlais 15 SS 5294
Llannefydd 31 SH 9770
Llannon 15 SN 5408
Llannor 30 SH 3537
Llanon 22 SN 5167
Llanpumsaint 15 SN 4129
Llanreithan 14 SM 8628
Llanrhaeadr 31 SJ 0763
Llanrhaeadr-ym-Mochnant 31 SJ 1226
Llanrhidian 15 SS 4992
Llanrhos 31 SH 7880
Llanrhyddlad 30 SH 3389
Llanrhystud 22 SN 5369
Llanrian 14 SM 8131
Llanrothal 16 SO 4618
Llanrug 30 SH 5363
Llanrwst 31 SH 7961
Llansadurnen 14 SN 2810
Llansadwrn (Dyfed) 15 SN 6931
Llansadwrn (Gwyn.) 30 SH 5575
Llansaint 15 SN 3808
Llansamlet 15 SS 6997
Llansannan 31 SH 9365
Llansannor 15 SS 9977
Llansantffraed 16 SO 1223
Llansantffraed-Cwmdeuddwr 23 SN 9667
Llansantffraed-in-Elvel 23 SO 0954
Llansantffraid 22 SN 5167
Llansantffraid Glan Conway 31 SH 8075
Llansantffraid-ym-Mechain 32 SJ 2220
Llansawel 15 SN 6136
Llansilin 32 SJ 2028
Llansoy 16 SO 4402
Llanspyddid 16 SO 0328
Llanstadwell 14 SM 9505
Llanstephan (Dyfed) 14 SN 3511
Llanstephan (Powys) 23 SO 1142
Llantarnam 16 ST 3093
Llanthony 16 SO 2827
Llantilio-Crossenny 16 SO 3914
Llantilio Pertholey 16 SO 3116
Llantrisant (Gwent) 16 ST 3996
Llantrisant (Mid Glam.) 16 ST 0483
Llantrithyd 16 ST 0472
Llantwit Fardre 16 ST 0785
Llantwit Major 15 SS 9768
Llantysilio 32 SJ 1943
Llanuwchllyn 31 SH 8730
Llanvaches 16 ST 4391
Llanvair-Discoed 16 ST 4492
Llanvapley 16 SO 3614
Llanvetherine 16 SO 3617
Llanveynoe 23 SO 3031
Llanvihangel Gobion 16 SO 3409
Llanvihangel-Ystern-Llewern 16 SO 4313
Llanwarne 16 SO 5028
Llanwddyn 31 SJ 0219
Llanwenog 15 SN 4945
Llanwern 16 ST 3688
Llanwinio 14 SN 2626
Llanwnda (Dyfed) 14 SM 9339
Llanwnda (Gwyn.) 30 SH 4758
Llanwnen 15 SN 5347
Llanwnog 23 SO 0293
Llanwrda 15 SN 7131
Llanwrin 22 SH 7803
Llanwrthwl 23 SN 9763
Llanwrtyd 15 SN 8647
Llanwrtyd Wells 15 SN 8746
Llanwyddelan 23 SJ 0801
Llanyblodwel 32 SJ 2322
Llanybri 14 SN 3312
Llanybyther 15 SN 5244
Llanycefn 14 SN 0923
Llanychaer Bridge 14 SM 9835
Llanycrwys 15 SN 6445
Llanymawddwy 31 SH 9019
Llanymynech 32 SJ 2620
Llanynghenedl 30 SH 3181
Llanynys 31 SJ 1062
Llanyre 23 SO 0462
Llanystumdwy 30 SH 4738
Llanywern 16 SO 1028
Llawhaden 14 SN 0717
Llawnt 32 SJ 2430
Llawryglyn 23 SN 9291
Llay 32 SJ 3255
Llechcynfarwy 30 SH 3881
Llechfaen 16 SO 0828
Llechryd (Dyfed) 14 SN 2243
Llechryd (Mid Glam.) 16 SO 1009
Llechrydau 32 SJ 2234
Lledrod (Clwyd) 32 SJ 2229
Lledrod (Dyfed) 22 SN 6470
Llidiadnenog 15 SN 5437
Llidiardau 30 SH 1929
Llithfaen 30 SH 3543
Llong 32 SJ 2562
Llowes 23 SO 1941
Llwydcoed 15 SN 9905
Llwyn 23 SO 2880
Llwyncelyn 22 SN 4459
Llwyndafydd 22 SN 3755
Llwynderw 23 SJ 2004
Llwyndyrys 30 SH 3741
Llwyngwril 22 SH 5909
Llwynhendy 15 SS 5599
Llwynmawr 32 SJ 2236
Llwynypia 15 SS 9993
Llynclys 32 SJ 2924
Llynfaes 30 SH 4178
Llysfaen 31 SH 8977
Llyswen 23 SO 1337
Llysworney 15 SS 9674
Llys-y-fran 14 SN 0424
Llywel 15 SN 8630
Loan 51 NS 9575
Loanend 53 NT 9450
Loanhead 51 NT 2765
Loans 50 NS 3431
Lochailort (Highld.) 54 NM 7682
Lochaline (Highld.) 54 NM 6744
Lochans 44 NX 0656
Locharbriggs 45 NX 9980
Lochawe (Strath.) 55 NN 1227
Lochboisdale (S. Uist) 63 NF 7820
Lochbuie (Strath.) 54 NM 6125
Lochcarron (Highld.) 59 NG 9039
Lochdonhead 54 NM 7333
Lochearnhead 56 NN 5823
Lochee 57 NO 3631
Lochend (Highld.) 67 ND 2668
Lochend (Highld.) 60 NH 5937
Locheport (N. Uist) 63 NF 8563
Lochfoot 45 NX 8973
Lochgair 49 NR 9290
Lochgarthside 60 NH 5219
Lochgelly 51 NT 1893
Lochgilphead 49 NR 8687
Lochgoilhead 55 NN 1901
Lochhill 61 NJ 2964
Lochinver (Highld.) 64 NC 0922
Lochlane 56 NN 8320
Loch Lubnaig 55 NN 5713
Lochluichart 64 NH 3262
Lochmaben 45 NY 0882
Lochnaw Castle 44 NW 9962
Lochore 56 NT 1796
Lochranza (Island of Arran) 49 NR 9350
Lochside (Grampn.) 57 NO 7464
Lochside (Highld.) 67 NC 8735
Loch Sionascaig 64 NC 1213
Loch Skealtar 63 NF 8968
Loch Skeen 51 NT 1716
Loch Skerrow 45 NX 6068
Loch Skiach 56 NN 9547
Lochskipport (South Uist) 63 NF 8238
Loch Tollaidh 64 NG 8478
Lochton 62 NO 7592
Lochwinnoch 50 NS 3558
Lochwood (Dumf. and Galwy.) 45 NY 0896
Lochwood (Strath.) 50 NS 6966
Lockengate 4 SX 0361
Lockerbie 45 NY 1381
Lockeridge 17 SU 1467
Lockerley 9 SU 2925
Locking 16 ST 3659
Lockington (Humbs.) 39 SE 9947
Lockington (Leic.) 33 SK 4628
Lockleywood 32 SJ 6828
Lockmaddy 63 NF 9168
Locks Heath 9 SU 5207
Lockton 43 SE 8489
Loddington (Leic.) 26 SK 7802
Loddington (Northants.) 26 SP 8178
Loddiswell 5 SX 7148
Loddon 29 TM 3698
Lode 20 TL 5362
Loders 7 SY 4994
Lodsworth 11 SU 9223
Lofthouse (N Yorks.) 42 SE 1073
Lofthouse (W Yorks.) 37 SE 3325
Loftus 43 NZ 7118
Logan 50 NS 5820
Logan Mains 44 NX 0942
Loggerheads 32 SJ 7336
Loggie 64 NH 1491
Logie (Fife.) 57 NO 4020
Logie (Grampn.) 62 NK 0356
Logie (Tays.) 57 NO 6963
Logie Coldstone 61 NJ 4304
Logie Hill 65 NH 7776
Logie Newton 62 NJ 6638
Logie Pert 57 NO 6664
Logierait 56 NN 9752
Login 14 SN 1623
Lolworth 20 TL 3664
Lonbain 58 NG 6853
Londesborough 39 SE 8645
London 12 TQ 3079
London Colney 19 TL 1603
Londonderry 42 SE 3087
Londonthorpe 34 SK 9537
Londubh 64 NG 8680
Long Ashton 16 ST 5470
Long Bennington 34 SK 8344
Longbenton 47 NZ 2668
Longborough 17 SP 1729
Long Bredy 7 SY 5690
Longbridge (Warw.) 26 SP 2662
Longbridge (W Mids.) 25 SP 0178
Longbridge Deverill 8 ST 8640
Long Buckby 26 SP 6267
Longburton 8 ST 6412
Long Clawson 34 SK 7227
Longcliffe 33 SK 2255
Long Common 9 SU 5014
Long Compton (Staffs.) 33 SJ 8522
Long Compton (Warw.) 18 SP 2832
Longcot 18 SU 2790
Long Crendon 18 SP 6908
Long Crichel 8 ST 9710
Longcroft 50 NS 7979
Longden 24 SJ 4306
Long Ditton 11 TQ 1666
Longdon (Here. and Worc.) 25 SO 8336
Longdon (Staffs.) 25 SK 0714
Longdon upon Tern 24 SJ 6215
Longdown 5 SX 8691
Longdowns 2 SW 7434
Long Drax 38 SE 6528
Long Duckmanton 33 SK 4371
Long Eaton 33 SK 4933
Longfield 12 TQ 6068
Longford (Derby.) 33 SK 2137
Longford (Glos.) 17 SO 8320
Longford (Gtr London) 11 TQ 0576
Longford (Salop) 32 SJ 6433
Longford (Salop) 32 SJ 7218
Longford (W Mids.) 26 SP 3583
Longforgan 57 NO 3129
Longformacus 52 NT 6957
Longframlington 47 NU 1201
Longham (Dorset) 8 SZ 0697
Longham (Norf.) 29 TF 9415
Long Hanborough 18 SP 4114
Long Hermiston 51 NT 1770
Longhirst 47 NZ 2289
Longhope (Glos.) 17 SO 6819
Longhorsley 47 NZ 1494
Longhoughton 53 NU 2414
Long Itchington 26 SP 4165
Long Lawford 26 SP 4775
Longley Green 24 SO 7350
Long Load 7 ST 4623
Longmanhill 62 NJ 7462
Long Marston (Herts.) 19 SP 8915
Long Marston (N Yorks.) 38 SE 4951
Long Marston (Warw.) 25 SP 1548
Long Marton 41 NY 6624
Long Melford 20 TL 8646
Longmoor Camp 9 SU 7930
Longmorn 61 NJ 2358
Long Newton (Cleve.) 42 NZ 3816
Long Newton (Glos.) 17 ST 9092
Longnewton 52 NT 5827
Longney 17 SO 7612
Longniddry 52 NT 4476
Longnor (Salop) 24 SJ 4800
Longnor (Staffs.) 33 SK 0864
Longparish 10 SU 4344
Long Preston 37 SD 8357
Longridge (Lancs.) 36 SD 6037
Longridge (Lothian) 51 NS 9462
Longriggend 50 NS 8270
Long Riston 39 TA 1242
Longsdon 33 SJ 9554
Longside 62 NK 0347
Longsleddale 40 NY 4902
Longslow 32 SJ 6535
Longstanton 20 TL 3966
Longstock 10 SU 3536
Long Stowe 20 TL 3054
Long Stratton 29 TM 1992
Long Street 26 SP 7947
Long Sutton (Hants.) 10 SU 7347
Long Sutton (Lincs.) 35 TF 4322
Long Sutton (Somer.) 7 ST 4625
Longthorpe 27 TL 1698
Longton (Lancs.) 36 SD 4725
Longton (Staffs.) 33 SJ 9043
Longtown (Cumbr.) 46 NY 3768
Longtown (Here. and Worc.) 16 SO 3228
Longville in the Dale 24 SO 5393
Long Whatton 33 SK 4723
Longwick 18 SP 7805
Long Wittenham 18 SU 5493
Longwitton 47 NZ 0788
Longwood 24 SJ 6007
Longworth 18 SU 3899
Longyester 52 NT 5465
Lonmore 58 NG 2646
Loose 12 TQ 7552
Loosley Row 18 SP 8100

Lootcherbrae 90 Melvaig

Lootcherbrae ... 62 ... NJ 6054
Lopcombe Corner ... 9 ... SU 2435
Lopen ... 7 ... ST 4214
Loppington ... 32 ... SJ 4629
Lorbottle ... 47 ... NU 0306
Lornty ... 56 ... NO 1746
Loscoe ... 33 ... SK 4247
Lossiemouth ... 61 ... NJ 2370
Lossit ... 48 ... NR 1856
Lostock Gralam ... 32 ... SJ 6874
Lostwithiel ... 4 ... SX 1059
Lothbeg ... 67 ... NC 9410
Lothersdale ... 37 ... SD 9545
Lothmore ... 67 ... NC 9611
Loudwater ... 19 ... SU 8990
Loughborough ... 34 ... SK 5319
Loughor ... 15 ... SS 5898
Loughton (Bucks.) ... 19 ... SP 8337
Loughton (Essex) ... 20 ... TQ 4296
Loughton (Salop) ... 24 ... SO 6183
Lound (Lincs.) ... 35 ... TF 0618
Lound (Notts.) ... 34 ... SK 6986
Lound (Suff.) ... 29 ... TM 5099
Lount ... 33 ... SK 3819
Louth ... 35 ... TF 3287
Love Clough ... 37 ... SD 8126
Lover ... 9 ... SU 2120
Loversall ... 38 ... SK 5798
Loves Green ... 20 ... TL 6404
Loveston ... 14 ... SN 0808
Lovington ... 7 ... ST 5931
Low Bradfield ... 37 ... SK 2691
Low Bradley ... 37 ... SE 0048
Low Braithwaite ... 40 ... NY 4242
Low Brunton ... 47 ... NY 9269
Low Burnham ... 38 ... SE 7702
Lowca ... 40 ... NX 9821
Low Catton ... 38 ... SE 7053
Low Coniscliffe ... 42 ... NZ 2514
Low Crosby ... 46 ... NY 4459
Lowdham ... 34 ... SK 6646
Low Dinsdale ... 42 ... NZ 3411
Low Eggborough ... 38 ... SE 5522
Lower Aisholt ... 7 ... ST 2035
Lower Assendon ... 18 ... SU 7484
Lower Beeding ... 11 ... TQ 2227
Lower Benefield ... 27 ... SP 9888
Lower Bentham ... 41 ... SD 6469
Lower Boddington ... 26 ... SP 4752
Lower Bullingham ... 24 ... SO 5038
Lower Cam ... 17 ... SO 7401
Lower Chapel ... 15 ... SO 0235
Lower Chute ... 10 ... SU 3153
Lower Cwmtwrch ... 15 ... SN 7710
Lower Darwen ... 36 ... SD 6824
Lower Down ... 23 ... SO 3384
Lower Dunsforth ... 38 ... SE 4464
Lower Farringdon ... 9 ... SU 7035
Lower Frankton ... 32 ... SJ 3732
Lower Froyle ... 10 ... SU 7544
Lower Gledfield ... 65 ... NH 5990
Lower Green ... 29 ... TF 9837
Lower Halstow ... 13 ... TQ 8567
Lower Hardres ... 13 ... TR 1453
Lower Heyford ... 18 ... SP 4824
Lower Higham ... 12 ... TQ 7172
Lower Hordley ... 32 ... SJ 3929
Lower Killeyan ... 48 ... NR 2743
Lower Langford ... 16 ... ST 4660
Lower Largo ... 57 ... NO 4102
Lower Lemington ... 18 ... SP 2134
Lower Lye ... 24 ... SO 4067
Lower Maes-coed ... 23 ... SO 3431
Lower Mayland ... 21 ... TL 9101
Lower Moor ... 25 ... SO 9847
Lower Nazeing ... 20 ... TL 3906
Lower Penarth ... 16 ... ST 1869
Lower Penn ... 25 ... SO 8696
Lower Pennington ... 9 ... SZ 3193
Lower Peover ... 32 ... SJ 7474
Lower Pitcalzean ... 65 ... NH 8070
Lower Quinton ... 25 ... SP 1847
Lower Shader ... 63 ... NB 3854
Lower Shelton ... 27 ... SP 9942
Lower Shiplake ... 10 ... SU 7779
Lower Shuckburgh ... 26 ... SP 4862
Lower Slaughter ... 17 ... SP 1622
Lower Stanton St. Quintin ... 17 ... ST 9180
Lower Sundon ... 19 ... TL 0526
Lower Swanwick ... 9 ... SU 4909
Lower Swell ... 17 ... SP 1725
Lower Tysoe ... 26 ... SP 3445
Lower Upham ... 9 ... SU 5219
Lower Vexford ... 7 ... ST 1135
Lower Weare ... 7 ... ST 4053
Lower Wield ... 10 ... SU 6340
Lower Winchendon ... 18 ... SP 7312
Lower Woodend ... 18 ... SU 8088
Lower Woodford ... 8 ... SU 1235
Lowesby ... 34 ... SK 7207
Lowestoft ... 29 ... TM 5493
Lowestoft End ... 29 ... TM 5394
Loweswater ... 40 ... NY 1421
Low Gate ... 47 ... NY 9064
Lowgill (Cumbr.) ... 41 ... SD 6297
Lowgill (Lancs.) ... 41 ... SD 6564
Low Ham ... 7 ... ST 4329
Low Hartsop ... 40 ... NY 4013
Low Hesket ... 46 ... NY 4646
Low Hesleyhurst ... 47 ... NZ 0997
Lowick (Cumbr.) ... 40 ... SD 2985
Lowick (Northants.) ... 27 ... SP 9781
Lowick (Northum.) ... 53 ... NU 0139
Low Mill ... 42 ... SE 6795
Low Moor ... 36 ... SD 7241
Lownie Moor ... 57 ... NO 4848
Low Redford ... 42 ... NZ 0731
Low Row (Cumbr.) ... 46 ... NY 5863
Low Row (N Yorks.) ... 41 ... SD 9897
Low Santon ... 39 ... SE 9312
Lowsonford ... 25 ... SP 1867
Low Street ... 29 ... TG 3424
Lowthorpe ... 39 ... TA 0860
Low Thurlton ... 29 ... TM 4299
Lowton ... 32 ... SJ 6197
Lowton Common ... 32 ... SJ 6397
Low Torry ... 51 ... NT 0086
Low Waters ... 50 ... NS 7353
Low Worsall ... 42 ... NZ 3909
Loxbeare ... 6 ... SS 9116
Loxhill ... 11 ... TQ 0037
Loxhore ... 6 ... SS 6138
Loxley ... 26 ... SP 2563
Loxton ... 16 ... ST 3755
Loxwood ... 11 ... TQ 0431
Lubenham ... 26 ... SP 7087
Luccombe ... 6 ... SS 9144
Luccombe Village ... 9 ... SZ 5880
Lucker ... 53 ... NU 1530
Luckett ... 4 ... SX 3873
Luckington ... 17 ... ST 8383
Lucklawhill ... 57 ... NO 4222
Luckwell Bridge ... 6 ... SS 9038
Lucton ... 24 ... SO 4364
Ludag ... 63 ... NF 7714
Ludborough ... 39 ... TF 2995
Ludchurch ... 14 ... SN 1411
Luddenden ... 37 ... SE 0425
Luddesdown ... 12 ... TQ 6766
Luddington ... 39 ... SE 8216
Ludford (Lincs.) ... 35 ... TF 1989
Ludford (Salop) ... 24 ... SO 5173
Ludgershall (Bucks.) ... 18 ... SP 6617
Ludgershall (Wilts.) ... 10 ... SU 2650
Ludgvan ... 2 ... SW 5033
Ludham ... 29 ... TG 3818
Ludlow ... 24 ... SO 5175
Ludwell ... 8 ... ST 9122
Ludworth ... 42 ... NZ 3641
Luffincott ... 4 ... SX 3394
Luffness ... 52 ... NT 4780
Lugar ... 50 ... NS 5821
Luggiebank ... 50 ... NS 7672
Lugton ... 50 ... NS 4152
Lugwardine ... 24 ... SO 5441
Luib ... 58 ... NG 5628
Lulham ... 24 ... SO 4041
Lullingstone Castle ... 12 ... TQ 5364
Lullington (Derby.) ... 33 ... SK 2513
Lullington (Somer.) ... 8 ... ST 7851
Lulsgate Bottom ... 16 ... ST 5065
Lulsley ... 24 ... SO 7455
Lumb ... 37 ... SE 0221
Lumby ... 38 ... SE 4830
Lumloch ... 50 ... NS 6369
Lumphanan ... 62 ... NJ 5804
Lumphinnans ... 51 ... NT 1692
Lumsdaine ... 53 ... NT 8769
Lumsden ... 61 ... NJ 4722
Lunan ... 57 ... NO 6851
Lunanhead ... 57 ... NO 4752
Luncarty ... 56 ... NO 0929
Lund (Humbs.) ... 39 ... SE 9648
Lund (N Yorks.) ... 38 ... SE 6532
Lundie (Tays.) ... 57 ... NO 2836
Lundin Links ... 57 ... NO 4002
Lunna ... 63 ... HU 4869
Lunning ... 63 ... HU 5066
Lunsford's Cross ... 12 ... TQ 7210
Lunt ... 36 ... SD 3401
Luntley ... 24 ... SO 3955
Luppitt ... 5 ... ST 1606
Lupton ... 41 ... SD 5581
Lurgashall ... 11 ... SU 9326
Lurgmore ... 60 ... NH 5937
Lusby ... 35 ... TF 3367
Luskentyre ... 63 ... NG 0699
Luss ... 50 ... NS 3592
Lusta ... 58 ... NG 2756
Lustleigh ... 5 ... SX 7881
Luston ... 24 ... SO 4863
Luthermuir ... 57 ... NO 6568
Luthrie ... 57 ... NO 3219
Luton (Beds.) ... 19 ... TL 0821
Luton (Devon.) ... 5 ... SX 9076
Luton (Kent) ... 12 ... TQ 7766
Lutterworth ... 26 ... SP 5484
Lutton (Devon.) ... 4 ... SX 5959
Lutton (Lincs.) ... 35 ... TF 4325
Lutton (Northants.) ... 27 ... TL 1187
Luxborough ... 7 ... SS 9738
Luxulyan ... 4 ... SX 0458
Lybster ... 67 ... ND 2435
Lydbury North ... 23 ... SO 3486
Lydcott ... 6 ... SS 6936
Lydd ... 13 ... TR 0421
Lydden ... 13 ... TR 2645
Lyddington ... 27 ... SP 8797
Lydd-on-Sea ... 13 ... TR 0819
Lydeard St. Lawrence ... 7 ... ST 1232
Lydford (Devon.) ... 4 ... SX 5084
Lydford (Somer.) ... 7 ... ST 5731
Lydgate ... 37 ... SD 9225
Lydham ... 23 ... SO 3391
Lydiard Millicent ... 17 ... SU 0986
Lydiate ... 36 ... SD 3604
Lydlinch ... 8 ... ST 7413
Lydney ... 17 ... SO 6203
Lydstep ... 14 ... SS 0898
Lye ... 25 ... SO 9284
Lye Green ... 19 ... SP 9703
Lyford ... 18 ... SU 3994
Lymbridge Green ... 13 ... TR 1243
Lyme Regis ... 7 ... SY 3492
Lyminge ... 13 ... TR 1641
Lymington ... 9 ... SZ 3295
Lyminster ... 11 ... TQ 0204
Lymm ... 32 ... SJ 6786
Lymore ... 9 ... SZ 2992
Lympne ... 13 ... TR 1235
Lympsham ... 16 ... ST 3454
Lympstone ... 5 ... SX 9984
Lynchat ... 60 ... NH 7801
Lyndhurst ... 9 ... SU 2907
Lyndon ... 27 ... SK 9004
Lyne ... 11 ... TQ 0166
Lyneal ... 32 ... SJ 4433
Lyneham (Oxon.) ... 18 ... SP 2720
Lyneham (Wilts.) ... 17 ... SU 0179
Lynemouth ... 47 ... NZ 2991
Lyne of Gorthleck ... 60 ... NH 5420
Lyne of Skene ... 62 ... NJ 7610
Lyness ... 63 ... ND 3094
Lyng (Norf.) ... 29 ... TG 0617
Lyng (Somer.) ... 7 ... ST 3328
Lynmouth ... 6 ... SS 7249
Lynsted ... 13 ... TQ 9461
Lynton ... 6 ... SS 7149
Lyon's Gate ... 8 ... ST 6605
Lyonshall ... 23 ... SO 3356
Lytchett Matravers ... 8 ... SY 9495
Lytchett Minster ... 8 ... SY 9593
Lyth ... 67 ... ND 2763
Lytham ... 36 ... SD 3727
Lytham St. Anne's ... 36 ... SD 3427
Lythe ... 43 ... NZ 8413
Lythes ... 63 ... ND 4589

Maaruig ... 63 ... NB 1906
Mabe Burnthouse ... 2 ... SW 7634
Mabie ... 45 ... NX 9570
Mablethorpe ... 35 ... TF 5085
Macclesfield ... 33 ... SJ 9173
Macduff ... 62 ... NJ 7064
Machany ... 56 ... NN 9015
Macharioch ... 48 ... NR 7309
Machen ... 16 ... ST 2189
Machrihanish ... 48 ... NR 6220
Machynlleth ... 22 ... SH 7401
Mackworth ... 33 ... SK 3137
Macmerry ... 52 ... NT 4372
Madderty ... 56 ... NN 9522
Maddiston ... 51 ... NS 9476
Madehurst ... 11 ... SU 9810
Madeley (Salop) ... 24 ... SJ 6904
Madeley (Staffs.) ... 32 ... SJ 7744
Madingley ... 20 ... TL 3960
Madley ... 24 ... SO 4138
Madresfield ... 24 ... SO 8047
Madron ... 2 ... SW 4532
Maenclochog ... 14 ... SN 0827
Maendy ... 15 ... ST 0176
Maentwrog ... 30 ... SH 6640
Maer ... 32 ... SJ 7938
Maerdy (Clwyd) ... 31 ... SJ 0144
Maerdy (Mid Glam.) ... 15 ... SS 9798
Maesbrook ... 32 ... SJ 3121
Maesbury Marsh ... 32 ... SJ 3125
Maes-glas ... 16 ... ST 2985
Maesgwynne ... 14 ... SN 2024
Maeshafn ... 32 ... SJ 2061
Maesllyn ... 15 ... SN 3644
Maesmynis ... 15 ... SO 0148
Maesteg ... 15 ... SS 8591
Maesybont ... 15 ... SN 5616
Maes-y-cwmmer ... 16 ... ST 1794
Magdalen Laver ... 20 ... TL 5108
Maggieknockater ... 61 ... NJ 3145
Magham Down ... 12 ... TQ 6111
Maghull ... 36 ... SD 3702
Magor ... 16 ... ST 4287
Maiden Bradley ... 8 ... ST 8038
Maidencombe ... 5 ... SX 9268
Maidenhead ... 19 ... SU 8881
Maiden Law ... 47 ... NZ 1749
Maiden Newton ... 7 ... SY 5997
Maidens ... 44 ... NS 2107
Maidford ... 26 ... SP 6052
Maids' Moreton ... 18 ... SP 7035
Maidstone ... 12 ... TQ 7656
Maidwell ... 26 ... SP 7477
Mail ... 63 ... HU 4228
Mains ... 60 ... NH 4239
Mains of Ardestie ... 57 ... NO 5034
Mains of Balhall ... 57 ... NO 5163
Mains of Ballindarg ... 57 ... NO 4051
Mains of Dalvey ... 61 ... NJ 1132
Mains of Drum ... 62 ... NO 8099
Mains of Melgund ... 57 ... NO 5456
Mains of Thornton ... 57 ... NO 6871
Mains of Throsk ... 50 ... NS 8690
Mainstone ... 23 ... SO 2687
Maisemore ... 17 ... SO 8121
Malborough ... 5 ... SX 7039
Malden ... 11 ... TQ 2166
Maldon ... 20 ... TL 8506
Malham ... 41 ... SD 9062
Mallaig ... 58 ... NM 6796
Malleny Mills ... 51 ... NT 1665
Mallwyd ... 22 ... SH 8612
Malmesbury ... 17 ... ST 9387
Malpas (Ches.) ... 32 ... SJ 4847
Malpas (Cornwall) ... 2 ... SW 8442
Maltby (Cleve.) ... 42 ... NZ 4613
Maltby (S Yorks.) ... 38 ... SK 5392
Maltby le Marsh ... 35 ... TF 4681
Malting Green ... 21 ... TL 9720
Maltman's Hill ... 13 ... TQ 9043
Malton ... 38 ... SE 7871
Malvern Link ... 24 ... SO 7848
Malvern Wells ... 24 ... SO 7742
Mamble ... 24 ... SO 6871
Manaccan ... 2 ... SW 7625
Manafon ... 23 ... SJ 1102
Manaton ... 5 ... SX 7481
Manby ... 35 ... TF 3986
Mancetter ... 26 ... SP 3196
Manchester ... 37 ... SJ 8397
Mancot ... 32 ... SJ 3267
Mandally ... 59 ... NH 2900
Manea ... 27 ... TL 4789
Manfield ... 42 ... NZ 2213
Mangersta ... 63 ... NB 0131
Mangotsfield ... 17 ... ST 6676
Manish (Harris) ... 63 ... NG 1089
Manish (Isle of Lewis) ... 63 ... NA 9513
Mankinholes ... 37 ... SD 9523
Manley ... 32 ... SJ 5071
Manmoel ... 16 ... SO 1703
Mannel ... 48 ... NL 9840
Manningford Bohune ... 17 ... SU 1357
Manningford Bruce ... 17 ... SU 1359
Manning's Heath ... 11 ... TQ 2028
Mannington ... 8 ... SU 0605
Manningtree ... 21 ... TM 1031
Mannofield ... 62 ... NJ 9104
Manorbier ... 14 ... SS 0698
Manorhill ... 52 ... NT 6632
Manorowen ... 14 ... SM 9336
Mansell Gamage ... 24 ... SO 3944
Mansell Lacy ... 24 ... SO 4245
Mansergh ... 41 ... SD 6082
Mansfield (Notts.) ... 34 ... SK 5361
Mansfield (Strath.) ... 50 ... NS 6214
Mansfield Woodhouse ... 34 ... SK 5363
Mansriggs ... 40 ... SD 2880
Manston ... 8 ... ST 8115
Manthorpe ... 35 ... TF 0616
Manton (Humbs.) ... 39 ... SE 9302
Manton (Leic.) ... 27 ... SK 8704
Manton (Wilts.) ... 17 ... SU 1768
Manuden ... 20 ... TL 4926
Maplebeck ... 34 ... SK 7160
Maple Cross ... 19 ... TQ 0392
Mapledurham ... 10 ... SU 6776
Mapledurwell ... 10 ... SU 6851
Maplehurst ... 11 ... TQ 1924
Mapleton ... 33 ... SK 1648
Mapperley ... 33 ... SK 4343
Mapperton ... 7 ... SY 5099
Mappleborough Green ... 25 ... SP 0866
Mappleton ... 39 ... TA 2244
Mappowder ... 8 ... ST 7105
Marazion ... 2 ... SW 5130
Marbury ... 32 ... SJ 5545
March ... 27 ... TL 4197
Marcham ... 18 ... SU 4596
Marchamley ... 32 ... SJ 5929
Marchbankwood ... 45 ... NY 0899
Marchington ... 33 ... SK 1330
Marchington Woodlands ... 33 ... SK 1128
Marchwiel ... 32 ... SJ 3547
Marchwood ... 9 ... SU 3809
Marcross ... 15 ... SS 9269
Marden (Here. and Worc.) ... 24 ... SO 5247
Marden (Kent) ... 12 ... TQ 7444
Marden (Wilts.) ... 17 ... SU 0857
Mardy ... 16 ... SO 3016
Marefield ... 34 ... SK 7408
Mare Green ... 7 ... ST 3326
Mareham le Fen ... 35 ... TF 2761
Mareham on the Hill ... 35 ... TF 2867
Maresfield ... 12 ... TQ 4624
Marfleet ... 39 ... TA 1329
Margam ... 15 ... SS 7887
Margaret Marsh ... 8 ... ST 8218
Margaret Roding ... 20 ... TL 5912
Margaretting ... 20 ... TL 6601
Margate ... 13 ... TR 3670
Margnaheglish ... 49 ... NS 0331
Marham ... 28 ... TF 7110
Marhamchurch ... 4 ... SS 2203
Marholm ... 27 ... TF 1402
Marian-glas ... 30 ... SH 5084
Mariansleigh ... 6 ... SS 7422
Marishader ... 58 ... NG 4963
Maristow ... 4 ... SX 4764
Mariveg ... 63 ... NB 4119
Mark ... 7 ... ST 3747
Markbeech ... 12 ... TQ 4842
Markby ... 35 ... TF 4878
Mark Causeway ... 7 ... ST 3547
Mark Cross ... 12 ... TQ 5831
Market Bosworth ... 26 ... SK 4003
Market Deeping ... 35 ... TF 1310
Market Drayton ... 32 ... SJ 6734
Market Harborough ... 26 ... SP 7387
Markethill ... 56 ... NO 2239
Market Lavington ... 17 ... SU 0154
Market Overton ... 34 ... SK 8816
Market Rasen ... 35 ... TF 1089
Market Stainton ... 35 ... TF 2279
Market Street ... 29 ... TG 2921
Market Weighton ... 39 ... SE 8741
Market Weston ... 29 ... TL 9877
Markfield ... 33 ... SK 4810
Markham ... 16 ... SO 1600
Markinch ... 57 ... NO 2901
Markington ... 42 ... SE 2864
Marksbury ... 17 ... ST 6662
Marks Tey ... 21 ... TL 9123
Markwell ... 4 ... SX 3658
Markyate ... 19 ... TL 0616
Marlborough ... 17 ... SU 1869
Marlcliff ... 25 ... SP 0950
Marldon ... 5 ... SX 8663
Marlesford ... 21 ... TM 3258
Marley Green ... 32 ... SJ 5745
Marlingford ... 29 ... TG 1208
Marloes ... 14 ... SM 7908
Marlow ... 19 ... SU 8587
Marlpit Hill ... 12 ... TQ 4447
Marnhull ... 8 ... ST 7718
Marnoch ... 62 ... NJ 5950
Marple ... 33 ... SJ 9588
Marr ... 38 ... SE 5105
Marrick ... 42 ... SE 0798
Marrister ... 63 ... HU 5464
Marros ... 14 ... SN 2008
Marsden ... 37 ... SE 0411
Marsett ... 41 ... SD 9086
Marsh ... 5 ... ST 2410
Marshall's Heath ... 19 ... TL 1515
Marsham ... 29 ... TG 1924
Marshaw ... 36 ... SD 5853
Marsh Baldon ... 18 ... SU 5699
Marshborough ... 13 ... TR 2958
Marshbrook ... 24 ... SO 4389
Marshchapel ... 39 ... TF 3598
Marshfield (Avon) ... 17 ... ST 7773
Marshfield (Gwent) ... 16 ... ST 2582
Marshgate ... 4 ... SX 1592
Marsh Gibbon ... 18 ... SP 6423
Marsh Green (Devon.) ... 5 ... SY 0493
Marsh Green (Kent) ... 12 ... TQ 4344
Marsh Green (Salop) ... 24 ... SJ 6014
Marshside ... 36 ... SD 3419
Marsh, The ... 23 ... SO 3197
Marshwood ... 7 ... SY 3899
Marske ... 42 ... NZ 1000
Marske-by-the-Sea ... 42 ... NZ 6322
Marston (Ches.) ... 32 ... SJ 6474
Marston (Here. and Worc.) ... 24 ... SO 3657
Marston (Lincs.) ... 34 ... SK 8943
Marston (Oxon.) ... 18 ... SP 5208
Marston (Staffs.) ... 25 ... SJ 8314
Marston (Staffs.) ... 33 ... SJ 9227
Marston (Warw.) ... 25 ... SP 2095
Marston (Wilts.) ... 17 ... ST 9656
Marston Green ... 25 ... SP 1685
Marston Magna ... 7 ... ST 5922
Marston Meysey ... 17 ... SU 1297
Marston Montgomery ... 33 ... SK 1338
Marston Moretaine ... 27 ... SP 9941
Marston on Dove ... 33 ... SK 2329
Marston St. Lawrence ... 26 ... SP 5342
Marston Stannett ... 24 ... SO 5655
Marston Trussell ... 26 ... SP 6986
Marstow ... 16 ... SO 5519
Marsworth ... 19 ... SP 9214
Marten ... 10 ... SU 2860
Marthall ... 32 ... SJ 8076
Martham ... 29 ... TG 4518
Martin (Hants.) ... 8 ... SU 0719
Martin (Lincs.) ... 35 ... TF 1259
Martin Drove End ... 8 ... SU 0420
Martinhoe ... 6 ... SS 6648
Martin Hussingtree ... 25 ... SO 8860
Martinscroft ... 32 ... SJ 6589
Martinstown ... 8 ... SY 6488
Martlesham ... 21 ... TM 2547
Martletwy ... 14 ... SN 0310
Martley ... 24 ... SO 7559
Martock ... 7 ... ST 4619
Marton (Ches.) ... 33 ... SJ 8468
Marton (Cleve.) ... 42 ... NZ 5115
Marton (Lincs.) ... 34 ... SK 8381
Marton (N Yorks.) ... 38 ... SE 4162
Marton (N Yorks.) ... 43 ... SE 7383
Marton (Salop) ... 23 ... SJ 2802
Marton (Warw.) ... 26 ... SP 4069
Marwood ... 6 ... SS 5437
Marybank ... 60 ... NH 4753
Maryburgh ... 60 ... NH 5456
Marygold ... 53 ... NT 8160
Maryhill ... 62 ... NJ 8245
Marykirk ... 57 ... NO 6865
Marylebone ... 36 ... SD 5807
Marypark ... 61 ... NJ 1938
Maryport ... 44 ... NX 1434
Maryport ... 40 ... NY 0336
Marystow ... 4 ... SX 4382
Mary Tavy ... 4 ... SX 5079
Maryton ... 57 ... NO 6856
Marywell (Grampn.) ... 62 ... NO 5896
Marywell (Tays.) ... 57 ... NO 6544
Masham ... 42 ... SE 2280
Mashbury ... 20 ... TL 6511
Mason ... 47 ... NZ 2073
Mastrick ... 62 ... NJ 9007
Matching ... 20 ... TL 5212
Matching Green ... 20 ... TL 5311
Matching Tye ... 20 ... TL 5111
Matfen ... 47 ... NZ 0371
Matfield ... 12 ... TQ 6541
Mathern ... 16 ... ST 5291
Mathon ... 24 ... SO 7345
Mathry ... 14 ... SM 8832
Matlaske ... 29 ... TG 1534
Matlock ... 33 ... SK 3060
Matlock Bath ... 33 ... SK 2958
Matson ... 17 ... SO 8316
Matterdale End ... 40 ... NY 3923
Mattersey ... 34 ... SK 6889
Mattingley ... 10 ... SU 7357
Mattishall ... 29 ... TG 0510
Mattishall Burgh ... 29 ... TG 0511
Mauchline ... 50 ... NS 4927
Maud ... 62 ... NJ 9247
Maugersbury ... 17 ... SP 1925
Maughold ... 43 ... SC 4991
Maulden ... 19 ... TL 0538
Maulds Meaburn ... 41 ... NY 6216
Maunby ... 42 ... SE 3486
Maund Bryan ... 24 ... SO 5550
Mautby ... 29 ... TG 4712
Mavesyn Ridware ... 25 ... SK 0817
Mavis Enderby ... 35 ... TF 3666
Mawbray ... 45 ... NY 0846
Mawdesley ... 36 ... SD 4914
Mawgan ... 2 ... SW 7024
Maw Green ... 25 ... SP 0197
Mawla ... 2 ... SW 6945
Mawnan ... 2 ... SW 7827
Mawnan Smith ... 2 ... SW 7728
Maxey ... 35 ... TF 1208
Maxstoke ... 26 ... SP 2386
Maxton ... 52 ... NT 6129
Maxwellheugh ... 52 ... NT 7333
Maxwellston ... 44 ... NS 2600
Maybole ... 44 ... NS 3009
Mayfield (E Susx) ... 12 ... TQ 5827
Mayfield (Staffs.) ... 33 ... SK 1545
Mayford ... 11 ... SU 9956
Maypole ... 16 ... SO 4716
Maypole Green ... 29 ... TM 4195
Maywick ... 63 ... HU 3724
Meadle ... 18 ... SP 8005
Meadowtown ... 23 ... SJ 3101
Meal Bank ... 41 ... SD 5495
Mealsgate ... 40 ... NY 2141
Mearbeck ... 41 ... SD 8160
Meare ... 7 ... ST 4541
Mears Ashby ... 26 ... SP 8366
Measham ... 33 ... SK 3312
Meathop ... 40 ... SD 4380
Meaux ... 39 ... TA 0939
Meavag ... 63 ... NG 1596
Meavy ... 4 ... SX 5467
Medbourne ... 26 ... SP 7993
Meddon ... 4 ... SS 2717
Medmenham ... 18 ... SU 8084
Medstead ... 10 ... SU 6537
Meerbrook ... 33 ... SJ 9860
Meer End ... 26 ... SP 2474
Meesden ... 20 ... TL 4432
Meeth ... 6 ... SS 5408
Meidrim ... 14 ... SN 2820
Meifod ... 23 ... SJ 1513
Meigle ... 57 ... NO 2844
Meikle Earnock ... 50 ... NS 7253
Meikleour ... 56 ... NO 1539
Meikle Strath ... 57 ... NO 6471
Meikle Tarty ... 62 ... NJ 9928
Meikle Wartle ... 62 ... NJ 7230
Meinciau ... 15 ... SN 4610
Meir ... 33 ... SJ 9342
Melbost ... 63 ... NB 4632
Melbourn (Cambs.) ... 20 ... TL 3844
Melbourne (Derby.) ... 33 ... SK 3825
Melbourne (Humbs.) ... 38 ... SE 7543
Melbury Bubb ... 7 ... ST 5906
Melbury Osmond ... 7 ... ST 5707
Melbury Sampford ... 7 ... ST 5705
Melchbourne ... 27 ... TL 0265
Melcombe Bingham ... 8 ... ST 7602
Meldon (Devon) ... 4 ... SX 5592
Meldon (Northum.) ... 47 ... NZ 1284
Meldreth ... 20 ... TL 3746
Melfort ... 54 ... NM 8314
Meliden ... 31 ... SJ 0580
Melin Court ... 15 ... SN 8201
Melin-y-coed ... 31 ... SH 8160
Melin-y-ddol ... 23 ... SJ 0807
Melin-y-grug ... 23 ... SJ 0507
Melin-y-wig ... 31 ... SJ 0448
Melkinthorpe ... 41 ... NY 5525
Melkridge ... 46 ... NY 7363
Melksham ... 17 ... ST 9063
Melldalloch ... 49 ... NR 9375
Melling (Lancs.) ... 41 ... SD 5970
Melling (Mers.) ... 36 ... SD 3800
Mellis ... 29 ... TM 0974
Mellon Charles ... 64 ... NG 8491
Mellon Udrigle ... 64 ... NG 8895
Mellor (Gtr Mches.) ... 33 ... SJ 9888
Mellor (Lancs.) ... 36 ... SD 6530
Mellor Brook ... 36 ... SD 6331
Mells ... 8 ... ST 7249
Melmerby (Cumbr.) ... 41 ... NY 6137
Melmerby (N Yorks.) ... 42 ... SE 0785
Melmerby (N Yorks.) ... 42 ... SE 3376
Melplash ... 7 ... SY 4797
Melrose ... 52 ... NT 5433
Melsetter ... 63 ... ND 2689
Melsonby ... 42 ... NZ 1908
Meltham ... 37 ... SE 0910
Melton ... 21 ... TM 2850
Meltonby ... 38 ... SE 7952
Melton Constable ... 29 ... TG 0433
Melton Mowbray ... 34 ... SK 7518
Melton Ross ... 39 ... TA 0610
Melvaig ... 64 ... NG 7486

Melverley 91 Nailstone

Melverley ... 23 ... SJ 3316
Melvich ... 67 ... NC 8864
Membury ... 7 ... ST 2703
Memsie ... 62 ... NJ 9762
Memus ... 57 ... NO 4258
Menabilly ... 4 ... SX 0951
Menai Bridge ... 30 ... SH 5572
Mendham ... 29 ... TM 2783
Mendlesham ... 21 ... TM 1065
Mendlesham Green ... 21 ... TM 0963
Menheniot ... 4 ... SX 2862
Mennock ... 45 ... NS 8008
Menston ... 37 ... SE 1743
Menstrie ... 56 ... NS 8596
Mentmore ... 19 ... SP 9019
Meole Brace ... 24 ... SJ 4811
Meonstoke ... 9 ... SU 6119
Meopham ... 12 ... TQ 6466
Meopham Station ... 12 ... TQ 6467
Mepal ... 27 ... TL 4481
Meppershall ... 19 ... TL 1336
Merbach ... 23 ... SO 3045
Mere (Ches.) ... 32 ... SJ 7281
Mere (Wilts.) ... 8 ... ST 8132
Mere Brow ... 36 ... SD 4118
Mereclough ... 37 ... SD 8730
Mere Green ... 25 ... SP 1298
Merevale ... 26 ... SP 2897
Mereworth ... 12 ... TQ 6553
Mergie ... 57 ... NO 7988
Meriden ... 26 ... SP 2482
Merkadale ... 58 ... NG 3831
Merkland ... 44 ... NX 2491
Merlin's Bridge ... 14 ... SM 9414
Merrington ... 32 ... SJ 4621
Merriott ... 7 ... ST 4412
Merrivale ... 4 ... SX 5475
Merrymeet ... 4 ... SX 2766
Mersham ... 13 ... TR 0539
Merstham ... 11 ... TQ 2953
Merston ... 11 ... SU 8903
Merstone ... 9 ... SZ 5285
Merther ... 2 ... SW 8644
Merthyr ... 14 ... SN 3520
Merthyr Cynog ... 15 ... SN 9837
Merthyr Dyfan ... 16 ... ST 1169
Merthyr Mawr ... 15 ... SS 8877
Merthyr Tydfil ... 16 ... SO 0406
Merthyr Vale ... 16 ... ST 0899
Merton (Devon.) ... 6 ... SS 5212
Merton (Gtr London) ... 11 ... TQ 2569
Merton (Norf.) ... 28 ... TL 9098
Merton (Oxon.) ... 18 ... SP 5717
Mervinslaw ... 52 ... NT 6713
Meshaw ... 6 ... SS 7519
Messing ... 21 ... TL 8918
Messingham ... 39 ... SE 8904
Metfield ... 29 ... TM 2980
Metheringham ... 35 ... TF 0661
Methil ... 57 ... NT 3699
Methley ... 37 ... SE 3826
Methlick ... 62 ... NJ 8537
Methven ... 56 ... NO 0225
Methwold ... 28 ... TL 7394
Methwold Hithe ... 28 ... TL 7195
Mettingham ... 29 ... TM 3689
Mevagissey ... 4 ... SX 0144
Mexborough ... 38 ... SK 4799
Mey ... 67 ... ND 2872
Meysey Hampton ... 17 ... SU 1199
Miavaig ... 63 ... NB 0834
Michaelchurch ... 16 ... SO 5125
Michaelchurch Escley ... 23 ... SO 3134
Michaelchurch-on-Arrow ... 23 ... SO 2450
Michaelston-le-Pit ... 16 ... ST 1573
Michaelston-y-Fedw ... 16 ... ST 2484
Michaelstow ... 4 ... SX 0778
Micheldever ... 10 ... SU 5138
Michelmersh ... 9 ... SU 3426
Mickfield ... 21 ... TM 1361
Mickleby ... 43 ... NZ 8013
Micklefield ... 38 ... SE 4433
Mickleham ... 11 ... TQ 1753
Mickleover ... 33 ... SK 3034
Mickleton (Durham) ... 41 ... NY 9623
Mickleton (Glos.) ... 25 ... SP 1543
Mickle Trafford ... 32 ... SJ 4469
Mickley ... 42 ... SE 2576
Mickley Square ... 47 ... NZ 0761
Mid Ardlaw ... 62 ... NJ 9464
Midbea ... 63 ... HY 4444
Mid Beltie ... 62 ... NJ 6200
Mid Cairncross ... 57 ... NO 4979
Middle Assendon ... 18 ... SU 7385
Middle Aston ... 18 ... SP 4726
Middle Barton ... 18 ... SP 4326
Middlebie ... 46 ... NY 2176
Middle Claydon ... 18 ... SP 7125
Middle Drums ... 57 ... NO 5957
Middleham ... 42 ... SE 1287
Middlehope ... 24 ... SO 4988
Middle Littleton ... 25 ... SP 0747
Middle Maes-coed ... 23 ... SO 3334
Middlemarsh ... 8 ... ST 6707
Middle Mill ... 14 ... SM 8025
Middle Rasen ... 35 ... TF 0889
Middlesbrough ... 42 ... NZ 4920
Middlesmoor ... 42 ... SE 0974
Middlestone Moor ... 42 ... NZ 2532
Middlestown ... 37 ... SE 2617
Middleton (Cumbr.) ... 41 ... SD 6286
Middleton (Derby.) ... 33 ... SK 1963
Middleton (Derby.) ... 33 ... SK 2755
Middleton (Essex) ... 20 ... TL 8639
Middleton (Grampn.) ... 62 ... NJ 8419
Middleton (Gtr Mches.) ... 37 ... SD 8606
Middleton (Hants.) ... 10 ... SU 4243
Middleton (Here. and Worc.) ... 24 ... SO 5469
Middleton (Lancs.) ... 36 ... SD 4258
Middleton (Lothian) ... 51 ... NT 3657
Middleton (Norf.) ... 28 ... TF 6616
Middleton (Northants.) ... 27 ... SP 8489
Middleton (Northum.) ... 53 ... NU 0024
Middleton (Northum.) ... 53 ... NU 1035
Middleton (Northum.) ... 47 ... NZ 0585
Middleton (N Yorks.) ... 43 ... SE 7885
Middleton (N Yorks. - W Yorks.) ... 37 ... SE 1249
Middleton (Salop) ... 32 ... SJ 3128
Middleton (Salop) ... 23 ... SO 2999
Middleton (Salop) ... 24 ... SO 5377
Middleton (Suff.) ... 21 ... TM 4267
Middleton (Tays.) ... 56 ... NO 1206
Middleton (Tiree) ... 48 ... NL 9443
Middleton (Warw.) ... 25 ... SP 1798
Middleton (W Yorks.) ... 37 ... SE 3027
Middleton Cheney ... 26 ... SP 4941
Middleton Green ... 33 ... SJ 9935
Middleton Hall ... 53 ... NT 9825
Middleton in Teesdale ... 41 ... NY 9425
Middleton-on-Sea ... 11 ... SU 9800
Middleton on the Hill ... 24 ... SO 5464
Middleton-on-the-Wolds ... 39 ... SE 9449
Middleton Priors ... 24 ... SO 6290
Middleton St. George ... 42 ... NZ 3412
Middleton Scriven ... 24 ... SO 6787
Middleton Stoney ... 18 ... SP 5323
Middleton Tyas ... 42 ... NZ 2205
Middletown ... 23 ... SJ 3012
Middle Tysoe ... 26 ... SP 3344
Middle Wallop ... 10 ... SU 2937
Middlewich ... 32 ... SJ 7066
Middle Winterslow ... 9 ... SU 2432
Middle Witchyburn ... 62 ... NJ 6356
Middle Woodford ... 8 ... SU 1136
Middlewood Green ... 21 ... TM 0961
Middleyard ... 50 ... NS 5132
Middlezoy ... 7 ... ST 3733
Middridge ... 42 ... NZ 2526
Midfield ... 66 ... NC 5864
Midge Hall ... 36 ... SD 5123
Midgeholme ... 46 ... NY 6458
Midgham ... 10 ... SU 5567
Midgley ... 37 ... SE 0226
Midhopestones ... 37 ... SK 2399
Midhurst ... 11 ... SU 8821
Midlem ... 52 ... NT 5227
Mid Sannox ... 49 ... NS 0145
Midsomer Norton ... 17 ... ST 6654
Mid Thundergay ... 49 ... NR 8846
Midtown ... 64 ... NG 8285
Midville ... 35 ... TF 3857
Mid Yell ... 63 ... HU 4991
Migvie ... 61 ... NJ 4306
Milborne Port ... 8 ... ST 6718
Milborne St. Andrew ... 8 ... SY 7997
Milborne Wick ... 8 ... ST 6620
Milbourne ... 47 ... NZ 1175
Milburn (Cumbr.) ... 41 ... NY 6529
Milbury Heath ... 17 ... ST 6690
Milcombe ... 18 ... SP 4134
Milden ... 21 ... TL 9546
Mildenhall (Suff.) ... 28 ... TL 7074
Mildenhall (Wilts.) ... 17 ... SU 2069
Milebrook ... 23 ... SO 3172
Milebush ... 12 ... TQ 7546
Mile Elm ... 17 ... ST 9968
Mile End ... 21 ... TL 9827
Mileham ... 28 ... TF 9119
Milesmark ... 51 ... NT 0688
Milfield ... 53 ... NT 9333
Milford (Derby.) ... 33 ... SK 3445
Milford (Staffs.) ... 33 ... SJ 9721
Milford (Surrey) ... 11 ... SU 9442
Milford Haven (Dyfed) ... 14 ... SM 9006
Milford on Sea ... 9 ... SZ 2891
Milkwall ... 17 ... SO 5809
Milland ... 9 ... SU 8228
Milland Marsh ... 9 ... SU 8326
Mill Bank ... 37 ... SE 0321
Millbounds ... 63 ... HY 5635
Millbreck ... 62 ... NK 0045
Millbridge ... 11 ... SU 8542
Millbrook (Beds.) ... 19 ... TL 0138
Millbrook (Corn.) ... 4 ... SX 4252
Millbrook (Hants.) ... 9 ... SU 4012
Millburn (Strath.) ... 50 ... NS 4429
Millcorner ... 12 ... TQ 8223
Milldens ... 57 ... NO 5450
Mill End (Bucks.) ... 18 ... SU 7885
Mill End (Herts.) ... 20 ... TL 3332
Millerhill ... 51 ... NT 3269
Miller's Dale ... 33 ... SK 1373
Mill Green (Essex) ... 20 ... TL 6400
Millgreen (Salop) ... 32 ... SJ 6727
Millheugh ... 50 ... NS 7551
Mill Hill ... 19 ... TQ 2292
Millholme ... 41 ... SD 5690
Millhouse ... 49 ... NR 9570
Millikenpark ... 50 ... NS 4162
Millington ... 39 ... SE 8351
Mill Lane ... 10 ... SU 7850
Millmeece ... 32 ... SJ 8333
Mill of Kingoodie ... 62 ... NJ 8425
Millom ... 40 ... SD 1780
Millport ... 49 ... NS 1655
Mill Street ... 29 ... TG 0118
Millthrop ... 41 ... SD 6691
Milltimber ... 62 ... NJ 8501
Millton of Auchriachan ... 61 ... NJ 1718
Millton of Corsindae ... 62 ... NJ 6809
Millton of Murtle ... 62 ... NJ 8702
Milltown (Derby.) ... 33 ... SK 3561
Milltown (Dumf. and Galwy.) ... 46 ... NY 3375
Milltown (Grampn.) ... 61 ... NJ 4616
Milltown (Grampn.) ... 62 ... NJ 5447
Milltown of Aberdalgie ... 56 ... NO 0720
Milltown of Auchindown ... 61 ... NJ 3540
Milltown of Campfield ... 62 ... NJ 6400
Milltown of Craigston ... 62 ... NJ 7655
Milltown of Edinvillie ... 61 ... NJ 2639
Milltown of Towie ... 61 ... NJ 4612
Milnathort ... 56 ... NO 1204
Milngavie ... 50 ... NS 5574
Milnrow ... 37 ... SD 9212
Milnthorpe ... 40 ... SD 4981
Milovaig ... 58 ... NG 1550
Milson ... 24 ... SO 6372
Milstead ... 13 ... TQ 9058
Milston ... 8 ... SU 1645
Milton (Cambs.) ... 20 ... TL 4762
Milton (Central) ... 55 ... NN 5001
Milton (Central) ... 50 ... NS 4490
Milton (Cumbr.) ... 46 ... NY 5560
Milton (Dumf. and Galwy.) ... 44 ... NX 2154
Milton (Dumf. and Galwy.) ... 45 ... NX 8470
Milton (Grampn.) ... 61 ... NJ 5163
Milton (Highld.) ... 67 ... ND 3451
Milton (Highld.) ... 59 ... NH 3055
Milton (Highld.) ... 60 ... NH 4930
Milton (Highld.) ... 60 ... NH 5749
Milton (Highld.) ... 65 ... NH 7674
Milton (Highld.) ... 60 ... NH 9553
Milton (Oxon.) ... 18 ... SP 4535
Milton (Oxon.) ... 18 ... SU 4892
Milton (Staffs.) ... 33 ... SJ 9050
Milton (Strath.) ... 50 ... NS 4274
Milton (Tays.) ... 56 ... NN 9138
Milton (Tays.) ... 57 ... NO 3843
Milton Abbas ... 8 ... ST 8001
Milton Abbot ... 4 ... SX 4079
Milton Bridge ... 51 ... NT 2363
Milton Bryan ... 19 ... SP 9730
Milton Clevedon ... 8 ... ST 6637
Milton Coldwells ... 62 ... NJ 9538
Milton Combe ... 4 ... SX 4866
Milton Damerel ... 4 ... SS 3810
Miltonduff ... 61 ... NJ 1760
Milton Ernest ... 27 ... TL 0156
Milton Green ... 32 ... SJ 4558
Milton Hill ... 18 ... SU 4790
Milton Keynes ... 27 ... SP 8939
Milton Lilbourne ... 17 ... SU 1860
Milton Malsor ... 26 ... SP 7355
Milton Morenish ... 56 ... NN 6135
Milton of Auchinhove ... 62 ... NJ 5503
Milton of Balgonie ... 57 ... NO 3100
Milton of Braicklaich ... 60 ... NH 7851
Milton of Campsie ... 50 ... NS 6576
Milton of Cushnie ... 61 ... NJ 5111
Milton of Lesmore ... 61 ... NJ 4628
Milton of Noth ... 61 ... NJ 5028
Milton of Potterton ... 62 ... NJ 9415
Milton of Tullich ... 61 ... NO 3897
Milton on Stour ... 8 ... ST 7928
Milton Regis ... 13 ... TQ 9064
Milton-under-Wychwood ... 18 ... SP 2618
Milverton ... 7 ... ST 1225
Milwich ... 33 ... SJ 9632
Milwr ... 32 ... SJ 1974
Minard ... 55 ... NR 9796
Minchinhampton ... 17 ... SO 8600
Mindrum ... 53 ... NT 8432
Minehead ... 7 ... SS 9746
Minera ... 32 ... SJ 2651
Minety ... 17 ... SU 0290
Minffordd ... 30 ... SH 5938
Mingary ... 63 ... NF 7426
Miningsby ... 35 ... TF 3264
Minions ... 4 ... SX 2671
Minishant ... 50 ... NS 3314
Minley Manor ... 10 ... SU 8157
Minnes ... 62 ... NJ 9423
Minnigaff ... 44 ... NX 4166
Minskip ... 42 ... SE 3864
Minstead ... 9 ... SU 2811
Minster (Kent) ... 13 ... TQ 9573
Minster (Kent) ... 13 ... TR 3164
Minsteracres ... 47 ... NZ 0255
Minsterley ... 24 ... SJ 3705
Minster Lovell ... 18 ... SP 3111
Minsterworth ... 17 ... SO 7717
Minterne Magna ... 8 ... ST 6504
Minting ... 35 ... TF 1873
Mintlaw ... 62 ... NK 0048
Minto ... 52 ... NT 5620
Minton ... 24 ... SO 4130
Minwear ... 14 ... SN 0413
Minworth ... 25 ... SP 1592
Mirbister ... 63 ... HY 3019
Mireland ... 67 ... ND 3160
Mirfield ... 37 ... SE 2019
Miserden ... 17 ... SO 9308
Miskin ... 16 ... ST 0481
Misson ... 38 ... SK 6895
Misterton (Leic.) ... 26 ... SP 5584
Misterton (Notts.) ... 38 ... SK 7694
Misterton (Somer.) ... 7 ... ST 4508
Mistley ... 21 ... TM 1231
Mitcham ... 11 ... TQ 2868
Mitcheldean ... 17 ... SO 6618
Mitchell ... 2 ... SW 8554
Mitchel Troy ... 16 ... SO 4910
Mitford ... 47 ... NZ 1786
Mithian ... 2 ... SW 7450
Mitton ... 25 ... SJ 8815
Mixbury ... 18 ... SP 6033
Mixon ... 33 ... SK 0457
Mobberley ... 32 ... SJ 7880
Moccas ... 24 ... SO 3542
Mochdre (Clwyd) ... 31 ... SH 8278
Mochdre (Powys) ... 23 ... SO 0788
Mochrum ... 44 ... NX 3446
Mockerkin ... 40 ... NY 0823
Modbury ... 5 ... SX 6551
Moddershall ... 33 ... SJ 9236
Moelfre (Clwyd) ... 32 ... SJ 1828
Moelfre (Gwyn.) ... 30 ... SH 5186
Moel Tryfan ... 30 ... SH 5155
Moffat ... 45 ... NT 0805
Mogerhanger ... 27 ... TL 1349
Moira ... 33 ... SK 3216
Molash ... 13 ... TR 0251
Mold ... 32 ... SJ 2363
Molehill Green ... 20 ... TL 5624
Molescroft ... 39 ... TA 0140
Molesworth ... 27 ... TL 0775
Molland ... 6 ... SS 8028
Mollington (Ches.) ... 32 ... SJ 3870
Mollington (Northants.) ... 26 ... SP 4347
Mollinsburn ... 50 ... NS 7171
Monachty ... 22 ... SN 5062
Monboddo ... 57 ... NO 7478
Mondynes ... 57 ... NO 7879
Monewden ... 21 ... TM 2358
Moneydie ... 56 ... NO 0629
Moniaive ... 45 ... NX 7791
Monifieth ... 57 ... NO 4932
Monikie ... 57 ... NO 4938
Monimail ... 57 ... NO 2914
Monington ... 14 ... SN 1344
Monken Hadley ... 19 ... TQ 2497
Monk Fryston ... 38 ... SE 5029
Monkhopton ... 24 ... SO 6293
Monkland ... 24 ... SO 4557
Monkleigh ... 4 ... SS 4520
Monknash ... 15 ... SS 9270
Monkokehampton ... 6 ... SS 5805
Monks Eleigh ... 21 ... TL 9647
Monks' Heath ... 33 ... SJ 8873
Monk Sherborne ... 10 ... SU 6056
Monkshill ... 62 ... NJ 7941
Monksilver ... 7 ... ST 0737
Monks Kirby ... 26 ... SP 4683
Monk Soham ... 21 ... TM 2165
Monkswood ... 16 ... SO 3403
Monkton (Devon.) ... 5 ... ST 1803
Monkton (Kent) ... 13 ... TR 2865
Monkton (Strath.) ... 50 ... NS 3527
Monkton (Tyne and Wear) ... 47 ... NZ 3463
Monkton Combe ... 17 ... ST 7761
Monkton Deverill ... 8 ... ST 8537
Monkton Farleigh ... 17 ... ST 8065
Monkton Heathfield ... 7 ... ST 2526
Monkton Up Wimborne ... 8 ... SU 0113
Monkwood ... 9 ... SU 6730
Monmouth ... 16 ... SO 5113
Monnington on Wye ... 24 ... SO 3743
Monreith ... 44 ... NX 3641
Monreith Mains ... 44 ... NX 3643
Montacute ... 7 ... ST 4916
Montford ... 24 ... SJ 4114
Montgarrie ... 62 ... NJ 5717
Montgomery ... 23 ... SO 2296
Montgreenan ... 50 ... NS 3343
Montrave ... 57 ... NO 3706
Montrose ... 57 ... NO 7157
Monxton ... 10 ... SU 3144
Monyash ... 33 ... SK 1566
Monymusk ... 62 ... NJ 6815
Monzie ... 56 ... NN 8725
Moonzie ... 57 ... NO 3317
Moorby ... 35 ... TF 2964
Moorcot ... 24 ... SO 3555
Moor Crichel ... 8 ... ST 9908
Moordown ... 8 ... SZ 0994
Moore ... 32 ... SJ 5584
Moorends ... 38 ... SE 6915
Moorhall ... 33 ... SK 3175
Moorhampton ... 24 ... SO 3846
Moorhouse (Cumbr.) ... 46 ... NY 3356
Moorhouse (Notts.) ... 34 ... SK 7566
Moorland or Northmoor Green ... 7 ... ST 3332
Moorlinch ... 7 ... ST 3936
Moor Monkton ... 38 ... SE 5056
Moor Nook ... 36 ... SD 6537
Moorsholm ... 43 ... NZ 6814
Moorside ... 37 ... SD 9507
Moor, The ... 12 ... TQ 7529
Moortown (Hants.) ... 9 ... SZ 4283
Moortown (Lincs.) ... 39 ... TF 0699
Morar ... 58 ... NM 6792
Morborne ... 27 ... TL 1391
Morchard Bishop ... 6 ... SS 7607
Morcombelake ... 7 ... SY 4093
Morcott ... 27 ... SK 9200
Morda ... 32 ... SJ 2827
Morden (Dorset) ... 8 ... SY 9195
Morden (Gtr London) ... 11 ... TQ 2567
Mordiford ... 24 ... SO 5637
Mordon ... 42 ... NZ 3326
More ... 23 ... SO 3491
Morebath ... 6 ... SS 9525
Morebattle ... 53 ... NT 7724
Morecambe ... 40 ... SD 4364
Morefield ... 64 ... NH 1195
Moreleigh ... 5 ... SX 7652
Morenish ... 56 ... NN 6035
Moresby ... 40 ... NX 9821
Morestead ... 9 ... SU 5125
Moreton (Dorset) ... 8 ... SY 8089
Moreton (Essex) ... 20 ... TL 5307
Moreton (Mers.) ... 32 ... SJ 2689
Moreton (Oxon.) ... 18 ... SP 6904
Moreton Corbet ... 32 ... SJ 5523
Moretonhampstead ... 5 ... SX 7586
Moreton-in-Marsh ... 25 ... SP 2032
Moreton Jeffries ... 24 ... SO 6048
Moreton Morrell ... 26 ... SP 3155
Moreton on Lugg ... 24 ... SO 5045
Moreton Pinkney ... 26 ... SP 5749
Moreton Say ... 32 ... SJ 6234
Moreton Valence ... 17 ... SO 7809
Morfa Bychan ... 30 ... SH 5437
Morfa Glas ... 15 ... SN 8606
Morfa Nefyn ... 30 ... SH 2840
Morgan's Vale ... 8 ... SU 1921
Morland ... 41 ... NY 6022
Morley (Derby.) ... 33 ... SK 3941
Morley (Durham) ... 42 ... NZ 1227
Morley (W Yorks.) ... 37 ... SE 2627
Morley Green ... 32 ... SJ 8282
Morley St. Botolph ... 29 ... TM 0799
Morningside ... 51 ... NT 2471
Morningthorpe ... 29 ... TM 2192
Morpeth ... 47 ... NZ 2085
Morphie ... 57 ... NO 7164
Morrey ... 33 ... SK 1218
Morriston ... 15 ... SS 6698
Morston ... 29 ... TG 0043
Mortehoe ... 6 ... SS 4545
Mortimer ... 10 ... SU 6564
Mortimer's Cross ... 24 ... SO 4263
Mortimer West End ... 10 ... SU 6363
Mortlake ... 11 ... TQ 2075
Morton (Avon) ... 17 ... ST 6491
Morton (Derby.) ... 33 ... SK 4060
Morton (Lincs.) ... 39 ... SK 8091
Morton (Lincs.) ... 35 ... TF 0924
Morton (Norf.) ... 29 ... TG 1217
Morton (Salop) ... 32 ... SJ 2824
Morton Bagot ... 25 ... SP 1164
Morton-on-Swale ... 42 ... SE 3292
Morvah ... 2 ... SW 4035
Morval ... 4 ... SX 2556
Morvich ... 59 ... NG 9621
Morville ... 24 ... SO 6694
Morwenstow ... 4 ... SS 2015
Morwick Hall ... 47 ... NU 2303
Mosborough ... 33 ... SK 4281
Moscow ... 50 ... NS 4840
Mosedale ... 40 ... NY 3532
Moseley (Here. and Worc.) ... 25 ... SO 8159
Moseley (W Mids) ... 25 ... SP 0883
Moss (Clwyd) ... 32 ... SJ 3052
Moss (Highld.) ... 54 ... NM 6868
Moss (S Yorks.) ... 38 ... SE 5914
Moss (Tiree) ... 48 ... NL 9644
Mossat ... 61 ... NJ 4719
Moss Bank (Cumbr.) ... 32 ... SJ 5198
Mossbank (Shetld.) ... 63 ... HU 4475
Mossburnford ... 52 ... NT 6616
Mossdale ... 45 ... NX 6571
Mossend ... 50 ... NS 7460
Mosside ... 57 ... NO 4252
Mossley ... 37 ... SD 9702
Moss Nook ... 32 ... SJ 8385
Moss of Barmuckity ... 61 ... NJ 2461
Moss Side ... 36 ... SD 3830
Mosston ... 57 ... NO 5444
Mosterton ... 7 ... ST 4505
Mostyn ... 31 ... SJ 1680
Motcombe ... 8 ... ST 8425
Motherwell ... 50 ... NS 7557
Mottingham ... 12 ... TQ 4272
Mottisfont ... 9 ... SU 3226
Mottistone ... 9 ... SZ 4083
Mottram in Logdendale ... 37 ... SJ 9995
Mouldsworth ... 32 ... SJ 5171
Moulin ... 56 ... NN 9459
Moulsecoomb ... 12 ... TQ 3307
Moulsford ... 18 ... SU 5984
Moulsoe ... 27 ... SP 9041
Moulton (Ches.) ... 32 ... SJ 6569
Moulton (Lincs.) ... 35 ... TF 3023
Moulton (Northants.) ... 26 ... SP 7866
Moulton (N Yorks.) ... 42 ... NZ 2303
Moulton (Suff.) ... 20 ... TL 6964
Moulton Chapel ... 35 ... TF 2918
Moulton Seas End ... 35 ... TF 3227
Mount (Corn.) ... 2 ... SW 7856
Mount (Corn.) ... 4 ... SX 1467
Mountain Ash ... 16 ... ST 0498
Mountain Cross ... 51 ... NT 1446
Mountain Water ... 14 ... SM 9224
Mountbenger ... 51 ... NT 3125
Mount Bures ... 21 ... TL 9032
Mountfield ... 12 ... TQ 7320
Mountgerald ... 65 ... NH 5661
Mount Hawke ... 2 ... SW 7147
Mountjoy ... 2 ... SW 8760
Mountnessing ... 20 ... TQ 6297
Mounton ... 16 ... ST 5193
Mount Pleasant ... 29 ... TM 5077
Mountsorrel ... 34 ... SK 5814
Mountstuart (Strath.) ... 49 ... NS 1059
Mousehole ... 2 ... SW 4626
Mouswald ... 45 ... NY 0672
Mow Cop ... 33 ... SJ 8557
Mowhaugh ... 53 ... NT 8120
Mowsley ... 26 ... SP 6489
Mowtie ... 57 ... NO 8388
Moy ... 55 ... NN 4282
Moy Hall ... 60 ... NH 7635
Moy House ... 61 ... NJ 0159
Moylgrove ... 14 ... SN 1244
Muasdale ... 48 ... NR 6840
Muchalls ... 62 ... NO 9091
Much Birch ... 24 ... SO 5030
Much Cowarne ... 24 ... SO 6147
Much Dewchurch ... 24 ... SO 4831
Muchelney ... 7 ... ST 4224
Much Hadham ... 20 ... TL 4319
Much Hoole ... 36 ... SD 4723
Muchlarnick ... 4 ... SX 2156
Much Marcle ... 24 ... SO 6533
Much Wenlock ... 24 ... SO 6199
Muckfoot ... 44 ... NX 2185
Mucking ... 20 ... TQ 6881
Mucklestone ... 32 ... SJ 7237
Muckleton ... 32 ... SJ 5821
Muckletown ... 62 ... NJ 5621
Muckton ... 35 ... TF 3781
Muddiford ... 6 ... SS 5638
Mudeford ... 8 ... SZ 1892
Mudford ... 7 ... ST 5719
Mudgley ... 7 ... ST 4445
Mugdock Resr ... 50 ... NS 5576
Mugeary ... 58 ... NG 4438
Mugginton ... 33 ... SK 2843
Muggleswick ... 47 ... NZ 0450
Muie ... 66 ... NC 6704
Muirdrum ... 57 ... NO 5637
Muirhead (Fife.) ... 57 ... NO 2805
Muirhead (Strath.) ... 50 ... NS 3530
Muirhead (Strath.) ... 50 ... NS 6869
Muirhead (Tays.) ... 57 ... NO 3434
Muirhouses ... 51 ... NT 0180
Muirkirk ... 50 ... NS 6927
Muir of Fowlis ... 62 ... NJ 5612
Muir of Ord ... 60 ... NH 5250
Muirshearlich ... 55 ... NN 1380
Muirskie ... 62 ... NO 8295
Muirtack (Grampn.) ... 62 ... NJ 8146
Muirtack (Grampn.) ... 62 ... NJ 9937
Muirton ... 65 ... NH 7463
Muirton of Ardblair ... 56 ... NO 1743
Muirton of Ballochy ... 57 ... NO 6462
Muirtown ... 56 ... NN 9211
Muiryfold ... 62 ... NJ 7651
Muker ... 41 ... SD 9198
Mulbarton ... 29 ... TG 1901
Mulben ... 61 ... NJ 3450
Mulgrave Castle ... 43 ... NZ 8412
Mulindry ... 48 ... NR 3659
Mullion ... 2 ... SW 6719
Mumbles, The ... 15 ... SS 6287
Mumby ... 35 ... TF 5174
Muncaster Castle ... 40 ... SD 1096
Munderfield Row ... 24 ... SO 6451
Munderfield Stocks ... 24 ... SO 6550
Mundesley ... 29 ... TG 3136
Mundford ... 28 ... TL 8093
Mundham (Norf.) ... 29 ... TM 3298
Mundham (W. Susx) ... 11 ... SU 8701
Mundon Hill ... 21 ... TL 8702
Mundurno ... 62 ... NJ 9413
Munerigie ... 59 ... NH 2602
Mungrisdale ... 40 ... NY 3630
Munlochy ... 60 ... NH 6453
Munsley ... 24 ... SO 6640
Munslow ... 24 ... SO 5187
Munslow Aston ... 24 ... SO 5086
Murcott ... 18 ... SP 5815
Murkle ... 67 ... ND 1668
Murlaggan (Highld.) ... 55 ... NN 3181
Murrow ... 35 ... TF 3707
Mursley ... 18 ... SP 8128
Murthill ... 57 ... NO 4657
Murthly ... 56 ... NO 0938
Murton (Cumbr.) ... 41 ... NY 7221
Murton (Durham) ... 47 ... NZ 3947
Murton (Northum.) ... 53 ... NT 9748
Murton (N Yorks.) ... 38 ... SE 6452
Musbury ... 7 ... SY 2794
Muscoates ... 43 ... SE 6880
Musselburgh ... 51 ... NT 3472
Muston (Leic.) ... 34 ... SK 8237
Muston (N Yorks.) ... 43 ... TA 0979
Mustow Green ... 25 ... SO 8774
Mutford ... 29 ... TM 4888
Muthill ... 56 ... NN 8616
Mutterton ... 5 ... ST 0304
Mybster ... 67 ... ND 1652
Myddfai ... 15 ... SN 7730
Myddle ... 32 ... SJ 4623
Mydroilyn ... 22 ... SN 4555
Mylor Bridge ... 2 ... SW 8036
Mynachlog-ddu ... 14 ... SN 1430
Myndtown ... 24 ... SO 3889
Mynytho ... 30 ... SH 3031
Myrebird ... 62 ... NO 7498
Mytchett ... 11 ... SU 8855
Mytholm ... 37 ... SD 9827
Mytholmroyd ... 37 ... SE 0125
Myton-on-Swale ... 38 ... SE 4366

Naburn ... 38 ... SE 5945
Nackington ... 13 ... TR 1554
Nacton ... 21 ... TM 2240
Nafferton ... 39 ... TA 0559
Nailsea ... 16 ... ST 4670
Nailstone ... 33 ... SK 4107

Nailsworth 92 North Tamerton

Nailsworth 17 ST 8499
Nairn 60 NH 8756
Nancegollan 2 SW 6632
Nanhoron 30 SH 2831
Nannau 30 SH 7420
Nannerch 31 SJ 1669
Nanpantan 34 SK 5017
Nanpean 2 SW 9556
Nant-ddu 15 SO 0015
Nanternis 22 SN 3756
Nantgaredig 15 SN 4921
Nantgarw 16 ST 1285
Nant-glas 23 SN 9965
Nantglyn 31 SJ 0061
Nantlle 30 SH 5053
Nantmawr 32 SJ 2424
Nantmel 23 SO 0366
Nantmor 30 SH 6046
Nantwich 32 SJ 6552
Nant-y-derry 16 SO 3306
Nantyffyllon 15 SS 8492
Nantyglo 16 SO 1911
Nant-y-moel 15 SS 9393
Naphill 19 SU 8496
Nappa 37 SD 8553
Napton on the Hill 26 SP 4661
Narberth 14 SN 1114
Narborough (Leic.) 26 SP 5497
Narborough (Norf.) 28 TF 7413
Nasareth 30 SH 4749
Naseby 26 SP 6878
Nash (Bucks.) 18 SP 7734
Nash (Gwent) 16 ST 3483
Nash (Here. and Worc.) 23 SO 3062
Nash (Salop) 24 SO 6071
Nash Lee 19 SP 8408
Nassington 27 TL 0696
Nasty 20 TL 3624
Nateby (Cumbr.) 41 NY 7706
Nateby (Lancs.) 36 SD 4644
Natland 40 SD 5289
Naughton 21 TM 0249
Naunton (Glos.) 17 SP 1123
Naunton (Here. and Worc.) 25 SO 8739
Naunton Beauchamp 25 SO 9652
Naust 64 NG 8283
Navenby 34 SK 9857
Navestock 20 TQ 5397
Navestock Side 20 TQ 5697
Nawton 42 SE 6584
Nayland 21 TL 9734
Nazeing 20 TL 4106
Neacroft 8 SZ 1897
Neal's Green 26 SP 3384
Neap 63 HU 5060
Near Cotton 33 SK 0646
Neasham 42 NZ 3210
Neath 15 SS 7597
Neatishead 29 TG 3421
Nebo (Dyfed) 22 SN 5465
Nebo (Gwyn.) 30 SH 4750
Nebo (Gwyn.) 31 SH 8356
Necton 28 TF 8709
Nedd 64 NC 1332
Nedging Tye 21 TM 0149
Needham 29 TM 2281
Needham Market 21 TM 0855
Needingworth 27 TL 3472
Neen Savage 24 SO 6777
Neen Sollars 24 SO 6572
Neenton 24 SO 6487
Nefyn 30 SH 3040
Neilston 50 NS 4657
Nelson (Lancs.) 37 SD 8737
Nelson (Mid Glam.) 16 ST 1195
Nelson Village 47 NZ 2577
Nemphlar 50 NS 8544
Nempnett Thrubwell 16 ST 5360
Nenthead 41 NY 7743
Nenthorn 52 NT 6837
Nercwys 32 SJ 2260
Nereabolls 48 NR 2255
Nerston 50 NS 6457
Nesbit 53 NT 9833
Ness (Ches.) 32 SJ 3075
Ness (N Yorks.) 43 SE 6878
Nesscliffe 32 SJ 3819
Neston (Ches.) 32 SJ 2877
Neston (Wilts.) 17 ST 8667
Nether Alderley 33 SJ 8476
Netheravon 8 SU 1448
Nether Blainslie 52 NT 5443
Netherbrae 62 NJ 7959
Nether Broughton 34 SK 6925
Netherburn 50 NS 7947
Nether Burrow 41 SD 6174
Netherbury 7 SY 4799
Netherby 46 NY 3971
Nether Cerne 8 SY 6698
Nether Compton 7 ST 5907
Nether Crimond 62 NJ 8222
Nether Dallachy 61 NJ 3663
Netherend 17 SO 5900
Nether Exe 6 SS 9300
Netherfield 12 TQ 7018
Netherhampton 8 SU 1029
Nether Handwick 57 NO 3641
Nether Haugh 38 SK 4196
Nether Howecleuch 51 NT 0312
Nether Kellet 40 SD 5067
Nether Kinmundy 62 NK 0444
Nether Kirkton 50 NS 4757
Nether Langwith 34 SK 5371
Netherlaw 45 NX 7445
Netherley 62 NO 8593
Nethermill 45 NY 0487
Nethermuir 62 NJ 9143
Nether Padley 33 SK 2478
Netherplace 50 NS 5155
Nether Poppleton 38 SE 5654
Netherseal 33 SK 2813
Nether Silton 42 SE 4592
Nether Stowey 7 ST 1939
Netherstreet 17 ST 9764
Netherthird 50 NS 5818
Netherthong 37 SE 1309
Netherton (Central) 50 NS 5579
Netherton (Devon.) 5 SX 8971
Netherton (Here. and Worc.) 25 SO 9941
Netherton (Mers.) 36 SD 3500
Netherton (Northum.) 47 NT 9907
Netherton (Tays.) 56 NO 1452
Netherton (Tays.) 57 NO 5457
Netherton (W Yorks.) 37 SE 2716
Nethertown (Cumbr.) 40 NX 9807
Nethertown (Island of Stroma) 67 ND 3578
Nether Wallop 9 SU 3036
Nether Whitacre 26 SP 2393
Netherwitton 47 NZ 1090
Nether Worton 18 SP 4230
Nethy Bridge 61 NJ 0020
Netley 9 SU 4508
Netley Marsh 9 SU 3312
Nettlebed 18 SU 7086
Nettlebridge 8 ST 6448
Nettlecombe 7 SY 5195
Nettleden 19 TL 0210
Nettleham 34 TF 0075
Nettlestead 12 TQ 6852
Nettlestead Green 12 TQ 6850
Nettlestone 9 SZ 6290
Nettleton (Lincs.) 39 TA 1000
Nettleton (Wilts.) 17 ST 8178
Neuk, The 62 NO 7397
Nevendon 20 TQ 7390
Nevern 14 SN 0840
New Abbey 45 NX 9665
New Aberdour 62 NJ 8863
New Addington 12 TQ 3863
New Alresford 9 SU 5832
New Alyth 57 NO 2447
New Annesley 34 SK 5153
Newark (Northants.) 27 TF 2100
Newark (Sanday) 63 HY 7242
Newark-on-Trent 34 SK 7953
New Arley 50 NS 7859
Newbald 39 SE 9136
New Bewick 53 NU 0620
Newbiggin (Cumbr.) 46 NY 5649
Newbiggin (Cumbr.) 41 NY 6228
Newbiggin (Cumbr.) 40 SD 2669
Newbiggin (Durham) 41 NY 9127
Newbiggin (N Yorks.) 41 SD 9591
Newbiggin (N Yorks.) 41 SD 9985
Newbiggin Common 41 NY 9131
Newbiggin-by-the Sea 47 NZ 3187
Newbigging (Strath.) 51 NT 0145
Newbigging (Tays.) 57 NO 2841
Newbigging (Tays.) 57 NO 4237
Newbigging (Tays.) 57 NO 4936
Newbiggin on Lune 41 NY 7005
Newbold (Derby.) 33 SK 3773
Newbold (Leic.) 33 SK 4018
Newbold on Avon 26 SP 4877
Newbold on Stour 26 SP 2446
Newbold Pacey 26 SP 2957
Newbold Verdon 26 SK 4403
New Bolingbroke 35 TF 3058
Newborough (Gwyn.) 30 SH 4265
Newborough (Northants.) 35 TF 2006
Newborough (Staffs.) 33 SK 1325
Newbottle 18 SP 5236
Newbourn 21 TM 2743
Newbridge (Clwyd) 32 SJ 2841
Newbridge (Corn.) 2 SW 4231
Newbridge (Gwent) 16 ST 2197
Newbridge (Hants.) 9 SU 2915
Newbridge (I. of W.) 9 SZ 4187
Newbridge (Lothian) 51 NT 1272
Newbridge-on-Usk 16 ST 3894
Newbridge on Wye 23 SO 0158
New Brighton 32 SJ 3093
New Brinsley 33 SK 4550
Newbrough 47 NY 8767
New Buckenham 29 TM 0890
Newburgh (Fife) 56 NO 2318
Newburgh (Grampn.) 62 NJ 9925
Newburgh (Lancs.) 36 SD 4810
Newburn 47 NZ 1765
Newbury 10 SU 4666
Newby (Cumbr.) 41 NY 5921
Newby (N Yorks.) 42 NZ 5012
Newby (N Yorks.) 41 SD 7269
Newby Bridge 40 SD 3686
Newby East 46 NY 4758
New Byth 62 NJ 8254
Newby West 46 NY 3653
Newby Wiske 42 SE 3687
Newcastle (Gwent) 16 SO 4417
Newcastle (Salop) 23 SO 2482
Newcastle Emlyn 14 SN 3040
Newcastleton 46 NY 4887
Newcastle-under-Lyme 33 SJ 8445
Newcastle upon Tyne 47 NZ 2464
Newchapel (Dyfed) 14 SN 2239
Newchapel (Staffs.) 33 SJ 8654
Newchapel (Surrey) 12 TQ 3642
Newchurch (Dyfed) 15 SN 3724
Newchurch (Gwent) 16 ST 4597
Newchurch (I. of W.) 9 SZ 5585
Newchurch (Kent) 13 TR 0531
Newchurch (Powys) 23 SO 2150
Newchurch in Pendle 37 SD 8239
New Clipstone 34 SK 5863
New Costessey 29 TG 1710
Newcott 5 ST 2309
New Cross 22 SN 6376
New Cumnock 50 NS 6113
New Deer 62 NJ 8846
Newdigate 11 TQ 2042
New Duston 26 SP 7162
New Earswick 38 SE 6155
New Edlington 38 SK 5399
New Ellerby 39 TA 1639
Newell Green 11 SU 8771
New Eltham 12 TQ 4573
New End 25 SP 0560
Newenden 12 TQ 8327
Newent 17 SO 7226
New Farnley 37 SE 2431
New Ferry 32 SJ 3385
Newfield (Durham) 42 NZ 2033
Newfield (Highld.) 65 NH 7877
New Fryston 38 SE 4526
Newgale 14 SM 8422
New Galloway 45 NX 6377
Newgate 29 TG 0443
Newgate Street 20 TL 3005
New Gilston 57 NO 4207
Newgord 63 HP 5706
Newgrounds 17 SO 7204
Newhall (Ches.) 32 SJ 6045
Newhall (Derby.) 33 SK 2821
Newham (Gtr London) 20 TQ 4082
Newham (Northum.) 53 NU 1728
Newham Hall 53 NU 1729
New Hartley 47 NZ 3076
Newhaven 12 TQ 4401
New Hedges 14 SN 1302
New Hey 37 SD 9311
New Holland 39 TA 0724
Newholm 43 NZ 8610
New Houghton (Derby.) 33 SK 4965
New Houghton (Norf.) 28 TF 7827
Newhouse 50 NS 7961
New Houses 41 SD 8073
New Hutton 41 SD 5691
New Hythe 12 TQ 7159
Newick 12 TQ 4121
Newington (Kent) 13 TQ 8665
Newington (Kent) 13 TR 1737
Newington (Oxon.) 18 SU 6196
New Inn (Gwent) 16 SO 4800
New Inn (Gwent) 16 ST 3099
New Inn (N Yorks.) 41 SD 8072
New Invention 23 SO 2976
New Kelso 59 NG 9442
New Lanark 50 NS 8742
Newland (Glos.) 16 SO 5509
Newland (Here. and Worc.) 24 SO 7948
Newland (N Yorks.) 38 SE 6824
Newlandrig 51 NT 3662
Newlands (Grampn.) 61 NJ 3051
Newlands (Northum.) 47 NZ 0955
Newlands of Geise 67 ND 0865
New Lane 36 SD 4212
New Leake 35 TF 4057
New Leeds 62 NJ 9954
New Longton 36 SD 5125
New Luce 44 NX 1764
Newlyn 2 SW 4628
Newlyn East 2 SW 8256
Newmachar 62 NJ 8819
Newmains 50 NS 8256
New Mains of Ury 57 NO 8787
Newmarket (Isle of Lewis) 63 NB 4235
Newmarket (Suff.) 20 TL 6463
New Marton 32 SJ 3334
Newmill (Borders) 52 NT 4510
New Mill (Corn.) 2 SW 4534
New Mill (Grampn.) 61 NJ 4352
New Mill (Herts.) 19 SP 9212
New Mill (W Yorks.) 37 SE 1608
Newmill of Inshewan 57 NO 4260
New Mills (Corn.) 2 SW 8952
New Mills (Derby.) 33 SK 0085
New Mills (Gwent) 16 SO 5107
Newmills (Lothian) 51 NT 1667
New Mills (Powys) 23 SJ 0901
Newmiln 56 NO 1230
Newmilns 50 NS 5337
New Milton 9 SZ 2495
New Moat 14 SN 0625
Newnham (Glos.) 17 SO 6911
Newnham (Hants.) 10 SU 7054
Newnham (Herts.) 19 TL 2437
Newnham (Kent) 13 TQ 9557
Newnham (Northants.) 26 SP 5859
Newnham Bridge 24 SO 6469
New Park 9 SU 2904
New Pitsligo 62 NJ 8855
New Polzeath 2 SW 9379
Newport (Devon) 6 SS 5631
Newport (Dyfed) 14 SN 0539
Newport (Essex) 20 TL 5234
Newport (Glos.) 17 ST 7097
Newport (Gwent) 16 ST 3187
Newport (Highld.) 67 ND 1224
Newport (Humbs.) 39 SE 8530
Newport (I. of W.) 9 SZ 4989
Newport (Norf.) 29 TG 5017
Newport (Salop) 32 SJ 7419
Newport-on-Tay 57 NO 4228
Newport Pagnell 27 SP 8743
Newpound Common 11 TQ 0627
New Prestwick 50 NS 3424
Newquay (Corn.) 2 SW 8161
New Quay (Dyfed) 22 SN 3859
New Rackheath 29 TG 2812
New Radnor 23 SO 2161
New Rent 40 NY 4536
New Romney 13 TR 0624
New Rossington 38 SK 6198
New Sauchie 50 NS 8993
New Scone 56 NO 1325
Newseat (Grampn.) 62 NJ 7033
Newseat (Grampn.) 62 NK 0749
Newsham (Northum.) 47 NZ 3079
Newsham (N Yorks.) 42 NZ 1010
Newsholme (Humbs.) 38 SE 7229
Newsholme (Lancs.) 37 SD 8451
New Silksworth 47 NZ 3853
Newstead (Borders) 52 NT 5634
Newstead (Northum.) 53 NU 1526
Newstead (Notts.) 34 SK 5252
New Stevenston 50 NS 7659
Newthorpe 38 SE 4632
Newtimber Place 11 TQ 2613
New Tolsta 63 NB 5348
Newton (Borders) 52 NT 6020
Newton (Cambs.) 35 TF 4314
Newton (Cambs.) 20 TL 4349
Newton (Ches.) 32 SJ 5059
Newton (Ches.) 32 SJ 5274
Newton (Cumbr.) 40 SD 2371
Newton (Dumf. and Galwy.) 45 NY 1194
Newton (Grampn.) 61 NJ 1663
Newton (Hants.) 9 SU 2322
Newton (Here. and Worc.) 23 SO 3433
Newton (Here. and Worc.) 24 SO 5054
Newton (Highld.) 64 NC 2331
Newton (Highld.) 67 ND 3449
Newton (Highld.) 60 NH 7448
Newton (Highld.) 65 NH 7866
Newton (Lancs.) 41 SD 5974
Newton (Lancs.) 36 SD 6950
Newton (Lincs.) 35 TF 0436
Newton (Lothian) 51 NT 0877
Newton (Mid Glam.) 15 SS 8377
Newton (Norf.) 28 TF 8315
Newton (Northants.) 27 SP 8883
Newton (North Uist) 63 NF 8977
Newton (Northum.) 47 NZ 0364
Newton (Notts.) 34 SK 6841
Newton (Staffs.) 33 SK 0325
Newton (Strath.) 55 NS 0498
Newton (Strath.) 50 NS 6560
Newton (Strath.) 51 NS 9331
Newton (Suff.) 21 TL 9140
Newton (Warw.) 26 SP 5378
Newton (W Glam.) 15 SS 6088
Newton (W Yorks.) 38 SE 4427
Newton Abbot 5 SX 8671
Newton Arlosh 46 NY 1955
Newton Aycliffe 42 NZ 2724
Newton Bewley 42 NZ 4626
Newton Blossomville 27 SP 9251
Newton Bromswold 27 SP 9966
Newton Burgoland 33 SK 3609
Newton by Toft 35 TF 0487
Newton Ferrers 4 SX 5447
Newton Flotman 29 TM 2198
Newtongarry Croft 62 NJ 5735
Newtongrange 51 NT 3364
Newton Harcourt 26 SP 6397
Newtonhill 62 NO 9193
Newton Kyme 38 SE 4644
Newton-le-Willows (Mers.) 32 SJ 5894
Newton-le-Willows (N Yorks.) 42 SE 2189
Newton Longville 19 SP 8431
Newton Mearns 50 NS 5456
Newtonmill 57 NO 6064
Newtonmore 60 NN 7199
Newton Mountain 14 SM 9807
Newton of Balcanquhal 56 NO 1510
Newton-on-Ouse 38 SE 5059
Newton-on-Rawcliffe 43 SE 8090
Newton-on-the-Moor 47 NU 1605
Newton on Trent 34 SK 8374
Newton Poppleford 5 SY 0889
Newton Purcell 18 SP 6230
Newton Regis 33 SK 2707
Newton Reigny 40 NY 4731
Newton St. Cyres 6 SX 8797
Newton St. Faith 29 TG 2117
Newton St. Loe 17 ST 7064
Newton St. Petrock 4 SS 4112
Newton Solney 33 SK 2825
Newton Stacey 10 SU 4040
Newton Stewart 44 NX 4165
Newton Toney 10 SU 2140
Newton Tracey 6 SS 5226
Newton under Roseberry 42 NZ 5613
Newton upon Derwent 38 SE 7149
Newton Valence 9 SU 7232
Newtown (Ches.) 32 SJ 6247
Newtown (Ches.) 33 SJ 9784
Newtown (Corn.) 2 SW 7323
Newtown (Cumbr.) 46 NY 5062
Newtown (Dorset) 8 SZ 0393
Newtown (Hants.) 9 SU 2710
Newtown (Hants.) 9 SU 3023
Newtown (Hants.) 10 SU 4763
Newtown (Hants.) 9 SU 6013
Newtown (Here. and Worc.) 24 SO 6145
Newtown (Highld.) 59 NH 3504
Newtown (I. of M.) 43 SC 3273
Newtown (I. of W.) 9 SZ 4290
New Town (Lothian) 52 NT 4470
Newtown (Northum.) 53 NT 9731
Newtown (Northum.) 47 NU 0300
Newtown (Northum.) 53 NU 0425
Newtown (Powys) 23 SO 1091
Newtown (Salop) 32 SJ 4831
Newtown (Staffs.) 33 SJ 9060
Newtown (Wilts.) 8 ST 9128
Newtown Linford 34 SK 5110
Newtown St. Boswells 52 NT 5731
New Tredegar 16 SO 1403
New Tupton 33 SK 3966
Newtyle 57 NO 2941
New Ulva 48 NR 7080
New Walsoken 35 TF 4709
New Waltham 39 TA 2804
New Wimpole 20 TL 3450
New Winton 52 NT 4271
New Yatt 18 SP 3713
New York (Lincs.) 35 TF 2455
New York (Tyne and Wear) 47 NZ 3270
Neyland 14 SM 9605
Nibley 17 ST 6882
Nicholashayne 7 ST 1015
Nicholaston 15 SS 5188
Nidd 42 SE 3060
Nigg (Grampn.) 62 NJ 9402
Nigg (Highld.) 65 NH 8071
Nightcott 6 SS 8925
Nine Ashes 20 TL 5902
Ninebanks 46 NY 7853
Ninfield 12 TQ 7012
Ningwood 9 SZ 3989
Nisbet 52 NT 6725
Niton 9 SZ 5076
Nitshill 50 NS 5160
Noak Hill 20 TQ 5493
Nobottle 26 SP 6763
Nocton 35 TF 0564
Noke 18 SP 5413
Nolton 14 SM 8718
No Man's Heath (Ches.) 32 SJ 5148
No Man's Heath (Warw.) 33 SK 2709
Nomansland (Devon) 6 SS 8313
Nomansland (Wilts.) 9 SU 2517
Noneley 32 SJ 4727
Nonington 13 TR 2552
Nook 46 NY 4679
Noran Water 57 NO 4860
Norbury (Ches.) 32 SJ 5547
Norbury (Derby.) 33 SK 1242
Norbury (Salop) 24 SO 3693
Norbury (Staffs.) 32 SJ 7823
Nordelph 28 TF 5501
Norden (Dorset) 8 SY 9483
Norden (Gtr Mches) 37 SD 8514
Nordley 24 SO 6998
Norham 53 NT 9047
Norley 32 SJ 5672
Norleywood 9 SZ 3597
Normanby (Humbs.) 39 SE 8716
Normanby (Lincs.) 34 SK 9988
Normanby (N Yorks.) 43 SE 7381
Normanby le Wold 39 TF 1294
Norman Cross 27 TL 1691
Normandy 11 SU 9251
Norman's Green 5 ST 0503
Normanton (Derby.) 33 SK 3433
Normanton (Lincs.) 34 SK 9446
Normanton (Notts.) 34 SK 7054
Normanton (W Yorks.) 37 SE 3822
Normanton le Heath 33 SK 3712
Normanton on Soar 34 SK 5123
Normanton on the Wolds 34 SK 6232
Normanton on Trent 34 SK 7868
Normoss 36 SD 3437
Norrington Common 17 ST 8864
Norris Hill 33 SK 3216
Northallerton 42 SE 3793
Northam (Devon.) 6 SS 4429
Northam (Hants.) 9 SU 4312
Northampton 26 SP 7561
North Aston 18 SP 4728
Northaw 19 TL 2802
North Baddesley 9 SU 3920
North Ballachulish 55 NN 0560
North Barrow 7 ST 6029
North Barsham 28 TF 9135
North Benfleet 20 TQ 7590
North Berwick 52 NT 5485
North Boarhunt 9 SU 6010
Northborough 35 TF 1508
Northbourne 13 TR 3352
North Bovey 5 SX 7483
North Bradley 17 ST 8554
North Brentor 4 SX 4781
North Buckland 6 SS 4740
North Burlingham 29 TG 3610
North Cadbury 8 ST 6327
North Cairn 44 NW 9770
North Carlton 34 SK 9477
North Cave 39 SE 8832
North Cerney 17 SP 0208
Northchapel 11 SU 9529
North Charford 8 SU 1919
North Charlton 53 NU 1622
Northchurch 19 SP 9708
North Cliffe 39 SE 8737
North Clifton 34 SK 8272
North Cotes 39 TA 3400
Northcott 4 SX 3392
North Cove 29 TM 4689
North Cowton 42 NZ 2803
North Crawley 27 SP 9244
North Cray 12 TQ 4972
North Creake 28 TF 8538
North Curry 7 ST 3125
North Dalton 39 SE 9352
North Dawn 63 HY 4803
North Deighton 37 SE 3851
North Duffield 38 SE 6837
North Elkington 35 TF 2890
North Elmham 29 TF 9820
North End (Avon) 16 ST 4167
Northend (Avon) 17 ST 7867
North End (Berks.) 10 SU 4063
Northend (Bucks.) 18 SU 7392
North End (Hants.) 9 SU 6502
Northend (Warw.) 26 SP 3852
North End (W Susx) 11 TQ 1209
North Erradale 64 NG 7481
North Fearns 58 NG 5835
North Ferriby 39 SE 9826
Northfield (Borders) 53 NT 9167
Northfield (Grampn.) 62 NJ 9008
Northfield (W Mids.) 25 SP 0179
Northfleet 12 TQ 6274
North Frodingham 39 TA 1053
North Green 29 TM 2288
North Grimston 39 SE 8467
North Haven (Grampn.) 62 NK 1138
North Hayling 9 SU 7203
North Heasley 6 SS 7333
North Heath 11 TQ 0621
North Hill (Corn.) 4 SX 2776
North Hinksey 18 SP 4806
North Holmwood 11 TQ 1646
North Huish 5 SX 7156
North Hykeham 34 SK 9465
Northiam 12 TQ 8324
Northill (Beds.) 27 TL 1446
Northington 10 SU 5637
North Kelsey 39 TA 0401
North Kessock 60 NH 6548
North Kilvington 42 SE 4285
North Kilworth 26 SP 6183
North Kingennie 57 NO 4736
North Kyme 35 TF 1452
North Lancing 11 TQ 1805
Northlands 35 TF 3453
Northleach 17 SP 1114
North Lee (Bucks.) 18 SP 8309
Northleigh (Devon.) 5 SY 1995
North Leigh (Oxon.) 18 SP 3813
North Leverton with Habblesthorpe 34 SK 7882
Northlew 6 SX 5099
North Littleton 25 SP 0847
North Lopham 29 TM 0383
North Luffenham 27 SK 9303
North Marden 9 SU 8015
North Marston 18 SP 7722
North Middleton 51 NT 3559
North Molton 6 SS 7329
Northmoor 18 SP 4202
Northmoor Green or Moorland 7 ST 3332
North Moreton 18 SU 5689
Northmuir 57 NO 3855
North Muskham 34 SK 7958
North Newbald 39 SE 9136
North Newington 18 SP 4139
North Newnton 17 SU 1257
North Newton 7 ST 2931
North Nibley 17 ST 7396
North Oakley 10 SU 5354
North Ockendon 20 TQ 5984
Northolt 19 TQ 1285
Northop 32 SJ 2468
Northop Hall 32 SJ 2767
North Ormsby 39 TF 2893
Northorpe (Lincs.) 39 SK 8996
Northorpe (Lincs.) 35 TF 0917
North Otterington 42 SE 3589
Northover 7 ST 5223
North Owersby 39 TF 0594
Northowram 37 SE 1127
North Perrott 7 ST 4709
North Petherton 7 ST 2832
North Petherwin 4 SX 2889
North Pickenham 28 TF 8606
North Piddle 25 SO 9654
North Poorton 7 SY 5197
North Queensferry 51 NT 1380
Northrepps 29 TG 2439
North Rigton 37 SE 2749
North Rode 33 SJ 8866
North Runcton 28 TF 6416
North Scale 40 SD 1769
North Scarle 34 SK 8466
North Seaton 47 NZ 2986
North Shian 54 NM 9143
North Shields 47 NZ 3468
North Shoebury 21 TQ 9286
North Shore 36 SD 3037
North Side 27 TL 2799
North Somercotes 39 TF 4296
North Stainley 42 SE 2876
North Stainmore 41 NY 8215
North Stifford 20 TQ 6080
North Stoke (Avon) 17 ST 7068
North Stoke (Oxon.) 18 SU 6186
North Stoke (W Susx) 11 TQ 0211
North Street (Berks.) 10 SU 6372
North Street (Hants.) 9 SU 6433
North Sunderland 53 NU 2131
North Tamerton 4 SX 3197

North Tawton 93 Pen-llyn

North Tawton	6	SS 6601
North Thoresby	39	TF 2998
North Tidworth	10	SU 2248
North Tolsta	63	NB 5347
Northton	63	NF 9889
North Tuddenham	29	TG 0413
North Walsham	29	TG 2730
North Waltham	10	SU 5546
North Warnborough	10	SU 7351
North Water Bridge	57	NO 6566
North Watten	67	ND 2458
Northway	25	SO 9234
North Weald Basset	20	TL 4904
North Whilborough	5	SX 8766
Northwich	32	SJ 6573
Northwick (Avon)	16	ST 5586
North Wick (Avon)	17	ST 5865
North Widcombe	17	ST 5758
North Willingham	35	TF 1688
North Wingfield	33	SK 4064
North Witham	34	SK 9221
Northwold	28	TL 7596
Northwood (Gtr London)	19	TQ 1090
Northwood (I. of W.)	9	SZ 4992
Northwood (Salop)	32	SJ 4633
Northwood Green	17	SO 7216
North Wootton (Dorset)	8	ST 6614
North Wootton (Norf.)	28	TF 6424
North Wootton (Somer.)	7	ST 5641
North Wraxall	17	ST 8174
North Wroughton	17	SU 1581
Norton (Ches.)	32	SJ 5581
Norton (Cleve.)	42	NZ 4421
Norton (Glos.)	17	SO 8624
Norton (Here. and Worc.)	25	SO 8750
Norton (Here. and Worc.)	25	SP 0447
Norton (Herts.)	19	TL 2234
Norton (I. of W.)	9	SZ 3489
Norton (Northants.)	26	SP 6063
Norton (Notts.)	34	SK 5772
Norton (N Yorks.)	38	SE 7971
Norton (N Yorks.)	33	SK 3581
Norton (Powys)	23	SO 3067
Norton (Salop)	24	SJ 5609
Norton (Salop)	24	SJ 7200
Norton (Salop)	24	SO 4581
Norton (Suff.)	21	TL 9565
Norton (S Yorks.)	38	SE 5415
Norton (Wilts.)	17	ST 8884
Norton (W Susx)	11	SU 9306
Norton Bavant	8	ST 9043
Norton Canes	25	SK 0108
Norton Canon	24	SO 3847
Norton Disney	34	SK 8859
Norton Ferris	8	ST 7936
Norton Fitzwarren	7	ST 1925
Norton Green	9	SZ 3388
Norton Hawkfield	17	ST 5964
Norton Heath	20	TL 6004
Norton in Hales	32	SJ 7038
Norton in the Moors	33	SJ 8951
Norton-Juxta-Twycross	33	SK 3207
Norton-le-Clay	38	SE 4071
Norton Lindsey	26	SP 2263
Norton Malreward	17	ST 6064
Norton St. Philip	17	ST 7755
Norton Subcourse	29	TM 4098
Norton sub Hamdon	7	ST 4615
Norwell	34	SK 7661
Norwell Woodhouse	34	SK 7462
Norwich	29	TG 2308
Norwick (Unst)	63	HP 6414
Norwood Green	11	TQ 1378
Norwood Hill	11	TQ 2443
Noseley	26	SP 7398
Noss Mayo	4	SX 5447
Nosterfield	42	SE 2780
Nostie	59	NG 8527
Notgrove	17	SP 1020
Nottage	15	SS 8278
Nottingham	34	SK 5741
Notton (Wilts.)	17	ST 9169
Notton (W Yorks.)	37	SE 3413
Nounsbrough	63	HU 2957
Nounsley	20	TL 7910
Noutard's Green	24	SO 7966
Nox	24	SJ 4010
Nuffield	18	SU 6687
Nunburnholme	39	SE 8548
Nuneaton	26	SP 3592
Nuneham Courtenay	18	SU 5599
Nun Monkton	38	SE 5057
Nunney	8	ST 7345
Nunnington	42	SE 6679
Nunnykirk	47	NZ 0892
Nunthorpe	42	NZ 5313
Nunton (Benbecula)	63	NF 7653
Nunton (Wilts.)	8	SU 1525
Nunwick	47	NY 8774
Nursling	9	SU 3615
Nursted	9	SU 7621
Nutbourne	11	TQ 0718
Nutfield	12	TQ 3150
Nuthall	34	SK 5144
Nuthampstead	20	TL 4134
Nuthurst	11	TQ 1926
Nutley	12	TQ 4427
Nutwell	38	SE 6303
Nybster	67	ND 3663
Nyetimber	11	SZ 8998
Nyewood	9	SU 8021
Nymet Rowland	6	SS 7108
Nymet Tracey	6	SS 7200
Nympsfield	17	SO 8000
Nynehead	7	ST 1422
Nyton	11	SU 9305
Oadby	26	SK 6200
Oad Street	13	TQ 8762
Oakamoor	33	SK 0544
Oakbank	51	NT 0866
Oakdale	16	ST 1898
Oake	7	ST 1525
Oaken	25	SJ 8502
Oakenclough	36	SD 5447
Oakengates	24	SJ 7010
Oakenshaw (Durham)	42	NZ 2036
Oakenshaw (W Yorks.)	37	SE 1727
Oakford (Devon.)	6	SS 9021
Oakford (Dyfed)	22	SN 4557
Oakgrove	33	SJ 9169
Oakham	34	SK 8509
Oakhanger	9	SU 7635
Oakhill	8	ST 6347
Oakington	20	TL 4164
Oaklands	31	SH 8158
Oakle Street	17	SO 7517
Oakley (Beds.)	27	TL 0153
Oakley (Bucks.)	18	SP 6412
Oakley (Fife.)	51	NT 0289
Oakley (Hants.)	10	SU 5650
Oakley (Suff.)	29	TM 1678
Oakley Green	11	SU 9376
Oakleypark	23	SN 9886
Oakridge	17	SO 9103
Oaks	24	SJ 4204
Oaksey	17	ST 9893
Oakthorpe	33	SK 3213
Oakwoodhill	11	TQ 1337
Oakworth	37	SE 0238
Oare (Kent)	13	TR 0062
Oare (Somer.)	6	SS 8047
Oare (Wilts.)	17	SU 1563
Oasby	34	TF 0039
Oathlaw	57	NO 4756
Oban	54	NM 8630
Obney	56	NO 0336
Oborne	8	ST 6518
Occlestone Green	32	SJ 6962
Occold	29	TM 1570
Ochertyre	56	NN 8323
Ochiltree	50	NS 5121
Ochtermuthill	56	NN 8216
Ockbrook	33	SK 4235
Ockham	11	TQ 0756
Ockle	54	NM 5570
Ockley	11	TQ 1640
Ocle Pychard	24	SO 5946
Odcombe	7	ST 5015
Oddingley	25	SO 9159
Oddington (Glos.)	18	SP 2225
Oddington (Oxon.)	18	SP 5514
Odell	27	SP 9658
Odiham	10	SU 7350
Odstock	8	SU 1426
Odstone	33	SK 3907
Offchurch	26	SP 3565
Offenham	25	SP 0546
Offham (E Susx)	12	TQ 4012
Offham (Kent)	12	TQ 6557
Offord Cluny	27	TL 2267
Offord Darcy	27	TL 2266
Offton	21	TM 0649
Offwell	5	SY 1999
Ogbourne Maizey	17	SU 1871
Ogbourne St. Andrew	17	SU 1872
Ogbourne St. George	17	SU 2074
Ogil	57	NO 4561
Ogle	47	NZ 1378
Ogmore	15	SS 8877
Ogmore-by-Sea	15	SS 8674
Ogmore Vale	15	SS 9490
Okeford Fitzpaine	8	ST 8010
Okehampton	6	SX 5895
Okehampton Camp	4	SX 5893
Okraquoy	63	HU 4331
Old	26	SP 7873
Old Aberdeen	62	NJ 9408
Old Alresford	9	SU 5834
Oldberrow	25	SP 1165
Old Bewick	53	NU 0621
Old Bolingbroke	35	TF 3564
Oldborough	6	SS 7706
Old Brampton	33	SK 3371
Old Bridge of Urr	45	NX 7767
Old Buckenham	29	TM 0691
Old Burghclere	10	SU 4657
Oldbury (Salop)	24	SO 7092
Oldbury (Warw.)	26	SP 3194
Oldbury (W Mids.)	25	SO 9889
Oldbury-on-Severn	17	ST 6092
Oldbury on the Hill	17	ST 8089
Old Byland	42	SE 5486
Oldcastle	16	SO 3224
Old Cleeve	7	ST 0342
Oldcoates	34	SK 5888
Old Colwyn	31	SH 8678
Old Dailly	44	NX 2299
Old Dalby	34	SK 6723
Old Deer	62	NJ 9747
Old Felixstowe	21	TM 3135
Oldfield	25	SO 8464
Old Fletton	27	TL 1997
Oldford	8	ST 7849
Old Hall (Highld.)	67	ND 2056
Old Hall, The (Humbs.)	39	TA 2717
Oldham	37	SD 9305
Oldhamstocks	53	NT 7470
Old Heath	21	TM 0122
Oldhurst	27	TL 3077
Old Hutton	41	SD 5688
Old Kea	2	SW 8441
Old Kilpatrick	50	NS 4673
Old Knebworth	19	TL 2320
Oldland	17	ST 6771
Old Leake	35	TF 4050
Old Malton	38	SE 7972
Oldmeldrum	62	NJ 8027
Old Milverton	26	SP 2967
Old Monkland	50	NS 7163
Old Newton	21	TM 0662
Oldpark	24	SJ 6909
Old Philpstoun	51	NT 0577
Old Radnor	23	SO 2559
Old Rayne	62	NJ 6728
Old Romney	13	TR 0325
Old Scone	56	NO 1226
Oldshore	66	NC 2059
Old Sodbury	17	ST 7581
Old Somerby	34	SK 9633
Oldstead	42	SE 5280
Old Town	47	NY 8891
Oldtown of Ord	62	NJ 6259
Old Warden	27	TL 1343
Oldways End	6	SS 8624
Old Weston	27	TL 0977
Oldwhat	62	NJ 8551
Old Windsor	11	SU 9874
Old Wives Lees	13	TR 0755
Olgrinmore	67	ND 0955
Oliver	51	NT 0924
Oliver's Battery	9	SU 4527
Ollaberry	63	HU 3680
Ollach	58	NG 5137
Ollerton (Ches.)	32	SJ 7776
Ollerton (Notts.)	34	SK 6567
Ollerton (Salop)	32	SJ 6425
Olney	27	SP 8851
Olton	25	SP 1282
Olveston	17	ST 6087
Ombersley	25	SO 8463
Ompton	34	SK 6865
Onchan	43	SC 4078
Onecote	33	SK 0555
Ongar Hill	28	TF 5724
Ongar Street	24	SO 3967
Onibury	24	SO 4579
Onich	55	NN 0261
Onllwyn	15	SN 8310
Onneley	32	SJ 7542
Onslow Village	11	SU 9849
Opinan (Highld.)	64	NG 7472
Opinan (Highld.)	64	NG 8796
Orby	35	TF 4967
Orchard	8	ST 8216
Orchard Portman	7	ST 2421
Orcheston	8	SU 0545
Orcop	16	SO 4726
Ord	58	NG 6113
Ordhead	62	NJ 6610
Ordiequish	61	NJ 3357
Ore	12	TQ 8311
Oreham Common	11	TQ 2214
Oreton	24	SO 6580
Orford (Ches.)	32	SJ 6090
Orford (Suff.)	21	TM 4250
Orgreave	25	SK 1415
Orlestone	13	TR 0034
Orleton (Here. and Worc.)	24	SO 4967
Orleton (Here. and Worc.)	24	SO 6967
Orlingbury	27	SP 8572
Ormesby	42	NZ 5317
Ormesby St. Margaret	29	TG 4915
Ormesby St. Michael	29	TG 4814
Ormiscaig	64	NG 8590
Ormiston	52	NT 4169
Ormsaigmore	54	NM 4763
Ormskirk	36	SD 4107
Orosay (Isle of Lewis)	63	NB 3612
Orphir	63	HY 3404
Orpington	12	TQ 4665
Orrell	36	SD 5203
Orrin Resr	60	NH 3850
Orrisdale Head	43	SC 3192
Orroland	45	NX 7746
Orsay	48	NR 1651
Orsett	20	TQ 6481
Orslow	24	SJ 8015
Orston	34	SK 7741
Orton (Cumbr.)	41	NY 6208
Orton (Northants.)	26	SP 8079
Orton Longueville	27	TL 1696
Orton-on-the-Hill	26	SK 3004
Orton Waterville	27	TL 1596
Orval	60	NM 3399
Orwell	20	TL 3650
Osbaldeston	36	SD 6431
Osbaston	26	SK 4204
Osborne	9	SZ 5194
Osborne Bay	9	SZ 5395
Osbournby	35	TF 0638
Oscroft	32	SJ 5066
Osdale	58	NG 3241
Osea Island	21	TL 9106
Ose River	58	NG 3442
Osgathorpe	33	SK 4219
Osgodby (Lincs.)	39	TF 0792
Osgodby (N Yorks.)	38	SE 6433
Osgodby (N Yorks.)	43	TA 0585
Oskaig	58	NG 5438
Oskamull	54	NM 4540
Osmaston	33	SK 1944
Osmington	8	SY 7282
Osmington Mills	8	SY 7381
Osmotherley	42	SE 4597
Osnaburgh or Dairsie	57	NO 4117
Ospringe	13	TQ 9960
Ossett	37	SE 2720
Ossington	34	SK 7564
Ostend	21	TQ 9397
Oswaldkirk	42	SE 6279
Oswaldtwistle	36	SD 7327
Oswestry	32	SJ 2829
Otford	12	TQ 5359
Otham	12	TQ 7954
Othery	7	ST 3831
Otley (Suff.)	21	TM 2055
Otley (W Yorks.)	37	SE 2045
Otterbourne	9	SU 4522
Otterburn (Northum.)	47	NY 8893
Otterburn (N Yorks.)	37	SD 8857
Otterburn Camp	47	NY 8995
Otter Ferry	49	NR 9384
Otterham	4	SX 1690
Ottershaw	11	TQ 0264
Otterswick (Yell)	63	HU 5185
Otterton	5	SY 0785
Ottery St. Mary	5	SY 0995
Ottringham	39	TA 2624
Oughtershaw	41	SD 8781
Oughtibridge	37	SK 3093
Oulston	38	SE 5474
Oulton (Cumbr.)	46	NY 2551
Oulton (Norf.)	29	TG 1328
Oulton (Staffs.)	33	SJ 9035
Oulton (Suff.)	29	TM 5194
Oulton (W Yorks.)	37	SE 3627
Oulton Broad	29	TM 5292
Oulton Street	29	TG 1527
Oundle	27	TL 0488
Ousby	41	NY 6134
Ousdale	67	ND 0620
Ousden	20	TL 7359
Ouseburn	38	SE 4461
Ousefleet	39	SE 8223
Ouston	47	NZ 2554
Outertown	63	HY 2310
Outgate	40	SD 3599
Outhgill	41	NY 7801
Outlane	37	SE 0817
Out Newton	39	TA 3822
Out Rawcliffe	36	SD 4041
Outwell	28	TF 5104
Outwood (Surrey)	12	TQ 3246
Outwood (W Yorks.)	37	SE 3223
Oval, The	17	ST 7363
Ovenden	37	SE 0727
Over (Avon)	17	ST 5882
Over (Cambs.)	27	TL 3770
Overbury	25	SO 9537
Over Haddon	33	SK 2066
Over Kellet	40	SD 5169
Over Kiddington	18	SP 4122
Over Norton	18	SP 3128
Overseal	33	SK 2915
Over Silton	42	SE 4593
Overstone	26	SP 8066
Overstrand	29	TG 2440
Overton (Clwyd)	32	SJ 3741
Overton (Dumf. and Galwy.)	45	NX 9864
Overton (Grampn.)	62	NJ 8714
Overton (Hants.)	10	SU 5149
Overton (Lancs.)	36	SD 4357
Overton (Salop)	24	SO 4972
Overton Green	32	SJ 7960
Overtown	50	NS 8052
Over Wallop	10	SU 2838
Over Whitacre	26	SP 2591
Overy Staithe	28	TF 8444
Oving (Bucks.)	18	SP 7821
Oving (W Susx)	11	SU 9005
Ovingdean	12	TQ 3503
Ovingham	47	NZ 0863
Ovington (Durham)	42	NZ 1314
Ovington (Essex)	20	TL 7742
Ovington (Hants.)	9	SU 5631
Ovington (Norf.)	29	TF 9202
Ovington (Northum.)	47	NZ 0663
Ower	9	SU 3216
Owermoigne	8	SY 7685
Owlswick	18	SP 7906
Owmby	34	SK 9987
Owslebury	9	SU 5123
Owston	34	SK 7708
Owston Ferry	39	SE 8000
Owstwick	39	TA 2732
Owthorpe	34	SK 6733
Oxborough	28	TF 7401
Oxenholme	40	SD 5390
Oxenhope	37	SE 0334
Oxen Park	40	SD 3187
Oxenton	25	SO 9531
Oxenwood	10	SU 3059
Oxford	18	SP 5305
Oxhill (Warw.)	26	SP 3145
Oxley	25	SJ 9002
Oxley's Green	12	TQ 6921
Oxnam	52	NT 7018
Oxshott	11	TQ 1460
Oxspring	37	SE 2601
Oxted	12	TQ 3852
Oxton (Borders)	52	NT 4953
Oxton (Notts.)	34	SK 6351
Oxwich	15	SS 4986
Oxwick	28	TF 9125
Oykel Bridge	66	NC 3800
Oyne	62	NJ 6725
Packington	33	SK 3614
Padanaram	57	NO 4251
Padbury	18	SP 7130
Paddington	19	TQ 2482
Paddlesworth	13	TR 1939
Paddockhaugh	61	NJ 2058
Paddock Wood	12	TQ 6645
Paddolgreen	32	SJ 5032
Padeswood	32	SJ 2761
Padiham	37	SD 7933
Padstow	2	SW 9175
Pagham	11	SZ 8897
Paglesham	21	TQ 9292
Paible (W Isles)	63	NF 7367
Paible (W Isles)	63	NG 0299
Paignton	5	SX 8960
Pailton	26	SP 4781
Painscastle	23	SO 1646
Painswick	17	SO 8609
Paisley	50	NS 4864
Pakefield	29	TM 5390
Pakenham	21	TL 9267
Pale	31	SH 9836
Palestine	10	SU 2640
Paley Street	11	SU 8776
Palgowan	44	NX 3783
Palgrave	29	TM 1178
Palmerstown	16	ST 1369
Palnackie	45	NX 8257
Palnure	44	NX 4563
Palterton	33	SK 4768
Pamber End	10	SU 6158
Pamber Green	10	SU 6059
Pamber Heath	10	SU 6262
Pamphill	8	ST 9900
Pampisford	20	TL 4948
Panbride	57	NO 5635
Pancrasweek	4	SS 2905
Pandy (Clwyd)	32	SJ 1935
Pandy (Gwent)	16	SO 3322
Pandy (Powys)	22	SH 9004
Pandy Tudur	31	SH 8564
Panfield	20	TL 7325
Pangbourne	10	SU 6376
Pannal	37	SE 3051
Pant	32	SJ 2722
Pant-glas (Gwyn.)	30	SH 4747
Pant Glas (Powys)	22	SN 7798
Pantgwyn	14	SN 2446
Pant Mawr	22	SN 8482
Panton	35	TF 1778
Pant-pastynog	31	SJ 0461
Pantperthog	22	SH 7504
Pant-y-dwr	23	SN 9875
Pant-y-ffridd	23	SJ 1502
Pantyffynnon	15	SN 6210
Panxworth	29	TG 3413
Papcastle	40	NY 1131
Papple	52	NT 5972
Papplewick	34	SK 5451
Papworth Everard	27	TL 2862
Papworth St. Agnes	27	TL 2664
Par	4	SX 0653
Parbold	36	SD 4911
Parbrook	7	ST 5736
Parc	30	SH 4486
Parcllyn	14	SN 2451
Pardshaw	40	NY 0924
Parham	21	TM 3060
Park (Grampn.)	62	NO 7798
Park (Strath.)	54	NM 9340
Park Corner	18	SU 6988
Parkend (Glos.)	17	SO 6108
Park End (Northum.)	47	NY 8775
Parkeston	21	TM 2332
Parkgate (Ches.)	32	SJ 2778
Parkgate (Ches.)	32	SJ 7874
Parkgate (Dumf. and Galwy.)	45	NY 0288
Park Gate (Hants.)	9	SU 5108
Parkgate (Surrey)	11	TQ 2043
Parkham	4	SS 3821
Parkham Ash	4	SS 3620
Parkhouse	16	SO 5002
Parkhurst	9	SZ 4991
Parkneuk	57	NO 7976
Parkstone	8	SZ 0491
Parley Common	8	SZ 0999
Parley Cross	8	SZ 0898
Parracombe	6	SS 6744
Parrog	14	SN 0439
Parson Drove	35	TF 3708
Partick	50	NS 5567
Partington	32	SJ 7191
Partney	35	TF 4168
Parton (Cumbr.)	40	NX 9720
Parton (Dumf. and Galwy.)	45	NX 6970
Parton (Glos.)	17	SO 8721
Partridge Green	11	TQ 1919
Parwich	33	SK 1854
Passenham	18	SP 7839
Paston	29	TG 3235
Patcham	12	TQ 3009
Patching	11	TQ 0806
Patchole	6	SS 6142
Patchway	17	ST 6082
Pateley Bridge	42	SE 1565
Pathhead (Fife.)	51	NT 2892
Pathhead (Grampn.)	57	NO 7363
Pathhead (Lothian)	51	NT 3964
Pathhead (Strath.)	50	NS 6114
Path of Condie	56	NO 0711
Patmore Heath	20	TL 4526
Patna	50	NS 4110
Patney	17	SU 0758
Patrick	43	SC 2482
Patrick Brompton	42	SE 2290
Patrington	39	TA 3122
Patrixbourne	13	TR 1855
Patterdale	40	NY 3915
Pattingham	25	SO 8299
Pattishall	26	SP 6654
Paul	2	SW 4627
Paulerspury	26	SP 7145
Paull	39	TA 1626
Paulton	17	ST 6456
Pauperhaugh	47	NZ 1099
Pavenham	27	SP 9955
Pawlett	7	ST 2942
Pawston	53	NT 8532
Paxford	25	SP 1837
Paxhill Park	12	TQ 3626
Paxton	53	NT 9352
Payhembury	5	ST 0801
Paythorne	37	SD 8251
Peacehaven	12	TQ 4101
Peachley	24	SO 8057
Peak Dale	33	SK 0976
Peak Forest	33	SK 1179
Peakirk	35	TF 1606
Pearsie	57	NO 3659
Peasedown St. John	17	ST 7057
Peasemore	10	SU 4576
Peasenhall	29	TM 3569
Peaslake	11	TQ 0844
Peasmarsh	13	TQ 8822
Peaston Bank	52	NT 4466
Peathill (Grampn.)	62	NJ 9365
Peat Hill (Tays.)	57	NO 5067
Peat Inn	57	NO 4509
Peatling Magna	26	SP 5992
Peatling Parva	26	SP 5889
Peaton	24	SO 5385
Pebmarsh	20	TL 8533
Pebworth	25	SP 1347
Pecket Well	37	SD 9929
Peckforton	32	SJ 5356
Peckleton	26	SK 4701
Pedmore	25	SO 9182
Pedwell	7	ST 4236
Peebles	51	NT 2540
Peel	43	SC 2484
Pegswood	47	NZ 2287
Pegwell Bay	13	TR 3563
Peinchorran	58	NG 5233
Peinlich	58	NG 4158
Pelaw	47	NZ 2962
Peldon	21	TL 9816
Pelsall	25	SK 0103
Pelton	47	NZ 2553
Pelutho	45	NY 1249
Pelynt	4	SX 2055
Pembrey	15	SN 4201
Pembridge	24	SO 3858
Pembroke	14	SM 9901
Pembroke Dock	14	SM 9603
Pembury	12	TQ 6240
Penallt	16	SO 5210
Penally	14	SS 1199
Penant	22	SN 5163
Penare	4	SW 9940
Penarth	16	ST 1871
Pen-bont Rhydybeddau	22	SN 6783
Penbryn	14	SN 2952
Pencader	15	SN 4436
Pencaitland	52	NT 4468
Pencarreg	15	SN 5345
Pencelli	16	SO 0925
Penclawdd	15	SS 5495
Pencoed (Mid Glam.)	15	SS 9581
Pen Coed (Powys.)	23	SH 9808
Pencombe	24	SO 5952
Pencoyd	16	SO 5126
Pencraig (Here. and Worc.)	17	SO 5621
Pencraig (Powys)	31	SJ 0427
Pendeen	2	SW 3834
Penderyn	15	SN 9408
Pendine	14	SN 2308
Pendlebury	37	SD 7802
Pendleton	37	SD 7539
Pendock	24	SO 7832
Pendoggett	4	SX 0279
Pendoylan	16	ST 0576
Penegoes	22	SH 7701
Pen-ffordd	14	SN 0722
Pengam	16	ST 1797
Penge	12	TQ 3570
Penhalvean	2	SW 7037
Penhow	16	ST 4290
Penhurst	12	TQ 6916
Peniarth	22	SH 6105
Penicuik	51	NT 2359
Penifiler	58	NG 4841
Peninver	48	NR 7524
Pen-isa'r-cwm	31	SJ 0018
Penisar Waun	30	SH 5564
Penistone	37	SE 2402
Penjerrick	2	SW 7730
Penketh	32	SJ 5687
Penkill	44	NX 2398
Penkridge	25	SJ 9214
Penley	32	SJ 4039
Penllergaer	15	SS 6199
Pen-llyn (Gwyn.)	30	SH 3482

Royal Leamington Spa 96 Seworgan

Royal Leamington Spa	26	SP 3166
Royal Tunbridge Wells	12	TQ 5839
Roybridge	55	NN 2781
Roydon (Essex)	20	TL 4009
Roydon (Norf.)	28	TF 7022
Roydon (Norf.)	29	TM 0980
Royston (Herts.)	20	TL 3541
Royston (S Yorks.)	37	SE 3611
Royton	37	SD 9207
Ruabon	32	SJ 3043
Ruaig	48	NM 0647
Ruan Lanihorne	2	SW 8942
Ruan Minor	2	SW 7115
Ruardean	17	SO 6117
Ruardean Woodside	17	SO 6216
Rubery	25	SO 9777
Ruckcroft	46	NY 5344
Ruckinge	13	TR 0233
Ruckland	35	TF 3378
Ruckley	24	SJ 5300
Ruddington	34	SK 5733
Rudge	8	ST 8252
Rudgeway	17	ST 6286
Rudgwick	11	TQ 0934
Rudhall	17	SO 6225
Rudry	16	ST 1986
Rudston	39	TA 0967
Rudyard	33	SJ 9557
Rufford	36	SD 4515
Rufforth	38	SE 5251
Rugby	26	SP 5075
Rugeley	33	SK 0418
Ruilick	60	NH 5046
Ruishton	7	ST 2624
Ruislip	19	TQ 0987
Ruislip Common	19	TQ 0789
Rumbling Bridge	56	NT 0199
Rumburgh	29	TM 3581
Rumford	2	SW 8970
Rumney	16	ST 2179
Runcorn	32	SJ 5182
Runcton	11	SU 8802
Runcton Holme	28	TF 6109
Runfold	11	SU 8747
Runhall	29	TG 0507
Runham	29	TG 4610
Runnington	7	ST 1121
Runswick	43	NZ 8016
Runtaleave	57	NO 2867
Runwell	20	TQ 7494
Rushall (Here. and Worc.)	24	SO 6434
Rushall (Norf.)	29	TM 1982
Rushall (Wilts.)	17	SU 1255
Rushall (W Mids.)	25	SK 0201
Rushbrooke	21	TL 8961
Rushbury	24	SO 5191
Rushden (Herts.)	20	TL 3031
Rushden (Northants.)	27	SP 9566
Rushford	29	TL 9281
Rush Green	20	TQ 5187
Rushlake Green	12	TQ 6218
Rushmere	29	TM 4987
Rushmere St. Andrew	21	TM 2046
Rushmoor	11	SU 8740
Rushock	25	SO 8871
Rusholme	37	SJ 8494
Rushton (Ches.)	32	SJ 5863
Rushton (Northants.)	27	SP 8483
Rushton (Salop)	24	SJ 6008
Rushton Spencer	33	SJ 9363
Rushwick	25	SO 8353
Rushyford	42	NZ 2828
Ruskie	56	NN 6200
Ruskington	35	TF 0850
Rusland	40	SD 3488
Rusper	11	TQ 2037
Ruspidge	17	SO 6512
Russell's Water	18	SU 7089
Rustington	11	TQ 0502
Ruston Parva	39	TA 0661
Ruswarp	43	NZ 8809
Rutherford	52	NT 6530
Rutherglen	50	NS 6161
Ruthernbridge	4	SX 0166
Ruthin	31	SJ 1257
Ruthrieston	62	NJ 9204
Ruthven (Grampn.)	61	NJ 5046
Ruthven (Highld.)	60	NH 8133
Ruthven (Tays.)	57	NO 2848
Ruthvoes	2	SW 9360
Ruthwell	45	NY 1067
Ruyton-XI-Towns	32	SJ 3922
Ryal	47	NZ 0174
Ryal Fold	36	SD 6621
Ryall	7	SY 4094
Ryarsh	12	TQ 6659
Rydal	40	NY 3606
Ryde	9	SZ 5992
Rye	13	TQ 9220
Rye Foreign	13	TQ 8822
Rye Harbour	13	TQ 9419
Ryhall	35	TF 0311
Ryhill	37	SE 3814
Ryhope	47	NZ 4152
Ryknild Street (Warw.) (ant.)	25	SP 0762
Rylstone	37	SD 9758
Ryme Intrinseca	7	ST 5810
Ryther	38	SE 5539
Ryton (Glos.)	24	SO 7232
Ryton (N Yorks.)	38	SE 7975
Ryton (Salop)	24	SJ 7502
Ryton (Tyne and Wear)	47	NZ 1564
Ryton-on-Dunsmore	26	SP 3874
Sabden	37	SD 7737
Sacombe	20	TL 3419
Sacriston	47	NZ 2447
Sadberge	42	NZ 3416
Saddell	49	NR 7832
Saddington	26	SP 6591
Saddle Bow	28	TF 6015
Saffron Walden	20	TL 5438
Saham Toney	28	TF 9002
Saighton	32	SJ 4462
St. Abbs	53	NT 9167
St. Agnes (Corn.)	2	SW 7150
St. Albans	19	TL 1507
St. Allen	2	SW 8250
St. Andrews	57	NO 5016
St. Andrews Major	16	ST 1471
St. Anne's (Lancs.)	36	SD 3129
St. Ann's (Dumf. and Galwy.)	45	NY 0793
St. Ann's Chapel	4	SX 4170
St. Anthony	2	SW 7725
St. Arvans	16	ST 5196
St. Asaph (Lanelwy)	31	SJ 0374
St. Athan	15	ST 0168
St. Austell	4	SX 0152
St. Bees	40	NX 9611
St. Blazey	4	SX 0654
St. Boswells	52	NT 5930
St. Breock	2	SW 9771
St. Breward	4	SX 0977
St. Briavels	16	SO 5504
St. Brides	14	SM 8010
St. Bride's Major	15	SS 8974
St. Brides Netherwent	16	ST 4289
St. Brides-super-Ely	16	ST 1078
St. Bride's Wentlooge	16	ST 2982
St. Budeaux	4	SX 4558
St. Buryan	2	SW 4025
St. Catherines	55	NN 1207
St. Clears	14	SN 2716
St. Cleer	4	SX 2468
St. Clement	2	SW 8443
St. Clether	4	SX 2084
St. Colmac	49	NS 0467
St. Columb Major	2	SW 9163
St. Columb Minor	2	SW 8362
St. Columb Road	2	SW 9059
St. Combs	62	NK 0563
St. Cross South Elmham	29	TM 2984
St. Cyrus	57	NO 7464
St. David's (Dyfed)	14	SM 7525
St. Davids (Fife.)	51	NT 1582
St. David's (Tays.)	56	NN 9420
St. Day	2	SW 7242
St. Dennis	2	SW 9558
St. Devereux	24	SO 4431
St. Dogmaels	14	SN 1646
St. Dogwells	14	SM 9728
St. Dominick	4	SX 3967
St. Donats	15	SS 9368
St. Edith's Marsh	17	ST 9764
St. Endellion	4	SW 9978
St. Enoder	2	SW 8956
St. Erme	2	SW 8449
St. Erth	2	SW 5435
St. Erth Praze	2	SW 5735
St. Ervan	2	SW 8870
St. Ewe	2	SW 9745
St. Fagans	16	ST 1177
St. Fergus	62	NK 0951
St. Fillans	56	NN 6924
St. Florence	14	SN 0801
St. Gennys	4	SX 1497
St. George (Clwyd)	31	SH 9775
St. George's (S Glam.)	16	ST 0976
St. Germans	4	SX 3557
St. Giles in the Wood	6	SS 5318
St. Giles-on-the-Heath	4	SX 3590
St. Harmon	23	SN 9872
St. Helena	29	TG 1816
St. Helen Auckland	42	NZ 1826
St. Helens (I. of W.)	9	SZ 6288
St. Helens (Mers.)	32	SJ 5095
St. Hilary (Corn.)	2	SW 5531
St. Hilary (S Glam.)	15	ST 0173
St. Illtyd	16	SO 2102
St. Ishmael's	14	SM 8307
St. Issey	2	SW 9271
St. Ive (Corn.)	4	SX 3167
St. Ives (Cambs.)	27	TL 3171
St. Ives (Corn.)	2	SW 5140
St. Ives (Dorset)	8	SU 1203
St. James South Elmham	29	TM 3281
St. John (Corn.)	4	SX 4053
St. Johns (Here. and Worc.)	25	SO 8453
St. John's (I. of M.)	43	SC 2781
St. John's Chapel	41	NY 8837
St. John's Fen End	28	TF 5311
St. John's Highway	28	TF 5314
St. John's Town of Dalry	45	NX 6281
St. Jude's	43	SC 3996
St. Just (Corn.)	2	SW 3631
St. Just (Corn.)	2	SW 8435
St. Katherines	62	NJ 7834
St. Keverne	2	SW 7821
St. Kew	4	SX 0276
St. Kew Highway	4	SX 0375
St. Keyne	4	SX 2460
St. Lawrence (Corn.)	4	SX 0466
St. Lawrence (Essex)	21	TL 9604
St. Lawrence (I. of W.)	9	SZ 5476
St. Leonards (Bucks.)	19	SP 9006
St. Leonards (Dorset)	8	SU 1002
St. Leonards (E Susx)	12	TQ 8009
St. Levan	2	SW 3722
St. Lythans	16	ST 1073
St. Mabyn	4	SX 0373
St. Margarets	24	SO 3534
St. Margaret's at Cliffe	13	TR 3644
St. Margaret's Bay	13	TR 3744
St. Margaret's Hope (Fife.)	51	NT 1181
St. Margaret's Hope (S. Ronaldsay)	63	ND 4493
St. Margaret South Elmham	29	TM 3183
St. Mark's	43	SC 2974
St. Martin (Corn.)	4	SX 2555
St. Martin's (Is. of Sc.)	2	SV 9215
St. Martin's (Salop)	32	SJ 3236
St. Martins (Tays.)	56	NO 1530
St. Martin's Green	2	SW 7324
St. Mary Bourne	10	SU 4250
St. Mary Church	15	ST 0071
St. Mary Cray	12	TQ 4767
St. Mary Hill	15	SS 9678
St. Mary in the Marsh	13	TR 0628
St. Marylebone	19	TQ 2881
St. Mary's (Orkney)	63	HY 4701
St. Mary's Bay	13	TR 0927
St. Mary's Grove	16	ST 4769
St. Mary's Hoo	12	TQ 8076
St. Mary's Isle	45	NX 6749
St. Mawes	2	SW 8433
St. Mawgan	2	SW 8765
St. Mellion	4	SX 3865
St. Mellons	16	ST 2281
St. Merryn	2	SW 8874
St. Mewan	4	SW 9951
St. Michael Caerhays	2	SW 9642
St. Michael Penkevil	2	SW 8542
St. Michaels (Here. and Worc.)	24	SO 5765
St. Michaels (Kent)	13	TQ 8835
St. Michael's Mount	2	SW 5130
St. Michael's on Wyre	36	SD 4640
St. Michael South Elmham	29	TM 3483
St. Minver	2	SW 9677
St. Monance	57	NO 5201
St. Neot (Corn.)	4	SX 1867
St. Neots (Cambs.)	27	TL 1860
St. Nicholas (Dyfed)	14	SM 9035
St. Nicholas (S Glam.)	16	ST 0874
St. Nicholas at Wade	13	TR 2666
St. Ninians	50	NS 7991
St. Osyth	21	TM 1215
St. Owen's Cross	16	SO 5324
St. Pauls Cray	12	TQ 4768
St. Paul's Walden	19	TL 1922
St. Peter's	13	TR 3668
St. Petrox	14	SR 9797
St. Pinnock	4	SX 2063
St. Quivox	50	NS 3723
St. Stephen (Corn.)	2	SW 9453
St. Stephens (Corn.)	4	SX 3285
St. Stephen's (Corn.)	4	SX 4158
St. Teath	4	SX 0680
St. Tudy	4	SX 0676
St. Twynnells	14	SR 9597
St. Vigeans	57	NO 6443
St. Wenn	2	SW 9664
St. Weonards	16	SO 4924
Saintbury	25	SP 1139
Saint Hill	12	TQ 3835
Salcombe	5	SX 7338
Salcombe Regis	5	SY 1488
Salcott	21	TL 9413
Sale	32	SJ 7990
Saleby	35	TF 4578
Sale Green	25	SO 9358
Salehurst	12	TQ 7424
Salem (Dyfed)	15	SN 6226
Salem (Dyfed)	22	SN 6684
Salem (Gwyn.)	30	SH 5456
Salen (Highld.)	54	NM 6864
Salen (Island of Mull)	54	NM 5743
Salesbury	36	SD 6732
Sales Point	21	TM 0209
Salford (Beds.)	27	SP 9339
Salford (Gtr Mches.)	37	SJ 7796
Salford (Oxon.)	18	SP 2828
Salford Priors	25	SP 0751
Salfords	11	TQ 2846
Salhouse	29	TG 3114
Saline	51	NT 0292
Salisbury	8	SU 1429
Sall	29	TG 1024
Sallachy (Highld.)	66	NC 5408
Sallachy (Highld.)	59	NG 9130
Salmonby	35	TF 3273
Salmond's Muir	57	NO 5837
Salperton	17	SP 0720
Salph End	27	TL 0752
Salsburgh	50	NS 8262
Salt	33	SJ 9527
Saltash	4	SX 4259
Saltburn	65	NH 7269
Saltburn-by-the-Sea	42	NZ 6621
Saltby	34	SK 8426
Saltcoats	49	NS 2441
Saltdean	12	TQ 3802
Salter	41	SD 6073
Salterforth	37	SD 8845
Saltergate	43	SE 8594
Salterswall	32	SJ 6267
Saltfleet	39	TF 4593
Saltfleetby All Saints	35	TF 4590
Saltfleetby St. Clements	39	TF 4591
Saltfleetby St. Peter	35	TF 4389
Saltford	17	ST 6867
Salthouse	29	TG 0743
Saltmarshe	38	SE 7824
Saltney	32	SJ 3864
Salton	43	SE 7180
Saltwick	47	NZ 1780
Saltwood	13	TR 1536
Salwarpe	25	SO 8762
Salwayash	7	SY 4596
Samala	63	NF 7962
Sambourne	25	SP 0561
Sambrook	32	SJ 7124
Samlesbury	36	SD 5829
Samlesbury Bottoms	36	SD 6229
Sampford Arundel	7	ST 1018
Sampford Brett	7	ST 0940
Sampford Courtenay	6	SS 6301
Sampford Peverell	7	ST 0214
Sampford Spiney	4	SX 5372
Samuelston	52	NT 4870
Sanaigmore	48	NR 2370
Sancreed	2	SW 4029
Sancton	39	SE 8939
Sand	63	HU 3447
Sandaig	58	NG 7102
Sandbach	32	SJ 7560
Sandbank	49	NS 1580
Sandbanks	8	SZ 0487
Sandend	62	NJ 5566
Sanderstead	12	TQ 3461
Sandford (Avon)	16	ST 4159
Sandford (Cumbr.)	41	NY 7216
Sandford (Devon.)	6	SS 8202
Sandford (Dorset)	8	SY 9289
Sandford (Strath.)	50	NS 7143
Sandfordhill	62	NK 1141
Sandford-on-Thames	18	SP 5301
Sandford Orcas	8	ST 6220
Sandford St. Martin	18	SP 4226
Sandgarth	63	HY 5215
Sandgate	13	TR 2035
Sandgreen	45	NX 5752
Sandhaven	62	NJ 9667
Sandhead	44	NX 0949
Sandhoe	47	NY 9766
Sandholme (Humbs.)	39	SE 8230
Sandholme (Lincs.)	35	TF 3337
Sandhurst (Berks.)	10	SU 8361
Sandhurst (Glos.)	17	SO 8223
Sandhurst (Kent)	12	TQ 8028
Sandhutton (N Yorks.)	42	SE 3881
Sand Hutton (N Yorks.)	38	SE 6958
Sandiacre	33	SK 4736
Sandilands	35	TF 5280
Sandiway	32	SJ 6070
Sandleheath	8	SU 1214
Sandleigh	18	SP 4501
Sandling	12	TQ 7558
Sandness	63	HU 1956
Sandon (Essex)	20	TL 7404
Sandon (Herts.)	20	TL 3234
Sandon (Staffs.)	33	SJ 9429
Sandown	9	SZ 5984
Sandplace	4	SX 2467
Sandridge (Herts.)	19	TL 1710
Sandridge (Wilts.)	17	ST 9465
Sandringham	28	TF 6928
Sandsend	43	NZ 8512
Sand Side	40	SD 2282
Sandsound	63	HU 3548
Sandtoft	38	SE 7408
Sandwich	13	TR 3358
Sandwick (Cumbr.)	40	NY 4219
Sandwick (Isle of Lewis)	63	NB 4432
Sandwick (Shetld.)	63	HU 4323
Sandwick (S. Ronaldsay)	63	ND 4389
Sandy	27	TL 1649
Sandycroft	32	SJ 3366
Sandygate	43	SC 3797
Sandy Lane	17	ST 9668
Sangobeg	66	NC 4266
Sanna	54	NM 4469
Sanquhar	45	NS 7809
Santon Bridge	40	NY 1001
Santon Downham	28	TL 8187
Sapcote	26	SP 4893
Sapey Common	24	SO 7064
Sapiston	28	TL 9175
Sapperton (Glos.)	17	SO 9403
Sapperton (Lincs.)	34	TF 0133
Saracen's Head	35	TF 3427
Sarclet	67	ND 3443
Sarisbury	9	SU 5008
Sarn (Mid Glam.)	15	SS 9083
Sarn (Powys)	23	SO 2090
Sarnau (Dyfed)	14	SN 3151
Sarnau (Dyfed)	14	SN 3318
Sarnau (Gwyn.)	31	SH 9739
Sarnau (Powys)	23	SJ 2315
Sarn-bach	30	SH 3026
Sarnesfield	24	SO 3750
Sarn Meyllteyrn	30	SH 2432
Saron (Dyfed)	15	SN 3738
Saron (Dyfed)	15	SN 6012
Sarratt	19	TQ 0499
Sarre	13	TR 2565
Sarsden	18	SP 2822
Satley	42	NZ 1143
Satterleigh	6	SS 6622
Satterthwaite	40	SD 3392
Sauchen	62	NJ 7010
Saucher	56	NO 1933
Sauchieburn	57	NO 6669
Sauchrie	50	NS 3014
Saughall	32	SJ 3669
Saughtree	46	NY 5696
Saul	17	SO 7409
Saundby	34	SK 7888
Saundersfoot	14	SN 1304
Saunderton	18	SP 7901
Saunton	6	SS 4537
Sausthorpe	35	TF 3869
Savalmore	66	NC 5908
Sawbridgeworth	20	TL 4814
Sawdon	43	SE 9485
Sawley (Derby.)	33	SK 4731
Sawley (Lancs.)	37	SD 7746
Sawley (N Yorks.)	42	SE 2467
Sawrey	40	SD 3695
Sawston	20	TL 4849
Sawtry	27	TL 1683
Saxby (Leic.)	34	SK 8220
Saxby (Lincs.)	34	TF 0086
Saxby All Saints	39	SE 9816
Saxelbye	34	SK 6921
Saxilby	34	SK 8875
Saxlingham	29	TG 0239
Saxlingham Nethergate	29	TM 2397
Saxmundham	21	TM 3863
Saxondale	34	SK 6839
Saxon Street	20	TL 6859
Saxtead	21	TM 2665
Saxtead Green	21	TM 2564
Saxthorpe	29	TG 1130
Saxton	38	SE 4736
Sayers Common	11	TQ 2618
Scackleton	38	SE 6472
Scadabay	63	NG 1792
Scaftworth	38	SK 6691
Scagglethorpe	39	SE 8372
Scalasaig	48	NR 3894
Scalby	43	TA 0090
Scaldwell	26	SP 7672
Scaleby	46	NY 4563
Scalebyhill	46	NY 4363
Scale Houses	46	NY 5845
Scales (Cumbr.)	40	NY 3426
Scales (Cumbr.)	40	SD 2772
Scalford	34	SK 7624
Scaling	43	NZ 7413
Scalloway	63	HU 4039
Scalpay (Harris)	63	NG 2395
Scalpay (Island of Skye)	58	NG 6030
Scamblesby	35	TF 2778
Scamodale	54	NM 8473
Scampston	39	SE 8575
Scampton	34	SK 9479
Scapa	63	HY 4309
Scar	63	HY 6745
Scarastavore	63	NG 0092
Scarborough	43	TA 0388
Scarcliffe	33	SK 4968
Scarcroft	37	SE 3540
Scardroy	59	NH 2151
Scarff	63	HU 2479
Scarfskerry	67	ND 2673
Scargill	42	NZ 0510
Scarinish	48	NM 0444
Scarisbrick	36	SD 3713
Scarning	29	TF 9512
Scarrington	34	SK 7341
Scarth Hill	36	SD 4206
Scartho	39	TA 2606
Scatsta	63	HU 3872
Scaur or Kippford	45	NX 8355
Scawby	39	SE 9605
Scawton	42	SE 5483
Scayne's Hill	12	TQ 3723
Scethrog	16	SO 1025
Scholar Green	32	SJ 8357
Scholes (W Yorks.)	37	SE 1507
Scholes (W Yorks.	37	SE 3736
Scleddau	14	SM 9434
Scole	29	TM 1579
Scolton	14	SM 9922
Sconser	58	NG 5232
Scoor	54	NM 4119
Scopwick	35	TF 0658
Scoraig	64	NH 0096
Scorborough	39	TA 0145
Scorrier	2	SW 7244
Scorton (Lancs.)	36	SD 5048
Scorton (N Yorks.)	42	NZ 2400
Sco Ruston	29	TG 2821
Scotby	46	NY 4454
Scotforth	36	SD 4759
Scothern	35	TF 0377
Scotland Gate	47	NZ 2584
Scotlandwell	56	NO 1801
Scotney Castle	12	TQ 6835
Scotsburn	65	NH 7275
Scotscraig	57	NO 4428
Scots' Gap	47	NZ 0486
Scotstown	54	NM 8263
Scotter	39	SE 8800
Scotterthorpe	39	SE 8701
Scotton (Lincs.)	39	SK 8899
Scotton (N Yorks.)	42	SE 1895
Scotton (N Yorks.)	37	SE 3259
Scottow	29	TG 2623
Scoughall	52	NT 6183
Scoulton	29	TF 9800
Scourie	66	NC 1544
Scousburgh	63	HU 3717
Scrabster	67	ND 0970
Scrainwood	47	NT 9909
Scrane End	35	TF 3841
Scraptoft	26	SK 6405
Scratby	29	TG 5115
Scrayingham	38	SE 7360
Scredington	35	TF 0940
Scremby	35	TF 4467
Scremerston	53	NU 0049
Screveton	34	SK 7343
Scriven	37	SE 3458
Scrooby	34	SK 6590
Scropton	33	SK 1930
Scrub Hill	35	TF 2355
Scruton	42	SE 2992
Sculthorpe	28	TF 8931
Scunthorpe	39	SE 8910
Seaborough	7	ST 4205
Seacombe	32	SJ 3190
Seacroft	35	TF 5660
Seafield	51	NT 0066
Seaford	12	TV 4899
Seaforth	32	SJ 3297
Seagrave	34	SK 6117
Seaham	47	NZ 4149
Seahouses	53	NU 2132
Seal	12	TQ 5556
Sealand	32	SJ 3268
Seamer (N Yorks.)	42	NZ 4910
Seamer (N Yorks.)	43	TA 0183
Seamill	49	NS 2047
Sea Palling	29	TG 4327
Searby	39	TA 0605
Seasalter	13	TR 0864
Seascale	40	NY 0301
Seathwaite (Cumbr.)	40	NY 2312
Seathwaite (Cumbr.)	40	SD 2296
Seaton (Corn.)	4	SX 3054
Seaton (Cumbr.)	40	NY 0130
Seaton (Devon.)	5	SY 2490
Seaton (Durham)	47	NZ 4049
Seaton (Humbs.)	39	TA 1646
Seaton (Leic.)	27	SP 9098
Seaton (Northum.)	47	NZ 3276
Seaton Carew	42	NZ 5229
Seaton Delaval	47	NZ 3075
Seaton Ross	38	SE 7741
Seaton Sluice	47	NZ 3376
Seave Green	42	NZ 5600
Seaview	9	SZ 6291
Seavington St. Mary	7	ST 3914
Seavington St. Michael	7	ST 4015
Sebergham	40	NY 3541
Seckington	33	SK 2607
Sedbergh	41	SD 6592
Sedbusk	41	SD 8891
Sedgeberrow	25	SP 0238
Sedgebrook	34	SK 8537
Sedgefield	42	NZ 3528
Sedgeford	28	TF 7136
Sedgehill	8	ST 8627
Sedgley	25	SO 9193
Sedgwick	40	SD 5186
Sedlescombe	12	TQ 7818
Seend	17	ST 9460
Seend Cleeve	17	ST 9260
Seer Green	19	SU 9691
Seething	29	TM 3197
Sefton	36	SD 3500
Seghill	47	NZ 2874
Seighford	33	SJ 8725
Seilebost	63	NG 0696
Seisdon	25	SO 8394
Selattyn	32	SJ 2633
Selborne	9	SU 7433
Selby	38	SE 6132
Selham	11	SU 9320
Selkirk	52	NT 4728
Sellack	17	SO 5627
Sellafirth	63	HU 5198
Sellindge	13	TR 0938
Selling	13	TR 0356
Sells Green	17	ST 9462
Selly Oak	25	SP 0482
Selmeston	12	TQ 5007
Selsdon	12	TQ 3562
Selsey	9	SZ 8593
Selsfield Common	12	TQ 3434
Selston	33	SK 4553
Selworthy	6	SS 9146
Semblister	63	HU 3350
Semer	21	TL 9946
Semington	17	ST 8960
Semley	8	ST 8926
Send	11	TQ 0155
Senghenydd	16	ST 1191
Sennen	2	SW 3525
Sennen Cove	2	SW 3425
Sennybridge	15	SN 9228
Sessay	38	SE 4575
Setchey	28	TF 6313
Setley	9	SU 3000
Settascarth	63	HY 3618
Setter (Shetld.)	63	HU 3954
Settle	41	SD 8263
Settrington	39	SE 8370
Sevenhampton (Glos.)	17	SP 0321
Sevenhampton (Wilts.)	17	SU 2090
Seven Kings	20	TQ 4586
Sevenoaks	12	TQ 5355
Sevenoaks Weald	12	TQ 5351
Seven Sisters	15	SN 8108
Severn Beach	16	ST 5384
Severn Stoke	25	SO 8544
Sevington	13	TR 0340
Sewards End	20	TL 5738
Sewerby	39	TA 2068
Seworgan	2	SW 7030

Sewstern 97 South Warnborough

Place	Page	Grid ref.
Sewstern	34	SK 8821
Sezincote	25	SP 1731
Shabbington	18	SP 6606
Shackerstone	33	SK 3706
Shackleford	11	SU 9345
Shadforth	42	NZ 3441
Shadingfield	29	TM 4383
Shadoxhurst	13	TQ 9737
Shaftesbury	8	ST 8622
Shafton	37	SE 3810
Shalbourne	10	SU 3163
Shalcombe	9	SZ 3985
Shalden	10	SU 6941
Shaldon	5	SX 9272
Shalfleet	9	SZ 4189
Shalford (Essex)	20	TL 7229
Shalford (Surrey)	11	TQ 0047
Shalford Green	20	TL 7127
Shallowford	6	SS 7144
Shalstone	18	SP 6436
Shamley Green	11	TQ 0344
Shandon	49	NS 2586
Shandwick	65	NH 8574
Shangton	26	SP 7196
Shanklin	9	SZ 5881
Shap	41	NY 5615
Shapwick (Dorset)	8	ST 9301
Shapwick (Somer.)	7	ST 4137
Shardlow	33	SK 4330
Shareshill	25	SJ 9406
Sharlston	37	SE 3818
Sharnbrook	27	SP 9959
Sharnford	26	SP 4891
Sharoe Green	36	SD 5332
Sharow	42	SE 3271
Sharpenhoe	27	TL 0630
Sharperton	47	NT 9503
Sharpness	17	SO 6702
Sharpthorne	12	TQ 3732
Sharrington	29	TG 0337
Shatterford	24	SO 7980
Shaughlaige-e-Quiggin	43	SC 3187
Shaugh Prior	4	SX 5463
Shavington	32	SJ 6951
Shaw (Berks.)	10	SU 4768
Shaw (Gtr Mches.)	37	SD 9308
Shaw (Wilts.)	17	ST 8865
Shawbost	63	NB 2646
Shawbury	32	SJ 5521
Shawell	26	SP 5480
Shawford	9	SU 4624
Shawforth	37	SD 8920
Shawhead	45	NX 8675
Shaw Hill	45	NX 5871
Shaw Mills	42	SE 2562
Shawwood	50	NS 5325
Shear Cross	8	ST 8642
Shearsby	26	SP 6291
Shebbear	4	SS 4309
Shebdon	32	SJ 7525
Shebster	67	ND 0164
Shedfield	9	SU 5512
Sheen	33	SK 1161
Sheepscombe	17	SO 8910
Sheepstor	4	SX 5567
Sheepwash	6	SS 4806
Sheepy Magna	26	SK 3201
Sheepy Parva	26	SK 3301
Sheering	20	TL 5013
Sheerness	13	TQ 9274
Sheet	9	SU 7524
Sheffield	33	SK 3587
Sheffield Bottom	10	SU 6469
Shefford	19	TL 1439
Sheinton	24	SJ 6104
Shelderton	24	SO 4077
Sheldon (Derby.)	33	SK 1768
Sheldon (Devon.)	5	ST 1208
Sheldon (W Mids.)	25	SP 1584
Sheldwich	13	TR 0156
Shelf	37	SE 1228
Shelfanger	29	TM 1083
Shelfield	25	SK 0302
Shelford	34	SK 6642
Shelley	37	SE 2011
Shellingford	18	SU 3193
Shellow Bowells	20	TL 6108
Shelsley Beauchamp	24	SO 7362
Shelsley Walsh	24	SO 7263
Shelton (Beds.)	27	TL 0368
Shelton (Norf.)	29	TM 2191
Shelton (Notts.)	34	SK 7744
Shelton Green	29	TM 2390
Shelve	23	SO 3399
Shelwick	24	SO 5243
Shenfield	20	TQ 6094
Shenington	26	SP 3642
Shenley	19	TL 1900
Shenley Brook End	19	SP 8335
Shenleybury	19	TL 1802
Shenley Church End	19	SP 8336
Shenmore	24	SO 3938
Shenstone (Here. and Worc.)	25	SO 8673
Shenstone (Staffs.)	25	SK 1004
Shenton	26	SK 3800
Shenval	61	NJ 2129
Shepherd's Green	18	SU 7183
Shepherdswell or Sibertswold	13	TR 2548
Shepley	37	SE 1909
Shepperdine	17	ST 6195
Shepperton	11	TQ 0867
Shepreth	20	TL 3947
Shepshed	33	SK 4719
Shepton Beauchamp	7	ST 4016
Shepton Mallet	7	ST 6143
Shepton Montague	8	ST 6731
Shepway	12	TQ 7753
Sheraton	42	NZ 4334
Sherborne (Dorset)	8	ST 6316
Sherborne (Glos.)	17	SP 1714
Sherborne St. John	10	SU 6155
Sherbourne	26	SP 2661
Sherburn (Durham)	42	NZ 3142
Sherburn (N Yorks.)	43	SE 9577
Sherburn in Elmet	38	SE 4933
Shere	11	TQ 0747
Shereford	28	TF 8829
Sherfield English	9	SU 2922
Sherfield on Loddon	10	SU 6757
Sherford	5	SX 7744
Sheriffhales	24	SJ 7512
Sheriff Hutton	38	SE 6566
Sheringham	29	TG 1543
Sherington	27	SP 8846
Shernborne	28	TF 7132
Sherrington	8	ST 9638
Sherston	17	ST 8585
Sherwood Green	6	SS 5520
Sheshader	63	NB 5534
Shettleston	50	NS 6464
Shevington	36	SD 5408
Shevington Moor	36	SD 5410
Sheviock	4	SX 3655
Shiel Bridge	59	NG 9318
Shieldaig	59	NG 8154
Shieldhill (Central)	50	NS 8976
Shielfoot	54	NM 6669
Shifnal	24	SJ 7407
Shilbottle	47	NU 1908
Shildon	42	NZ 2226
Shillingford (Devon.)	7	SS 9723
Shillingford (Oxon.)	18	SU 5992
Shillingford St. George	5	SX 9087
Shillingstone	8	ST 8211
Shillington	19	TL 1234
Shillmoor (Northum.)	47	NT 8807
Shiltenish	63	NB 2819
Shilton (Oxon.)	18	SP 2608
Shilton (Warw.)	26	SP 4084
Shimpling (Norf.)	29	TM 1583
Shimpling (Suff.)	20	TL 8551
Shimpling Street	20	TL 8652
Shiney Row	47	NZ 3252
Shinfield	10	SU 7368
Shinness	66	NC 5314
Shipbourne	12	TQ 5952
Shipdham	29	TF 9607
Shipham	16	ST 4457
Shiphay	5	SX 8965
Shiplake	10	SU 7678
Shipley (Salop)	24	SO 8095
Shipley (W Susx)	11	TQ 1422
Shipley (W Yorks.)	37	SE 1337
Shipmeadow	29	TM 3789
Shippon	18	SU 4898
Shipston on Stour	26	SP 2540
Shipton (Glos.)	17	SP 0318
Shipton (N Yorks.)	38	SE 5558
Shipton (Salop)	24	SO 5591
Shipton Bellinger	10	SU 2345
Shipton Gorge	7	SY 4991
Shipton Green	9	SU 8000
Shipton Moyne	17	ST 8889
Shipton-on-Cherwell	18	SP 4716
Shiptonthorpe	39	SE 8543
Shipton-under-Wychwood	18	SP 2717
Shirburn	18	SU 6995
Shirdley Hill	36	SD 3612
Shirebrook	34	SK 5267
Shirehampton	16	ST 5276
Shiremoor	47	NZ 3171
Shirenewton	16	ST 4793
Shire Oak	25	SK 0504
Shirland	33	SK 3958
Shirley (Derby.)	33	SK 2141
Shirley (Hants.)	9	SU 4114
Shirley (W Mids.)	25	SP 1277
Shirl Heath	24	SO 4359
Shirrell Heath	9	SU 5714
Shirwell	6	SS 5937
Shiskine	49	NR 9129
Shobdon	24	SO 3961
Shobrooke	6	SS 8600
Shocklach	32	SJ 4348
Shoeburyness (Essex)	21	TQ 9384
Sholden	13	TR 3552
Sholing	9	SU 4511
Shop (Corn.)	4	SS 2214
Shop (Corn.)	2	SW 8773
Shoreditch	20	TQ 3284
Shoreham	12	TQ 5261
Shoreham-by-Sea	11	TQ 2105
Shoresdean	53	NT 9546
Shoreswood	53	NT 9446
Shoretown	65	NH 6161
Shorncote	17	SU 0296
Shorne	12	TQ 6970
Short Cross	23	SJ 2605
Shortgate	12	TQ 4915
Short Heath (Leic.)	33	SK 3014
Short Heath (W Mids.)	25	SP 0992
Shortlanesend	2	SW 8047
Shortless	50	NS 4335
Shorwell	9	SZ 4582
Shoscombe	17	ST 7156
Shotesham	29	TM 2599
Shotgate	20	TQ 7692
Shotley Bridge	47	NZ 0752
Shotley Gate	21	TM 2433
Shotley Street	21	TM 2335
Shottenden	13	TR 0454
Shottermill	11	SU 8732
Shottery	25	SP 1854
Shotteswell	26	SP 4245
Shottisham	21	TM 3144
Shottle	33	SK 3149
Shotton (Clwyd)	32	SJ 3069
Shotton (Durham)	42	NZ 4139
Shotton (Northum.)	53	NT 8430
Shotton Colliery	42	NZ 3941
Shotts	50	NS 8760
Shotwick	32	SJ 3371
Shouldham	28	TF 6708
Shouldham Thorpe	28	TF 6607
Shoulton	24	SO 8058
Shrawley	24	SO 8064
Shrewley	25	SP 2167
Shrewsbury	24	SJ 4912
Shrewton	8	SU 0643
Shripney	11	SU 9302
Shrivenham	18	SU 2489
Shropham	29	TL 9893
Shroton or Iwerne Courtney	8	ST 8512
Shrub End	21	TL 9723
Shucknall	24	SO 5842
Shudy Camps	20	TL 6244
Shulishader	63	NB 5334
Shurdington	17	SO 9118
Shurlock Row	10	SU 8374
Shurrery	67	ND 0458
Shurton	7	ST 2044
Shustoke	26	SP 2290
Shute	5	SY 2597
Shut End	25	SO 9089
Shutford	18	SP 3840
Shuthonger	25	SO 8935
Shutlanger	26	SP 7249
Shuttington	26	SK 2505
Shuttlewood	33	SK 4672
Sibbertoft	26	SP 6782
Sibdon Carwood	24	SO 4083
Sibertswold or Shepherdswell	13	TR 2548
Sibford Ferris	18	SP 3537
Sibford Gower	18	SP 3537
Sible Hedingham	20	TL 7734
Sibsey	35	TF 3551
Sibson (Cambs.)	27	TL 0997
Sibson (Leic.)	26	SK 3500
Sibthorpe	34	SK 7645
Sicklesmere	21	TL 8760
Sicklinghall	37	SE 3548
Sidbury (Devon.)	5	SY 1491
Sidbury (Salop)	24	SO 6885
Sidcup	12	TQ 4672
Siddington (Ches.)	33	SJ 8470
Siddington (Glos.)	17	SU 0399
Sidestrand	29	TG 2539
Sidford	5	SY 1390
Sidinish	63	NF 8763
Sidlesham	9	SZ 8599
Sidley	12	TQ 7409
Sidmouth	5	SY 1287
Siefton	24	SO 4883
Sigford	5	SX 7773
Sigglesthorne	39	TA 1545
Silchester	10	SU 6462
Sileby	34	SK 6015
Silecroft	40	SD 1281
Silian	15	SN 5751
Silkstone Common	37	SE 2904
Silksworth	47	NZ 3752
Silk Willoughby	35	TF 0542
Silloth	45	NY 1153
Sillyearn	61	NJ 5254
Silpho	43	SE 9692
Silsden	37	SE 0446
Silsoe	19	TL 0835
Silverburn	51	NT 2060
Silverdale (Lancs.)	40	SD 4674
Silverdale (Staffs.)	32	SJ 8146
Silver End (Beds.)	27	TL 0942
Silver End (Essex)	20	TL 8019
Silverford	62	NJ 7764
Silverley's Green	29	TM 2976
Silverstone	26	SP 6644
Silverton	6	SS 9502
Silwick (Shetld.)	63	HU 2942
Simonburn	47	NY 8773
Simonsbath	6	SS 7739
Simonstone	37	SD 7734
Simprim	53	NT 8545
Simpson	27	SP 8836
Sinclairston	50	NS 4716
Sinderby	42	SE 3481
Sinderhope	47	NY 8452
Sindlesham	10	SU 7769
Singleton (Lancs.)	36	SD 3838
Singleton (W Susx)	11	SU 8713
Singlewell or Ifield	12	TQ 6471
Sinnahard	61	NJ 4713
Sinnington	43	SE 7485
Sinton Green	25	SO 8160
Sipson	11	TQ 0877
Sirhowy	16	SO 1410
Sissinghurst	12	TQ 7937
Siston	17	ST 6875
Sithney	2	SW 6329
Sittenham	65	NH 6574
Sittingbourne	13	TQ 9163
Six Ashes	24	SO 6988
Sixhills	35	TF 1787
Six Mile Bottom	20	TL 5756
Sixpenny Handley	8	ST 9917
Sizewell	21	TM 4762
Skaill (Orkney)	63	HY 2318
Skaill (Orkney)	63	HY 5806
Skares	50	NS 5217
Skarpigarth	63	HU 2049
Skateraw	52	NT 7375
Skaw (Whalsay)	63	HU 5866
Skeabost	58	NG 4148
Skeabrae	63	HY 2720
Skeeby	42	NZ 1902
Skeffington	26	SK 7402
Skeffling	39	TA 3619
Skegby	33	SK 4961
Skegness	35	TF 5663
Skelberry	63	HU 3916
Skelbo	65	NH 7895
Skeldyke	35	TF 3337
Skellingthorpe	34	SK 9272
Skellister	63	HU 4654
Skelmanthorpe	37	SE 2210
Skelmersdale	36	SD 4605
Skelmonae	62	NJ 8839
Skelmorlie	49	NS 1967
Skelmuir	62	NJ 9842
Skelpick	66	NC 7355
Skelton (Cleve.)	42	NZ 6518
Skelton (Cumbr.)	40	NY 4335
Skelton (N Yorks.)	42	NZ 0900
Skelton (N Yorks.)	42	SE 3568
Skelton (N Yorks.)	38	SE 5656
Skelwith Bridge	40	NY 3503
Skendleby	35	TF 4369
Skenfrith	16	SO 4520
Skerne	39	TA 0455
Skeroblingarry	48	NR 7026
Skerray	66	NC 6563
Sketty	15	SS 6293
Skewen	15	SS 7297
Skewsby	38	SE 6270
Skeyton	29	TG 2425
Skidbrooke	39	TF 4393
Skidby	39	TA 0133
Skigersta	63	NB 5461
Skilgate	7	SS 9827
Skillington	34	SK 8925
Skinburness	45	NY 1255
Skinidin	58	NG 2247
Skinningrove	43	NZ 7119
Skipness	49	NR 8957
Skipsea	39	TA 1655
Skipton	37	SD 9851
Skipton-on-Swale	42	SE 3679
Skipwith	38	SE 6538
Skirling	51	NT 0739
Skirmett	18	SU 7789
Skirpenbeck	38	SE 7457
Skirwith (Cumbr.)	41	NY 6132
Skirwith (N Yorks.)	41	SD 7073
Skirza	67	ND 3868
Skulamus	58	NG 6722
Skullomie	66	NC 6161
Skye of Curr	61	NH 9924
Slack	37	SD 9828
Slackhall	33	SK 0781
Slackhead	61	NJ 4063
Slad	17	SO 8707
Slade	6	SS 5046
Slade Green	12	TQ 5276
Slaggyford	46	NY 6752
Slaidburn	36	SD 7152
Slaithwaite	37	SE 0714
Slaley	47	NY 9757
Slamannan	50	NS 8573
Slapton (Bucks.)	19	SP 9320
Slapton (Devon.)	5	SX 8244
Slapton (Northants.)	26	SP 6346
Slattocks	37	SD 8808
Slaugham	11	TQ 2528
Slawston	26	SP 7794
Sleaford (Hants.)	10	SU 8037
Sleaford (Lincs.)	35	TF 0645
Sleagill	41	NY 5919
Sleapford	24	SJ 6315
Sledge Green	25	SO 8134
Sledmere	39	SE 9364
Sleightholme	41	NY 9510
Sleights	43	NZ 8607
Slepe	8	SY 9293
Slickly	67	ND 2966
Sliddery	49	NR 9322
Sliemore	61	NJ 0320
Sligachan	58	NG 4829
Slimbridge	17	SO 7303
Slindon (Staffs.)	32	SJ 8232
Slindon (W Susx)	11	SU 9608
Slinfold	11	TQ 1131
Slingsby	38	SE 6974
Slioch (Grampn.)	62	NJ 5638
Slip End	19	TL 0818
Slipton	27	SP 9479
Slockavullin	54	NR 8297
Sloley	29	TG 2924
Sloothby	35	TF 4970
Slough	11	SU 9779
Slyne	40	SD 4765
Smailholm	52	NT 6436
Smallbridge	37	SD 9114
Smallburgh	29	TG 3324
Smallburn (Grampn.)	62	NK 0141
Smallburn (Strath.)	50	NS 6827
Small Dole	11	TQ 2112
Smalley	33	SK 4044
Smallfield	12	TQ 3243
Small Hythe	13	TQ 8930
Smallridge	7	ST 3001
Smardale	41	NY 7308
Smarden	13	TQ 8842
Smearisary	54	NM 6477
Smeatharpe	5	ST 1910
Smeeth	13	TR 0739
Smeeton Westerby	26	SP 6792
Smerclate	63	NF 7415
Smerral	67	ND 1733
Smethwick	25	SP 0288
Smisby	33	SK 3419
Smithfield	46	NY 4465
Smithincott	7	ST 0611
Smithton	60	NH 7145
Snailbeach	24	SJ 3702
Snailwell	20	TL 6467
Snainton	43	SE 9182
Snaith	38	SE 6422
Snape (N Yorks.)	42	SE 2684
Snape (Suff.)	21	TM 3959
Snape Street	21	TM 3958
Snarestone	33	SK 3409
Snarford	35	TF 0482
Snargate	13	TQ 9928
Snave	13	TR 0130
Snead	23	SO 3191
Sneaton	43	NZ 8907
Sneaton Thorpe	43	NZ 9006
Snelland	35	TF 0780
Snelston	33	SK 1543
Snettisham	28	TF 6834
Snishival	63	NF 7534
Snitter	47	NU 0203
Snitterby	39	SK 9894
Snitterfield	25	SP 2159
Snitton	24	SO 5575
Snodhill	23	SO 3140
Snodland	12	TQ 7061
Snowshill	25	SP 0933
Soberton	9	SU 6016
Soberton Heath	9	SU 6014
Soham	28	TL 5973
Soldon Cross	4	SS 3210
Soldridge	9	SU 6534
Sole Street	13	TR 0949
Solihull	25	SP 1479
Sollas	63	NF 8074
Sollers Dilwyn	24	SO 4255
Sollers Hope	24	SO 6033
Sollom	36	SD 4518
Solva	14	SM 8024
Somerby	34	SK 7710
Somercotes	33	SK 4253
Somerford Keynes	17	SU 0195
Somerley	9	SZ 8198
Somerleyton	29	TM 4897
Somersall Herbert	33	SK 1335
Somersby	35	TF 3472
Somersham (Cambs.)	27	TL 3677
Somersham (Suff.)	21	TM 0848
Somerton (Norf.)	29	TG 4719
Somerton (Oxon.)	18	SP 4928
Somerton (Somer.)	7	ST 4828
Sompting	11	TQ 1605
Sonning	10	SU 7575
Sonning Common	10	SU 7080
Sopley	8	SZ 1596
Sopworth	17	ST 8286
Sorbie	44	NX 4346
Sordale	67	ND 1462
Sorisdale	48	NM 2763
Sorn	50	NS 5526
Sornhill	50	NS 5134
Sortat	67	ND 2863
Sotby	35	TF 2078
Sots Hole	35	TF 1164
Sotterly	29	TM 4584
Soughton	32	SJ 2466
Soulbury	19	SP 8827
Soulby	41	NY 7410
Souldern	18	SP 5231
Souldrop	27	SP 9861
Sound (Shetld.)	63	HU 3850
Sound (Shetld.)	63	HU 4640
Soundwell	17	ST 6574
Sourhope	53	NT 8420
Sourin	63	HY 4331
Sourton	4	SX 5390
Soutergate	40	SD 2281
South Acre	28	TF 8014
Southall	19	TQ 1280
South Alloa	50	NS 8791
Southam (Glos.)	17	SO 9725
Southam (Warw.)	26	SP 4161
South Ambersham	11	SU 9120
Southampton	9	SU 4212
South Ballachulish	55	NN 0559
South Bank	42	NZ 5220
South Barrow	7	ST 6027
South Benfleet	20	TQ 7785
Southborough	12	TQ 5842
Southbourne (Dorset)	8	SZ 1491
Southbourne (W Susx)	9	SU 7705
South Brent	5	SX 6960
Southburgh	29	TG 0004
South Burlingham	29	TG 3708
South Cadbury	8	ST 6325
South Cairn	44	NW 9768
South Carlton	34	SK 9476
South Cave	39	SE 9231
South Cerney	17	SU 0497
South Chard	7	ST 3205
South Charlton	53	NU 1620
Southchurch	21	TQ 9186
South Cliffe	39	SE 8736
South Clifton	34	SK 8270
Southcott	6	SX 5495
South Cove	29	TM 5081
South Creake	28	TF 8536
South Croxton	34	SK 6810
South Dalton	39	SE 9645
South Darenth	12	TQ 5669
South Duffield	38	SE 6733
Southease	12	TQ 4205
South Elkington	35	TF 2988
South Elmsall	38	SE 4711
South End (Berks.)	10	SU 5970
South End (Cumbr.)	40	SD 2063
Southend (Strath.)	48	NR 6908
Southend-on-Sea	21	TQ 8885
Southerndown	15	SS 8874
Southerness	45	NX 9754
South Erradale	64	NG 7471
Southery	28	TL 6294
South Fambridge	20	TQ 8694
South Fawley	10	SU 3979
South Ferriby	39	SE 9820
Southfleet	12	TQ 6171
Southgate (Gtr London)	20	TQ 3093
Southgate (Norf.)	28	TF 6833
Southgate (Norf.)	29	TG 1324
South Green	20	TQ 6893
South-haa	63	HU 3688
South Hall	49	NS 0672
South Hanningfield	20	TQ 7497
South Harting	9	SU 7819
South Hayling	9	SZ 7299
South Heath	19	SP 9102
South Heighton	12	TQ 4503
South Hetton	47	NZ 3745
South Hiendley	37	SE 3812
South Hill	4	SX 3272
South Hole	4	SS 2219
South Holmwood	11	TQ 1745
South Hornchurch	20	TQ 5283
South Hylton	47	NZ 3556
Southill	27	TL 1442
South Kelsey	39	TF 0398
South Kilvington	42	SE 4283
South Kilworth	26	SP 6082
South Kirkby	38	SE 4410
South Kirkton	62	NJ 7405
South Kyme	35	TF 1749
South Lancing	11	TQ 1804
Southleigh (Devon)	5	SY 2093
South Leigh (Oxon.)	18	SP 3908
South Leverton	34	SK 7881
South Littleton	25	SP 0746
South Lochboisdale	63	NF 7817
South Lopham	29	TM 0481
South Luffenham	27	SK 9402
South Malling	12	TQ 4211
South Marston	17	SU 1987
South Milford	38	SE 4931
South Milton	5	SX 7042
South Mimms	19	TL 2200
Southminster	21	TQ 9599
South Molton	6	SS 7125
South Moor	47	NZ 1952
South Moreton	18	SU 5688
South Muskham	34	SK 7957
South Newington	18	SP 4033
South Newton	8	SU 0834
South Normanton	33	SK 4456
South Norwood	12	TQ 3468
South Nutfield	12	TQ 3048
South Ockendon	20	TQ 5982
Southoe	27	TL 1864
Southolt	21	TM 1968
South Ormsby	35	TF 3675
Southorpe	27	TF 0803
South Otterington	42	SE 3787
Southowram	37	SE 1123
South Oxhey	19	TQ 1193
South Perrott	7	ST 4706
South Petherton	7	ST 4316
South Petherwin	4	SX 3182
South Pickenham	28	TF 8504
South Pool	5	SX 7740
Southport	36	SD 3316
South Radworthy	6	SS 7432
South Raynham	28	TF 8723
Southrepps	29	TG 2536
South Reston	35	TF 4082
Southrey	35	TF 1366
Southrop	17	SP 1903
Southrope	10	SU 6744
South Runcton	28	TF 6308
South Scarle	34	SK 8463
Southsea	9	SZ 6498
South Shian	54	NM 9042
South Shields	47	NZ 3667
South Shore	36	SD 3033
South Skirlaugh	39	TA 1439
South Somercotes	39	TF 4193
South Stainley	42	SE 3063
South Stoke (Avon)	17	ST 7461
South Stoke (Oxon.)	18	SU 6083
South Stoke (W Susx)	11	TQ 0210
South Street	12	TQ 3918
South Tawton	6	SX 6594
South Thoresby	35	TF 4077
South Tidworth	10	SU 2347
South Town (Hants.)	9	SU 6536
Southwaite	46	NY 4445
South Walsham	29	TG 3613
Southwark	12	TQ 3278
South Warnborough	10	SU 7247

Tillycorthie 100 Upper Scoulag

Tillycorthie 62 NJ 9123
Tillyfourie 62 NJ 6412
Tillygarmond 62 NO 6393
Tillygreig 62 NJ 8823
Tilmanstone 13 TR 3051
Tilney All Saints 28 TF 5618
Tilney High End 28 TF 5617
Tilney St. Lawrence 28 TF 5414
Tilshead 8 SU 0347
Tilstock 32 SJ 5337
Tilston 32 SJ 4551
Tilstone Fearnall 32 SJ 5660
Tilsworth 19 SP 9724
Tilton on the Hill 26 SK 7405
Timberland 35 TF 1158
Timbersbrook 33 SJ 8962
Timberscombe 6 SS 9542
Timble 37 SE 1752
Timperley 32 SJ 7988
Timsbury (Avon) 17 ST 6658
Timsbury (Hants.) 9 SU 3424
Timworth Green 28 TL 8669
Tincleton 8 SY 7691
Tindale 46 NY 6159
Tingewick 18 SP 6533
Tingley 37 SE 2826
Tingrith 19 TL 0032
Tinhay 4 SX 4085
Tinshill 37 SE 2540
Tinsley 33 SK 3990
Tintagel 4 SX 0588
Tintern Parva 16 SO 5200
Tintinhull 7 ST 5019
Tintwistle 37 SK 0297
Tinwald 45 NY 0081
Tinwell 34 TF 0006
Tipperty 62 NJ 9627
Tipton 25 SO 9592
Tipton St. John 5 SY 0991
Tiptree 21 TL 8916
Tirabad 15 SN 8741
Tirley 17 SO 8328
Tirphil 16 SO 1303
Tirril 40 NY 5026
Tir y mynach 23 SH 9302
Tisbury 8 ST 9429
Tissington 33 SK 1752
Titchberry 4 SS 2427
Titchfield 9 SU 5305
Titchmarsh 27 TL 0279
Titchwell 28 TF 7543
Tithby 34 SK 6936
Titley 23 SO 3260
Titlington 53 NU 1015
Tittensor 33 SJ 8738
Tittleshall 28 TF 8920
Tiverton (Ches.) 32 SJ 5560
Tiverton (Devon.) 6 SS 9512
Tivetshall St. Margaret 29 TM 1787
Tivetshall St. Mary 29 TM 1686
Tixall 33 SJ 9722
Tixover 27 SK 9700
Toab (Shetld.) 63 HU 3811
Tobermory 54 NM 5055
Toberonochy 54 NM 7408
Tobson 63 NB 1438
Tocher 62 NJ 6932
Tockenham 17 SU 0379
Tockenham Wick 17 SU 0381
Tockholes 36 SD 6623
Tockington 17 ST 6186
Tockwith 38 SE 4652
Todber 8 ST 7919
Toddington (Beds.) 19 TL 0129
Toddington (Glos.) 25 SP 0432
Todenham 18 SP 2436
Todhills 46 NY 3663
Todmorden 37 SD 9324
Todwick 33 SK 4984
Toft (Cambs.) 20 TL 3655
Toft (Ches.) 32 SJ 7676
Toft (Lincs.) 35 TF 0617
Toft Monks 29 TM 4295
Toft next Newton 35 TF 0488
Toftrees 28 TF 8927
Toftwood 29 TF 9811
Togston 47 NU 2401
Tokavaig 58 NG 6012
Tokers Green 10 SU 7077
Tolland 7 ST 1032
Tollard Royal 8 ST 9417
Toller Fratrum 7 SY 5797
Toller Porcorum 7 SY 5697
Tollerton (Notts.) 34 SK 6134
Tollerton (N Yorks.) 38 SE 5164
Tollesbury 21 TL 9510
Tolleshunt D'Arcy 21 TL 9312
Tolleshunt Major 21 TL 9011
Toll of Birness 62 NK 0034
Tolob 63 HU 3811
Tolpuddle 8 SY 7994
Tolstachaolais 63 NB 1938
Tolworth 11 TQ 1965
Tomatin 60 NH 8028
Tombreck 60 NH 6934
Tomdoun 59 NH 1501
Tomich (Highld.) 59 NH 3127
Tomich (Highld.) 60 NH 5348
Tomich (Highld.) 65 NH 7071
Tomintoul (Grampn.) 61 NJ 1618
Tomintoul (Grampn.) 61 NO 1490
Tomnavoulin 61 NJ 2026
Ton 16 SO 3301
Tonbridge 12 TQ 5845
Tondu 15 SS 8984
Tong (Isle of Lewis) 63 NB 4436
Tong (Salop) 24 SJ 7907
Tonge 33 SK 4123
Tongham 11 SU 8848
Tongland 45 NX 6953
Tongue 66 NC 5957
Tongwynlais 16 ST 1581
Tonna 15 SS 7798
Tonwell 20 TL 3317
Tonypandy 15 SS 9992
Tonyrefail 15 ST 0188
Toot Baldon 18 SP 5600
Toot Hill (Essex) 20 TL 5102
Toot Hill (Hants.) 9 SU 3718
Topcliffe 42 SE 3976
Topcroft 29 TM 2693
Topcroft Street 29 TM 2692
Toppesfield 20 TL 7337
Toppings 36 SD 7213
Topsham 5 SX 9788
Torbay 5 SX 8962
Torbeg 49 NR 8929
Torbryan 5 SX 8266
Torcastle 55 NN 1378
Torcross 5 SX 8242
Tore 60 NH 6052
Torhousemuir 44 NX 3957
Torksey 34 SK 8378
Torlum (Benbecula) 63 NF 7850
Torlundy 55 NN 1477
Tormarton 17 ST 7678
Tormitchell 44 NX 2394
Tormore 49 NR 8932
Tormsdale 67 ND 1350
Tornagrain 60 NH 7649
Tornahaish 61 NJ 2908
Tornaveen 62 NJ 6106
Torness (Highld.) 60 NH 5727
Torpenhow 40 NY 2039
Torphichen 51 NS 9672
Torphins 62 NJ 6202
Torpoint 4 SX 4355
Torquay 5 SX 9164
Torquhan 52 NT 4447
Torran (Island of Raasay) 58 NG 5949
Torran (Strath.) 54 NM 8704
Torrance 50 NS 6174
Torridon 59 NG 9055
Torrin 58 NG 5720
Torrisdale (Highld.) 66 NC 6761
Torrish 67 NC 9718
Torrisholme 40 SD 4464
Torroble 66 NC 5904
Torry (Grampn.) 61 NJ 4339
Torry (Grampn.) 62 NJ 9404
Torryburn 51 NT 0286
Torrylin 49 NR 9621
Torterston 62 NK 0747
Torthorwald 45 NY 0378
Tortington 11 TQ 0005
Tortworth 17 ST 6992
Torvaig 58 NG 4944
Torver 40 SD 2894
Torwood 50 NS 8484
Torworth 34 SK 6586
Toscaig 58 NG 7138
Toseland 27 TL 2362
Tosside 37 SD 7655
Tostock 21 TL 9563
Totaig 58 NG 2050
Tote 58 NG 4149
Totegan 67 NC 8268
Totland 9 SZ 3286
Totley 33 SK 3179
Totnes 5 SX 8060
Toton 34 SK 5034
Totscore 58 NG 3866
Tottenham 20 TQ 3491
Tottenhill 28 TF 6310
Totteridge 19 TQ 2494
Totternhoe 19 SP 9921
Tottington 37 SD 7712
Totton 9 SU 3513
Tournaig 64 NG 8783
Toux (Grampn.) 62 NJ 5458
Toux (Grampn.) 62 NJ 9850
Tovil 12 TQ 7554
Toward 49 NS 1368
Towcester 26 SP 6948
Towednack 2 SW 4838
Tower Hamlets 20 TQ 3582
Towersey 18 SP 7305
Towie 61 NJ 4412
Towiemore 61 NJ 3945
Tow Law 42 NZ 1139
Town End (Cambs.) 27 TL 4195
Town End (Cumbr.) 40 SD 4483
Townend (Strath.) 50 NS 4076
Townhead 45 NX 6946
Townhead of Greenlaw 45 NX 7465
Townhill 51 NT 1089
Townshend 2 SW 5932
Town Street 28 TL 7786
Town Yetholm 53 NT 8228
Towthorpe 38 SE 6258
Towton 38 SE 4839
Towyn (Clwyd) 31 SH 9779
Towyn (Gwyn.) 22 SH 5800
Toynton All Saints 35 TF 3964
Toynton Fen Side 35 TF 3961
Toynton St. Peter 35 TF 4063
Toy's Hill 12 TQ 4751
Trabboch 50 NS 4321
Trabbochburn 50 NS 4621
Traboe 2 SW 7421
Tradespark (Highld.) 60 NH 8656
Tradespark (Orkney) 63 HY 4408
Trafford Park 37 SJ 7996
Trallong 15 SN 9629
Tranent 52 NT 4072
Trantlemore 67 NC 8853
Tranwell 47 NZ 1883
Trapp 15 SN 6519
Traprain 52 NT 5975
Traquair 51 NT 3334
Trawden 37 SD 9138
Trawsfynydd 30 SH 7035
Trealaw 15 SS 9992
Treales 36 SD 4432
Trearddur Bay 30 SH 2478
Treaslane 58 NG 3953
Trebartha 4 SX 2677
Trebarwith 4 SX 0585
Trebetherick 2 SW 9377
Treborough 7 ST 0036
Trebudannon 2 SW 8961
Treburley 4 SX 3477
Trecastle 15 SN 8729
Trecwn 14 SM 9632
Trecynon 15 SN 9903
Tredavoe 2 SW 4528
Tre-ddiog 14 SM 8928
Tredegar 16 SO 1409
Tredington 26 SP 2543
Tredinnick 2 SW 9270
Tredomen 23 SO 1231
Tredunnock 16 ST 3795
Treen 2 SW 3923
Treeton 33 SK 4387
Trefdraeth 30 SH 4070
Trefecca 23 SO 1431
Trefeglwys 23 SN 9690
Trefenter 22 SN 6068
Treffgarne 14 SM 9523
Treffynnon 14 SM 8428
Trefil 16 SO 1212
Trefilan 22 SN 5457
Trefnannau 23 SJ 2015
Trefnant 31 SJ 0570
Trefonen 32 SJ 2526
Trefor 30 SH 3779
Trefriw 31 SH 7763
Tregadillett 4 SX 2983
Tregaian 30 SH 4579
Tregare 16 SO 4110
Tregaron 22 SN 6759
Tregarth 30 SH 6067
Tregeare 4 SX 2486
Tregeiriog 31 SJ 1733
Tregele 30 SH 3592
Tregidden 2 SW 7523
Treglemais 14 SM 8229
Tregole 4 SX 1998
Tregonetha 2 SW 9563
Tregony 2 SW 9244
Tregoyd 23 SO 1937
Tre-groes 15 SN 4044
Tregurrian 2 SW 8465
Tregynon 23 SO 0999
Trehafod 16 ST 0491
Treharris 16 ST 1097
Treherbert 15 SS 9398
Trelawnyd 31 SJ 0879
Trelech 14 SN 2830
Trelech a'r Betws 14 SN 3026
Treleddyd-fawr 14 SM 7528
Trelewis 16 ST 1197
Trelights 2 SW 9879
Trelill 4 SX 0477
Trellech 16 SO 5005
Trelleck Grange 16 SO 4901
Trelogan 31 SJ 1180
Trelystan 23 SJ 2603
Tremadog 30 SH 5640
Tremail 4 SX 1686
Tremain 14 SN 2348
Tremaine 4 SX 2388
Tremar 4 SX 2568
Trematon 4 SX 3959
Tremeirchion 31 SJ 0773
Trenance 2 SW 8567
Trenarren 4 SX 0348
Trench 24 SJ 6913
Treneglos 4 SX 2088
Trenewan 4 SX 1753
Trent 7 ST 5918
Trentham 33 SJ 8640
Trentishoe 6 SS 6448
Treoes 15 SS 9478
Treorchy 15 SS 9596
Tre'r-ddol 22 SN 6592
Tresaith 14 SN 2751
Trescott 25 SO 8497
Trescowe 2 SW 5731
Tresham 17 ST 7991
Tresillian 2 SW 8646
Tresinwen 14 SM 9040
Tresmeer 4 SX 2387
Tressait 56 NN 8160
Tresta (Fetlar) 63 HU 6190
Tresta (Shetld.) 63 HU 3650
Treswell 34 SK 7779
Trethurgy 4 SX 0355
Tretio 14 SM 7829
Tretire 16 SO 5124
Tretower 16 SO 1821
Treuddyn 32 SJ 2458
Trevalga 4 SX 0889
Trevanson 2 SW 9772
Trevarren 2 SW 9160
Trevarrick 2 SW 9843
Trevellas 2 SW 7452
Treverva 2 SW 7531
Trevethin 16 SO 2802
Trevigro 4 SX 3369
Trevine 14 SM 8432
Treviscoe 2 SW 9455
Trevone 2 SW 8975
Trevor 30 SH 3746
Trewarmett 4 SX 0686
Trewarthenick 2 SW 9044
Trewassa 4 SX 1486
Trewellard 2 SW 3733
Trewen 4 SX 2583
Trewidland 4 SX 2560
Trewint 4 SX 1897
Trewithian 2 SW 8737
Trewoon 4 SW 9952
Treyford 9 SU 8218
Trickett's Cross 8 SU 0801
Trimdon 42 NZ 3634
Trimdon Colliery 42 NZ 3835
Trimdon Grange 42 NZ 3735
Trimingham 29 TG 2738
Trimley 21 TM 2736
Trimley St. Mary 21 TM 2737
Trimpley 24 SO 7978
Trimsaran 15 SN 4504
Trimstone 6 SS 5043
Trinant 16 SO 2000
Tring 19 SP 9211
Trinity 52 NO 6061
Trislaig 55 NN 0874
Trispen 2 SW 8450
Tritlington 47 NZ 2092
Trochry 56 NN 9740
Troedyraur 14 SN 3245
Troedyrhiw 16 SO 0702
Trofarth 31 SH 8571
Troon (Corn.) 2 SW 6638
Troon (Strath.) 50 NS 3230
Troston 28 TL 8972
Trottiscliffe 12 TQ 6460
Trotton 9 SU 8322
Troutbeck 40 NY 4103
Troutbeck Bridge 40 NY 4000
Trowbridge 17 ST 8557
Trow Green 17 SO 5706
Trowle Common 17 ST 8358
Trows 52 NT 6932
Trowse Newton 29 TG 2406
Trudoxhill 8 ST 7443
Trull 7 ST 2122
Trumisgarry 63 NF 8674
Trumpan 58 NG 2261
Trumpet 24 SO 6539
Trumpington 20 TL 4455
Trunch 29 TG 2834
Truro 2 SW 8244
Trusham 5 SX 8582
Trusley 33 SK 2535
Trusthorpe 35 TF 5183
Trysull 25 SO 8494
Tubney 18 SU 4498
Tuckenhay 5 SX 8156
Tuddenham (Suff.) 28 TL 7371
Tuddenham (Suff.) 21 TM 1948
Tudeley 12 TQ 6245
Tudhoe 42 NZ 2635
Tudweiloig 30 SH 2336
Tuffley 17 SO 8315
Tugby 26 SK 7601
Tugford 24 SO 5587
Tullibody 50 NS 8595
Tullich (Highld.) 65 NH 8576
Tullich (Strath.) 55 NN 0815
Tullich Muir 65 NH 7373
Tulliemet 56 NN 9952
Tulloch (Grampn.) 57 NO 7671
Tulloch (Highld.) 65 NH 6192
Tullochgorm 49 NR 9695
Tulloes 57 NO 5145
Tullybannocher 56 NN 7521
Tullyfergus 56 NO 2149
Tullynessle 62 NJ 5519
Tumble 15 SN 5411
Tumby 35 TF 2359
Tumby Woodside 35 TF 2657
Tummel Bridge 56 NN 7659
Tunstall (Humbs.) 39 TA 3032
Tunstall (Kent) 13 TQ 8961
Tunstall (Lancs.) 41 SD 6073
Tunstall (Norf.) 29 TG 4107
Tunstall (N Yorks.) 42 SE 2195
Tunstall (Staffs.) 33 SJ 8551
Tunstall (Suff.) 21 TM 3655
Tunstead 29 TG 3022
Tunworth 10 SU 6748
Tupsley 24 SO 5340
Turgis Green 10 SU 6959
Turin 57 NO 5352
Turkdean 17 SP 1017
Tur Langton 26 SP 7194
Turnastone 24 SO 3536
Turnberry 44 NS 2005
Turnditch 33 SK 2946
Turner's Hill 12 TQ 3435
Turners Puddle 8 SY 8293
Turnworth 8 ST 8107
Turriff 62 NJ 7249
Turton Bottoms 36 SD 7315
Turvey 27 SP 9452
Turville 18 SU 7691
Turville Heath 18 SU 7391
Turweston 18 SP 6037
Tushingham cum Grindley 32 SJ 5246
Tutbury 33 SK 2129
Tutnall 25 SO 9870
Tutshill 16 ST 5394
Tuttington 29 TG 2227
Tuxford 34 SK 7370
Twatt (Orkney) 63 HY 2624
Twatt (Shetld.) 63 HU 3252
Twechar 50 NS 6975
Tweedmouth 53 NT 9952
Tweedsmuir 51 NT 1024
Twelveheads 2 SW 7642
Twenty 35 TF 1520
Twerton 17 ST 7263
Twickenham 11 TQ 1473
Twigworth 17 SO 8421
Twineham 11 TQ 2519
Twinhoe 17 ST 7359
Twinstead 20 TL 8637
Twiss Green 32 SJ 6595
Twitchen (Devon) 6 SS 7830
Twitchen (Salop) 24 SO 3679
Two Bridges 4 SX 6075
Two Dales 33 SK 2762
Two Gates 25 SK 2101
Twycross 26 SK 3305
Twyford (Berks.) 10 SU 7975
Twyford (Bucks.) 18 SP 6626
Twyford (Hants.) 9 SU 4724
Twyford (Leic.) 34 SK 7210
Twyford (Norf.) 29 TG 0124
Twyford Common 24 SO 5135
Twynholm 45 NX 6654
Twyning 25 SO 8936
Twyning Green 25 SO 9037
Twynllanan 15 SN 7524
Twyn-y-Sheriff 16 SO 4005
Twywell 27 SP 9578
Tyberton 24 SO 3739
Tyburn 25 SP 1490
Tycroes 15 SN 6010
Tycrwyn 31 SJ 1018
Tydd Gote 35 TF 4518
Tydd St. Giles 35 TF 4216
Tydd St. Mary 35 TF 4418
Ty-hen 30 SH 1731
Tyldesley 36 SD 6902
Tyler Hill 13 TR 1460
Tylers Green 19 SU 9094
Tylorstown 15 ST 0195
Tylwch 23 SN 9780
Ty-mawr 31 SH 9047
Ty-nant (Clwyd) 31 SH 9944
Ty-nant (Gwyn.) 31 SH 9026
Tyndrum 55 NN 3330
Tyneham 8 SY 8880
Tynehead 51 NT 3959
Tynemouth (Tyne and Wear) 47 NZ 3468
Tynewydd 15 SS 9399
Tyninghame 52 NT 6179
Tynribbie 54 NM 9446
Tynron 45 NX 8093
Tyn-y-ffridd 31 SJ 1230
Tyn-y-graig 15 SO 0149
Ty'n-y-groes 31 SH 7771
Tyringham 27 SP 8547
Tythegston 15 SS 8578
Tytherington (Avon) 17 ST 6788
Tytherington (Ches.) 33 SJ 9175
Tytherington (Somer.) 8 ST 7744
Tytherington (Wilts.) 8 ST 9140
Tytherleigh 7 ST 3203
Tywardreath 4 SX 0854
Tywyn 31 SH 7878
Tywyn Trewan 30 SH 3175

Uachdar 63 NF 7955
Ubbeston Green 29 TM 3271
Ubley 16 ST 5257
Uckerby 42 NZ 2402
Uckfield 12 TQ 4721
Uckington 17 SO 9224
Uddingston 50 NS 6960
Uddington 50 NS 8633
Udimore 13 TQ 8718
Udny Green 62 NJ 8726
Udstonhead 50 NS 7047
Uffcott 17 SU 1277
Uffculme 7 ST 0612
Uffington (Lincs.) 35 TF 0608
Uffington (Oxon.) 18 SU 3089
Uffington (Salop) 24 SJ 5313
Ufford (Northants.) 27 TF 0904
Ufford (Suff.) 21 TM 2953
Ufton 26 SP 3762
Ufton Nervet 10 SU 6367
Ugborough 5 SX 6755
Uggeshall 29 TM 4580
Ugglebarnby 43 NZ 8707
Ugley 20 TL 5128
Ugley Green 20 TL 5227
Ugthorpe 43 NZ 7911
Uig (Isle of Lewis) 63 NB 0534
Uig (Isle of Skye) 58 NG 1952
Uig (Isle of Skye) 58 NG 3963
Uigshader 58 NG 4246
Uisken 54 NM 3819
Ulbster 67 ND 3241
Ulceby (Humbs.) 39 TA 1014
Ulceby (Lincs.) 35 TF 4272
Ulcombe 13 TQ 8449
Uldale 40 NY 2536
Uley 17 ST 7898
Ulgham 47 NZ 2392
Ullapool 64 NH 1294
Ullenhall 25 SP 1267
Ullenwood 17 SO 9416
Ulleskelf 38 SE 5140
Ullesthorpe 26 SP 5087
Ulley 33 SK 4687
Ullingswick 24 SO 5950
Ullinish 58 NG 3237
Ullock 40 NY 0724
Ulpha 40 SD 1993
Ulrome 39 TA 1656
Ulsta 63 HU 4680
Ulverston 40 SD 2878
Umberleigh 6 SS 6023
Unapool 64 NC 2333
Underbarrow 40 SD 4692
Underhoull 63 HP 5704
Under River 12 TQ 5552
Underwood 33 SK 4750
Undy 16 ST 4386
Unifirth 63 HU 2856
Union Mills 43 SC 3578
Unstone 33 SK 3777
Upavon 17 SU 1354
Up Cerne 8 ST 6502
Upchurch 13 TQ 8467
Upcott 23 SO 3250
Upend 20 TL 7058
Up Exe 6 SS 9302
Uphall 51 NT 0571
Upham (Devon.) 6 SS 8808
Upham (Hants.) 9 SU 5320
Up Hatherley 17 SO 9120
Uphill (Avon) 16 ST 3158
Up Hill (Kent) 13 TR 2140
Up Holland 36 SD 5105
Uplawmoor 50 NS 4355
Upleadon 17 SO 7527
Upleatham 42 NZ 6319
Uplees 13 TQ 9964
Uploman 7 ST 0115
Uplyme 7 SY 3293
Upminster 20 TQ 5686
Up Nately 10 SU 6951
Upnor 12 TQ 7470
Upottery 5 ST 2007
Uppark 9 SU 7717
Upper Affcot 24 SO 4486
Upper Ardchronie 65 NH 6188
Upper Arley 24 SO 7680
Upper Astrop 18 SP 5137
Upper Basildon 10 SU 5976
Upper Beeding 11 TQ 1910
Upper Benefield 27 SP 9789
Upper Boddington 26 SP 4853
Upper Borth 22 SN 6088
Upper Breinton 24 SO 4640
Upper Broughton 34 SK 6826
Upper Brow Top 36 SD 5258
Upper Bucklebury 10 SU 5368
Upper Caldecote 27 TL 1645
Upper Chapel 15 SO 0040
Upper Chute 10 SU 2953
Upper Clatford 10 SU 3543
Upper Clynnog 30 SH 4746
Upper Cokeham 11 TQ 1605
Upper Coll 63 NB 4539
Upper Cwmtwrch 15 SN 7611
Upper Dallachy 61 NJ 3662
Upper Dean 27 TL 0467
Upper Denby 37 SE 2207
Upper Derraid 61 NJ 0233
Upper Dicker 12 TQ 5510
Upper Elkstone 33 SK 0559
Upper End 33 SK 0876
Upper Ethie 65 NH 7663
Upper Farringdon 9 SU 7135
Upper Framilode 17 SO 7510
Upper Froyle 10 SU 7542
Upper Gravenhurst 19 TL 1136
Upper Green 10 SU 3663
Upper Hackney 33 SK 2961
Upper Hale 11 SU 8448
Upper Hambleton 34 SK 8907
Upper Hardres Court 13 TR 1550
Upper Hartfield 12 TQ 4634
Upper Heath 24 SO 5685
Upper Helmsley 38 SE 6956
Upper Heyford 18 SP 4926
Upper Hill 24 SO 4753
Upper Hopton 37 SE 1918
Upper Hulme 33 SK 0160
Upper Inglesham 17 SU 2096
Upper Killay 15 SS 5892
Upper Knockando 61 NJ 1843
Upper Lambourn 10 SU 3180
Upper Langwith 34 SK 5169
Upper Lochton 62 NO 6997
Upper Longdon 25 SK 0614
Upper Lydbrook 17 SO 6015
Upper Maes-coed 23 SO 3335
Uppermill 37 SD 9906
Upper Minety 17 SU 0091
Upper North Dean 19 SU 8598
Upper Poppleton 38 SE 5554
Upper Quinton 25 SP 1746
Upper Sanday 63 HY 5303
Upper Sapey 24 SO 6863
Upper Scoulag 49 NS 1059

Upper Seagry 101 West Halton

Upper Seagry 17 ST 9580
Upper Shelton 27 SP 9943
Upper Sheringham 29 TG 1441
Upper Skelmorlie 49 NS 1968
Upper Slaughter 17 SP 1523
Upper Soudley 17 SO 6610
Upper Stondon 19 TL 1535
Upper Stowe 26 SP 6456
Upper Street (Hants.) 8 SU 1418
Upper Street (Norf.) 29 TG 3516
Upper Sundon 19 TL 0527
Upper Swell 17 SP 1726
Upper Tasburgh 29 TM 2095
Upper Tean 33 SK 0139
Upperthong 37 SE 1208
Upper Tillyrie 56 NO 1006
Upperton 11 SU 9522
Upper Tooting 11 TQ 2772
Upper Town (Avon) 16 ST 5265
Uppertown (Island of Stroma) 67 ND 3576
Upper Tysoe 26 SP 3343
Upper Upham 10 SU 2277
Upper Wardington 26 SP 4946
Upper Weald 18 SP 8037
Upper Weedon 26 SP 6258
Upper Wield 10 SU 6238
Upper Winchendon 18 SP 7414
Upper Woodford 8 SU 1237
Uppingham 27 SP 8699
Uppington 24 SJ 5909
Upsall 42 SE 4587
Upshire 20 TL 4100
Up Somborne 9 SU 3932
Upstreet 13 TR 2262
Up Sydling 8 ST 6201
Upton (Berks.) 11 SU 9879
Upton (Bucks.) 18 SP 7711
Upton (Cambs.) 27 TL 1778
Upton (Ches.) 32 SJ 4069
Upton (Dorset) 8 SY 9893
Upton (Hants.) 10 SU 3555
Upton (Hants.) 9 SU 3716
Upton (Lincs.) 34 SK 8686
Upton (Mers.) 32 SJ 2687
Upton (Norf.) 29 TG 3912
Upton (Northants.) 26 SP 7160
Upton (Northants.) 27 TF 1000
Upton (Notts.) 34 SK 7354
Upton (Notts.) 34 SK 7476
Upton (Oxon.) 18 SU 5186
Upton (Somer.) 7 SS 9928
Upton (W Yorks.) 38 SE 4713
Upton Bishop 17 SO 6427
Upton Cheyney 17 ST 6969
Upton Cressett 24 SO 6592
Upton Cross 4 SX 2872
Upton Grey 10 SU 6948
Upton Hellions 6 SS 8303
Upton Lovell 8 ST 9440
Upton Magna 24 SJ 5512
Upton Noble 8 ST 7139
Upton Pyne 6 SX 9197
Upton St. Leonards 17 SO 8615
Upton Scudamore 8 ST 8647
Upton Snodsbury 25 SO 9454
Upton upon Severn 25 SO 8540
Upton Warren 25 SO 9267
Upwaltham 11 SU 9413
Upware 28 TL 5370
Upwell 28 TF 5002
Upwey 8 SY 6684
Upwood 27 TL 2582
Uradale 63 HU 4137
Urafirth (Shetld.) 63 HU 3078
Urchal 60 NH 7544
Urchany 60 NH 8849
Urchfont 17 SU 0356
Urdimarsh 24 SO 5249
Ure 63 HU 2180
Urgha 63 NG 1799
Urishay Common 23 SO 3137
Urlay Nook 42 NZ 4014
Urmston 37 SJ 7695
Urquhart 61 NJ 2860
Urra 42 NZ 5702
Urray 60 NH 5053
Urswick 40 SD 2674
Ushaw Moor 42 NZ 2342
Usk 16 SO 3701
Usselby 39 TF 0993
Utley 37 SE 0542
Uton 6 SX 8298
Utterby 39 TF 3093
Uttoxeter 33 SK 0933
Uwchmynydd (Gwyn.) 30 SH 1425
Uwch-mynydd (Gwyn) 30 SH 6419
Uxbridge 19 TQ 0583
Uyeasound (Unst) 63 HP 5901
Uzmaston 14 SM 9714

Valley 30 SH 2979
Valleyfield 51 NT 0086
Valsgarth 63 HP 6413
Valtos (Island of Skye) 58 NG 5163
Valtos (Isle of Lewis) 63 NB 0936
Vange 20 TQ 7287
Vardre 15 SN 6902
Varteg 16 SO 2506
Vatten 58 NG 2843
Vaul 48 NM 0448
Vauld, The 24 SO 5349
Vaynol Hall 30 SH 5369
Vaynor 16 SO 0410
Veensgarth 63 HU 4244
Velindre (Dyfed) 14 SN 1039
Velindre (Dyfed) 14 SN 3538
Velindre (Powys) 23 SO 1836
Veness (Eday) 63 HY 5729
Venn Ottery 23 SJ 3309
Venn Ottery 5 SY 0791
Ventnor 9 SZ 5677
Vernham Dean 10 SU 3356
Vernham Street 10 SU 3457
Vernolds Common 24 SO 4780
Verwig 14 SN 1849
Verwood 8 SU 0908
Veryan 2 SW 9139
Vicarage 5 SY 2088
Vickerstown 40 SD 1868
Victoria 4 SW 9961
Vidlin 63 HU 4765
Viewpark 50 NS 7161
Villavin 6 SS 5816
Vinehall Street 12 TQ 7520
Vine's Cross 12 TQ 5917
Virginia Water 11 SU 9967
Virginstow 4 SX 3792
Vobster 8 ST 7048
Voe (Shetld.) 63 HU 4062
Vowchurch 24 SO 3636
Voxter 63 HU 3769
Voy 63 HY 2515

Wackerfield 42 NZ 1522
Wacton 29 TM 1891
Wadborough 25 SO 8947
Waddesdon 18 SP 7416
Waddingham 39 SK 9896
Waddington (Lancs.) 36 SD 7243
Waddington (Lincs.) 34 SK 9764
Wadebridge 4 SW 9972
Wadeford 7 ST 3110
Wadenhoe 27 TL 0083
Wadesmill 20 TL 3517
Wadhurst 12 TQ 6431
Wadshelf 33 SK 3171
Wadworth 38 SK 5697
Waen Fach 23 SJ 2017
Wainfleet All Saints 35 TF 4959
Wainfleet Bank 35 TF 4759
Wainhouse Corner 4 SX 1895
Wainscott 12 TQ 7471
Wainstalls 37 SE 0428
Waitby 41 NY 7507
Wakefield 37 SE 3320
Wakerley 27 SP 9599
Wakes Colne 21 TL 8928
Walberswick 29 TM 4974
Walberton 11 SU 9705
Walcot (Lincs.) 35 TF 0535
Walcot (Lincs.) 35 TF 1256
Walcot (Salop) 24 SJ 5912
Walcot (Salop) 23 SO 3485
Walcot (Warw.) 25 SP 1258
Walcote 26 SP 5683
Walcott (Norf.) 29 TG 3632
Walden 41 SE 0082
Walden Head 41 SD 9880
Walden Stubbs 38 SE 5516
Walderslade 12 TQ 7563
Walderton 9 SU 7910
Walditch 7 SY 4892
Waldridge 47 NZ 2549
Waldingfield 21 TM [illegible]
Waldron 12 TQ 5419
Wales 33 SK 4782
Walesby (Lincs.) 39 TF 1392
Walesby (Notts.) 34 SK 6870
Walford (Here. and Worc.) 24 SO 3872
Walford (Here. and Worc.) 17 SO 5820
Walford (Salop) 32 SJ 4320
Walgherton 32 SJ 6948
Walgrave 26 SP 8071
Walkden 36 SD 7303
Walker 47 NZ 2864
Walkerburn 51 NT 3637
Walker Fold 36 SD 6742
Walkeringham 38 SK 7692
Walkerith 38 SK 7892
Walkern 19 TL 2926
Walker's Green 24 SO 5248
Walkerton 56 NO 2301
Walkhampton 4 SX 5369
Walkington 39 SE 9936
Walk Mill 37 SD 8629
Wall (Northum.) 47 NY 9168
Wall (Staffs.) 25 SK 0906
Wallacetown 50 NS 3422
Wallasey 32 SJ 2992
Wall Bank 24 SO 5092
Wallend 13 TQ 8775
Walling Fen 39 SE 8829
Wallingford 18 SU 6089
Wallington (Gtr London) 11 TQ 2863
Wallington (Hants.) 9 SU 5806
Wallington (Herts.) 19 TL 2933
Wallis 14 SN 0125
Walliswood 11 TQ 1138
Walls 63 HU 2449
Wallsend 47 NZ 2766
Wallyford 51 NT 3671
Walmer 13 TR 3750
Walmer Bridge 36 SD 4724
Walmersley 37 SD 8013
Walmley 25 SP 1393
Walpole 29 TM 3674
Walpole Highway 28 TF 5113
Walpole St. Andrew 28 TF 5017
Walpole St. Peter 28 TF 5016
Walsall 25 SP 0198
Walsall Wood 25 SK 0403
Walsden 37 SD 9322
Walsgrave on Sowe 26 SP 3781
Walsham le Willows 29 TM 0071
Walsoken 35 TF 4710
Walston 51 NT 0545
Walterstone 16 SO 3425
Waltham (Humbs.) 39 TA 2503
Waltham (Kent) 13 TR 1148
Waltham Abbey 20 TL 3800
Waltham Chase 9 SU 5614
Waltham on the Wolds 34 SK 8025
Waltham St. Lawrence 10 SU 8276
Walthamstow 20 TQ 3788
Walton (Bucks.) 27 SP 8936
Walton (Cumbr.) 46 NY 5264
Walton (Derby.) 33 SK 3569
Walton (Leic.) 26 SP 5987
Walton (Powys) 23 SO 2559
Walton (Salop) 32 SJ 5818
Walton (Somer.) 7 ST 4636
Walton (Suff.) 21 TM 2935
Walton (Warw.) 26 SP 2853
Walton (W Yorks.) 37 SE 3516
Walton (W Yorks.) 38 SE 4447
Walton Cardiff 25 SO 9032
Walton East 14 SN 0123
Walton-in-Gordano 16 ST 4273
Walton-le-Dale 36 SD 5627
Walton-on-Thames 11 TQ 1066
Walton-on-the-Hill (Staffs.) 33 SJ 9520
Walton on the Hill (Surrey) 11 TQ 2255
Walton on the Naze 21 TM 2521
Walton on the Wolds 34 SK 5919
Walton-on-Trent 33 SK 2118
Walton West 14 SM 8713
Walworth 42 NZ 2218
Walwyn's Castle 14 SM 8711
Wambrook 7 ST 2907
Wanborough 17 SU 2082
Wandsworth 11 TQ 2673
Wangford 29 TM 4679
Wanlip 34 SK 5910
Wanlockhead 50 NS 8712
Wansford (Cambs.) 27 TL 0799
Wansford (Humbs.) 39 TA 0656
Wanstead 20 TQ 4087
Wanstrow 8 ST 7141
Wanswell 17 SO 6801
Wantage 18 SU 4087
Wapley 17 ST 7179
Wappenbury 26 SP 3769
Wappenham 26 SP 6245
Warbleton 12 TQ 6018
Warborough 18 SU 6093
Warboys 27 TL 3080
Warbstow 4 SX 2090
Warburton 32 SJ 7089
Warcop 41 NY 7415
Warden 13 TR 0271
Ward Green 21 TM 0564
Wardington 26 SP 4946
Wardlaw Hill 50 NS 6822
Wardle (Ches.) 32 SJ 6057
Wardle (Gtr Mches.) 37 SD 9116
Wardley 27 SK 8300
Wardlow 33 SK 1874
Wardy Hill 27 TL 4782
Ware 20 TL 3614
Wareham 8 SY 9287
Warehorne 13 TQ 9832
Warenford 53 NU 1328
Waren Mill 53 NU 1534
Warenton 53 NU 1030
Wareside 20 TL 3915
Waresley 27 TL 2454
Warfield 11 SU 8872
Wargrave 10 SU 7878
Warham All Saints 29 TF 9441
Warham St. Mary 29 TF 9441
Wark (Northum.) 53 NT 8238
Wark (Northum.) 47 NY 8576
Warkleigh 6 SS 6422
Warkton 27 SP 8980
Warkworth 47 NU 2406
Warlaby 42 SE 3591
Warland 37 SD 9419
Warleggan 4 SX 1569
Warley 25 SP 0086
Warlingham 12 TQ 3658
Warmfield 37 SE 3720
Warmingham 32 SJ 7161
Warmington (Northants.) 27 TL 0791
Warmington (Warw.) 26 SP 4147
Warminster 8 ST 8644
Warmsworth 38 SE 5400
Warmwell 8 SY 7585
Warndon 25 SO 8856
Warnford 9 SU 6223
Warnham 11 TQ 1633
Warninglid 11 TQ 2526
Warren (Ches.) 33 SJ 8870
Warren (Dyfed) 14 SR 9397
Warren Row 10 SU 8180
Warren Street 13 TQ 9253
Warrington (Bucks.) 27 SP 8954
Warrington (Ches.) 32 SJ 6088
Warsash 9 SU 4905
Warslow 33 SK 0858
Warsop 34 SK 5667
Warter 39 SE 8750
Warthill 38 SE 6755
Wartling 12 TQ 6509
Wartnaby 34 SK 7123
Warton (Lancs.) 36 SD 4028
Warton (Lancs.) 40 SD 4972
Warton (Northum.) 47 NU 0002
Warton (Warw.) 26 SK 2803
Warwick (Cumbr.) 46 NY 4656
Warwick (Warw.) 26 SP 2865
Warwick Bridge 46 NY 4756
Wasbister 63 HY 3932
Washaway 4 SX 0369
Washbourne 5 SX 7954
Washfield 6 SS 9315
Washfold 42 NZ 0502
Washford 7 ST 0441
Washford Pyne 6 SS 8111
Washingborough 34 TF 0170
Washington (Tyne and Wear) 47 NZ 3356
Washington (W Susx) 11 TQ 1212
Wasing 10 SU 5764
Waskerley 47 NZ 0545
Wasperton 26 SP 2659
Wass 42 SE 5579
Watchet 7 ST 0743
Watchfield (Oxon.) 18 SU 2490
Watchfield (Somer.) 7 ST 3446
Watchgate 40 SD 5399
Water 37 SD 8425
Waterbeach 20 TL 4965
Waterbeck 46 NY 2477
Waterden 28 TF 8835
Water End (Herts.) 19 TL 0310
Water End (Herts.) 19 TL 2304
Waterfall 33 SK 0851
Waterfoot (Lancs.) 37 SD 8321
Waterfoot (Strath.) 50 NS 5654
Waterford 20 TL 3114
Waterhead (Cumbr.) 40 NY 3703
Waterhead (Strath.) 50 NS 5411
Waterheads 51 NT 2451
Waterhouses (Durham) 42 NZ 1841
Waterhouses (Staffs.) 33 SK 0850
Wateringbury 12 TQ 6853
Wateringhouse 63 ND 3090
Waterloo (Dorset) 8 SZ 0194
Waterloo (Mers.) 32 SJ 3297
Waterloo (Norf.) 29 TG 2219
Waterloo (Strath.) 50 NS 8153
Waterloo (Tays.) 56 NO 0636
Waterlooville 9 SU 6809
Water Meetings 51 NS 9513
Watermillock 40 NY 4322
Water Newton 27 TL 1097
Water Orton 25 SP 1791
Waterperry 18 SP 6206
Waterrow 7 ST 0525
Watersfield 11 TQ 0115
Waterside (Strath.) 44 NS 4308
Waterside (Strath.) 50 NS 4843
Waterside (Strath.) 50 NS 5160
Waterside (Strath.) 50 NS 6773
Waterstock 18 SP 6305
Waterston 14 SM 9306
Water Stratford 18 SP 6534
Waters Upton 32 SJ 6319
Water Yeat 40 SD 2889
Watford (Herts.) 19 TQ 1196
Watford (Northants.) 26 SP 6069
Wath (N Yorks.) 42 SE 1467
Wath (N Yorks.) 42 SE 3277
Wath Upon Dearne 38 SE 4300
Watlington (Norf.) 28 TF 6211
Watlington (Oxon.) 18 SU 6994
Watnall Chaworth 33 SK 4946
Watten 67 ND 2454
Wattisfield 29 TM 0174
Wattisham 21 TM 0151
Watton (Humbs.) 39 TA 0150
Watton (Norf.) 28 TF 9100
Watton-at-Stone 20 TL 3019
Wattston 50 NS 7770
Wattstown 15 ST 0194
Waunarlwydd 15 SS 6095
Waunfawr 30 SH 5259
Wavendon 19 SP 9137
Waverton (Ches.) 32 SJ 4663
Waverton (Cumbr.) 46 NY 2247
Wawne 39 TA 0836
Waxham 29 TG 4326
Waxholme 39 TA 3229
Wayford 7 ST 4006
Way Village 6 SS 8810
Wealdstone 19 TQ 1689
Weare 7 ST 4152
Weare Giffard 6 SS 4721
Weasenham All Saints 28 TF 8421
Weasenham St. Peter 28 TF 8522
Weaverham 32 SJ 6173
Weaverthorpe 39 SE 9670
Webheath 25 SP 0266
Weddington 26 SP 3693
Wedhampton 17 SU 0557
Wedmore 7 ST 4347
Wednesbury 25 SP 0095
Wednesfield 25 SJ 9400
Weedon 18 SP 8118
Weedon Bec 26 SP 6259
Weedon Lois 26 SP 6047
Weeford 25 SK 1404
Week 6 SS 7316
Weekley 27 SP 8880
Week St. Mary 4 SX 2397
Weeley 21 TM 1422
Weeley Heath 21 TM 1520
Weem 56 NN 8449
Weeping Cross 33 SJ 9421
Weeting 28 TL 7788
Weeton (Lancs.) 36 SD 3834
Weeton (W Yorks.) 37 SE 2846
Weir 37 SD 8724
Welbeck Colliery Village 34 SK 5869
Welborne 29 TG 0610
Welbourn 34 SK 9654
Welburn 38 SE 7168
Welbury 42 NZ 3902
Welby 34 SK 9738
Welches Dam 27 TL 4786
Welcombe 4 SS 2218
Weldon 27 SP 9289
Welford (Berks.) 10 SU 4073
Welford (Northants.) 26 SP 6480
Welford-on-Avon 25 SP 1552
Welham 26 SP 7692
Welham Green 19 TL 2305
Well (Hants.) 10 SU 7646
Well (Lincs.) 35 TF 4473
Well (N Yorks.) 42 SE 2682
Welland 24 SO 7940
Wellesbourne Hastings 26 SP 2755
Wellesbourne Mountford 26 SP 2755
Well Hill (Kent) 12 TQ 4963
Welling 12 TQ 4575
Wellingborough 27 SP 8968
Wellingham 28 TF 8722
Wellingore 34 SK 9856
Wellington (Here. and Worc.) 24 SO 4948
Wellington (Salop) 24 SJ 6411
Wellington (Somer.) 7 ST 1320
Wellington Heath 24 SO 7140
Wellow (Avon) 17 ST 7358
Wellow (I. of W.) 9 SZ 3887
Wellow (Notts.) 34 SK 6666
Wells 7 ST 5445
Wellsborough 26 SK 3602
Wells-Next-The-Sea 28 TF 9143
Wells of Ythan 62 NJ 6338
Wellwood 51 NT 0888
Welney 28 TL 5294
Welshampton 32 SJ 4334
Welsh Bicknor 17 SO 5917
Welsh End 32 SJ 5035
Welsh Frankton 32 SJ 3633
Welsh Hook 14 SM 9327
Welsh Newton 16 SO 4918
Welshpool (Trallwng) 23 SJ 2207
Welsh St. Donats 15 ST 0276
Welton (Cumbr.) 46 NY 3544
Welton (Humbs.) 39 SE 9527
Welton (Lincs.) 34 TF 0079
Welton (Northants.) 26 SP 5865
Welton le Marsh 35 TF 4768
Welton le Wold 35 TF 2787
Welwick 39 TA 3421
Welwyn 19 TL 2316
Welwyn Garden City 19 TL 2412
Wem 32 SJ 5129
Wembdon 7 ST 2837
Wembley 19 TQ 1985
Wembury 4 SX 5148
Wembworthy 6 SS 6609
Wemyss Bay 49 NS 1869
Wenallt 31 SH 9842
Wendens Ambo 20 TL 5136
Wendlebury 18 SP 5519
Wendling 29 TF 9213
Wendover 19 SP 8708
Wendron 2 SW 6731
Wendy 20 TL 3247
Wenhaston 29 TM 4275
Wennington (Cambs.) 27 TL 2379
Wennington (Essex) 20 TQ 5381
Wennington (Lancs.) 41 SD 6169
Wensley (Derby.) 33 SK 2661
Wensley (N Yorks.) 42 SE 0989
Wentbridge 38 SE 4817
Wentnor 24 SO 3892
Wentworth (Cambs.) 27 TL 4878
Wentworth (S Yorks.) 37 SK 3898
Wenvoe 16 ST 1272
Weobley 24 SO 4051
Weobley Marsh 24 SO 4151
Wereham 28 TF 6801
Wergs 25 SJ 8601
Wernrheolydd 16 SO 3913
Werrington (Devon.) 4 SX 3287
Werrington (Northants.) 27 TF 1703
Werrington (Staffs.) 33 SJ 9647
Wervin 32 SJ 4171
Wesham 36 SD 4132
Wessington 33 SK 3757
West Acre 28 TF 7715
West Allerdean 53 NT 9646
West Alvington 5 SX 7243
West Anstey 6 SS 8527
West Ashby 35 TF 2672
West Ashling 9 SU 8007
West Ashton 17 ST 8755
West Auckland 42 NZ 1826
West Bagborough 7 ST 1633
West Barns 52 NT 6578
West Barsham 28 TF 9033
West Bay (Dorset) 7 SY 4690
West Beckham 29 TG 1339
Westbere 13 TR 1961
West Bergholt 21 TL 9527
West Bexington 7 SY 5386
West Bilney 28 TF 7115
West Blatchington 11 TQ 2706
Westbourne (Dorset) 8 SZ 0690
Westbourne (W Susx) 9 SU 7507
West Bradenham 29 TF 9209
West Bradford 36 SD 7444
West Bradley 7 ST 5536
West Bretton 37 SE 2813
West Bridgford 34 SK 5837
West Bromwich 25 SP 0091
West Buckland (Devon.) 6 SS 6510
West Buckland (Somer.) 7 ST 1720
West Burrafirth 63 HU 2557
West Burton (N Yorks.) 41 SE 0186
West Burton (W Susx) 11 TQ 0014
Westbury (Bucks.) 18 SP 6235
Westbury (Salop) 24 SJ 3509
Westbury (Wilts.) 8 ST 8751
Westbury Leigh 8 ST 8649
Westbury-on-Severn 17 SO 7114
Westbury-sub-Mendip 7 ST 5049
Westby 36 SD 3731
West Caister 29 TG 5011
West Calder 51 NT 0163
West Camel 7 ST 5724
West Challow 18 SU 3688
West Charleton 5 SX 7542
West Chelborough 7 ST 5405
West Chevington 47 NZ 2297
West Chiltington 11 TQ 0918
West Clandon 11 TQ 0452
West Cliffe 13 TR 3445
Westcliff-on-Sea 20 TQ 8685
West Coker 7 ST 5113
Westcombe 8 ST 6739
West Compton (Dorset) 7 SY 5694
West Compton (Somer.) 7 ST 5942
Westcote 17 SP 2120
Westcott (Bucks.) 18 SP 7117
Westcott (Devon) 5 ST 0104
Westcott (Surrey) 11 TQ 1348
Westcott Barton 18 SP 4224
West Cross 15 SS 6189
West Curry 4 SX 2893
West Curthwaite 46 NY 3248
Westdean (E Susx) 12 TV 5299
West Dean (Wilts.) 9 SU 2526
West Dean (W Susx) 9 SU 8512
West Deeping 35 TF 1009
West Derby 32 SJ 3993
West Dereham 28 TF 6500
West Ditchburn 53 NU 1320
West Down (Devon.) 6 SS 5142
West Down (Wilts.) 8 SU 0648
West Drayton (Gtr London) 11 TQ 0679
West Drayton (Notts.) 34 SK 7074
West End (Avon) 16 ST 4469
West End (Beds.) 27 SP 9853
West End (Hants.) 9 SU 4614
West End (Herts.) 20 TL 3306
West End (Norf.) 29 TG 4911
West End (N Yorks.) 37 SE 1457
West End (Oxon.) 18 SP 4204
West End (Surrey) 11 SU 9461
West End Green 10 SU 6661
Wester Clynekirton 67 NC 8906
Wester Culbeuchly Crofts 62 NJ 6562
Westerdale (Highld.) 67 ND 1251
Westerdale (N Yorks.) 42 NZ 6605
Westerdale Moor 42 NZ 6502
Wester Denoon 57 NO 3543
Westerfield (Shetld.) 63 HU 3551
Westerfield (Suff.) 21 TM 1747
Wester Fintray 62 NJ 8116
Westergate 11 SU 9305
Wester Gruinards 65 NH 5292
Westerham 12 TQ 4454
Westerleigh 17 ST 6979
Wester Lonvine 65 NH 7172
Wester Skeld 63 HU 2943
Wester Teaninich 65 NH 6267
Westerton 57 NO 6654
Wester Wick 63 HU 2842
West Farleigh 12 TQ 7152
West Felton 32 SJ 3425
Westfield (Caithness) 67 ND 0564
Westfield (E Susx) 12 TQ 8115
Westfield (Lothian) 51 NS 9372
Westfield (Norf.) 29 TF 9909
West Firle 12 TQ 4707
Westgate (Durham) 41 NY 9038
Westgate (Humbs.) 38 SE 7707
Westgate (Norf.) 29 TF 9740
Westgate on Sea 13 TR 3270
West Geirinish 63 NF 7741
West Ginge 18 SU 4386
West Grafton 10 SU 2460
West Green 10 SU 7456
West Grimstead 8 SU 2026
West Grinstead 11 TQ 1721
West Haddlesey 38 SE 5526
West Haddon 26 SP 6371
West Hagbourne 18 SU 5187
Westhall (Cumbr.) 46 NY 5667
Westhall (Suff.) 29 TM 4280
West Hallam 33 SK 4341
West Halton 39 SE 9020

Westham 102 Witham

Westham (E Susx)	12	TQ 6404
West Ham (Gtr London)	20	TQ 4081
Westham (Somer.)	7	ST 4046
Westhampnett	11	SU 8706
West Handley	33	SK 3977
West Hanney	18	SU 4092
West Hanningfield	20	TQ 7399
West Hardwick	38	SE 4118
West Harnham	8	SU 1229
West Harptree	16	ST 5556
West Hatch	7	ST 2820
Westhay	7	ST 4342
Westhead	36	SD 4407
West Heath	11	SU 8556
West Helmsdale	67	ND 0114
West Hendred	18	SU 4488
West Heslerton	39	SE 9175
Westhide	24	SO 5844
West Hill	5	SY 0694
West Hoathly	12	TQ 3632
West Holme	8	SY 8885
Westhope (Here. and Worc.)	24	SO 4651
Westhope (Salop)	24	SO 4786
West Horndon	20	TQ 6288
Westhorpe (Lincs.)	35	TF 2131
Westhorpe (Suff.)	29	TM 0469
West Horrington	7	ST 5747
West Horsley	11	TQ 0753
West Hougham	13	TR 2640
Westhoughton	36	SD 6505
Westhouse	41	SD 6673
Westhouses	33	SK 4257
West Humble	11	TQ 1652
West Hyde	19	TQ 0391
West Ilsley	10	SU 4682
Westing	63	HP 5705
West Itchenor	9	SU 7900
West Kennet	17	SU 1167
West Kilbride	49	NS 2048
West Kingsdown	12	TQ 5762
West Kington	17	ST 8077
West Kirby	32	SJ 2186
West Knighton	8	SY 7387
West Knoyle	8	ST 8532
Westlake	5	SX 6253
West Langdon	13	TR 3247
West Langwell	66	NC 6909
West Lavington (Wilts.)	8	SU 0052
West Lavington (W Susx)	11	SU 8920
West Layton	42	NZ 1409
West Leake	34	SK 5226
Westleigh (Devon)	6	SS 4628
Westleigh (Devon)	7	ST 0517
Westleton	29	TM 4469
West Lexham	28	TF 8417
Westley (Salop)	24	SJ 3507
Westley (Suff.)	20	TL 8264
Westley Waterless	20	TL 6256
West Lilling	38	SE 6465
Westlington	18	SP 7610
West Linton (Borders)	51	NT 1551
Westlinton (Cumbr.)	46	NY 3964
West Littleton	17	ST 7575
West Looe	4	SX 2553
West Lulworth	8	SY 8280
West Lutton	39	SE 9269
West Lynn	28	TF 6120
West Mains	51	NS 9550
West Malling	12	TQ 6857
West Malvern	24	SO 7646
West Marden	9	SU 7613
West Markham	34	SK 7272
Westmarsh	13	TR 2761
West Marton	37	SD 8850
West Meon	9	SU 6424
West Mersea	21	TM 0112
Westmeston	12	TQ 3313
Westmill	20	TL 3627
West Milton	7	SY 5096
West Monkton	7	ST 2528
West Moors	8	SU 0802
Westmuir (Tays.)	57	NO 3652
West Muir (Tays.)	57	NO 5661
Westness (Rousay)	63	HY 3829
Westnewton (Cumbr.)	45	NY 1344
West Newton (Norf.)	28	TF 6927
West Norwood	12	TQ 3171
West Ogwell	5	SX 8170
Weston (Avon)	17	ST 7266
Weston (Berks.)	10	SU 3973
Weston (Ches.)	32	SJ 5080
Weston (Ches.)	32	SJ 7252
Weston (Dorset)	8	SY 6870
Weston (Hants.)	9	SU 7221
Weston (Herts.)	19	TL 2630
Weston (Lincs.)	35	TF 2925
Weston (Northants.)	26	SP 5847
Weston (Notts.)	34	SK 7767
Weston (Salop)	32	SJ 5628
Weston (Salop)	24	SO 5993
Weston (Staffs.)	33	SJ 9727
Weston (W Yorks.)	37	SE 1747
Weston Beggard	24	SO 5841
Weston by Welland	26	SP 7791
Weston Colville	20	TL 6153
Weston Favell	26	SP 7862
Weston Green	20	TL 6252
Weston Heath	24	SJ 7813
Weston Hills	35	TF 2821
Westoning	19	TL 0332
Weston-in-Gordano	16	ST 4474
Weston Jones	32	SJ 7524
Weston Longville	29	TG 1116
Weston Lullingfields	32	SJ 4224
Weston-on-the-Green	18	SP 5318
Weston-on-Trent	33	SK 4027
Weston Patrick	10	SU 6946
Weston Rhyn	32	SJ 2835
Weston Subedge	25	SP 1240
Weston-super-Mare	16	ST 3261
Weston Turville	19	SP 8511
Weston-under-Lizard	24	SJ 8010
Weston under Penyard	17	SO 6323
Weston under Wetherley	26	SP 3569
Weston Underwood (Bucks.)	27	SP 8650
Weston Underwood (Derby.)	33	SK 2942
Westonzoyland	7	ST 3534
West Overton	17	SU 1367
Westow	38	SE 7565
West Parley	8	SZ 0997
West Peaston	52	NT 4265
West Peckham	12	TQ 6452
West Pennard	7	ST 5438
West Pentire	2	SW 7760
Westport	7	ST 3819
West Putford	4	SS 3515
West Quantoxhead	7	ST 1141
West Rainton	47	NZ 3246
West Rasen	35	TF 0589
West Raynham	28	TF 8725
Westrigg	50	NS 9067
West Row	28	TL 6775
West Rudham	28	TF 8127
West Runton	29	TG 1842
Westruther	52	NT 6349
Westry	27	TL 3998
West Saltoun	52	NT 4667
West Sandwick	63	HU 4488
West Scrafton	42	SE 0783
West Stafford	8	SY 7289
West Stoke	9	SU 8208
West Stonesdale	41	NY 8802
West Stoughton	7	ST 4149
West Stour	8	ST 7822
West Stourmouth	13	TR 2562
West Stow	28	TL 8170
West Stowell	17	SU 1362
West Street	13	TQ 9054
West Tanfield	42	SE 2778
West Tarbert	49	NR 8467
West Thorney	9	SU 7602
West Thurrock	12	TQ 5877
West Tilbury	12	TQ 6677
West Tisted	9	SU 6429
West Tofts	56	NO 1134
West Torrington	35	TF 1381
West Town	16	ST 4767
West Tytherley	9	SU 2730
West Tytherton	17	ST 9474
West Walton	35	TF 4713
West Walton Highway	28	TF 4912
Westward	46	NY 2744
Westward Ho[	6	SS 4329
Westwell (Kent)	13	TQ 9947
Westwell (Oxon.)	18	SP 2210
Westwell Leacon	13	TQ 9647
West Wellow	9	SU 2818
West Wemyss	51	NT 3294
West Wick (Avon)	16	ST 3661
Westwick (Cambs.)	20	TL 4265
Westwick (Norf.)	29	TG 2727
West Wickham (Cambs.)	20	TL 6149
West Wickham (Gtr London)	12	TQ 3866
West Winch	28	TF 6316
West Wittering	9	SZ 7999
West Witton	42	SE 0688
Westwood (Devon)	5	SY 0199
Westwood (Wilts.)	17	ST 8158
West Woodburn	47	NY 8986
West Woodhay	10	SU 3962
West Woodlands	8	ST 7743
Westwoodside	38	SK 7499
West Worldham	9	SU 7436
West Wratting	20	TL 6052
West Wycombe	18	SU 8394
West Yell	63	HU 4582
Wetheral	46	NY 4654
Wetherby	38	SE 4048
Wetherden	21	TM 0062
Wetheringsett	21	TM 1266
Wethersfield	20	TL 7131
Wethersta	63	HU 3565
Wetherup Street	21	TM 1464
Wetley Rocks	33	SJ 9649
Wettenhall	32	SJ 6261
Wetton	33	SK 1055
Wetwang	39	SE 9359
Wetwood	32	SJ 7733
Wexcombe	10	SU 2758
Weybourne	29	TG 1143
Weybread	29	TM 2480
Weybridge	11	TQ 0764
Weydale	67	ND 1464
Weyhill	10	SU 3146
Weymouth	8	SY 6778
Whaddon (Bucks.)	18	SP 8034
Whaddon (Cambs.)	20	TL 3546
Whaddon (Glos.)	17	SO 8313
Whaddon (Wilts.)	8	SU 1926
Whale	40	NY 5221
Whaley	34	SK 5171
Whaley Bridge	33	SK 0181
Whaligoe	67	ND 3240
Whalley	36	SD 7335
Whalton	47	NZ 1281
Wham	41	SD 7762
Whaplode	35	TF 3224
Whaplode Drove	35	TF 3113
Whaplode Fen	35	TF 3220
Wharfe	41	SD 7869
Wharles	36	SD 4435
Wharncliffe Side	37	SK 2994
Wharram le Street	39	SE 8666
Wharton (Ches.)	32	SJ 6666
Wharton (Here. and Worc.)	24	SO 5055
Whashton	42	NZ 1406
Whatcombe	8	ST 8301
Whatcote	26	SP 2944
Whatfield	21	TM 0246
Whatley	8	ST 7347
Whatlington	12	TQ 7618
Whatstandwell	33	SK 3354
Whatton	34	SK 7439
Whauphill	44	NX 4049
Whaw	41	NY 9804
Wheatacre	29	TM 4594
Wheathampstead	19	TL 1713
Wheatley (Hants.)	10	SU 7840
Wheatley (Notts.)	34	SK 7685
Wheatley (Oxon.)	18	SP 5905
Wheatley Hill	42	NZ 3839
Wheatley Lane	37	SD 8337
Wheaton Aston	25	SJ 8412
Wheatsheaf	32	SJ 3253
Wheddon Cross	6	SS 9238
Wheedlemont	61	NJ 4726
Wheelerstreet	11	SU 9440
Wheelock	32	SJ 7458
Wheelton	36	SD 6021
Wheldrake	38	SE 6744
Whelford	17	SU 1698
Whelpley Hill	19	TL 0004
Whenby	38	SE 6369
Whepstead	20	TL 8358
Wherstead	21	TM 1540
Wherwell	10	SU 3840
Wheston	33	SK 1376
Whetsted	12	TQ 6546
Whetstone	26	SP 5597
Whicham	40	SD 1382
Whichford	18	SP 3134
Whickham	47	NZ 2061
Whiddon Down	5	SX 6992
Whigstreet	57	NO 4844
Whilton	26	SP 6364
Whim	51	NT 2153
Whimple	5	SY 0497
Whimpwell Green	29	TG 3829
Whinburgh	29	TG 0009
Whinnyfold	62	NK 0733
Whippingham	9	SZ 5193
Whipsnade	19	TL 0117
Whipton	5	SX 9493
Whissendine	34	SK 8214
Whissonsett	28	TF 9123
Whistley Green	10	SU 7974
Whiston (Mers.)	32	SJ 4791
Whiston (Northants.)	27	SP 8560
Whiston (Staffs.)	25	SJ 8914
Whiston (Staffs.)	33	SK 0347
Whiston (S Yorks.)	33	SK 4489
Whitbeck	40	SD 1184
Whitbourne	24	SO 7156
Whitburn (Lothian)	51	NS 9464
Whitburn (Tyne and Wear)	47	NZ 4061
Whitby (Ches.)	32	SJ 4075
Whitby (N Yorks.)	43	NZ 8911
Whitchurch (Avon)	17	ST 6167
Whitchurch (Bucks.)	18	SP 8020
Whitchurch (Devon)	4	SX 4972
Whitchurch (Dyfed)	14	SM 8025
Whitchurch (Hants.)	10	SU 4648
Whitchurch (Here. and Worc.)	16	SO 5417
Whitchurch (Oxon.)	10	SU 6377
Whitchurch (Salop)	32	SJ 5441
Whitchurch (S Glam.)	16	ST 1680
Whitchurch Canonicorum	7	SY 3995
Whitcott Keysett	23	SO 2782
Whitebrook	16	SO 5306
Whitecairns	62	NJ 9218
White Chapel	36	SD 5542
Whitechurch	14	SN 1436
White Coppice	36	SD 6119
White Court	20	TL 7421
Whitecraig (Lothian)	51	NT 3570
Whitecroft	17	SO 6106
Whitecross	51	NS 9676
Whiteface	65	NH 7189
Whitefield (Gtr Mches.)	37	SD 8005
Whitefield (Tays.)	56	NO 1734
Whiteford	62	NJ 7126
Whitehall	63	HY 6528
Whitehaven	40	NX 9718
Whitehill (Hants.)	9	SU 7934
Whitehills	62	NJ 6565
Whitehouse (Grampn.)	62	NJ 6214
Whitehouse (Strath.)	49	NR 8161
Whitekirk	52	NT 5981
White Lackington	8	SY 7198
White Ladies Aston	25	SO 9252
Whiteley Village	11	TQ 0962
Whitemans Green	12	TQ 3025
Whitemire	60	NH 9854
Whitemoor	2	SW 9757
White Notley	20	TL 7818
Whiteparish	9	SU 2423
Whiterashes	62	NJ 8523
White Roding	20	TL 5613
Whiterow	67	ND 3548
Whiteshill	17	SO 8307
Whiteside (Lothian)	51	NS 9667
Whitesmith	12	TQ 5214
Whitestaunton	7	ST 2810
Whitestone	6	SX 8694
White Waltham	11	SU 8577
Whiteway	17	SO 9110
Whitewell	36	SD 6546
Whitewreath	61	NJ 2356
Whitfield (Glos.)	17	ST 6791
Whitfield (Kent)	13	TR 3146
Whitfield (Northants.)	26	SP 6039
Whitfield (Northum.)	46	NY 7758
Whitford	31	SJ 1477
Whitgift	39	SE 8022
Whitgreave	33	SJ 8928
Whithorn	44	NX 4440
Whiting Bay (Island of Arran)	49	NS 0425
Whitington	28	TL 7199
Whitland	14	SN 1916
Whitletts	50	NS 3622
Whitley (Berks.)	10	SU 7170
Whitley (Ches.)	32	SJ 6178
Whitley (N Yorks.)	38	SE 5521
Whitley Bay	47	NZ 3572
Whitley Chapel	47	NY 9257
Whitley Row	12	TQ 5052
Whitlock's End	25	SP 1076
Whitminster	17	SO 7708
Whitmore	32	SJ 8041
Whitnage	7	ST 0215
Whitnash	26	SP 3263
Whitney	23	SO 2647
Whitrigg (Cumbr.)	40	NY 2038
Whitrigg (Cumbr.)	46	NY 2257
Whitsbury	8	SU 1218
Whitsome	53	NT 8650
Whitson	16	ST 3783
Whitstable	13	TR 1166
Whitstone	4	SX 2698
Whittingham	53	NU 0611
Whittingslow	24	SO 4288
Whittington (Derby.)	33	SK 3975
Whittington (Glos.)	17	SP 0120
Whittington (Here. and Worc.)	25	SO 8582
Whittington (Here. and Worc.)	25	SO 8752
Whittington (Lancs.)	41	SD 5976
Whittington (Salop)	32	SJ 3230
Whittington (Staffs.)	25	SK 1508
Whittlebury	26	SP 6943
Whittle-le-Woods	36	SD 5822
Whittlesey	27	TL 2797
Whittlesford	20	TL 4748
Whitton (Cleve.)	42	NZ 3822
Whitton (Humbs.)	39	SE 9024
Whitton (Northum.)	47	NU 0501
Whitton (Powys)	23	SO 2667
Whitton (Salop)	24	SO 5772
Whitton (Suff.)	21	TM 1447
Whittonditch	10	SU 2872
Whittonstall	47	NZ 0757
Whitwell (Derby.)	34	SK 5276
Whitwell (Herts.)	19	TL 1821
Whitwell (I of W.)	9	SZ 5277
Whitwell (Leic.)	34	SK 0208
Whitwell (N Yorks.)	42	SE 2899
Whitwell-on-the-Hill	38	SE 7265
Whitwick	33	SK 4316
Whitwood	38	SE 4124
Whitworth	37	SD 8818
Whixall	32	SJ 5034
Whixley	38	SE 4457
Whorlton (Durham)	42	NZ 1014
Whorlton (N Yorks.)	42	NZ 4802
Whygate	46	NY 7675
Whyle	24	SO 5560
Whyteleafe	12	TQ 3358
Wibdon	17	ST 5797
Wibtoft	26	SP 4787
Wichenford	24	SO 7860
Wichling	13	TQ 9256
Wick (Avon)	17	ST 6972
Wick (Dorset)	8	SZ 1591
Wick (Here. and Worc.)	25	SO 9645
Wick (Highld.)	67	ND 3650
Wick (S Glam.)	15	SS 9272
Wick (Shetld.)	63	HU 4439
Wick (Wilts.)	8	SU 1621
Wick (W Susx)	11	TQ 0203
Wicken (Cambs.)	28	TL 5770
Wicken (Northants.)	26	SP 7439
Wicken Bonhunt	20	TL 5033
Wickenby	35	TF 0882
Wickersley	38	SK 4891
Wickford	20	TQ 7593
Wickham (Berks.)	10	SU 3971
Wickham (Hants.)	9	SU 5711
Wickham Bishops	20	TL 8412
Wickhambreaux	13	TR 2158
Wickhambrook	20	TL 7454
Wickhamford	25	SP 0642
Wickham Market	21	TM 3056
Wickhampton	29	TG 4205
Wickham St. Paul	20	TL 8336
Wickham Skeith	29	TM 0969
Wickham Street (Suff.)	20	TL 7554
Wickham Street (Suff.)	29	TM 0869
Wicklewood	29	TG 0702
Wickmere	29	TG 1633
Wick Rissington	17	SP 1821
Wick St. Lawrence	16	ST 3665
Wickwar	17	ST 7288
Widdington	20	TL 5331
Widdrington	47	NZ 2595
Widecombe In the Moor	5	SX 7176
Wide Open	47	NZ 2472
Widewall	63	ND 4391
Widford (Essex)	20	TL 6905
Widford (Herts.)	20	TL 4115
Widmerpool	34	SK 6327
Widnes	32	SJ 5185
Wigan	36	SD 5805
Wiggaton	5	SY 1093
Wiggenhall St. Germans	28	TF 5914
Wiggenhall St. Mary Magdalen	28	TF 5911
Wiggenhall St. Mary the Virgin	28	TF 5814
Wigginton (Herts.)	19	SP 9410
Wigginton (N Yorks)	38	SE 5958
Wigginton (Oxon.)	18	SP 3833
Wigginton (Staffs.)	25	SK 2106
Wigglesworth	37	SD 8056
Wiggonby	46	NY 2953
Wiggonholt	11	TQ 0616
Wighill	38	SE 4746
Wighton	29	TF 9339
Wigmore (Here. and Worc.)	24	SO 4169
Wigmore (Kent)	12	TQ 8063
Wigsley	34	SK 8570
Wigsthorpe	27	TL 0482
Wigston	26	SP 6099
Wigtoft	35	TF 2636
Wigton	46	NY 2548
Wigtown	44	NX 4355
Wilbarston	26	SP 8188
Wilberfoss	38	SE 7350
Wilburton	27	TL 4875
Wilby (Norf.)	29	TM 0389
Wilby (Northants.)	27	SP 8666
Wilby (Suff.)	29	TM 2472
Wilcot	17	SU 1461
Wildboarclough	33	SJ 9868
Wilden	27	TL 0955
Wildhern	10	SU 3550
Wildsworth	39	SK 8097
Wilford	34	SK 5637
Wilkesley	32	SJ 6241
Wilkhaven	65	NH 9486
Wilkieston	51	NT 1168
Willand	5	ST 0310
Willaston (Ches.)	32	SJ 3277
Willaston (Ches.)	32	SJ 6752
Willen	27	SP 8741
Willenhall (W Mids.)	25	SO 9698
Willenhall (W Mids.)	26	SP 3676
Willerby (Humbs.)	39	TA 0230
Willerby (N Yorks.)	43	TA 0079
Willersey	25	SP 1039
Willersley	23	SO 3147
Willesborough	13	TR 0441
Willesden	19	TQ 2284
Willett	7	ST 1033
Willey (Salop)	24	SO 6799
Willey (Warw.)	26	SP 4984
Williamscot	26	SP 4745
Willian	19	TL 2230
Willimontswick	46	NY 7763
Willingale	20	TL 5907
Willingdon	12	TQ 5902
Willingham (Cambs.)	27	TL 4070
Willingham (Lincs.)	34	SK 8784
Willington (Beds.)	27	TL 1150
Willington (Derby.)	33	SK 2928
Willington (Durham)	42	NZ 1935
Willington (Tyne and Wear)	47	NZ 3167
Willington (Warw.)	18	SP 2638
Willington Corner	32	SJ 5367
Willitoft	38	SE 7434
Williton	7	ST 0740
Willoughby (Lincs.)	35	TF 4772
Willoughby (Warw.)	26	SP 5167
Willoughby-on-the-Wolds	34	SK 6325
Willoughby Waterleys	26	SP 5792
Willoughton	39	SK 9293
Wilmcote	25	SP 1658
Wilmington (Devon.)	5	SY 2199
Wilmington (E Susx)	12	TQ 5404
Wilmington (Kent)	12	TQ 5372
Wilmslow	33	SJ 8480
Wilnecote	26	SK 2201
Wilpshire	36	SD 6832
Wilsden	37	SE 0035
Wilsford (Lincs.)	34	TF 0043
Wilsford (Wilts.)	17	SU 1057
Wilsford (Wilts.)	8	SU 1339
Wilshamstead	27	TL 0643
Wilsill	42	SE 1864
Wilson	33	SK 4024
Wilsthorpe	35	TF 0913
Wilstone	19	SP 9014
Wilton (Borders)	52	NT 4914
Wilton (Cleve.)	42	NZ 5819
Wilton (N Yorks.)	43	SE 8582
Wilton (Wilts.)	8	SU 0931
Wilton (Wilts.)	10	SU 2661
Wimbish	20	TL 5936
Wimbish Green	20	TL 6035
Wimbledon	11	TQ 2470
Wimbledon Park	11	TQ 2472
Wimblington	27	TL 4192
Wimborne Minster	8	SZ 0199
Wimborne St. Giles	8	SU 0212
Wimbotsham	28	TF 6205
Wimpstone	25	SP 2148
Wincanton	8	ST 7128
Wincham	32	SJ 6675
Winchburgh	51	NT 0874
Winchcombe	17	SP 0228
Winchelsea	13	TQ 9017
Winchelsea Beach	13	TQ 9115
Winchester	9	SU 4829
Winchfield	10	SU 7654
Winchmore Hill (Bucks.)	19	SU 9394
Winchmore Hill (Gtr London)	20	TQ 3195
Wincle	33	SJ 9565
Windermere (Cumbr.)	40	SD 4198
Winderton	26	SP 3240
Windlesham	11	SU 9363
Windley	33	SK 3045
Windmill Hill (E Susx)	12	TQ 6412
Windmill Hill (Somer.)	7	ST 3116
Windrush	17	SP 1913
Windsor	11	SU 9676
Windygates	57	NO 3400
Wineham	11	TQ 2320
Winestead	39	TA 2924
Winfarthing	29	TM 1085
Winford	16	ST 5364
Winforton	23	SO 2947
Winfrith Newburgh	8	SY 8084
Wing (Bucks.)	19	SP 8822
Wing (Leic.)	27	SK 8903
Wingate (Durham)	42	NZ 4036
Wingates (Gtr Mches.)	36	SD 6507
Wingates (Northum.)	47	NZ 0995
Wingerworth	33	SK 3867
Wingfield (Beds.)	19	SP 9926
Wingfield (Suff.)	29	TM 2276
Wingfield (Wilts.)	17	ST 8256
Wingham	13	TR 2457
Wingrave	19	SP 8719
Winkburn	34	SK 7158
Winkfield	11	SU 9072
Winkfield Row	11	SU 9071
Winkhill	33	SK 0651
Winkleigh	6	SS 6308
Winksley	42	SE 2471
Winless	67	ND 3054
Winmarleigh	36	SD 4748
Winnersh	10	SU 7870
Winscales	40	NY 0226
Winscombe	16	ST 4157
Winsford (Ches.)	32	SJ 6566
Winsford (Somer.)	6	SS 9034
Winsham	7	ST 3706
Winshill	33	SK 2623
Winskill	41	NY 5835
Winslade	10	SU 6547
Winsley	17	ST 7960
Winslow	18	SP 7627
Winson	17	SP 0908
Winster (Cumbr.)	40	SD 4193
Winster (Derby.)	33	SK 2460
Winston (Durham)	42	NZ 1416
Winston (Suff.)	21	TM 1861
Winstone	17	SO 9609
Winswell	6	SS 4913
Winterborne Clenston	8	ST 8302
Winterborne Herringston	8	SY 6887
Winterborne Houghton	8	ST 8104
Winterborne Kingston	8	SY 8697
Winterborne Monkton (Dorset)	8	SY 6787
Winterborne Stickland	8	ST 8304
Winterborne Whitechurch	8	SY 8399
Winterborne Zelston	8	SY 8997
Winterbourne	17	ST 6480
Winterbourne Abbas	7	SY 6190
Winterbourne Bassett	17	SU 1074
Winterbourne Dauntsey	8	SU 1734
Winterbourne Earls	8	SU 1633
Winterbourne Gunner	8	SU 1735
Winterbourne Monkton (Wilts.)	17	SU 0972
Winterbourne Steepleton	8	SY 6289
Winterbourne Stoke	8	SU 0740
Winterburn	37	SD 9358
Winteringham	39	SE 9222
Winterley	32	SJ 7457
Wintersett	37	SE 3815
Winterslow	9	SU 2232
Winterton	39	SE 9218
Winterton-on-Sea	29	TG 4919
Winthorpe (Lincs.)	35	TF 5665
Winthorpe (Notts.)	34	SK 8156
Winton (Cumbr.)	41	NY 7810
Winton (Dorset)	8	SZ 0894
Wintringham	39	SE 8873
Winwick (Cambs.)	27	TL 1080
Winwick (Ches.)	32	SJ 6092
Winwick (Northants.)	26	SP 6273
Wirksworth	33	SK 2854
Wirswall	32	SJ 5444
Wisbech	35	TF 4609
Wisbech St. Mary	35	TF 4208
Wisborough Green	11	TQ 0526
Wiseton	34	SK 7189
Wishaw (Strath.)	50	NS 7954
Wishaw (Warw.)	25	SP 1794
Wispington	35	TF 2071
Wissett	29	TM 3679
Wistanstow	24	SO 4385
Wistanswick	32	SJ 6629
Wistaston	32	SJ 6853
Wiston (Dyfed)	14	SN 0218
Wiston (Strath.)	51	NS 9531
Wiston (W Susx)	11	TQ 1512
Wistow (Cambs.)	27	TL 2781
Wistow (N Yorks.)	38	SE 5835
Wiswell	36	SD 7437
Witcham	27	TL 4680
Witchampton	8	ST 9806
Witchford	28	TL 5078
Witham	20	TL 8114

 British Tourist Authority
239 Old Marylebone Road London NW1 5QT England

BTA OVERSEAS OFFICES

Enquiries from prospective overseas visitors to Britain will be welcome at the offices of the British Tourist Authority in the following countries:

ARGENTINA
Av Cordoba 645 (piso 2)
1054 Buenos Aires
☎ 392–9955

AUSTRALIA
171 Clarence Street
Sydney NSW 2000
☎ 29–8627

BELGIUM
23 Place Rogierplein 23
1000 Brussels
☎ 218 67 70

BRAZIL
Avenida Ipiranga 318–A
12° Andar conj 1201
01046 Sao Paulo–SP
☎ 257–1834

CANADA
151 Bloor Street
West Suite 460
Toronto
Ontario M5S IT3
☎ (416) 925–6326

DENMARK
PO Box 46
1002 Copenhagen
☎ 12–07–93

FRANCE
6 Place Vendome
75001 Paris
☎ 2964760

GERMANY
Neue Mainzer str 22
6000 Frankfurt a M
☎ (0611) 23 64 28

HOLLAND
Leidseplein 5
Amsterdam
☎ (020) 234667

ITALY
Via S Eufemia 5
00187 Rome
☎ 6785548

JAPAN
Tokyo Club Building (Room 246)
2–6 3–chome
Kasumigaseki
Chiyoda-ku Tokyo 100
☎ 581 3603

MEXICO
Tiber 103 6–piso
Mexico 5D F
☎ 511 39 27

NEW ZEALAND
Box 3655
Wellington
☎ 843–233

NORWAY
Postboks 1781 Vika
Oslo 1
☎ (02) 41 18 49

SOUTH AFRICA
Union Castle Building
36 Loveday Street
Box 3256 Johannesburg
☎ 838 1881

SPAIN
Torre de Madrid 6/4
Plaza de Espana
Madrid 13
☎ 241–1396

SWEDEN
For visitors :
Malmskillnadsgatan 42 (1st floor)
For mail : Box 40 097
S–103 42 Stockholm 40
☎ 08–21–24–44

SWITZERLAND
Limmatquai 78
8001 Zurich
☎ 01/47 42 77

USA
680 Fifth Avenue
New York NY 10019
☎ (212) 581–4700

612 South Flower Street
Los Angeles CA 90017
☎ (213) 623–8196

John Hancock Center (suite 2450)
875 North Mitchigan Avenue
Chicago IL 60611
☎ (312) 787–0490

INFORMATION FOR VISITORS TO BRITAIN

The following tourist organisations will be able to give advice and directions on how best to enjoy your holiday in Britain:

British Tourist Authority
'Welcome to Britain' Tourist Information Centre
64 St James's Street
London SW1A 1NF
☎ 01–629 9191

*English Tourist Board
4 Grosvenor Gardens
London SW1W 0DU

Northern Ireland Tourist Board
River House
48 High Street
Belfast BT1 2DS
☎ Belfast 31221/46609

*Scottish Tourist Board
23 Ravelston Terrace
Edinburgh EH4 3EU

*Wales Tourist Board
Llandaff
Cardiff CF5 2YZ

London Tourist Board
26 Grosvenor Gardens
London SW1W 0DU
☎ 01–730 0791

* written enquiries only

BREAKDOWNS –

WHAT TO DO TO OBTAIN FREE BREAKDOWN SERVICE

1 Check 'Route Planning Maps' on pages (ii) (iii) and (iv) for location of nearest Breakdown Service Centre

2 Look at opposite page for telephone number of that Centre. Note whether it is open for service at the time you are phoning. Telephone (on motorway use SOS phone and ask Police for AA service).

If the centre is closed, ring the nearest that is open and they will process your call

3 **Have these details ready.**

AA membership number
Exact location of vehicle
Make,year,registration number
Trouble (if known)
Whether automatic transmission
Whether under manufacturer's warrenty

4 Return and remain with vehicle

IMPORTANT NOTES

A If an AA garage is used, show your membership certificate to the mechanic and sign the garage report card after completion. If the garage is not authorised to carry out repairs under guarantee, it may be necessary for you to arrange delivery to an authorised distributor/dealer

B If you do not have your membership certificate, pay the garage, obtain receipt and send with covering details to The Automobile Association, Breakdown Service Accounts, Fanum House, Basingstoke, Hants